ALCOHOL IN AFRICA
Mixing Business, Pleasure, and Politics

Edited by
Deborah Fahy Bryceson

HEINEMANN
Portsmouth, NH

Heinemann
A division of Reed Elsevier Inc.
361 Hanover Street
Portsmouth, NH 03801–3912
www.heinemann.com

Offices and agents throughout the world

ISBN 0–325–07115–2 (Heinemann cloth)

British Library Cataloguing in Publication Data is available.

Library of Congress Cataloging-in-Publication Data

Alcohol in Africa : mixing business, pleasure, and politics / edited by Deborah Fahy Bryceson.
p. cm.
Includes bibliographical references and index.
ISBN 0–325–07115–2 (alk. paper)
1. Drinking of alcoholic beverages—Africa. 2. Alcoholism—Africa. 3. Alcoholic beverage industry—Africa. 4. Africa—Social life and customs. I. Bryceson, Deborah Fahy.
HV5638.A43 2002
394.1'3'096—dc21 2002024063

Printed in the United States of America on acid-free paper.

06 05 04 03 02 SB 1 2 3 4 5 6 7 8 9

Copyright Acknowledgments

The editor and publisher gratefully acknowledge permission to reprint the following material: Chapter 8 is an edited version of Jon Abbink's "Competing Practices of Drinking and Power: Alcoholic 'Hegemonism' in Southern Ethiopia," *Northeast African Studies* 4(3) (N.S.), 1988, pp. 7–22. Used by permission.

Contents

Preface vii

PART I: INTRODUCTION 1

Chapter 1: Alcohol in Africa: Substance, Stimulus, and Society 3
Deborah Fahy Bryceson

Chapter 2: Changing Modalities of Alcohol Usage 23
Deborah Fahy Bryceson

PART II: BUSINESS INTERESTS 53

Chapter 3: For Women and Children: An Economic History of Brewing among the Nyakyusa of Southwestern Tanzania 55
Justin Willis

Chapter 4: Liquid Gold of a Lost Kingdom: The Rise of *Waragi* Production in Kibaale District, Uganda 75
Nite Baza Tanzarn

Chapter 5: Brewers, Woodfuel, and Donors: An Awkward Silence as the Fires Blaze 93
Michael K. McCall

PART III: POLITICAL CONTESTS 115

Chapter 6: Diluting Drinks and Deepening Discontent: Colonial Liquor Controls and Public Resistance in Windhoek, Namibia 117
Jan-Bart Gewald

Chapter 7: Living on the Proceeds of a Grog Shop: Liquor Revenue in Nigeria 139
Simon Heap

Chapter 8: Drinking, Prestige, and Power: Alcohol and Cultural Hegemony in Maji, Southern Ethiopia 161
Jon Abbink

Chapter 9: Democracy's Heady Brew: Cashew Wine and the Authority of the Elders among the Balanta in Guinea-Bissau 179
Roy van der Drift

Chapter 10: Drinking Mothers Feeding Children: Market Women and Gender Politics in Kilimanjaro, Tanzania 197
Tuulikki Pietilä

PART IV: SOCIAL COMFORTS AND DISCOMFORTS 213

Chapter 11: Drinking with Friends: Popular Culture, the Working Poor, and Youth Drinking in Independent Ghana 215
Emmanuel Akyeampong

Chapter 12: To Drink or Not to Drink: Beer Brewing, Rituals, and Religious Conversion in Maane, Burkina Faso 231
Sabine Luning

Chapter 13: Modernity's Limits: Pentecostalism and the Moral Rejection of Alcohol in Malawi 249
Rijk van Dijk

PART V: CONCLUSION 265

Chapter 14: Pleasure and Pain: The Ambiguity of Alcohol in Africa 267
Deborah Fahy Bryceson

Index 293

About the Contributors 303

Preface

Quite innocently, this book began life as a short half-day seminar at the African Studies Centre (ASC), Leiden, The Netherlands, in June 1997. Was it the novelty of Internet communication or the topic itself that led to the ripple effects that followed? Whatever the case, several parties stepped forward with the admission that they too had been writing recently on the subject of alcohol. It soon became apparent that there was a critical mass of authors to produce this book.

The original impulse to hold a seminar on alcohol, organized by Nina Tellegen and myself, was triggered by findings from several rural income-diversification studies coordinated within the De-agrarianization and Rural Employment (DARE) research program at the ASC. The studies showed that the expansion of brewing and distilling activities was common to many rural areas throughout Sub-Saharan Africa over the last two decades. Reviewing the literature and soliciting papers on alcohol production and consumption in countries not covered by the DARE program started as a way of double-checking our findings, but inexorably led to the complex interplay of social and political phenomena associated with the growing alcohol economy in urban as well as rural areas.

This book has benefited from the insightful observations and suggestions of many people along the way, including Andrew Byerly, Sara Franceys, Lukas Goslinga, Raufu Mustapha, Margaret Niger-Thomas, Christine Obbo, Gerda Rossel, Gabriel Rugalema and Mohamed Salih. Nina Tellegen assisted with the workshop organization, read and commented on the chapters, and consulted some key Internet brewery sites. Special thanks go to Sjaan van Marrewijk and Ella Verkaik-Steenvoorden of the ASC library. The number and, in some cases, obscurity of the references that they managed to find were pivotal to the literature review. Ann Reeves put a great deal of time into the book. Her deft copyediting work has rendered a large and highly diverse text far more accessible to a general readership. Claire Taylor compiled the index.

Infrastructural and financial support for this book came from the African Studies Centre, Leiden, and the Research and Development Division at the Netherlands Ministry of Foreign Affairs and is gratefully acknowledged.

Deborah Fahy Bryceson
African Studies Centre
Leiden, The Netherlands

PART I
Introduction

1

Alcohol in Africa

Substance, Stimulus, and Society

Deborah Fahy Bryceson

The topic of alcohol has a chameleon character—frivolous or weighty—depending on the light in which its intrinsic nature is viewed. In Africa, studies of changing alcohol usage are similar, sometimes darkly pessimistic and foreboding, and at other times light, even exuberant. Given the vagaries of perception, it is probably unwise to assume that evolving patterns of usage simply mirror social transformations.

Alcohol is a ubiquitous part of everyday life, particularly in rural communities where its production and distribution are closely intertwined with consumption. As a medium for communication with the ancestors, it has always had a central place in African religious belief. And in urban and rural areas alike, drinking provides a focal point for relaxation and socializing. Alcohol's stimulating effect on social exchange has long been appreciated, with the oral cultural inheritance of agrarian societies throughout the continent putting a premium on face-to-face social exchange. Indeed, the range of human emotions kindled by alcohol, from celebratory happiness to dark despair, and from bonhomie to violent revenge, imparts drama and enigma to the comparative study of alcohol usage. And to this alluring cocktail can be added the calculating maneuvers of the alcohol industry and state officials maximizing sales and fiscal revenue from alcohol.

The study of alcohol usage strategically situates the analyst in a broad concourse of religious, political, economic, psychological, social and physiological phenomena, raising a myriad of methodological possibilities and problems. Nonetheless, academic research on alcohol in Africa until recently has been restricted primarily to anthropologists. Their interest was sparked by a material culture perspective, or as a by-product of general ethnographic studies. The notion of alcohol usage as a reflection of society in general emanates from these studies.

Academic concentration has been placed on alcohol's utilization and the meaning and control people vested in alcohol, but this is only half the story. As a material stimulant, alcohol has a causal force that acts on people. Thus, alcohol is a reflexive and not simply a reflective substance through which African society can be analyzed.[1] This point becomes evident in the chapters to follow, written by authors hailing from a variety of disciplines. Their themes are wide-ranging, dealing not only with how people use alcohol, but also with how alcohol affects people.

There is no doubt that the ubiquity of alcohol affords a wealth of comparison within Africa, and between Africa and the outside world. However, the record of observation has to be treated with caution. The intrinsic nature of alcohol, its ingestion in the human body, and its power to alter states of consciousness incite controversy. Studies of alcohol usage may be inadvertently or stridently underscored by value judgments regarding the balance between alcohol's positive and negative effects on the drinker and the wider society. Furthermore, non-Africans have written the bulk of the literature on African alcohol. Their vantage point may be influenced by value judgments emanating from their own societies. Or wishing to compensate for their allochthone status, they may uncritically immerse themselves in the value judgments of the local society. In any case, few societies can be expected to generate a uniformity of attitude regarding alcohol. Strong variance of opinion will exist among drinkers themselves, drinkers' families and community support networks, people seeking to control drinking patterns, and, not least, the social scientists attempting to objectively document alcohol usage. This book is anchored in the view that objectivity is impossible in such a highly contested arena. Instead a wide variety of case studies, disciplinary perspectives and value judgments are offered.

This chapter provides general background about alcohol's utilitarian value in African society, followed by a schematic presentation of the major disciplinary approaches in African alcohol studies. The book's four main parts are then outlined, with brief summaries of the individual chapters.

A HIGHLY VALUED SUBSTANCE

Alcohol is and has been a valued substance in Sub-Saharan Africa for centuries. Its imputed value varies in form from culture to culture. In some cultures, institutional efforts have been made to deny or denigrate its perceived worth. Nonetheless, its psychoactive qualities lend it added value above and beyond its thirst-quenching utility and the cost of the labor and raw materials to make it. This section explores the multiple facets of its valuation.

Religious and Symbolic Value

While the precise symbolism associated with alcohol varies from one rural ethnic community to another, strong symbolic content is generally attached to the production, distribution and consumption of traditional alcoholic beverages (Luning, Chapter 12). African traditional drinks are, first and foremost, the thick, cloudy grain beers of the savannah areas of East and southern Africa and the Sahelian zone, and the palm and banana wines of the higher rainfall areas, especially in Central and West Africa as well as coastal areas (e.g., Parkin 1972; Saul 1981; Herlehy 1984; Anigbo 1990; Moukolo 1990; Rekdal 1996). Even in societies heavily influenced by Islam or Christianity, alcohol's role in traditional ritual surfaces irrepressibly, often interlaced with more recent religious attitudes toward alcohol. Anomalous practices exist side by side, compartmentalized into traditional, ancestrally influenced versus nontraditional secular drinks or ways of preparing alcohol (Luning, Chapter 12). Interestingly, West Africa's long exposure to imported spirits has resulted in the extension of traditional symbolism to imported drinks (Akyeampong, Chapter 11; van den Bersselaar 1998; Nti 1998).[2] By contrast, the more recently adopted urban-manufactured drinks, notably the clear, bottled lager beers, are generally associated with modernity and freedom from ancestral spirits.

The symbolic content of traditional alcoholic drinks may stem from a number of different factors. First, the drinks are produced from plants considered to be vital staple foods essential to the well-being of the population. Second, the preparation of the drinks entails achieving specified changes in the observable chemical and physical properties of the foodstuff. Finally, the resultant drink has the power to produce altered states of consciousness in the consumer. The pervasive practice of calling on the intercession of the ancestors to sanction production, distribution and consumption of alcohol may be linked to the uncertainty and seemingly supernatural changes associated with producing and consuming alcohol, as well as the perceived overall importance of the plant used to make the alcohol to the group's material survival.

Likewise, traditional emphasis on sharing and group cooperation in beer and palm-wine production and consumption serves to reaffirm a society's corporate welfare (Ngokwey 1987; Anigbo 1990).[3] While it is no exaggeration to state that the rich ritual content of drinking events harbors an essential realm of spiritual existence, the rituals tend to belie tensions embedded in the moral order. Frequently, the contrast between male and female identities as well as distinctions of rank and power are represented in the rituals (Ngokwey 1987). Drinking occasions can be used to construct an ideal, ordered world in which people are seen to symbolically accept their place in a convivial environment. Nonetheless, such occasions can have embedded within them the antithesis to the ideal, local people's own construction of why the ideal is so difficult to attain in daily life (Karp 1980).

Social and Psychological Value

The intensely social nature of drinking surfaces as one of the most salient themes of the African literature. Alcohol and intoxication are conceptualized as a stimulus that "provide[s] material and symbolic means for the achievement of a heightened sense of sociability" (Partanen 1991: 221). The analogy of social interaction as a liquid flow emphasizes the oneness of alcohol and sociability and relates to the recurrent theme of "powerful liquids," notably blood, alcohol and water (van Dijk, Chapter 13; Netting 1964). Alcoholic drinks are seen to strengthen social ties with family ancestors and within the extended family. They are used to celebrate important social occasions, rites of passages like marriage, funerals and widowhood (McAllister 1986; Anigbo 1990), and friendship pacts (Herlehy 1984), but their use at special events is usually quantitatively surpassed by everyday usage. Drinking serves as a ubiquitous leisure activity across the class spectrum, especially among men, and demarcates the separation of leisure time from work. Furthermore, drinking locations function as major nodes for meeting people and exchanging both vital and mundane information.

Drinking as a social pastime in a relaxed environment takes a range of forms. One's class, gender and age identity are communicated by where, what and how one drinks, and whether or not one gets drunk. Cultural norms structure drinking events. The age at which one starts drinking is often highly significant. Akyeampong documents how young men in Kumasi are attracted to hard drinking as a way of proving their masculinity

(Chapter 11). Sanctions against women drinking too much or drinking specific types of alcohol are widespread (Pietilä, Chapter 10).[4]

The major class divide is between local home brews and distilled liquors as opposed to manufactured bottled alcohol. Since the independence era, drinking clear, bottled lager has been the hallmark of membership in the educated urban middle class. More than a class fissure, the price differential between bottled beer and informal-sector brews is the boundary between rural, rustic ways and urban sophistication.

Last, but certainly not least, drinking affords considerable psychic value. As the numerous drinking scenes of African novelists evocatively depict, alcohol stimulates emotional feelings that momentarily make one's existence seem more vivid and even liberating (e.g., Themba 1972; Mwangi 1973; Okri 1991). Van der Drift (Chapter 9) documents the camaraderie of men across the generations during impromptu rural drinking sessions. Similarly, Kumasi's hard-drinking young men participate in an urban popular culture in which men of all ages are bound together by poverty and the use of alcohol (Akyeampong, Chapter 11). Alcoholically joyful, creative exchanges have been described as "poor man's opera" for those who do not have the financial means to procure more expensive aesthetic experiences or exhilarating pastimes (Partanen 1991: 234).

Economic and Political Value

The high economic value placed on alcohol derives, in the first instance, from the fact that traditionally fermented alcoholic drinks made especially of sorghum/millet and palm wine provided basic food and drink. The Zulu king Cetshwayo in 1881 reported to the Native Laws and Customs Commission that beer was the food of the Zulus (la Hausse 1988). A century later, Botswanan households were estimated to consume 15–20 percent of all grain in the form of sorghum beer (Haggblade 1992: 395). Such high intakes are not restricted to southern Africa. An estimated 50 percent of family grain consumption was consumed in the form of beer during the 1970s in Ouagadougou, Upper Volta (now Burkina Faso) (Saul 1981).

Men were and still are more likely to consume their grain intake in the form of beer than are women and children. However, traditional forms of thick, cloudy sorghum and millet beers have a relatively low alcohol content, on average only 2–5 percent, making the boundary between alcohol and nutritional gruel difficult to determine. Traditionally, women and children drank the nutritious gruel. Furthermore, these beverages provided liquid refreshment in places where the water supply was unsafe. Not surprisingly, alcoholic drinks often gained a reputation for being healthy or even medicinal, a reputation that extended to other alcoholic drinks regardless of their actual content, as Tanzarn notes in the case of distilled Ugandan *waragi* (Chapter 4).

Historically, alcohol has provided a medium of exchange, facilitating economic reciprocity within the community in the form of barter (Hedlund and Lundahl 1984). Brewing for work parties exceeded that for rituals in Zambian villages during the 1950s and early 1960s (Colson and Scudder 1988). In the rural areas of Transkei, South Africa, work parties persist, although the exchange of beer for labor is not a straightforward barter exchange. The beer functions as a symbolic pledge, signifying the labor beneficiary's willingness to make a return labor contribution in the future, although it would be misleading to impute strict calculation in such exchanges (McAllister 2001).

Any consideration of the economic utilization of alcohol in Africa has necessarily to take account of the widespread use of alcohol as a currency in early European trading conquests and labor recruitment (Dumett 1974; Pirio 1982). Alcohol's utility as a currency is enhanced by its infinitely divisible nature. In seventeenth-century West Africa, distilled liquor, in the form of brandy, rum and gin, rapidly became a major trading good in exchange for slaves. From an early period in South Africa, spirits and later wine tots were used as a method of payment for manual labor (van Onselen 1976; la Hausse 1988; Ambler and Crush 1992; Scully 1992).

The state has had a strong fiscal interest in alcohol dating back to early colonial penetration. In Nigeria, import duties on alcohol provided the bulk of the state's fiscal revenue (Heap, Chapter 7). Gradually, domestic alcohol production displaced imports, and other forms of liquor taxation had to be devised. The difficulty of licensing and collecting tax from alcohol producers in the ubiquitous informal sector has been instrumental in some national governments throwing support behind alcohol control legislation and industrial production at the expense of the cottage industry (McCall, Chapter 5; Wolcott 1974; Haggblade 1987, 1992; Ambler and Crush 1992). Interventionist states, notably those of southern Africa, favored the erection of production and distribution monopolies. The South African beer hall became a model for urban beer distribution in the region during the first half of the twentieth century, generating revenues for building apartheid urban infrastructure in the name of African welfare (Ambler and Crush 1992; Parry 1992; Gewald, Chapter 6). Postcolonial African states were similarly bent on establishing alcohol monopolies to facilitate tax revenues for funding their ambitious national development programs or setting up joint ventures with multinational breweries like Heineken and Guinness (e.g., Nigeria: Heap, Chapter 7; Zaire: Schatzberg 1980; Cameroon: Diduk 1993).

ALCOHOL STUDIES IN AFRICA: MORAL REFORMERS VERSUS SOCIAL SCIENCE OBSERVERS

It is difficult to summarize the vast, diffuse literature on alcohol in Africa that has accumulated over the past century. In the last fifteen years, some valuable bibliographies have been published which can help interested readers get their bearings (Molamu and Kebede Gessesse 1988; Curto 1989; Heap 1994/95). This section schematically reviews the major disciplinary approaches and areas of contention that have emerged in the literature, notably the polarization between anthropologists' "constructive drinking" perspective as opposed to the "problem drinking" perspective of the medical and social welfare literature.

Integrative Drinking: Anthropologists Versus Colonial Moralists

The anthropological literature on alcohol is interwoven with an overt unease with past colonial moral injunctions and current theories of alcohol-induced disease. Describing anthropology's contribution to alcohol studies, Heath (1987a: 18) adopts a defensive tone: "the long term strength of anthropological studies has been that they have paid attention not only to 'alcoholism' but rather to alcohol as an artefact and to the complex of attitudes, values, and actions that are associated with it."

The discipline of anthropology congealed during the era of European colonial empire, at a time when the international temperance movement was in its heyday. The discipline was largely apprenticed to the colonial states' need to understand their "native subjects." Colonial anthropologists had to tread a narrow path between missionaries' passionate temperance attitudes (Gewald, Chapter 6) and colonial states and employers who were often swayed by more instrumental concerns connected with alcohol's labor-recruiting and revenue potential.

One of the best strategies was simply avoiding the topic. Anthropologists rarely ventured into the study of alcohol. Existing documentation tends to be a by-product of more general ethnographic studies. In the postcolonial period of the 1970s, anthropologists started focusing on alcohol usage, broadening awareness of its multiple symbolic meanings and functions in African societies (e.g., O'Laughlin 1973; Hagaman 1977; van Beek 1978; McAllister 1985, 1986). Selection of case study areas has been weighted toward rural rather than urban communities. On balance, their work stresses alcohol's role as a facilitator of sociability, alcohol rituals' symbolic mediation of social order, alcohol usage patterns' demarcation of social status, and the material culture associated with alcohol production, distribution and consumption. A wealth of evidence has been amassed to support the "integrative drinking" thesis. Douglas's (1987) term "constructive drinking" goes even further in emphasizing alcohol's positive role in local African societies.

By contrast, there are anthropologists who broke ranks and began writing of alcohol's disintegrative social impact on rural areas. Interestingly, these were anthropologists who undertook restudies of locations that they had documented in the past. Colson and Scudder (1988) returned to a Zambian village after twenty-five years, and Monica Wilson (1977) observed Nyakyusa society in southern Tanzania after an interval of thirty years. In both cases, they recorded the comparatively divisive role of alcohol and generational struggles over alcohol control.

During the 1990s, postmodernist themes reverberated in anthropological studies. Endeavoring to counter the dualism posited between tradition and modernity, they stressed the contemporaneous plurality of different drinking mores and styles (Luning and van Dijk in this volume; Green 1999). Generally, a cacophony of drinking practices has been observed to coexist in mutual harmony, lending weight to an integrative rather than a disintegrative drinking interpretation. Analytical attention has focused on how people rationalize these disparate alcohol consumption patterns. The study of symbolic mediation is primarily related to the sphere of consumption rather than production. Furthermore, the village as a unit of analysis has often been subdivided into specific ethnic, religious, gender, age or economically stratified groups reflecting the increasing social complexity of local communities. "Integrative drinking," no longer contained within the boundaries of small-scale homogeneous local communities, has become plural but retains a sense of social harmony. But this is not always the case, as Abbink (Chapter 8) illustrates in the case of Maji, a small town in southern Ethiopia. Here drinking patterns reflect ethnic tensions and fear of "the other," notably "the drunken other."

Problem Drinking: Medical and Social Policy Perspectives

During the postcolonial period, medical practitioners and researchers dealing with social welfare and relying on conventional survey and quantitative data-gathering techniques generated another literature on African drinking. Their more applied policy focus has been biased toward urban rather than rural areas. Although their studies have incorporated background information generated by anthropologists, their findings are often at odds with the "constructive drinking" perspective. Some have leveled trenchant criticism at anthropologists (Singer 1986).[5]

In turn, the problem drinking literature is criticized for superimposing the notion of addiction and a substance-led approach that hinges on Western individualist concepts of personal escape or deviance (Douglas 1987; Heath 1987a). This is seen to be contrary to the highly social drinking patterns evidenced in rural and urban Africa.[6] Heath (1987b) stresses that anthropologists deal with average modal drinking patterns of an entire study population, whereas the applied alcohol researchers focus on the deviant "problem drinkers." Beyond the differences in focus, there is the more fundamental divide between anthropologists who treat alcohol as an object of control conforming to cultural norms, or less forcefully, a mirror reflecting cultural patterns, and the applied alcohol researchers who attribute an independent causal force to alcohol. However, as Partanen (1991: 245) notes, the concept of causality is restrictively employed: "[A]lcohol is attributed causal power not because of its intrinsic properties, but insofar as its use can be regulated and its effects can be dealt with." Hence, alcohol problems are largely synonymous with human failure in terms of lack of social control or individual willpower.

The applied alcohol studies literature is not as profuse but has the advantage of providing much-needed data on actual drinking practices, types of drinks, and quantities and rates of consumption, as well as documenting morbidity connected with heavy drinking. Most of the literature exists in the form of unpublished survey reports, and its geographical coverage is heavily biased toward southern Africa.[7] Heavy drinking among a significant segment of the urban population is a general finding (Reader and May 1971; Haworth, Mwanalushi and Todd 1981; Molamu and Manyeneng 1988; Pomuti and Eiseb 1990; Obot 1990, 1993). Efforts made to relate findings on drinking practices to hospital admissions, traffic accidents and family welfare are hindered by a lack of reliable statistics.

Given its policy orientation, the literature combines factual reporting with advocacy for the need to address the policymakers' and the public's lack of awareness of and indifference to alcohol abuse. Policy recommendations tend to be directed primarily at educating the public and only secondarily at government efforts to regulate alcohol supply or pricing. These measures are realistic in the context of a policy environment best characterized by a shrug of the shoulders, as illustrated by Partanen's (1991) interviews with key informants in Kenya during the mid-1980s:

> [T]he respondents professed no particular interest in stiffer government controls relating to the availability or the use of alcohol, nor in the medical treatment of alcoholics . . . alcohol-related problems were not perceived primarily as health problems . . . in comparison with infant mortality, infectious disease, or malnutrition, the prevention and treatment of alcohol problems had low priority on the public health agenda. Problematic drinking was more often linked with the erosion of traditional values and with poverty. . . . "How can you tell the people not to drink if you cannot give them jobs?" asks one interviewee. (Partanen 1991: 19–20)

Drinking Struggles: Social and Political Historians' View

Recent apathy toward alcohol policy undoubtedly reflects the relatively unregulated markets and laissez-faire approach of most Sub-Saharan African governments. Historically, however, there is ample evidence of political contestation over alcohol in Africa. As a highly valued good, state or market control over alcohol production afforded the acquisition of power, influence and money. In the mid-1970s, social and political historians began documenting the intricate drinking struggles waged between the state and capitalist employers versus African working populations (van Onselen 1976; la Hausse 1988; Ambler 1991; Crush and Ambler 1992; Akyeampong 1996; Gewald, Chapter 6).

Historians cannot ignore the important function alcohol played in mobilizing workforces in a continent with no legacy of wage labor and where acute labor scarcity prevailed. The manipulation of the supply of alcohol at farm and firm levels by employers revealed a cynical drive for profit (van Onselen 1976; Crush 1992; Edgecombe 1992; Scully 1992). However, as Ambler and Crush (1992: 11) observe, "[D]rinking must be conceived not simply as a weapon of domination but also as a relatively autonomous form of cultural expression and thus a potent form of resistance." The heavy drinking patterns of southern African waged laborers, first cultivated then repressed by state and market forces, coalesced into a drinking subculture with its own momentum. Resistance to state regulatory control was fierce.

More akin to the applied alcohol studies analysts, social and political historians recognize alcohol's inherent capacity to incite dispute over its control, lending alcohol a motive power that is traceable through the clash of opposing interests. Disharmony rather than harmony tends to be the salient theme when these struggles are traced through time. The vested interests of the state and/or capital are pitted against the population. Within the population, splintering along class, ethnic, gender and generational lines over alcohol distribution and consumption generates internal conflict (Willis, Abbink, van der Drift and Pietilä in this volume; Nelson 1982; Bradford 1992).

Tracing alcohol as an object of contestation against the backdrop of national labor transformations, Africanization, urbanization and corporate investment strategies not only provides a more panoramic view of the role of alcohol in society, but also demonstrates the progression of ever-changing societal responses to alcohol. While cynical efforts to utilize alcohol to further capitalist profit and state revenue maximization readily belie policies in the name of the worker or public welfare, popular movements' large-scale concerns for family welfare and social integrity are often compromised by micro-level economic need or lifestyle preferences. Reversing the coin, publicly unsanctioned alcohol-related activities such as women's illegal brewing have often been highly beneficial to family provisioning at the micro-level (Willis, Chapter 3; McCall 1996). The clash of competing interests and sacrificed principles emerge as key themes from the social and political historians' study of alcohol.

ALCOHOL IN AFRICAN SOCIETY: PIECING TOGETHER A BROADER PICTURE THROUGH MULTIPLE LENSES

The three discourses outlined above have provided a wealth of insights, yet have existed largely in isolation from one another. Their non-intersection has diverted attention from comparative study of alcohol usage throughout Sub-Saharan Africa. Common historical trends and significant diverging tendencies related to production and consumption patterns have gone unnoticed. This collection outlines the continental mosaic of drinking patterns and their reconfiguration over time. The cross-disciplinary nature of the articles urges the reader to consider drinking in Africa in terms of context, introducing such matters as the emergence of drinking cultures and the ways in which alcohol becomes a vehicle for contesting change and power relations. A dialogue between anthropology and history emerges which highlights contradictory tendencies of social harmony and discord over alcohol usage. The medical and social welfare literature contributes insights pertaining to the relative weighting of alcohol's social benefits and costs.

This collection's continent-wide[8] panoply of case studies encompasses Guinea-Bissau, Ghana, Burkina Faso, Nigeria, Ethiopia, Tanzania, Uganda, Malawi and Namibia. Chapter 2 sketches changing modalities of alcohol usage in the colonial and postcolonial period before turning to recent tendencies that have surfaced during the neoliberal period of the past two decades.

In any edited collection, there is a need to group material for ease of reading. In this volume, there are no rigid boundaries between the parts. The reader will find many overlapping topics. Nonetheless, the chapters are grouped within economic, political and sociological sections, affording consideration of individual case studies from contrasting disciplinary perspectives.

Before moving to the case studies, Chapter 2 provides a historical overview, tracing the progression of technical innovation in alcohol production and its adoption by growing ranks of cottage-industry producers throughout Sub-Saharan Africa. Local brewing and distilling activities expanded massively as people scrambled to earn cash during the economic crisis of the 1980s. Demand for less costly alcohol swelled supply from the informal sector. During the 1990s, economic liberalization and privatization policies gave multinational corporations a firm footing in the African market for bottled beer and other alcoholic drinks. Drinking patterns became highly variable depending on the consumer's income standing and rural or urban ties. Until now, the literature on African alcohol usage has restrictively consisted of isolated case studies that have generally noted local and regional expansion of supply and demand without providing an aggregate overview or analyzing the significance of expanding supply for the continent as a whole.

Part II, entitled "Business Interests," explores alcohol as an economic resource, its production and sale, and how it has affected local and national economies. Alcohol has proven its economic value in gift exchange, in rationing schemes to privileged groups of people, in institutionally controlled incentive schemes, and in commodity markets. Willis's chapter affords readers a century-long timeline tracing locally brewed beer's utilization within a gift economy of male elders in southern Tanzania through to its current commodification. With the benefit of technical innovations, beer brewing now forms the basis of an extensive local economy from which women earn cash income to maintain their children. As a social historian, Willis documents how alcohol has been a continuous focus of contestation between men and women and between different age groups through the twentieth century.

Tanzarn's chapter also adopts a historical timeframe tracing the economic decline and political marginality of Kibaale District in Uganda, where the local banana crop faced commercial ruin as the poor state of repair of local roads precluded exports to regional urban markets. Under the circumstances, the distillation of bananas into *waragi*, now a renowned export of the area, has been a boon to the local economy. Nonetheless, social costs have ensued in the form of alcoholism and gender conflict over export earnings.

In Chapter 5, McCall provides a valuable compendium of findings from around the continent to demonstrate the environmental implications of cottage brewing, a widely overlooked dimension of alcohol production. He argues that national governments and the international donor community largely ignore the environmental problems associated with the enormous aggregate scale of local brewing enterprises. They are torn between supporting the need for local income generation on the one hand, and the perceived moral compromise involved in encouraging alcohol consumption on the other.

Part III turns to the political contests between the state and producers or consumers, or among drinkers and brewers along age, gender, ethnic and class divides. Manifestations of alcohol's value surface at household, community, regional and national levels. African nation-states have capitalized on its taxation potential and sought to exercise power over where, when and how people drink.

Gewald demonstrates how alcohol became a political football, almost impossible for the Namibian colonial state to control from above, when cottage brewing was readily accessible to the broad masses of the poor. Different aspirant local groups aligned with the state in the name of moral rectitude, but older women beer brewers and young male drinkers successfully circumvented official supply restrictions, proving to be an invincible force in Windhoek's townships.

In Chapter 7, Heap reveals how Nigerian colonial finance relied on alcohol import duties during the early stages of colonial rule. Alcohol tax revenues were transformed as alcohol production became more nationally based. Nonetheless, the state continued to be subjected to heavy criticism by temperance advocates who saw the state's taxation policies as a morally compromised license for drunkenness.

Moving away from national politics to the arena of current ethnic tension, Abbink shows how informal ethnically differentiated drinking patterns in southern Ethiopia are woven into a local discourse mirroring interethnic power politics at a national level. Against the backdrop of Ethiopia's current national experiment in ethnic separatism, this discourse centers on ethnic drinking styles heavily laced with attitudes of cultural superiority and inferiority.

Van der Drift's Guinea-Bissau case study provides striking contrast. Here drink unites rather than divides anomalous groups of people. In the face of traditional taboos on youth drinking, male elders and youth experimented with new communal drinking patterns. Newfound rural prosperity connected with cashew-nut production has produced a welcome side-effect, a potent distillate of the cashew fruit, *cana*, which adds to the merriment and frequency of drinking occasions. But in the aftermath of Guinea-Bissau's 1999 coup, van der Drift asks whether the egalitarian drinking alliance of elders and youth and associated talk of democracy introduced under structural adjustment were more superficial than many would care to believe. Possibly generational, gender and other social divides ran deeper and eventually had to erupt.

Pietelä, citing northern Tanzania case study material, documents ongoing gender antagonisms, and demonstrates how economically successful market women avert their menfolk's resentment of their businesses and leisure-time drinking. By limiting their drinking to certain evening hours and neighborhood locations, they avoid drawing attention to personal enjoyment, emphasizing instead the hard labor of their working day and the maternal sacrifice they endure to keep their children well fed. This contrasts with men's more open public drinking.

Part IV, "Social Comforts and Discomforts," explores the symbolic meaning associated with alcohol usage and the community controls exerted on alcohol production and consumption. A wealth of cultural meanings and special lexicons is embedded in alcohol's utilitarian usage and political control. It is true that alcohol's association with the ancestors is not invoked as frequently as before, and its role in ceremonial events has waned as commodity exchange replaces gift exchange. Nonetheless, drinking remains a central social activity and a source of commensality in both rural and urban settings throughout the continent. The psychochemical properties of alcohol continue to be a focus of social concern, prompting community sanctions and controls.

Akyeampong describes Ghanaian youth's drinking camaraderie and their celebration of alcoholic prowess in Accra in circumstances of rampant urban unemployment and limited life chances. Their drinking activities, characterized by strong group solidarity, do not prevent individuals within the group from eventually charting successful careers. Propitious circumstances befall some of the young drinkers, prompting them to move on, making their days of heavy drinking simply a memory of a carefree past, while those left behind face ever-narrowing prospects of escaping economic deprivation.

In the Sahelian setting of Maane in Burkina Faso, Luning explores traditional beliefs and attitudes to brewing that are overlaid with new, sometimes oppositional, religious affiliations of Protestantism and Catholicism. Yet local pragmatism and flexibility serve to dilute the effect of religious conversion, making Catholic attitudes to alcohol in particular much more tolerant than might otherwise be expected.

Van Dijk examines more brittle attitudes to alcohol consumption among Christian fundamentalists in Blantyre, Malawi. He demonstrates how alcohol is depicted as a defiling liquid associated with African extended family interaction that must be avoided by those desiring salvation in heaven and success on earth.

Building on the insights gleaned from these case studies, the concluding chapter turns to the darker side of alcohol consumption. Current institutional control of heavy drinking in the face of the widespread informalization of production and expansion of supply over the past two decades is considered. The focus is on how states, markets and community institutions influence drinking practices, serving to preclude or encourage individuals and communities crossing the fine line between the exuberance of social drinking and the misery of excess.

NOTES

1. Partanen (1991: 216) notes that the notion of "the transparency of alcohol does not fully take into account its role in social life. . . . The crucial question . . . is: How does the presence of alcohol in social situations alter the nature of interaction? . . . [how are] the forces of society and culture . . . 'refracted' when they pass through the medium of alcohol?"

2. McAllister (personal communication, 2000) notes that the first few drops of bottled brandy are often offered to the ancestors in the Ciskei and Transkei, a custom probably linked to the Dutch East Indies Company's introduction of brandy into South Africa in the seventeenth century (Ambler and Crush 1992).

3. Preindustrial societies in Europe similarly insisted on the social nature of alcohol. Drinking alone was taboo (Adler 1991).

4. In some ethnic groups, only postmenopausal women were traditionally free to drink (Sangree 1962).

5. Room (1984: 170) criticized "the disparity between the ethnographic and other alcohol literatures . . . [which] . . . reflects a systematic bias in the modern ethnographic literature against the full recognition of alcohol problems in the cultures under study."

6. Partanen (1991: 248) perceptively remarks that escape does not have to be private. "Collective misfortunes" can lead to collective loss of meaning in life, and the search for collective solace in the form of alcohol consumption.

7. Southern Africa accounts for 53 percent of the references in Molamu and Kebede Gessesse's (1988) bibliography on African alcohol and alcoholism. References for Nigeria (21 percent) and Kenya (11 percent) are also salient.

8. Throughout this book, "continent" refers to Sub-Saharan Africa.

REFERENCES

Adler, M. 1991. "From Symbolic Exchange to Commodity Consumption: Anthropological Notes on Drinking as a Symbolic Practice." In Susanna Barrows and Robin Room (eds.), *Drinking Behaviour and Belief in Modern History.* Berkeley and Los Angeles: University of California Press, 377–98.

Akyeampong, E.K. 1996. *Drink, Power, and Cultural Change: A Social History of Alcohol in Ghana, c. 1800 to Recent Times.* Portsmouth, NH: Heinemann; Oxford: James Currey.

Ambler, C.H. 1991. "Drunks, Brewers, and Chiefs." In Susanna Barrows and Robin Room (eds.), *Drinking Behaviour and Belief in Modern History.* Berkeley and Los Angeles: University of California Press, 165–83.

Ambler, C.H., and J. Crush. 1992. "Alcohol in Southern African Labor History." In J. Crush and C.H. Ambler (eds.), *Liquor and Labor in Southern Africa.* Athens: Ohio University Press, 1–55.

Anigbo, O.A.C. 1990. "Palm Wine as Social Processes: The Igbo Experience." *Africana Marburgensia* 23 (2): 3–23.

Beek, W.E.A. van. 1978. "Bierbrouwers in de Bergen: De Kapsiki en Higi van Noord-Kameroen en Noordoost Nigeria." Ph.D. thesis, Utrecht University.

Bersselaar, D. van den. 1998. "In Search of Igbo Identity: Language, Culture and Politics in Nigeria, 1900–1966." Ph.D. thesis. Leiden University.

Bradford, H. 1992. "'We Women Will Show Them': Beer Protests in the Natal Countryside, 1929." In J. Crush and C.H. Amber (eds.), *Liquor and Labor in Southern Africa.* Athens: Ohio University Press, 208–34.

Colson, E., and T. Scudder. 1988. *For Prayer and Profit: The Ritual, Economic and Social Importance of Beer in Gwembe District, Zambia, 1950–1982.* Stanford, CA: Stanford University Press.

Crush, J. 1992. "The Construction of Compound Authority: Drinking at Havelock, 1938–1944." In J. Crush and C.H. Ambler (eds.), *Liquor and Labor in Southern Africa.* Athens: Ohio University Press, 367–94.

Crush, J., and C.H. Ambler. 1992. *Liquor and Labor in Southern Africa*. Athens: Ohio University Press.

Curto, J. 1989. "Alcohol in Africa: A Preliminary Compilation of the Post-1875 Literature." *A Current Bibliography on African Affairs* 21 (1): 3–31.

Diduk, S. 1993. "European Alcohol, History, and the State in Cameroon." *African Studies Review* 36 (10): 1–42.

Douglas, M. 1987. "A Distinctive Anthropological Perspective." In M. Douglas (ed.), *Constructive Drinking: Perspectives on Drink from Anthropology*. Cambridge: Cambridge University Press, 3–15.

Dumett, R.E. 1974. "The Social Impact of the European Liquor Trade on the Akan of Ghana (Gold Coast and Asante): 1875–1910." *Journal of Interdisciplinary History* 5 (1): 69–101.

Edgecombe, R. 1992. "The Role of Alcohol in Labor Acquisition and Control on the Natal Coal Mines, 1911–1938." In J. Crush and C.H. Ambler (eds.), *Liquor and Labor in Southern Africa*. Athens: Ohio University Press, 187–207.

Green, M. 1999. "Trading on Inequality: Gender and the Drinks Trade in Southern Tanzania." *Africa* 69 (3): 404–25.

Hagaman, B.L. 1977. "Beer and Matriliny: The Power of Women in a West African Society." Ph.D. thesis, Northeastern University.

Haggblade, S. 1987. "Vertical Considerations of Choice-of-Technique Studies: Evidence from Africa's Indigenous Beer Industry." *Economic Development and Cultural Change* 35: 723–42.

———. 1992. "The Shebeen Queen and the Evolution of Botswana's Sorghum Beer Industry." In J. Crush, and C.H. Ambler (eds.), *Liquor and Labor in Southern Africa*. Athens: Ohio University Press, 395–412.

Hausse, P. la. 1988. *Brewers, Beerhalls and Boycotts: A History of Liquor in South Africa*. Johannesburg: Ravan Press.

Haworth, A., M. Mwanalushi, and D. Todd. 1981. *Community Response to Alcohol-Related Problems in Zambia*. Lusaka: University of Zambia, Institute for African Studies, Community Health Research Unit.

Heap, S. 1994/95. "Alcohol in Africa: A Supplementary List of Post-1875 Literature." *A Current Bibliography on African Affairs* 26 (1): 1–14.

Heath, D.B. 1987a. "A Decade of Development in the Anthropological Study of Alcohol Use: 1970–1980." In M. Douglas (ed.), *Constructive Drinking: Perspectives on Drink from Anthropology*. Cambridge: Cambridge University Press, 16–69.

———. 1987b. "Anthropology and Alcohol Studies: Current Issues." *Annual Review of Anthropology* 16: 99–120.

Hedlund, M., and M. Lundahl. 1984. "The Economic Role of Beer in Rural Zambia." *Human Organization* 43: 61–65.

Herlehy, T.J. 1984. "Ties that Bind: Palm Wine and Blood Brotherhood at the Kenya Coast during the Nineteenth Century." *International Journal of African Historical Studies* 17: 285–308.

Karp, I. 1980. "Beer Drinking and Social Experience in an African Society: An Essay in Formal Sociology." In I. Karp and C.S. Bird (eds.), *Explorations in African Systems of Thought.* Bloomington: Indiana University Press, 83–119.

McAllister, P. 1985. "Beasts to Beer Pots—Migrant Labor and Ritual Change in Willowvale District, Transkei." *African Studies* 44 (2): 121–35.

———. 1986. "'Releasing the Widow'—Xhosa Beer Drink Oratory and Status Change." *African Studies* 45 (2): 171–97.

———. 2001. *Building the Homestead: Agriculture, Labour and Beer in South Africa's Transkei.* Leiden: African Studies Centre/Ashgate.

McCall, M. 1996. "Rural Brewing, Exclusion and Development Policy-Making." *Gender and Development* 4 (3): 29–38.

Molamu, L., and Kebede Gessesse. 1988. *Alcohol and Alcoholism in Africa: A Bibliography.* Gaborone: University College of Botswana, National Institute of Development Research and Documentation Unit.

Molamu, L., and W.G. Manyeneng. 1988. *Alcohol Use and Abuse in Botswana: Report of a Study.* Gaborone: Health Education Unit.

Moukolo, A. 1990. "Alcohol and Its Main Functions in the Congo." In J. Maula, M. Lindblad, and C. Tigerstedt (eds.), *Alcohol in Developing Countries.* Helsinki: Nordic Council for Alcohol and Drug Research, 127–33.

Mwangi, M. 1973. *Kill Me Quick.* London: Heinemann Educational Books.

Nelson, N. 1982. "'Women Must Help Each Other': The Operation of Personal Networks among Buzaa Beer Brewers." In P. Caplan and J. Bujra (eds.), *Women United, Women Divided.* Bloomington: Indiana University Press, 77–98.

Netting, R.M. 1964. "Beer as a Locus of Value among the West African Kofyar." *American Anthropologist* 66 (2): 375–84.

Ngokwey, N. 1987. "Varieties of Palm Wine among the Lele of the Kasai." In M. Douglas (ed.), *Constructive Drinking: Perspectives on Drink from Anthropology.* Cambridge: Cambridge University Press, 113–21.

Nti, K. 1998. "The Role of Alcohol in the 1905 Conflict between the Anaafo and Ntsin Asafo Companies of Cape Coast." *Transactions of the Historical Society of Ghana*, New Series 2: 49–55.

Obot, I.S. 1990. "Substance Abuse, Health and Social Welfare in Africa: An Analysis of the Nigerian Experience." *Social Science and Medicine* 6 (31): 699–704.

———. 1993. *Drinking Behaviour and Attitudes in Nigeria: A General Population Survey in the Middlebelt Region.* Jos: University of Jos, Centre for Development Studies.

Okri, B. 1991. *Famished Road.* London: Cape.

O'Laughlin, B. 1973. "Mbum Beer Parties: Structures of Production and Exchange in an African Social Formation." Ph.D. thesis, Yale University.

Onselen, C. van. 1976. "Randlords and Rotgut, 1886–1905: An Essay on the Role of Alcohol in the Development of European Imperialism and South African Capitalism." *History Workshop Journal* 2: 32–89.

Parkin, D.J. 1972. *Palms, Wine, and Witnesses: Public Spirit and Private Gain in an African Farming Community*. San Francisco: Chandler.

Parry, R. 1992. "The 'Durban System' and the Limits of Colonial Power in Salisbury, 1890–1935." In J. Crush and C.H. Ambler (eds.), *Liquor and Labor in Southern Africa.* Athens: Ohio University Press, 139–61.

Partanen, J. 1991. *Sociability and Intoxication: Alcohol and Drinking in Kenya, Africa, and the Modern World.* Helsinki: Finnish Foundation for Alcohol Studies, vol. 39.

Pirio, G.R. 1982. "Commerce, Industry and Empire: The Making of Modern Portuguese Colonialism in Angola and Mozambique." Ph.D. thesis, University of California, Los Angeles.

Pomuti, A., and G. Eiseb. 1990. *Alcohol Abuse: A Southern Namibian Survey.* Windhoek: Namibian Institute for Social and Economic Research.

Reader, D.H., and J. May. 1971. *Drinking Patterns in Rhodesia: Highfield African Township Salisbury.* Salisbury: University of Rhodesia.

Rekdal, O.B. 1996. "Money, Milk and Sorghum Beer: Change and Continuity among the Iraqw of Tanzania." *Africa* 66 (3): 367–85.

Room, R. 1984. "Alcohol and Ethnography: A Case of Problem Deflation?" *Current Anthropology* 25 (2): 169–91.

Sangree, W.H. 1962. "The Social Functions of Beer Drinking in Bantu Tiriki." In D.J. Pittman and C.R. Snyder (eds.), *Society, Culture, and Drinking Patterns.* New York: John Wiley & Sons, 6–21.

Saul, M. 1981. "Beer, Sorghum and Women: Production for the Market in Rural Upper Volta." *Africa* 51 (3): 746–64.

Schatzberg, M. 1980. *Politics and Class in Zaire: Bureaucracy, Business and Beer in Lisala.* New York: African Publishing Company.

Scully, P. 1992. "Liquor and Labor in the Western Cape, 1870–1900." In J. Crush and C.H. Ambler (eds.), *Liquor and Labor in Southern Africa.* Athens: Ohio University Press, 56–77.

Singer, M. 1986. "Toward a Political-Economy of Alcoholism: The Missing Link in the Anthropology of Drinking." *Social Science and Medicine* 23 (2): 113–30.

Themba, C. 1972. *The Will to Die.* London: Heinemann.

Wilson, M. 1977. *For Men and Elders: Change in the Relations of Generations and of Men and Women among the Nyakyusa-Ngonde People, 1875–1971.* London: International African Institute.

Wolcott, H.F. 1974. *The African Beer Gardens of Bulawayo.* New Brunswick, NJ: Rutgers Center of Alcohol Studies.

2

Changing Modalities of Alcohol Usage

Deborah Fahy Bryceson

Alcohol drinking modalities are defined here as patterns of drinking and the accompanying norms, attitudes and values associated with drinking and intoxication. The modalities reflect political, economic and cultural change in the wider society and roughly correspond to differences in economic livelihood and social lifestyle. In Africa, where livelihoods have undergone tremendous transformation over the past century, drinking modalities serve as barometers of socioeconomic change.

Long before colonial penetration, Africans produced and consumed alcoholic drinks, unlike the indigenous peoples of Australia and North America. In a geographical landmass as large as Sub-Saharan Africa, enormous variation is to be expected. Nonetheless, a general characterization of the continent's precolonial agrarian communities' alcohol modalities has emerged based on oral history and explorers' accounts. In the absence of counter-evidence, it is employed as a baseline for the study of changing consumption patterns (e.g., Sangree 1962; Ambler 1991; Partanen 1991; Colson and Scudder 1988). The first section of this chapter sketches the contours of a drinking modality believed to have been widely prevalent prior to colonialism. The following sections trace changes in production, distribution and consumption patterns during the colonial and postcolonial periods.

THE PRECOLONIAL "SPECIAL" MODALITY

Insofar as one can argue that a precolonial drinking modality existed, its defining features were characterized by social, physical and environmental constraints on alcohol consumption. "Special" seems a suitable designation since it highlights the fact that alcohol was not an everyday consumption item in most people's lives in precolonial Africa.

First, the indigenous alcoholic drinks of Africa were fermented, not distilled. Sorghum and millet beers and palm wines dominated, and they were usually of low ethanol content, generally between 2 and 4 percent (McCall 1996). These drinks could not be conserved and had to be drunk within a day or two of production.

Second, alcohol production and consumption tended to be highly seasonal, especially with respect to the grain-based beers (Sangree 1962; Colson and Scudder 1988; Ambler 1991). The pattern of ceremonial festivities and drinking occasions was based on the agricultural cycle (Luning, Chapter 12). The peak came in the wake of a successful grain harvest when there was real cause for celebration and giving thanks to the ancestors. This was a period of relaxation following months of labor-intensive agricultural planting, weeding and harvesting. Drinking represented a clear demarcation between work and leisure, seasonally rather than diurnally delineated. Due to its temporal concentration, the drinking may well have had an air of abandon about it, with heavy binge drinking for several days until the supply of beer ran out. This was not unusual or frowned upon (Ambler 1991). However, Colson and Scudder (1988) stressed that the amount of grain allocated to brewing would have been constrained by practical considerations of the community's grain requirements until the next harvest. Hence, beer availability on these occasions would have been strictly rationed until improved rural transport introduced the possibility of grain purchase throughout the year (Heap 2000).[1]

Many family and community celebrations such as weddings and puberty rites would have been deliberately scheduled to take place in the postharvest period when the availability of ingredients for alcohol production was assured (Luning, Chapter 12). Alcohol could appear out of season at other occasions like funerals and, given its close association with the ancestors, it was not surprisingly a feature of wakes.

The other feature of the traditional drinking modality is that alcohol was strongly associated with male elders, who held the highest status in Africa's rural communities. Older men received preferential access to alcohol.

The drinking of low ethanol–content alcohol, woven into special communitywide ceremonies and occasions marking life-cycle passage, constituted an intensely social event. Cannabis, another stimulant found in Africa, had a different profile. When it was used, it tended to be a private solace rarely found in public ceremonies (Colson and Scudder 1988). Alcohol, on the other hand, was so fundamentally associated with social exchange between contemporaries as well as with the ancestors that drinking alone could be considered morally depraved (Sangree 1962; Karp 1980).

The relevance of the special drinking modality as a composite construct faded during the colonial period, as an array of drinking modalities began to surface.

REVAMPING PRODUCTION, 1880–1980

The century spanning the colonial and early postcolonial period witnessed an escalation in the variety, scale, rate and reliability of alcohol production and ethanol strength. By its nature, home-based production of alcohol is subject to constant experimentation. As a chemical process taking place outside a controlled laboratory setting, variable outcomes are inevitable, and the producer must constantly struggle to preclude brewing failure (McCall, Chapter 5). During the colonial period, new crops were introduced, previously adopted crops were more widely disseminated, and improvements in transport led to the availability of new food items. Some of these began to be added to or substituted for the more traditional ingredients in alcohol recipes. The displacement of sorghum and millet by maize was most notable. Throughout much of East and southern Africa, higher-yielding maize was edging out the lower-yielding indigenous sorghums and millets. Not surprisingly, maize increasingly became the primary grain in alcohol production, often facilitating the discovery of faster brewing techniques (la Hausse 1988). As brewing became more commercialized, these time savings offered brewers better business prospects. Women producers were at the center of the growth of alcohol as a cottage industry, first in urban areas and later throughout rural Africa (Hellman 1948; Nelson 1982; Hedlund and Lundahl 1984; Malahleha 1985; Eales 1989; la Hausse 1992; Redding 1992; Maula 1997; Glazer 1997; Green 1999; Lentz 1999).

At the turn of the century, sugar became readily available in towns, and its ethanol-enhancing properties were quickly exploited, as Gewald

(Chapter 6) documents for Windhoek. Gradually, this innovation spread to rural areas as well (Willis, Chapter 3). Fermented sugar drinks tended to boost alcohol content to 6–8 percent and offered value for money for those seeking intoxication. It was these new experimental drinks concentrated in the urban areas, rather than the traditional rural brews, that colonial officialdom endeavored to curb (Gewald, Chapter 6). At the same time, distillation techniques were spreading, fanned in West Africa by colonial government attempts to curtail or ban importation of European distilled drinks like gin and whisky that had been a feature of the area since the trans-Atlantic slave trade of the seventeenth to nineteenth centuries (Akyeampong 1996). In East and southern Africa, distillation techniques were often spread by worldly-wise returning soldiers or contract laborers who appreciated their get-drunk-quickly quality despite the dangers of producing alcohol using sometimes suspect ingredients and relatively primitive equipment that, under the pressurized conditions of the distilling process, was liable to explode (Tanzarn, Chapter 4). The production of distilled drinks was generally banned in rural and urban areas on health and safety grounds.

Colonial paternalism, which reached its pinnacle in the settler and mining zones of British-dominated southern Africa, inevitably led to state production of officially authorized brews. To ensure a market for its product, the state outlawed local cottage alcohol production, subjecting women brewers and distillers to campaigns of harassment.[2] Gewald's (Chapter 6) case study reveals the racist and political machinations that so often accompanied these "for their own good" state undertakings. The aim was to produce a beer that African drinkers, particularly male laborers in urban areas and mining compounds, would be willing to drink. Popularizing a nutritious, relatively low alcohol content like that found in home brews was the goal. South Africa pioneered this effort, and other southern African colonies followed.[3] To be attractive to African drinkers, these state-produced opaque beers had to sell at relatively low prices, because they faced competition from tantalizing, higher alcohol-content home brews and the distilled drinks of clandestine shebeens (la Hausse 1988).[4] By contrast, in Francophone Africa the manufacture of beer by private enterprises was more pronounced (Ivory Coast: Domergue 1985; Zaire: Ngindu 1982).

In the first two decades after national independence, the industrial production of alcohol expanded rapidly throughout the continent. State monopolies figured prominently in these instances but for different reasons. Official thinking of the time saw industrialization as the lynchpin of rapid economic development. Alcohol manufacture, perhaps more than any other form of industrial production, offered reliable and quick profits despite the innumerable handicaps faced by African industry (Mphaisha 1986/87). A ready market and the natural import barrier inherent in perishable beer in heavy bottles made it not only profit-making, but also revenue-generating for fledging young African governments in search of fiscal funding for their ambitious economic development plans (Heap 1996). Nonetheless, as national economic enterprises there were drawbacks, best exemplified by the ballooning of import costs associated with the meteoric rise of breweries from seven to thirty-four during Nigeria's postindependence oil boom of the late 1970s and early 1980s. High import costs were embedded in the beer brewing package: turnkey factories using state-of-the-art brewing technology and barley that could not be grown in the tropics (Kortteinen 1990; Odejide et al. 1990).

Some governments, notably those in East Africa, followed the South African model and manufactured opaque beer, generically known as *chibuku*. Far more significant, however, was the manufacture of clear lager beer. This beer, often three to four times more expensive than *chibuku* and ten times as expensive as a homemade brew, became the drink of the budding African middle class.

Postcolonial governments eager to establish state-owned breweries actively sought to expand the urban population's consumption of bottled beer while limiting their consumption of informal-sector products. Nelson (1982) describes the stringent enforcement measures in the squatter settlements of Nairobi and the solidarity of women brewers in the face of sporadic police raids. Brewers had to contend with on-duty police law enforcement and off-duty customers.

In Ghana, by contrast, a long-standing battle between government enforcement officers and urban women *akpeteshie* gin distillers appeared to turn in favor of the women with the legalization of *akpeteshie*. In fact, Kwame Nkrumah's ambitious postindependent government had its eye on the gin's potentially lucrative tax revenues. But the distillers were far from eager to pay license fees and be taxed (Akyeampong 1996).

RESTRUCTURING CONSUMPTION, 1880–1980: FROM CEREMONIAL TO RECREATIONAL LEISURE

Alcohol consumption increased in terms of the widening availability and array of alcoholic drinks, their increasing alcoholic strength, the proportion of the community drinking, and the amount drunk on an annual

Table 2.1
Types of Drinks and Their Average Alcoholic Content

Drink type[1] and production source	Alcoholic content (% alcohol/vol.)	Usual measure (ml)	Alcoholic content/drink (ml)	Units of alcohol per drink	Relative economic cost
A Home-brewed beer[2] & sap wine	2.4	780 or less	19	4	non-monetized
B Commercial cottage-industry brew[3]	6.9	225	16	3	very cheap
C Commercial manufactured opaque beer[4]	3.0	780	24	5	cheap
D Commercial manufactured bottled beer[5]	4.0	375	15	3	expensive
E Commercial cottage-industry distilled drinks[6]	20.0	225	45	9	cheap per unit of alcohol
F Commercial distilled imports[7]	40.0	24	10	2	very expensive

Source: Haworth, Mwanalushi and Todd 1981: 3.10, 2.23.

Notes:

[1]The drinks named below, illustrative of each drink type, are drawn from a 1981 Zambian survey by Haworth et al. They have a local equivalent in most African countries with roughly similar alcohol content levels.

[2]Traditional fermented home brews usually use sorghum and/or maize and have a low alcohol content. In Zambia, they include the "near beer" *munkoyo* or *mukonde* (0.6–2.7%) and *mutete* (2.3–4.2%). In South Africa, these brews were historically referred to as "kaffir beer" or *utshwala* and *bojalwa* in Botswana. In East Africa and Ethiopia, respectively, the generic terms are *pombe* and *bordé*. Traditional drinks found elsewhere in Africa include sorghum (Guinea corn) beer in West Africa, banana beers in East Africa (*mbege*), and a wide range of sap wines made from coconut palms (e.g., *tembo* in East Africa), bamboo (*ulanzi* in East Africa and *tombo* in Nigeria) and oil palms (*Elaéis guineensis* and the raphia palm *Raphia hookeri* in West Africa) (Heap 1999). Other food items are also used for fermentation, such as honey *wanzuki* in East Africa (Maula 1997) and *t'ädj* in Ethiopia (Abbink, Chapter 8).

[3]*Mbamba* is a collective name for illicitly brewed drinks with varying alcoholic contents: *mbamba* (6–8%), *skokiaan* (5%), *solopi*, a sugar and yeast mixture requiring less than a day's preparation with unpleasant hangover effects (4–8%). In South Africa a wide array of drinks are concocted with fermented yeast or sugar, including *khali*, *skokiaan*, *shimeya* and *babaton*.

[4]In Zambia, these opaque beers include Lusaka and Kafue beer (3.5–5.5%), whereas in East Africa they are generally referred to as *chibuku*.

(continued)

[5]Bottled lager beer.
[6]Cottage-industry–produced African gin *kachasu* (15–31%) and some of the distilled drinks of other countries have been recorded with alcoholic contents of up to 40%. *Sodabi* is distilled palm wine drunk in Benin. Distilled alcohols in East Africa include *gongo, waragi* and *chang'aa* and in Ethiopia *katikala* (30–50%). In West Africa, African gin goes under various names including *akpeteshie* (Ghana), *ogogoro* or *kaikai* (Nigeria) and *afofo* (Cameroon). *Cana* is the distilled cashew drink of Guinea-Bissau.
[7]*Euro* is a generic name for typical imported European distilled drinks including whisky, gin and brandy.

per capita basis. In the process, the purpose of drinking was gradually transformed. Formerly limited to public ceremonies where relatively few imbibed, drinking became a communally shared leisure pastime in which broader sections of the community participated. Drinking took on new temporal dimensions as well. Previously limited by seasonal supply, the market now offered year-round availability, although drinking was constrained by the formal working day for those with jobs. Their drinking peaked at weekends, with the frequency of after-work evening drinks depending on one's affluence (Crush 1992).

Differentiated consumption patterns began to coalesce around a proliferating array of drinks distinguished by their production source, price and varying alcoholic content. Table 2.1 groups these different drinks into six main types.

Not all drink categories were present everywhere, but the general applicability of this drinks typology can be used as the basis for constructing a stylized five-category schema of drinking modalities indicative of the trends and differentiated drinking patterns that had emerged by the early postcolonial period (Table 2.2). These drinking modalities are observable to varying degrees in most African countries to the present. They evolved alongside processes of urbanization and economic class formation during the colonial period and in the first decades after independence.

Rural Ceremonial and Gift Exchange Drinking Modality (I)

Although rural drinking modalities dominated in the 1880–1980 period, the distributive form of drinking was drastically altered as the influence of the cash nexus spread. Ceremonial (I) and commoditized (II) alcohol consumption coexisted in most rural areas, but as time passed, the former was progressively displaced by the latter (e.g., Luning, Chapter 12). The consensually agreed distribution of alcohol in favor of older men began to

Table 2.2
Schema of Drinking Modalities in the Post-Independence Period, 1960–1980

	Rural Peasant			*Urban Classes*	
	I	II	III	IV	V
Drinking modalities	Ceremonial and gift exchange	Commoditized	Working-class commoditized	Middle-class commoditized	Elite commoditized
Type of alcoholic drink	almost exclusively traditional fermented beers & sap wine	primarily fermented beers & wine + some distilled drinks	primarily fermented beers & wine + some distilled drinks	primarily manufactured bottled beer	manufactured beers, wines & distilled drinks
Production source	home-made rural product	local rural cottage-industry	primarily local urban cottage-industry	local urban factory manufacture	local urban factory & imported manufacture
Consump-tion trend	contracting	expanding relative to (I)	expanding with growth of urban population	rapidly expanding	expanding in countries with large income disparities

Source: Author's compilation.

erode. Once distribution became commoditized, beer consumption could no longer be kept within the bounds of traditional ascriptive norms. The rights and responsibilities associated with gender and age, the well-worn fracture lines of the rural community, started to be renegotiated.

However, ceremonial and exchange beer production still held sway in communities where agricultural cashcropping had been sidestepped or short-circuited. Ironically, South Africa, the continent's most economically advanced country, had many rural communities where agricultural commodity production was virtually nonexistent (McAllister 2001). Most were labor reserves where remittances and pensions provided some cash inflow. The lack of surpluses of grain and the restricted money supply largely precluded commoditized beer production. These societies were not characterized by a traditional special drinking modality, because the ceremonies and exchange forms were relatively recent innovations reflecting continual negotiation about the status between community members. They acknowledged not only the privileges of old age, but also the power of cash earners such as young migrant laborers. Traditional features like single-sex drinking, especially among men, were more marked than in other rural communities.

Rural Commoditized Drinking Modality (II)

The rural societies characterized primarily by this drinking modality became more prevalent than those of the ceremonial gift exchange modality (e.g., Willis, Tanzarn and McCall in this volume). While the direction of change emanated from designated ceremonial prestation within the local community toward commodity purchase within and beyond the immediate community, alcohol distribution displayed many variants.

In East and especially southern Africa, young men's work-related access to alcohol increased when they became part of the colonial wage labor force. The tedium of life in a single-sex work compound, earning low bachelor wages, was assuaged by employers' efforts to supplement wages with alcohol payments in kind or provisions to facilitate laborers' indirect access to alcohol.

African peasant cashcropping spread during the 1920s and 1930s, but depressed international commodity prices and colonial government tax demands left little disposable income from peasants' cashcrop earnings. This began to change in the 1950s when an international commodity boom following the Korean War raised peasant producer prices at the same time as the surge in African nationalist aspirations kept colonial tax demands in check. Several studies (Willis, Chapter 3; Haggblade 1992) note the rapid growth of beer brewing enterprises in response to rising rural commercial demand.

Colson and Scudder (1988) documented the initiation of women's cottage beer production in Gwembe District, Zambia. As a remote, subsistence-based economy experiencing periodic grain shortfalls, local communities tried to safeguard their grain supply, and brewing was seasonally restricted to that of a primarily ceremonial nature. In the early 1950s, the provision of a road and a shop with assorted consumer goods gave women the impetus to brew for cash. Concern about grain shortages was alleviated by the possibility of purchasing grain year-round. Such purchases afforded the opportunity to brew on a far larger scale than would have been possible using locally generated grain supplies.

A gender struggle evolved in the process of beer's commoditization. Rural women, who had been largely excluded from colonial-directed cashcropping, saw the sale of alcoholic drinks as a way to wrest some of the local cash income out of men's hands. Men, however, were eager to hold on to the trappings of the traditional uncommoditized economy in the form of free tasting rights (Nkhoma 1987; Lentz 1999).

Drinking became informalized, narrowing social distances in most rural areas as commoditized consumption of alcohol increasingly displaced gift and ceremonial exchange drinking. Willis (Chapter 3) traces this process in southern Tanzania. In general, as the sale of alcoholic drinks moved away from the brewer's home to more commercial premises, the decorum of traditional ritual drinking and good-neighborliness eroded and drinkers felt far less inhibited. So too, the growing involvement of youth in village drinking reduced status recognition and ceremonial norms (Ambler 1991). In rural Uganda, it was noted that

> [t]here is a trend from less to more public display of drunkenness, aggressiveness, and sexuality . . . people in the traditional setting say they drink "to be polite," "to visit with one another." In the more modern bars people say "to get drunk." . . . The "informalisation" of consumption patterns has various implications. (Robbins and Pollnac 1969: 280)

Urban Working- and Middle-Class Drinking Modalities (III & IV)

Rural and urban differences in drinking modalities became marked during the 1960s and 1970s. Urban migration fueled by the Africanization of white-collar segments of the economy gave educated Africans disposable incomes hitherto unrealized. But alcohol had just as strong a pull on the relatively uneducated, whose job prospects were far less promising. Beyond southern Africa, urban drinking habits during the period under consideration have not been extensively documented. Partanen's (1991) and Akyeampong's (1996) studies of drinking and cultural change in Kenya and Ghana stand out as notable exceptions. In the urban setting, both have identified three distinct drinking modalities based on congealing divisions between the working, middle and elite classes (Table 2.2).

In southern Africa, South Africa and Zambia have received the most coverage. South Africa's apartheid history makes it an extreme nonrepresentative example, whereas Zambia, where both rural and urban drinking modalities have been observed, more closely reflects conditions pertaining to the rest of Sub-Saharan Africa. Colson and Scudder's (1988) in-depth anthropological and historical study of rural drinking is supplemented by Haworth et al.'s 1981 WHO-sponsored survey of drinking patterns in three settings: a working-class neighborhood and a middle-class (though somewhat economically mixed) neighborhood of Lusaka, as well as a village within relatively easy reach of Lusaka. This survey provides one of the few comparative studies of Sub-Saharan Africa's three most common commoditized drinking modalities, namely, that of rural peasants (II), and the working (III) and middle classes (IV) (Table 2.2). It is useful to reflect on Haworth et al.'s findings before considering how Zambian drinking modalities contrast with patterns found elsewhere in Sub-Saharan Africa.

Zambian intermodal differences were based more on what people drank than on how they drank. Income played a decisive role. While rural peasants drank inexpensive locally produced cottage-industry beer, working-class drinkers relied primarily on cheap manufactured *chibuku*, and middle-class drinkers preferred more expensive bottled lager beer, a sign of having made it financially, distancing themselves from rustic consumption patterns.[5]

Zambia had a long history of beer halls that were replaced by less institutionalized taverns and bars for higher-income earners, but the legacy of single-sex drinking groups was strongly evident in all three modalities. Drinking with members of the opposite sex was not common, but drinking with one's spouse was even more infrequent, probably because of the strong association between drinking occasions and opportunities for extramarital sex, especially in urban areas. Formerly, women who frequented the beer halls were assumed to be prostitutes. In the 1960s and 1970s, it became more acceptable for women to drink publicly, although a certain social stigma lingered. Middle-aged men with family responsibilities reported drinking less than other men. Nonetheless, the major variation in quantities drunk related to differences in gender rather than age.

Polarized drinking habits, described as "all-or-none" by Haworth et al. (1981), were marked. About half of the adult population drank heavily, whereas the other half reported themselves to be abstainers. Haworth et al. caution that it was not always clear what "abstaining" meant, and generally it could not be equated with never drinking. A substantial segment of the population tended to avoid alcohol, in contrast to another large segment who actively sought to consume considerable quantities of alcohol, "drinking to get drunk." This was no doubt related to an increasing availability of alcoholic drinks as well as the prevailing practice of not eating while drinking so as to maximize alcohol absorption. Amounts drunk during drinking sessions and the frequency of drinking were generally high, especially among rural peasants.[6]

There are, of course, severe limitations on the inferences that can be drawn from the Zambian intermodal comparison for the rest of Sub-Saharan Africa. Zambia, as part of the southern African labor migration zone, has a history soaked in institutional (both government and employer) interference in local people's alcohol consumption patterns. The widespread use of leisure time for heavy drinking was hardly a historical accident for the population of this region given their comparatively proletarianized and urbanized livelihoods, as well as the brutal manner in which the proletarianization process unfolded. Furthermore, the manufacturing sector of beer and in particular *chibuku* was far more developed in this region than elsewhere. The multinational corporation Lonrho developed a string of twenty breweries in small towns throughout Zambia in the mid-1970s with a wide rural outreach (Rogerson and Tucker 1985).[7] Lager beer and especially *chibuku* were not only readily available but also reasonably priced, as in Zimbabwe (Reader and May 1971), South Africa (Crush and Ambler 1992) and Botswana (Molamu and Manyeneng 1988).

The disparate evidence of the middle-class drinking modality found in other African countries where industrial breweries had started manufacturing clear lager beer after independence was remarkably similar across the continent. As a drink, lager beer served with roasted meat in East Africa or some spicy dish like pepper soup in West Africa could provide after-work sustenance far into the night for the white-collar rank and file of rapidly expanding government bureaucracies and commercial spheres.[8] The bars frequented played the local popular music of the time, highlife music in West Africa and Congo jazz in East Africa, such that disco music or even live bands provided the background music to conversations of the primarily male drinkers. Careers could be facilitated through the choice of drinking partners or topics of conversation. Furthermore, the bars offered ample opportunities for sexual fulfillment (Vuorela 1979; Glazer 1997). Many men developed a characteristic beer belly (*kitambi* in Kiswahili), a mark of success and enjoyment of the good life. These middle-class men were savoring the fruits of independence in the form of leisure-filled beer drinking (Vuorela 1979; Schatzberg 1980; Partanen 1991; Akyeampong 1996; Glazer 1997).

An increase in lager beer consumption among up-and-coming South African blacks also began to surface in the 1960s, replacing reliance on the commercial so-called kaffir beer (*chibuku*) so heavily associated with South

African state repression. South African Breweries, among others, had embarked on widespread advertising campaigns following the lifting of alcohol prohibition to "engineer a taste transfer" of black consumers from sorghum to lager beers (Rogerson and Hart 1986; Rogerson 1990). With their more educated clientele, shebeens became important nodes for urban black artistic and political expression, inspiring black musicians and writers, the *marabi* culture.

By contrast, across the continent working-class drinkers could not afford lager beer except on rare occasions. They were reliant on cottage industry–produced beers or distilled drinks. In Kenya, an estimated 37 percent of alcohol consumption nationally was illegally distilled *chang'aa* (Nout 1981, quoted in Partanen 1991). In Ghana, *akpeteshie* gin was the favorite. Cheap and powerful, *akpeteshie* gave value for money in terms of getting drunk fast, but it was as much the conviviality of male drinking groups as the alcohol itself that made drinking a major social pastime among Ghanaian urban working-class men. In and out of employment, one's neighborhood drinking companions could provide needed social backup to see one through lean times. Akyeampong (1996) notes that such bars also served as centers for mobilizing strike action during turbulent periods in Ghana's political history.

Urban Elite Drinking Modality (V)

The type of alcohol consumed and the setting in which it is consumed are the hallmarks of each modality. The elite class, consisting primarily of the highest echelons of government officialdom, adopted international consumption patterns long before the term "globalization" came into vogue. They drank imported European distilled alcoholic drinks like whisky and cognac, which they had acquired on foreign trips or could purchase at the up-market international tourist hotels built in the decades immediately after independence. They distinguished themselves from all the other modalities by seeking secluded drinking settings in the cocktail lounges of the tourist hotels or in their own homes with friends. Akyeampong (1996) notes with irony that in Ghana these drinkers numbered among Nkrumah's socialist vanguard.

The importance of distilled drinks among the working classes was less pronounced outside West Africa, where the early appearance of imported distilled drinks and the backlash effects generated by prohibition during the early part of the twentieth century had led to far earlier reliance on an informal-sector distilled drink supply. In this sense, Ghana was a pacesetter, not only with respect to being the first African country to gain independence from colonial rule. Features of its alcohol consumption pattern were to gain more general continental significance in the decades to come.

TWISTS AND TURNS OF THE NEOLIBERAL ERA: ALCOHOL AS ECONOMIC SALVATION AND FREEDOM

The protracted economic and political upheavals of the 1980s and 1990s reverberated through alcohol production and consumption patterns. Tendencies of preceding decades accelerated: drink preference moved increasingly toward higher alcoholic content, the drinking population continued to expand and embraced more women, and collapsing class formations and new rural-urban relations gave rise to fluctuating, often unexpected patterns of alcoholic drink supply.

Sub-Saharan Africa's economic crisis, precipitated by two successive oil-price spirals, one in the mid-1970s and the other in 1979, seriously undermined the viability of peasant agriculture. The spiraling costs of transporting the relatively low, uncapitalized agricultural output of widely scattered peasant households to centers of urban demand and ports caused the already inefficient parastatals that transported and processed such crops to buckle. This had a domino effect on the urban economy. As agriculture floundered, the relative affluence of urban government and parastatal employees quickly dissolved. National governments fell into debt and became subject to the conditionality of structural adjustment programs enforced by the World Bank and the International Monetary Fund (IMF) (Bryceson 2000b).

The Surge in Urban and Rural Cottage Production During the 1980s

The inflationary effects of the oil crisis hit urban dwellers, especially formal sector wage earners, extremely hard.[9] The rapidly declining purchasing power of male heads of households, combined with job redundancies, led to a burgeoning informal sector. Formal sector employees resorted to work in the informal sector during or after their official office hours to help make up the shortfall in income, while other family members, notably unemployed wives, entered the informal sector in droves on a full- or part-time basis. Most, without educational qualifications or technical training, were forced to offer goods or services that were an extension of their home-making skills, such as beer brewing or distilling (e.g., Bryceson 2000b; Tanzania: Tripp 1997; Lesotho: Mapetla and Machai 1997; Cameroon: Niger-Thomas 2000; Sudan: Huby 1994).

The economic crisis and the imposition of structural adjustment policies spread throughout Sub-Saharan Africa during the 1980s. The situation in Dar es Salaam, Tanzania, is cited here to illustrate how the general economic trend affected alcohol production patterns and drinking modalities. In Tripp's 1987–88 survey of two neighborhoods in Dar es Salaam, roughly 5 percent of the residents engaged in alcohol production. This corroborates with Maula's (1997) 1988 Dar es Salaam survey findings showing 6.7 percent and 4.2 percent of women and men, respectively, supporting themselves by brewing.

The mushrooming of household-based alcohol production units was linked to dramatic changes in alcohol demand and supply. Dar es Salaam, not unlike many African capital cities, had a state-run brewery with a monopoly on the supply of bottled lager beer. As the purchasing power of the city's middle-class beer-drinking stratum declined,[10] the market for the far cheaper alcohol products[11] of the informal sector expanded (Kilima 1983). Middle-class drinkers rubbed shoulders with the working class:

> Ten years ago it was shameful for a university graduate to visit a *Pombe*-bar [local cottage-brewed beer], and if he did it, he would sit drinking behind the house or otherwise try to hide himself. Now they have to drink *Pombe* because they have no more money to buy [bottled] beer. (Kilima 1988, communication quoted in Maula 1997: 189)

A Dar es Salaam senior civil servant remarked:

> I have so many friends. They are used to having three or four bottles each when we meet after the office is closed. Now beer has become very expensive. They cannot have three, four bottles every day. So they turn to stronger drinks. If they can find bottled whisky or something which is not too expensive they drink that, but very often they drink *gongo*. And they get sick. They look worse with every day taking that stuff. It is a tragedy. Government has to increase the production of beer and set lower prices, otherwise . . . (Quoted in Beckman 1988: 102)

The economic crisis was marked by increasing industrial undercapacity as countries did not have sufficient foreign exchange to import vital spare parts or inputs into the manufacturing process to keep factories in production.[12] The production of state-owned beer factories, which provided reliable and much-needed revenues for the state, was often given priority in foreign exchange allocation. In Lusaka during the 1980s, the beer factory was among the last of the government parastatals to collapse (Glazer 1997). The gradual drying up of bottled beer supplies gave the informal sector space for market expansion (Abbink, Akyeampong and Tanzarn in this volume; Huby 1994).[13]

While the Food and Agriculture Organization (FAO) estimated that 90 percent of alcohol available in Tanzania was in the form of traditional brews, Maula's (1997) Dar es Salaam survey indicates that only half of total consumption was fermented traditional brews, 35 percent was distilled drinks, and the remainder was beer and wine in 1988.[14] The bottled-beer market, formerly so prevalent and reflective of urban modernity, was shrinking and being replaced by relatively cheap distilled drinks from cottage industries.[15] The higher alcoholic content was attractive to drinkers experiencing hard times. Furthermore, the 1980s were a period of sometimes protracted grain shortages in the capital, so distilled alcohol, requiring less grain than beer, made economic sense (Bryceson 1990). The illegality of producing such alcohol was being mitigated by economic liberalization policies (Tripp 1997).[16] In conformity with international financial institutions' emphasis on open markets, and sensitive to the need to encourage income-earning activities for economically distressed households, municipal and local rural governments eased, if not abandoned, controls on so-called illicit alcohol production (Carlson 1992).

With economic conditions reminiscent of the 1930s depression, the 1980s were nonetheless a period of alcoholic abandon in Dar es Salaam. Liberalization rather than prohibition of the trade in alcohol prevailed. Employment opportunities were highly stratified. At one end, bar owners with large premises, almost invariably male and often operating their businesses as a sideline to formal sector work, reaped profits without having any direct involvement in alcohol production. A bar owner usually subcontracted the brewing work to several brewers who guaranteed deliveries of ready-made beer or, alternatively, he simply rented space to brewers who sold beer on his premises.[17] The brewers shouldered the costs of defective brews. Barmaids were at the bottom of the earnings spectrum. Many were very young and were hired by the bar owner not only to serve drinks but to attract male customers and encourage them to drink more (Tanzania Gender Networking Programme 1993). Maula (1997) describes the situation of Dar es Salaam barmaids as "especially precarious," noting that:

> together with the old female brewers they seem to form the most vulnerable operators in the local alcohol economy. These women are not always paid even the minimum wages and they have to support themselves through gifts from men, i.e., sort of semi- or "traditional" prostitution. . . . This was evident in the cases of some bar-owners who had such barmaids and refused to discuss their wages. One of the bar-owners actually responded in a hostile manner that the women were "satisfied if they get a man for a night." (Maula 1997: 181)

It is impossible to get an accurate picture of relative sources of urban alcohol supply. In Dar es Salaam, roughly one in twenty adults were engaged in some form of alcohol production, so a substantial portion of the city's supplies may have been obtained *in situ*. However, surpluses of distilled alcohol were being produced in rural areas, some of which was consumed locally, but increasing amounts were likely to have been exported.

Historically, many rural areas had gained the reputation of being authentic sources of supply for a particular alcoholic beverage, having had the advantage of being subject to less policing of bans on alcohol production. Tanzarn (Chapter 4) argues that Kibaale District in Uganda built up its reputation during the economic crisis and began successfully specializing in the production of easily transportable and nonperishable distilled drinks to urban markets.[18]

During the 1980s, peasant households throughout much of the continent faced a collapse of crop marketing infrastructure and the removal of subsidized productive inputs. Vast numbers of peasant producers were left without markets or with low, nonremunerative prices for their traditional export crops in line with declining world market primary commodity prices. Few peasant farmers were as fortunate as the Balanta of Guinea-Bissau described by van der Drift (Chapter 9), who found a viable nontraditional crop, namely, cashew nut, and guaranteed prices for their output. The most pronounced tendency was for peasant producers to seek alternatives to agriculture. Male heads of households, who had historically been the chief cash-earners in families, along with their wives and other household members, became involved in nonagricultural income diversification (Bryceson 1999a, 1999b). Rural alcohol production represented an important income-diversifying activity, particularly for women (Tanzarn, Chapter 4; McCall 1996; Nkhoma 1987; Niger-Thomas 2000; Green 1999). Many rural women had no other marketable skills, and alcohol production represented a lucrative, if not their only, option.[19]

Most significantly, preparation of traditional fermented drinks was giving way to the relatively newer distilled drinks as sale commodities

(Otieno et al. 1979). Colson and Scudder (1988) had already observed this in the early 1980s in Zambia. A decade later, 72 percent of the women in Tellegen's (1997) Malawian village surveys engaged in distilling the sugar-based *kachasu*, while only 25 percent brewed the traditional *masese* fermented maize drink. The proliferating number of women inundated the market and depressed prices, benefiting the consumers, while producers barely covered their costs (see also Nkhoma-Wamunza 1992; Lentz 1999). This generated social tension among the competing women producers that they were reluctant to admit due to the cultural premium placed on cooperation.

In general, the 1980s were years of economic shock and reorientation in rural Africa. Within local agricultural commodity markets there were a number of reasons why grain and starchy staples like bananas could readily be diverted from food stores to alcohol production. On the supply side, many areas lost their existing markets and had to find ways to dispose of surplus food crops and opted to do so by brewing (Bryceson 1999a). Alternatively, crops like brewing banana or stands of bamboo for making fermented *ulanzi* were substituted for food crops because they fetched higher prices, especially in remote areas where private traders were loath to travel (Tanzarn, Chapter 4; Beckman 1988; Carlson 1992; Kangasniemi 1996). Rural areas that had been receiving *chibuku* and bottled beer from urban factories faced depleted supplies. On the demand side, the costs of bottled beer became prohibitive for rural salaried employees like teachers and health workers. Thus, local alcohol supply and demand were militating for the increased use of staple food products in rural alcohol production. In a period of fluctuating and often depressed agricultural prices, the use of local agricultural crops to produce alcohol gave peasant households the benefit of higher returns from value-added production.

People's changing work lives influenced demand for locally provisioned alcohol. Many enjoyed more leisure time as their agricultural labor subsided. Those who turned to trade or service-sector activities enjoyed idle time between sales, and time invested in social drinking constituted a useful way of gathering local market information. As Pietilä (Chapter 10) demonstrates, women's trading activities in Kilimanjaro gave them not only cash in hand but also the opportunity to relax after working hours. Niger-Thomas (2000) records that entrepreneurial-minded women's *njangi* (saving societies) often fined their members for late loan repayment in crates of beer rather than cash. The beer constituted "Item 11" of their societies' meeting agendas: a social hour when women could enjoy each other's company and indulge in otherwise prohibitively expensive bottled beer-drinking. Other observers (Uganda: Tanzarn, Chapter 4; Kenya: Otieno et al. 1979; Zambia: Colson and Scudder 1988; Cameroon: Diduk 1993; Tanzania: Green 1999) have noted that female drinking was becoming more prevalent.

Finally, the depressed economic circumstances and livelihood uncertainties of the 1980s gave rural dwellers ample reason to seek escape in alcohol. Peasant agriculture held few immediate or long-range economic prospects (Bryceson 2000b). African farmers' commodity production, combined with its subsistence orientation and low-yielding, unstandardized agricultural output and high transport costs, was the antithesis of the growing dominance of agro-industrial production in the world's agricultural commodity trade circuits. In the face of global competition, African peasant farmers had the classic need for a drink, be it in the form of light-hearted social drinking to take one's mind off one's problems or heavier drinking to get drunk with the power to temporarily erase all cares.

Economic Liberalization and Privatization of the 1990s

The implementation of structural adjustment and economic liberalization policies, well advanced in most countries by the 1990s, did not trigger the promised economic recovery. Despite international financial institutions' eagerness to identify countries following the "right policies," each of the countries cited as models could barely sustain its lauded position for more than a year or two. One by one, Ghana, Tanzania and Uganda lost their praiseworthy status and were mired in debt. Structural adjustment had effected profound change. Occupational restructuring away from peasant agriculture and the erosion of formal sector employment largely undermined the relevance of the three-sector model of the postcolonial economy. The once distinct and readily identifiable rural peasant, urban formal, and urban informal sectors were meshing into one amorphous liberalized sector in which people responded to risks and opportunities primarily on the basis of ad hoc decision-making rather than as part of a vocational career path (Bryceson 1999a). However, this ill-defined liberalized sector was rapidly becoming highly stratified. People's occupational opportunities were not determined merely by being in the right place at the right time. Existing asset holdings were decisive, and those who entered the marketplace with capital assets and skills had a strong advantage. As African economies began to privatize in conformity with World Bank and IMF conditionality, these factors became even more critical.

Public wealth was transferred into private hands, spurring wealth differentiation. While the 1980s had been extremely difficult years for all but those at the pinnacle of the economic pyramid, the 1990s were years when one's economic ascent or descent depended on how strategically one was positioned to grab the opportunities thrown up by liberalization and the privatization bonanza.

As successive countries' reform programs gained donor approval and national markets were opened to foreign investment, there was a surge in bottled beer sales. The African middle classes reclaimed their role as "modern" consumers.[20] Their eagerness to drink lager beer was no doubt in part due to the protracted period during which it had been beyond their reach.[21] The timing of this middle-class recovery varied. There were notable stragglers and inconsistent performers. For example, the privatized Zambian Breweries, holding a monopoly on the country's clear beer production, reported a dip in unit sales in 1998 which contrasted with a 27 percent increase the preceding year. This dramatic false start in consumption levels was attributed to the recession induced by the government's inability to agree on the sale of its copper mines to the multinational mining corporation giant Anglo-American (Zambian Breweries 2000). Clearly, lager beer sales were a sensitive indicator of the economic standing of the middle class and the national economy.

By the late 1990s, most of the large national breweries had been privatized and were actively developing new products and seeking new markets. In Central and East Africa, South African Breweries (SAB)[22] had become the major player, vacuuming up shares in former nationalized breweries with the aim of boosting the low per capita average lager beer consumption of East Africa (7.5 liters) toward that of South Africa (57 liters) (Tanzanian Breweries Ltd. 2000). In West Africa, where multinational corporations like Guinness and Heineken had long had a foothold in national breweries,[23] the outlook was equally optimistic for the breweries.[24]

Corporate expansion of this nature was bound to make incursions into the informal sector's cottage-brewing market, not unlike the process that was well advanced in South Africa and progressing in Botswana, Namibia and Zimbabwe and various West Africa countries (McCall, Chapter 5; Rogerson and Tucker 1985; Rogerson 1990; Haggblade 1992; Saul 1981; Diduk 1993). An examination of the southern African market is revealing. There were clear indications that manufactured *chibuku* had lost part of its market share to clear beer. It had become the drink of the elderly. Youth were repelled by its associations with the racist policies of the past and its lower alcoholic content.

Haggblade's (1992) work in Botswana provides a valuable glimpse of the dynamics at work as corporate breweries strategically set out to gain market share. His work focuses on the strategy of the Lonrho-owned Botswana Breweries to increase its factory-produced *chibuku*. Given the country's mineral wealth, purchasing power was relatively buoyant, and through a carefully constructed advertising campaign Botswana Breweries managed to overcome the tarnished image of *chibuku* as an old man's drink. Despite Botswana Breweries' willingness to effect profit-sharing with local councils and local distributors, the overall effect of the growth of factory brewing was to undermine the livelihoods of women brewers and to deepen economic inequality:

> Due to the introduction of Chibuku, full-time brewing employment—including home and factory brewing plus all retailing—dropped roughly 30 percent. At the same time, because of partial foreign ownership and the higher import content of Chibuku, national brewing and retailing income declined by about 6 percent. And income distribution worsened considerably. The rise of factory brewing has consequently transferred earnings from poor and middle-income groups to the very wealthy, from women to men, and from rural to urban areas. (Haggblade 1992: 409)

Comparing the operations of home brewing using trade malt with factory brewing distributed through licensed bars in Botswana, Haggblade (1987) showed the former to be superior on both efficiency and equity grounds. Lower costs and employment absorption were cottage brewing's obvious strengths.[25]

Despite the clear economic advantages of home brewing, case study evidence of the 1990s suggests that home brewing was being encroached upon by factory production, generating labor displacement. Nelson's (1997) restudy of women in a Nairobi shantytown, Mathare Valley, is illustrative. In the 1970s, approximately 4 out of every 5 women, an estimated 1,000 women, were brewing *buzaa* maize beer for a livelihood. But, by the 1990s, a South African multinational firm was manufacturing *chibuku*, and the women beer brewers' market had been replaced by male entrepreneurs owning roughly ten large bars with commercial licenses to sell factory-produced *chibuku*.[26] Only a few women dared to sell locally distilled *chang'aa* gin or marijuana, both of which were easier to conceal from the police than beer.

Throughout Sub-Saharan Africa, brewing corporations' plans to extend lager consumption were succeeding in the face of two major constraints: the extremely low—and in some cases declining—purchasing power of the majority of the population, and the high transport costs of supply to rural areas. Given the immense size of the alcohol drinks market, it is surprising that there is so little documentation of this economic takeover.

SURMISING CONTINENTAL TRENDS IN ALCOHOL SUPPLY

The extent of cottage alcohol production in rural and urban areas across the continent cannot be estimated with any accuracy. Studies of alcohol consumption tend to be highly localized and rarely quantify production and consumption of different alcoholic drinks and their sources of supply. Nonetheless, hypothesizing the changing magnitude of different factory and cottage-produced alcohol is a useful exercise if only to provoke debate and interest in this massive, but largely ignored, segment of the continent's economy. Thus Figure 2.1, on the basis of rural/urban populations, various national estimates of consumption, and individual case study evidence, juxtaposes the different components of alcohol consumption to provide a stylized overview of drinking tendencies in Sub-Saharan Africa during the twentieth century.

It highlights the fact that African alcohol consumption during this period was overwhelmingly dominated by rural home or cottage-brewed supplies primarily because the bulk of the population were peasant farmers. Urbanization and national independence in the 1960s began to alter the basic equation, but only gradually. Urban cottage-brewed and distilled drinks that had been slowly gaining ground during the colonial period began edging forward. Lager beer also became a significant component. The plunge in purchasing power in the 1980s resulted in a crash in lager beer production while boosting cottage-distilled drink production. The latter achieved inroads into urban supply channels, with a detrimental domino effect for rural firewood supplies and the environment (McCall, Chapter 5). The most recent development, the resurgence of lager beer, does not necessarily undermine the cottage-distilled drinks sector. Several case studies suggest that hard drinking is escalating in rural areas (Abbink, Tanzarn and van der Drift in this volume; Colson and Scudder 1988).

Africa's alcohol economy cannot be characterized as a stark dualism between traditional and modern sectors. There is a dichotomy between cottage- and factory-produced supply, and there are still marked contrasts in most countries between rural and urban drink preferences. However, these locational contrasts are disappearing as African populations become more urban and as rural/urban contrasts blur. Consumption patterns dur-

Figure 2.1
Schematic Representation of African Alcohol Consumption

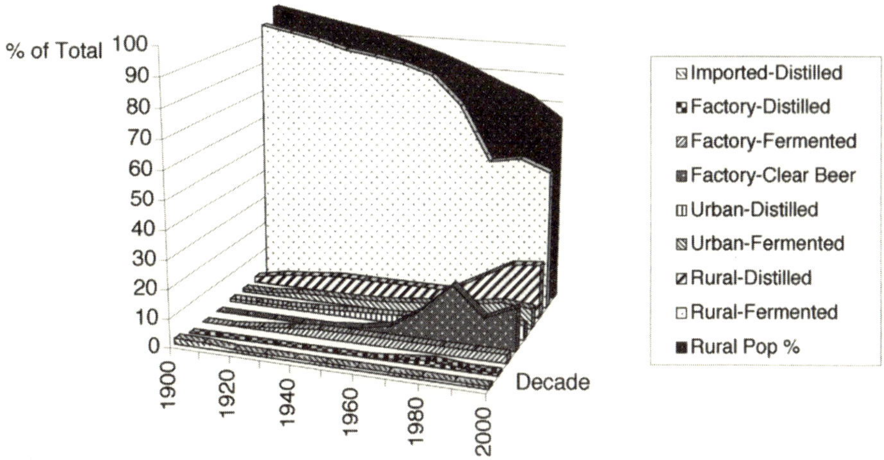

ing the 1980s and 1990s experienced radical change and increasingly moved away from rural/urban dualities toward stratified drinking patterns determined overwhelmingly by income. At a glance, African drinking modalities are capable of revealing a subtle picture of social class differentiation in the making.

NOTES

1. The supply of palm wine, in contrast to grain beer, would have been continuous throughout the year, although it would have been limited by day-to-day tree sap availability and a diurnal pattern of tapping and drinking times.

2. In the racist environment of the day, African women in southern African towns were stereotyped by officialdom as "immoral," assumed to be out of wedlock and earning their livelihood as prostitutes and/or disreputable liquor sellers (e.g., Eales 1989).

3. In effect, it entailed the colonial state carving out an exclusive vertical monopoly in the cities and areas of employed labor, stretching from factory production down to retailing drinks in state beer halls.

4. To this day the commercial giant, South African Breweries, bears the hallmark of this historical legacy, claiming to be the world's lowest-cost beer producer, although, like its government predecessor, it is essentially a monopoly accounting

for 98 percent of South Africa's domestic malt beer production (South Africa, Department of Trade and Industry, June 1998. "South African Beer: Big Lion, Small Cage," *The Economist*, 12–18 August 2000).

5. There was a wide price differential between rural peasant and urban white-collar drinks. For example, Haggblade (1992) observed that cottage-brewed sorghum beer was selling for only 10–15 percent of the cost of clear lager beer in Botswana.

6. Zambian survey respondents who reported getting drunk one or more times per week were: rural peasants—61 percent (men), 29 percent (women); urban working class—42 percent (men), 24 percent (women); and urban middle class—38 percent (men), 37 percent (women). The average percentage of those who consumed more than 9 cl pure alcohol on their last drinking occasion was 75 percent (men) and 55 percent (female) (Haworth et al. 1981).

7. It should be noted that although such a sophisticated distribution network extending to the rural areas was unusual, it was not unique. Diduk (1993) describes a similar transnational corporation-backed system in Cameroon capable of providing regular weekly bottled beer deliveries to remote rural localities.

8. Walsh and Grant (1985) provide figures showing a phenomenal percentage increase in beer consumption in liters per capita between 1960 and 1981: Cameroon (562%), Congo (893%), Gabon (1025%), Ivory Coast (506%), Kenya (248%) and Namibia (274%).

9. For example, in Tanzanian urban areas between 1973 and 1983, the minimum wage index fell from 101 to 39 (Bryceson 1990). Thus, in the early 1980s, two decades after independence and the establishment of minimum wage levels pegged to cover family needs, workers found their real earnings had regressed to pre–World War II bachelor wage levels.

10. In neighboring Uganda, inflation had seriously eroded urban access to bottled beer during the 1980s (Heald 1986).

11. Methods of production were being revamped with the addition of additives like coins, detergents and plant extracts to hasten fermentation. Inexperienced younger people were taking part in the production process (Kilonzo 1990).

12. For example, Nigeria, which had experienced a meteoric increase in beer factory expansion during the oil boom of the 1970s, suffered declines of between 30 and 50 percent in factory capacity during the late 1980s (Adejemilua 1989).

13. "Production and distribution of Castle and *chibuku* became more unreliable during the course of the 1980s, while at the same time towns grew in size and poverty . . . brewers followed the general trend in informal-sector expansion and at least partially make up for declining production by Zambia breweries" (Glazer 1997: 154).

14. Estimates of average annual per capita pure alcohol consumption in Dar es Salaam of 5.4 liters were 70 percent higher than an estimate of the national average (Kilonzo 1989, cited in Maula 1997). This study was primarily based in a Muslim coastal area, so it could have resulted in an underestimation of total national rural consumption.

15. Tanzania Breweries had been operating at undercapacity from 1976 onwards (Kilima 1983).

16. Due to an outbreak of cholera in 1977, the Dar es Salaam City Council prohibited the sale of all local liquors, but this ruling was barely enforced (Kilima 1983).

17. Maula's (1997) survey revealed that the women brewers were often younger and less experienced than had previously been the norm, and they were joined by male brewers. Overcrowding was readily apparent in this easy-entry sector of the informal economy.

18. Tanzanian examples of growing alcohol specialization include *buzaa* production in Amani, where sugarcane was boiled down to paste, cheaply transported to Kilimanjaro, then distilled for the country's northern urban market (Hakizumwami 1995, in McCall 1999). Carlson (1992) recorded the expansion of *konyagi* (banana distillate) production in the 1980s among rural Haya communities who supplied nearby Bukoba town.

19. Haggblade (1992) emphasized the vast size of the female cottage sorghum beer industry, estimated in the early 1980s to account for roughly 30 percent of all Botswanan households' income, making it the largest nonfarm income-generating activity in the country.

20. For example, Niger's Braniger brewery experienced a fall in production between 1989 and 1996 of 40 percent, whereas Tanzania Breweries Ltd. increased its sales volume by 150 percent in the first three years after privatization in 1993. Similarly, Crevejas de Moçambique Limitada (CDM) was privatized in 1996 and increased its sales volume fourfold in the six months that followed (www.skolinternational.com, 16 March 2000).

21. It should be noted that preference for lager beer is by no means restricted to the middle classes, but financial cost is the main barrier to it becoming the drink of the masses. In Botswana, a country whose mineral wealth helped it to escape economic crisis, lager beer was the population's usual drink, almost twice as popular as wine, and three times more so than various traditional drinks (Molamu and Manyeneng 1988).

22. SAB's corporate empire was expanding at lightning speed. As of 1998, in addition to its interests in breweries in Botswana, Swaziland, Lesotho, Tanzania, Uganda, Zambia, Mozambique, Angola, Malawi, Zimbabwe and the Seychelles, it had plans to set up production units in Ethiopia, Namibia, Kenya and Ivory Coast. Meanwhile, to mark its multinational status, SAB transferred its primary listing from the Johannesburg to the London Stock Exchange in 1999 and is currently on course to become the biggest brewer in eastern Europe and the Baltic states (www.skolinternational.com).

23. In Nigeria there have never been any national government-owned breweries, but many regional state-owned breweries folded in the 1990s, leaving Guinness and Nigerian Breweries as the two dominant players.

24. According to *The Economist* (3 June 2000) in an article entitled "More than Expected: Investment in Africa," contrary to general opinion, Africa was receiving

some direct foreign investment, especially in World Bank–endorsed countries like Ghana, Mali, Zimbabwe, Uganda and Tanzania, where "[m]ost of the money went into oil and mining, but, in these countries, investors diversified into areas such as agriculture and *brewing* [my emphasis] as well."

25. Similarly, in Maula's (1997) Benin and Tanzania case studies, the economic importance of cottage brewing's labor creation among the urban poor, notably women, and often female heads of households, was stressed.

26. As McCall (personal communication, 2000) points out, homebrew and *chibuku* both have a restricted shelf life of one to two days. Transport is a constraint, and they are ideal products for small-scale female enterpreneurs dealing in small quantities and low profit margins. The corporate takeover of this sphere of the beer market and reliance on larger-scale male distributors are a double blow to women producers. Malahleha (1985) reports that Lesotho women brewers successfully weathered an attempt by South African manufacturers to enter their beer market in the early 1980s.

REFERENCES

Adejemilua, F. 1989. "Trends in the Nigerian Brewing Industry." *Modern Brewery Age* 23: 27–31.

Akyeampong, E.K. 1996. *Drink, Power, and Cultural Change: A Social History of Alcohol in Ghana, c. 1800 to Recent Times*. Portsmouth, NH: Heinemann; Oxford: James Currey.

Ambler, C.H. 1991. "Drunks, Brewers, and Chiefs." In S. Barrows and R. Room (eds.), *Drinking: Behavior and Belief in Modern History*. Berkeley and Los Angeles: University of California Press, 165–83.

Beckman, V. 1988. *Alcohol: Another Trap for Africa*. Örebro: Bokförlaget Libris.

Bryceson, D.F. 1990. *Food Insecurity and the Social Division of Labor in Tanzania, 1919–1985*. London: Macmillan.

———. 1999a. "African Rural Labor, Income Diversification and Livelihood Approaches: A Long-Term Development Perspective." *Review of African Political Economy* 80: 171–89.

———. 1999b. *Sub-Saharan Africa Betwixt and Between: Rural Livelihood Practices and Policies*. Leiden: Afrika-Studiecentrum, Working Paper 43.

———. 2000a. "African Peasants' Centrality and Marginality: Rural Labor Transformations." In D.F. Bryceson, C. Kay and J. Mooij (eds.), *Disappearing Peasantries? Rural Labor in Africa, Asia and Latin America*. London: Intermediate Technology Publications, 37–80.

———. 2000b. "Disappearing Peasantries? Rural Labor Redundancy in the Neoliberal Era and Beyond." In D.F. Bryceson, C. Kay and J. Mooij (eds.), *Disappearing Peasantries? Rural Labor in Africa, Asia and Latin America*. London: Intermediate Technology Publications, 299–326.

Carlson, R.G. 1992. "Symbolic Mediation and Commoditization: A Critical Examination of Alcohol Use among the Haya of Bukoba, Tanzania." *Medical Anthropology* 15: 41–62.

Colson, E., and T. Scudder. 1988. *For Prayer and Profit: The Ritual, Economic and Social Importance of Beer in Gwembe District, Zambia, 1950–1982*. Stanford: Stanford University Press.

Crush, J. 1992. "The Construction of Compound Authority: Drinking at Havelock, 1938–1944." In J. Crush and C. Ambler (eds.), *Liquor and Labor in Southern Africa*. Athens: Ohio University Press, 367–94.

Crush, J., and C. Ambler (eds.). 1992. *Liquor and Labor in Southern Africa*. Athens: Ohio University Press.

Diduk, S. 1993. "European Alcohol, History, and the State in Cameroon." *African Studies Review* 36 (10): 1–42.

Domergue, D. 1985. "Histoire d'une entreprise industrielle privée en Afrique de l'Ouest: La Société des Brasseries de la Cote d'Ivoire (Bracodi), 1949–1970." *Annales de l'Université d'Abidjan*, Série I: Histoire, 159–81.

Eales, K. 1989. "Patriarchs, Passes and Privileges." In P. Bonner, I. Hofmeyr, D. James and T. Lodge (eds.), *Holding Their Ground*. Johannesburg: Ravan Press, 105–39.

Glazer, I.M. 1997. "Alcohol and Politics in Urban Zambia: The Intersection of Gender and Class." In G. Mikell (ed.), *African Feminism: The Politics of Survival in Sub-Saharan Africa*. Philadelphia: University of Pennsylvania Press, 142–58.

Green, M. 1999. "Trading on Inequality: Gender and the Drinks Trade in Southern Tanzania." *Africa* 69 (3): 404–25.

Haggblade, S. 1987. "Vertical Considerations of Choice-of-Technique Studies: Evidence from Africa's Indigenous Beer Industry." *Economic Development and Cultural Change* 35: 723–42.

———. 1992. "The Shebeen Queen and the Evolution of Botswana's Sorghum Beer Industry." In J. Crush and C. Ambler (eds.), *Liquor and Labor in Southern Africa*. Athens: Ohio University Press, 395–412.

Hakizumwami, E. 1995. "Field Notes on *Boha* Brewing from Sugarcane, East Usambaras, Tanzania." Enschede, the Netherlands: ITC.

Hausse, P. la. 1988. *Brewers, Beerhalls and Boycotts: A History of Liquor in South Africa*. Johannesburg: Ravan Press.

———. 1992. "Drink and Cultural Innovation in Durban: The Origins of the Beerhall in South Africa, 1902–1916." In J. Crush and C. Ambler (eds.), *Liquor and Labor in Southern Africa*. Athens: Ohio University Press, 78–114.

Haworth, A., M. Mwanalushi and D. Todd. 1981. *Community Response to Alcohol-Related Problems in Zambia*. Lusaka: University of Zambia, Institute for African Studies, Community Health Research Unit.

Heald, S. 1986. "Mafias in Africa: The Rise of Drinking Companies and Vigilante Groups in Bugisu District, Uganda." *Africa* 56 (4): 446–66.

Heap, S. 1996. "Before *Star*: The Import Substitution of Western-Style Alcohol in Nigeria, 1870–1970." *African Economic History* 24: 69–89.

———. 1999. "The Quality of Liquor in Nigeria during the Colonial Era." *Itinerario* 23 (2): 29–47.

———. 2000. "Transport and Liquor in Colonial Nigeria." *Journal of Transport History* 21 (1): 28–53.

Hedlund, M., and M. Lundahl. 1984. "The Economic Role of Beer in Rural Zambia." *Human Organization* 43: 61–65.

Hellman, E. 1948. *Rooiyard: A Sociological Survey of an Urban Native Slumyard.* Capetown: Oxford University Press.

Huby, G. 1994. "Drinking and the Management of Problem Drinking among the Bari, Southern Sudan." In M. MacDonald (ed.), *Gender, Drink and Drugs*. Oxford: Berg, 235–47.

Kangasniemi, J. 1996. "Bananas in Rwanda: Wasteful Brewing or Food Security for the Poor." Paper presented at the African Local Economy Seminar, University of Helsinki.

Karp, I. 1980. "Beer Drinking and Social Experience in an African Society: An Essay in Formal Sociology." In I. Karp and C.S. Bird (eds.), *Explorations in African Systems of Thought*. Bloomington: Indiana University Press, 83–119.

Kilima, M. 1983. "Study on the Pattern of Alcohol Production, Consumption and Resulting Problems in Dar es Salaam." In B.A. Coche (ed.), *Mental Health: Proceedings of the 22nd Postgraduate KCMC Seminar*. Moshi, Tanzania: Kilimanjaro Christian Medical Centre, 87–102.

Kilonzo, G.P. 1990. "Production and Consumption of Alcohol in Tanzania and Alcohol-Related Accidents." In J. Maula, M. Lindblad and C. Tigerstedt (eds.), *Alcohol in Developing Countries.* Helsinki: Nordic Council for Alcohol and Drug Research, 185–92 .

Kortteinen, T. 1990. "Alcohol and Urbanisation in Africa." In J. Maula, M. Lindblad and C. Tigerstedt (eds.), *Alcohol in Developing Countries.* Helsinki: Nordic Council for Alcohol and Drug Research, 36–58.

Lentz, C. 1999. "Alcohol Consumption Between Community Ritual and Political Economy: Case Studies from Ecuador and Ghana." In C. Lentz (ed.), *Changing Food Habits: Case Studies from Africa, South America and Europe*. Germany: Harwood Academic Publishers, 155–79.

Malahleha, G.M. 1985. "Liquor Brewing: A Cottage Industry in Lesotho Shebeens." *Journal of Eastern African Research and Development* 15: 45–55.

Mapetla, M., and P. Machai. 1997. "Beer Brewing as a Survival Strategy in Urban Lesotho." In A. Larsson, M. Mapetla and A. Schlyter (eds.), *Changing Gender Relations in Southern Africa: Issues of Urban Life*. Roma, Lesotho: Institute of Southern African Studies.

Maula, J. 1997. *Small-Scale Production of Food and Traditional Alcoholic Beverages in Benin and Tanzania: Implications for the Promotion of Female Entrepreneurship.* Helsinki: Finnish Foundation for Alcohol Studies, vol. 43.

Maula, J., M. Lindblad and C. Tigerstedt (eds.). 1990. *Alcohol in Developing Countries*. Helsinki: Nordic Council for Alcohol and Drug Research.

McAllister, P. 2001. *Building the Homestead: Agriculture, Labour and Beer in South Africa's Transkei*. Leiden: African Studies Centre/Ashgate.

McCall, M. 1996. "Rural Brewing, Exclusion and Development Policy-Making." *Gender and Development* 4 (3): 29–38.

———. 1999. "Bibliography on African Beer and Brewing." Mimeo. Enschede, the Netherlands.

Molamu, L., and W.G. Manyeneng. 1988. *Alcohol Use and Abuse in Botswana: Report of a Study*. Gaborone: Health Education Unit.

Mphaisha, C.J.J. 1986/87. "Public Enterprise and Industrialisation: The Case of Zambia Breweries Limited." *Ufahamu* 15 (1–2): 152–63.

Nelson, N. 1982. "Women Must Help Each Other: The Operation of Personal Networks among Buzaa Beer Brewers." In P. Caplan and J. Bujra (eds.), *Women United, Women Divided*. Bloomington: Indiana University Press, 77–98.

———. 1997. "How Women and Men Got By and Still Get By (Only Not So Well): The Gender Division of Labor in a Nairobi Shanty-Town." In J. Gugler (ed.), *Cities in the Developing World: Issues, Theory and Policy*. Oxford: Oxford University Press, 156–70.

Ngindu, K.M. 1982. *Programmation commerciale et prise de décision financière dans une industrie: Cas d'une brasserie*. Kinshasa: Institut de Recherches Economiques.

Niger-Thomas, M. 2000. "Buying Futures: The Upsurge of Female Entrepreneurship Crossing the Formal-Informal Sector Divide in Southwest Cameroon." Ph.D. thesis, Leiden University.

Nkhoma, A.G. 1987. "Beer-Brewing in Utengule-Usangu Village." In B. Koda, M. Mbilinyi, A. Muro, A. Nkebukwa, A. Nkhoma, Z. Tumbo-Masabo and U. Vuorela (eds.), *Women's Initiatives in the United Republic of Tanzania*. Geneva: International Labor Office, 32–42.

Nkhoma-Wamunza, A. 1992. "The Informal Sector: A Strategy for Survival in Tanzania." In D.R.F. Taylor and F. MacKenzie (eds.), *Development from Within: Survival in Rural Africa*. London: Routledge, 197–213.

Nout, M.J.R. 1981. "Aspects of the Manufacture and Consumption of Kenyan Traditional Fermented Beverages." Ph.D. thesis, Wageningen University.

Odejide, O.A., J.U. Ohaeri and B.A. Ikuesan, with M.L. Adelekan. 1990. "A Need for Cross-Cultural Collaborative Research Activities: The Promotion of Alcohol Research in Nigeria." In J. Maula, M. Lindblad and C. Tigerstedt (eds.), *Alcohol in Developing Countries*. Helsinki: Nordic Council for Alcohol and Drug Research, 59–69.

Otieno, B., J.A. Owola and P. Oduor. 1979. "A Study of Alcoholism in a Rural Setting in Kenya." *East African Medical Journal* 56 (12): 665–70.

Partanen, J. 1991. *Sociability and Intoxication: Alcohol and Drinking in Kenya, Africa, and the Modern World*. Helsinki: Finnish Foundation for Alcohol Studies, vol. 39.

Reader, D.H., and Joan May. 1971. *Drinking Patterns in Rhodesia: Highfield African Township, Salisbury*. Salisbury: University of Rhodesia.

Redding, S. 1992. "Beer Brewing in Umtata: Women, Migrant Labor, and Social Control in a Rural Town." In J. Crush and C. Ambler (eds.), *Liquor and Labor in Southern Africa*. Athens: Ohio University Press, 235–51.

Robbins, M.C., and R.B. Pollnac. 1969. "Drinking Patterns and Acculturation in Rural Buganda." *American Anthropologist* 71: 277–85.

Rogerson, C. 1990. "Consumerism, the State, and the Informal Sector: Shebeens in South Africa's Black Townships." In D. Drakakis-Smith (ed.), *Economic Growth and Urbanization in Developing Areas*. London: Routledge, 287–303.

Rogerson, C., and D.M. Hart. 1986. "The Survival of the 'Informal Sector': The Shebeens of Black Johannesburg." *GeoJournal* 12: 153–66.

Rogerson, C., and B. Tucker. 1985. "Commercialization and Corporate Capital in the Sorghum Beer Industry of Central Africa." *Geoforum* 16: 357–68.

Sangree, W.H. 1962. "The Social Functions of Beer Drinking in Bantu Tiriki." In D.J. Pittman and C.R. Snyder (eds.), *Society, Culture, and Drinking Patterns*. New York: John Wiley & Sons, 6–21.

Saul, M. 1981. "Beer, Sorghum and Women: Production for the Market in Rural Upper Volta." *Africa* 51 (3): 746–64.

Schatzberg, M. 1980. *Politics and Class in Zaire: Bureaucracy, Business and Beer in Lisala*. New York: African Publishing Company.

Tanzania Breweries Ltd. 2000. www.theexpress.com/express69/tbl/tbl.htm, 5 March.

Tanzania Gender Networking Programme (TGNP). 1993. *Gender Profile of Tanzania*. Dar es Salaam: TGNP.

Tellegen, Nina. 1997. *Rural Enterprises in Malawi: Necessity or Opportunity?* African Studies Centre Research Series 12. Aldershot: Ashgate.

Tripp, A. 1997. *Changing the Rules: The Politics of Liberalization and the Urban Informal Economy in Tanzania*. Berkeley and Los Angeles: University of California Press.

Vuorela, U. 1979. "Women's Role in Production and Reproduction: Some Reflections on Relationships Between Men and Women in Tanzania and Finland." Paper presented at the BRALUP Workshop on Women's Studies and Development, University of Dar es Salaam, 24–29 September.

Walsh, B., and M. Grant. 1985. *Public Implications of Alcohol Production and Trade*. Geneva: World Health Organisation.

Zambian Breweries. 2000. www.pangaeapartners.dom/zbrew.htm, 5 March.

PART II
Business Interests

3

For Women and Children

An Economic History of Brewing among the Nyakyusa of Southwestern Tanzania

Justin Willis

The importance of brewing as a source of income for African women has been noted in a number of historical and sociological studies (Akyeampong 1996; Harries 1994; Nelson 1982). Such studies have often associated commercial brewing and distillation by women with the emergence of female-headed households—mostly in urban areas, but also in rural areas as a consequence of labor migration by men (Redding 1992; Haggblade 1992). There has been a note of celebration in much of this work, emphasizing the financial autonomy, even independence, that women have derived from making and selling alcohol, and setting female success as income-earners in the context of official hostility and men's attempts to subordinate them. Brewing emerges in this literature as a kind of triumph against oppression (Bradford 1992; Bonner 1992). Through brewing, it has been argued, African women have defied colonial and postcolonial states and achieved a kind of freedom.

A quite different approach can be found in another body of literature that focuses on the decline of "integrated"traditional drinking and posits alcohol as a powerful engine of social disruption. For writers of this genre, the commercialization of women's brewing has been not a triumph but a major step toward moral breakdown, and it has brought no lasting gains for women (Colson and Scudder 1988; Beckman 1988).

This study of the changing economics of beer brewing among the Nyakyusa of southwestern Tanzania is intended as an examination of the validity of these contrasting views of the benefits derived by women from brewing.[1] It seeks to set brewing clearly in the context of other changes. The systems of state authority within which brewers operate have changed over the last hundred years. Techniques of brewing have also changed greatly, and Nyakyusa women have shown considerable adaptability and enterprise in altering the ways in which they make beer. Most important, the fields of conflict over the use of household resources have shifted, as have the possibilities for investment. It is only in the light of these changes that the real significance for women of the commercialization of brewing can be understood.

THE NYAKYUSA: GENERATIONAL AND GENDER DYNAMICS

The area in question lies at the north end of Lake Nyasa. It is a well-watered region, and offers a remarkable variety of climate and landscape in a small area. Local people compare the shoreline of Lake Nyasa with the coast of East Africa; it is hot and humid, and densely covered with fruit trees. Only a few kilometers north, the land rises steeply to an area of ridges and high mountains where it can be remarkably cold at times. The area is fertile and predominantly given over to agriculture. The region is now divided into two administrative districts, Rungwe (the higher area) and Kyela (the lake shore), and throughout the population is quite dense by Tanzanian standards. Despite some historical differences in language and culture, the population has, during this century, come to be known collectively as the Nyakyusa.

A surprising number of researchers have visited the Nyakyusa region over the years. Apart from its natural beauty, it has a special attraction for academics: a social system in which age rather than lineage was the dominant organizational principle of settlement, for men at least. Nyakyusa men lived in villages that were composed of their age-mates, not of kin, and each new generation of men founded new settlements separate from those of their fathers. Monica and Godfrey Wilson studied this system in the 1930s, and a succession of books by Monica Wilson on the subject has given the Nyakyusa a modest degree of fame in ethnographic circles (Wilson 1957, 1959, 1977). Scholars have since criticized some aspects of Wilson's argument but not the basic description of a population that lived in age villages (Charsley 1969; Wright 1972). The past tense is used intentionally, as the system largely broke down during the first half of the twentieth century. This change was associated with a series of transformations: a growth in population, the development of permanent tree crops of cash value in the highlands, and the development and subsequent curtailment of labor migrancy, with men leaving the area to work in the nearby Lupa Goldfield or across the border in the Copperbelt. Monica Wilson's last book expounded the thesis that beer, and changes in the way it has been produced and consumed, were central to this transformation. In particular, she argued that the growth of a commerce in locally brewed beer had undermined the authority of men and elders: "What brings disrespect is beer," as one Nyakyusa man succinctly put it (Wilson 1977).

Wilson thus highlighted intergenerational tensions in her study of Nyakyusa society. These were and are bound up with intragenerational and gender conflicts. The households headed by elder Nyakyusa men were arenas of conflict over resources. Certain things—notably cattle and millet—were the property of the head, and were controlled and managed by him. Until the mid-twentieth century, and to a degree thereafter, these were the investment capital of an economy that focused on the accumulation of social relationships, and the elaboration of networks of claim and obligation. There was constant tension between young men and their fathers over the use of these resources.

Many Nyakyusa men were polygynous, and in polygynous households each wife's "house"was a separate entity with its own fields and stores. A man's wife worked in his millet fields alongside other wives, but she grew all other crops in her own fields, which she worked and harvested alone. There was no "house-property"complex: each wife and her children controlled the various crops they grew, but had no special claim over cattle or millet, which belonged solely to the household head. When a young man wished to marry, he and his mother had to ask for cattle from his father, hoping for generosity. Each wife and her children were in competition with other wives for a share of scarce investable resources. Men competed with their half-brothers as well as their fathers.

When a household head died, the situation could become even tenser. In the past, women could not inherit, and even now they are rarely able to exercise their legal right to do so. Their own long-term security rests on the success of their children, especially their sons. Over the course of the twentieth century, changes in intergenerational relationships have meant that a son of the deceased, rather than one of his brothers, is more likely to inherit. But in either case, inheritance was (and usually still is) wholesale: there was no division between the "houses"of various wives. The heir took over all the investment resources, as well as all the obligations, of the deceased. "The others have no rights," as one man told me.[2] Whether the heir was an uncle or a half-brother, the children of the deceased could usually expect little help from him, as his first concern would be to help his own full brothers and sons. The possibility of effective disinheritance when a household head died lent a particular urgency to the competition between young and old, and between wives and half-brothers, over household resources. These tensions were the context for the development of commercial beer brewing among the Nyakyusa.

FREE BEER: PRECOLONIAL BREWING

Almost all Nyakyusa now insist that the brewing of beer for sale is a recent phenomenon, and many profess to recall a childhood in which beer was not sold. "In the past there was no market for selling beer, they just made it to drink themselves."[3] There is reason to believe that commercial brewing is a little older than they argue, but there is no evidence of a commerce in beer before the start of colonial rule in the 1890s. Before 1890, brewing was women's work, and it remains so today. The beer was *kimpumu*, a brew made solely from eleusine millet. There was a considerable amount of exchange trade in the region, and constant processes of giving and receiving created complex ties of obligation and affiliation among the population. But beer was only involved in these patterns of exchange in certain restricted ways. Beer apparently did not play a role in barter. Earthenware pots and iron were bartered for foodstuffs, particularly millet. Livestock were sometimes involved in barter, but cattle in particular were usually involved in more complex kinds of exchange, creating enduring obligations—forms of investment in people. Rights to cattle were constantly transferred in bridewealth payments, compensation for injuries, or fines.

Women were excluded from many of these exchange and investment processes since they had no control over cattle and millet. Other crops were harvested and stored by women, but millet was grown in fields worked by all of a man's wives, and was stored by him (Wilson 1977). If a man wanted beer to be made, he would give one of his wives sufficient millet from his store for the purpose. Such beer might be drawn into the kind of transfers through which men made and marked social obligations, and accumulated social capital. Beer was regularly provided by men to their in-laws in particular. But women brewed only for their husbands, and with their permission. Women could become involved in barter for small items for the everyday needs of the household, exchanging bananas or chickens for salt or pots, but they had no control over the transactions in cattle, millet and beer through which men invested in social relationships.

BEER FOR DIGGING: BREWING IN THE EXCHANGE ECONOMY, 1890–1930

The area came under effective German rule in 1893 and remained under German control until 1916, when the British captured it. During the German period, token money came into fairly general circulation. It would seem likely that there was something of a collapse of the cash economy during the chaotic years from 1916 to 1918,[4] but cash again began to circulate widely in the 1920s, though barter continued to be important in small-scale transactions.[5] It was mainly men who had access to money through wage labor and the sale of millet and occasionally cattle; and men also continued to control the transfers of cattle, which remained the principal way of investing in social relationships.

There was little technical change in beer brewing before 1930. Maize slowly became more important as a food crop, alongside finger millet, but it did not replace millet in the making of beer. Mechanical grinders were very rare, and hand-grinding maize for beer brewing was considered to require an excessive amount of labor. Beer continued to be made from millet, in earthenware vessels or bamboo baskets, and in small quantities of perhaps 40 liters at a time. The process took about seven days altogether but, apart from grinding the millet, actually required little concentrated labor.[6] Beginning in the German period, there was some beer for sale that was made and sold at home by women. Unfortunately, there is no record of how lucrative beer selling was in this period.

While a few women derived a cash income from beer in this period, there was another new use for beer, one which affected rather more women, and which emphasized their economic subordination. In Nyakyusa society, men were responsible for preparing ground for planting by hoeing it; women planted, weeded and reaped. During the first decades of the twentieth century, men started to use beer as a way of rewarding other men who came to help them hoe. They would invite neighbors to hoe with them, and then would give a beer party for all those involved. The beer was made by their wives. "The millet belonged to the husband. If there was need, he called them [wives] to bring their containers, and shared some out, giving each one some to go and make beer for digging."[7] This innovation derived from the former practice—particularly associated with chiefs—of rewarding participants of work parties with food. It was the use of beer, to try and draw more participants, which distinguished this new practice. Men were thus able either to do less work themselves in their wives' fields or in their own millet fields—or they were able to hoe more land, especially for millet growing. In the latter case, this served to increase the amount of labor required of women, in planting and weeding; and it relied on beer made by women.

This form of labor mobilization was not, at this time, available to women. In planting, tending and harvesting those crops that were under her control, each of a man's wives could call only on her own or her daughters' labor. And women could not, before the 1930s, turn beer into labor as men could by inviting others to help them work.

EARNING FROM BEER: BREWING FROM THE 1930s TO THE 1950s

The Nyakyusa economy underwent tremendous change in this period. There was a big growth in labor migrancy, with men going to work in the nearby goldfields of Chunya, in the northern Rhodesian Copperbelt, or in South Africa. It would seem that in the 1940s and 1950s probably the majority of young Nyakyusa men spent some time working for wages outside the area. Women were not involved in this kind of migrancy for wages, though some did go to work in the informal sector that serviced these labor forces, and a few went as wives of male miners, specifically to the Copperbelt. There was, at the same time, a considerable growth in the local food market, particularly as the labor force at the Chunya goldfields grew.[8] The cultivation of cash crops, especially coffee, also expanded greatly, partly as a result of official encouragement.[9] Coffee offered a new arena for conflict over household resources as well as a new source of income, as old and young, and men and women, disputed access to land and control over permanent tree crops.

With these changes, the amount of money in circulation rapidly increased locally. And a major share of this money was in the hands of young men, who were the main wage earners deriving their income from migrant labor. Young men now had access to resources in a way that old men did not, and tensions between generations took on new aspects. One of these was alcoholic: young men invaded the privileges of age by buying the beer that formerly had been gifted by older men. This was the "disrespect"of which Wilson's informants complained.

This period brought technical change in the making of beer, as well as a new demand for beer for cash. The increased availability of mechanical grinders and of sugar both had considerable effect. "That is development: long ago there were few of us and we did not have things like machines for grinding maize or millet. We used the traditional grindstone, where we ground millet. You cannot grind maize with that. Now beer has spread all over the place, because the machines help them to grind."[10] Migrant workers acquired a taste for new kinds of thin beer in which maize was the principal source of starch. Migrant laborers also observed the techniques of quickly preparing stronger alcoholic drinks through the use of granulated sugar (a popular means of increasing the potency of weak, officially supplied beer in South African mine compounds).

From the 1930s, a drink called *kangara*, made from soured chaff and sugar, became common in Nyakyusa despite attempts at official prohibition.[11] New kinds of beers, called in Swahili *pombe za maji* or "watery beers," based on maize, became the staple of domestic commercial brewing. These were more difficult to make than *kimpumu* as they involved boiling up the "porridge"of the beer for many hours, and straining it at the end of the process. They also tended to be more alcoholic, because the boiling produced a gelatinization of the starch that speeded the enzymatic processes through which starch was converted to sugar and made available for fermentation. A given amount of grain would produce more "watery" beer than *kimpumu*, and so this shift made brewing at least potentially more profitable, if harder work. "I saw that watery beer generated more money. There was not much money in *kimpumu*. That one is full of water, we put water in and it becomes more."[12]

This watery beer was—except in Tukuyu Town and the smaller settlement of Kyela—sold in the homes of the women who made it for a clientele consisting largely of neighbors. There was only minimal official interference in this. Native Authority rules, promulgated in 1940, demanded that any brewer obtain a license at a cost of 10 Tanzanian shillings (Tsh) a month, but these rules were not enforced in practice.[13] Only in Tukuyu and in Kyela were license fees collected, with drinking limited to specified locations. In Tukuyu, there was a government "beer hall"of the kind common over much of eastern and southern Africa, while in Kyela there were three privately owned beer shops.[14]

It is difficult to judge the profitability of the business at this time, as there are few figures, but those that do exist suggest that brewing was a relatively good source of income. In 1934 a "pot"of beer (which is unlikely to have exceeded 20 liters in volume) sold at Tsh 1.[15] Wages in casual labor at this time were 50 cents a day, while a teacher in a village school earned Tsh 5 a month. A woman could earn Tsh 5 a month picking coffee or Tsh 2 by selling a sack of maize or beans.[16]

Outside the towns, brewers paid no dues to the authorities. Women struggled with their husbands to control the income from brewing. Generally, they seem to have been successful. Oral testimony now suggests that in fact there was less conflict than might have been expected when women started to demand payment for beer. This lack of conflict is both remarkable and revealing. It seems partly to have been because women who began to brew for sale often bought the grain with which they brewed. By avoiding any demands on household resources, they implicitly asserted their right to control the proceeds.

The attitude of men to commercial brewing by their wives was also governed by another factor: the new and constantly rising cash costs of maintaining a household. Small items previously bartered—oil, pots, salt, knives, some foodstuffs—now had to be purchased. And there were new costs: school fees for the still small number who sent their children to school, donations to the church offertory, and clothes. In 1930 a relatively small number of Nyakyusa women wore cloth garments. By 1955 almost all did, at least some of the time. "We are the ones who started wearing clothes," one woman, born around 1920, told me.[17] Another said, "I used to brew to get food to eat; when I had earned from beer you would find I had bought food and clothes."[18] And so the daily costs of the household, in cash terms, grew. According to informants, this influenced male attitudes to female brewing. "[My husband] was happy when I brought money. Oh thank you. It helped us, for example if we were sick."[19] Women had already begun to sell maize and beans. Selling beer was more lucrative, and most husbands accepted and even welcomed it, as it brought cash into the household.

In some cases, men provided the small capital needed for their wives to start brewing beer for sale. "I saw that my wife had no clothes. I would give her millet and tell her to use that millet to make beer. If she wanted to continue after making a profit, we had to go to buy millet from another person so that she could continue making beer."[20] The corollary of this was, however, that it was widely expected that although the cash earned from brewing did not pass through men's hands, it was used primarily to support the households they headed. A particular pattern in the control of cash income and expenditure was established. Men controlled the larger part of the cash income, and particularly those parts that arrived in lump sums, such as the accumulated wages migrant laborers brought back with them when they completed their contract, or the yield from the sale of a year's coffee crop. It was these lump sums that helped to change the terms of intergenerational conflict between men. The money might be used to marry a new wife, to build a brick and corrugated-iron house, to buy cattle, or to buy coffee bushes or access to land on which to plant coffee.

Women's cash income came in a trickle and was spent largely on clothes or on the daily needs of the household. It might indeed be argued that despite the intrusion of cash, and women's ability to earn cash through brewing, the pattern established by the early 1950s was remarkably similar to that of the precolonial period. Men controlled accumulation and investment, while women bore the day-to-day burden of maintaining the household.

But there was a significant difference. Women's access to a cash income, however small, allowed one new kind of investment: investment in the upbringing, and especially the education, of children. It was in this way that commercial brewing affected the terms of the ongoing conflict within Nyakyusa society over a basic issue and the extent to which each wife of a man could claim a distinct share of the household's resources for her children. Women could not usually earn enough from brewing to pay bridewealth for their sons. But for those who chose to take it, the government school in Tukuyu and the numerous mission schools in the area offered a way to try to build the fortunes of their children.

There was, moreover, one group of women who accumulated more material forms of capital from brewing in the 1950s. These were the urban women of Tukuyu, who sold maize-based "watery" beer in the "club" established on the edge of the township (attractively sited next to the graveyard, and a brisk walk from where most people lived). The exact system under which beer was sold changed somewhat over the years, as there was limited room in the club, which had six "windows"—each a little hatch through which one or two women could sell. At one time women took turns selling their beer; then for a period the whole building was licensed to one man who allowed women to brew and sell there in return for a fee. Then the license was issued for three-month periods to three or four women at a time. Each of these women, it would seem, allowed others to brew and sell. There were about 40 women involved in brewing in the early 1950s. Many of them had Muslim names, and they called themselves Waswahili, which in this context distinguished them as townspeople.[21] Some were single women, migrants from elsewhere in Tanganyika, or Nyakyusa women who were divorced or widowed. One man neatly expressed the way that young men's access to cash propelled the financial independence of these women: "Those who used to make that beer were those who came from the village and went to the town. They went to live there without husbands. Those Swahili were the townspeople! They stayed in the town without any work apart from making beer according to their ability. . . . For us who were working, when we came from work we drank their beer and gave them money."[22] As these women themselves explained (in petitioning the District Commissioner for the issue of licenses), "As you know, Sir, we old ones of the town have no hope of getting money to pay our head tax and even house tax except for doing our best to make beer and sell it at a good price."[23]

I interviewed one of these women who had done well enough from the business to do rather more than this: she had built two houses that she rented out.[24] She was in an unusually good position, as her mother (another urban woman) had left her land in the town. Her case is illustrative of the profit possible from brewing in the town, where there was a strong demand for beer and where competition was controlled by the government's desire to limit drinking to the club.[25] She stressed the importance of having a brewing income for raising children: "I started because my mother had died and I did not have anybody to help me. I knew life would be hard with the children so I started making beer."[26]

"THE GOVERNMENT BROUGHT THE CLUBS": TAXMEN AND MIDDLEMEN, 1950–1980

In 1950 there were beer clubs only in Tukuyu and Kyela. Over the next three decades clubs came to be established over the entire area and the selling of beer in the home came to an end. This was a complex process, and in some respects it was driven by the concerns of women brewers. Ultimately, however, the change was not to the advantage of women.

In the early 1950s, some women felt that removing beer selling from the home to a more evidently commercial atmosphere would reduce the problem of debts. Women faced constant difficulties with men who took beer and later refused to pay. Some women thought that men would feel less able to resist payment by invoking their "traditional" right to free beer if they were drinking in a club. "It is business. The women found the business to be better as people did not ask for credit in the clubs. At home many people come who know you and are used to you and ask for credit. When you go to the clubs, most of the people are not used to you. Therefore the people who used to sell beer at home switched to the clubs."[27]

There were other reasons too for the move to clubs. Some women brewers feared the potential for violent arguments when selling beer at their homes. Women brewers themselves established a number of the first village clubs for their beer sales. Once this process had begun, it was further encouraged by the local authorities, who saw in the establishment of clubs the possibility of closer control of drinking and, perhaps more important, more efficient control of the collection of revenue for the burgeoning structures of local government councils. "The government was concerned that people were drinking beer, but they did not know where. They therefore allowed people to build and everybody who had built a club had to pay tax. . . . So that is why they say it is the government that brought the clubs because it wanted to get some income."[28] Rural councils, established at the beginning of the 1950s, began to collect license fees from commercial women brewers.[29]

Throughout the 1950s, more and more clubs opened. Some were started by groups of women, but impressionistic evidence suggests that rather more were started by men who obtained a license, established a club, and then either charged women a fee to sell their beer there, or sold beer for them, keeping a portion of the proceeds for themselves. The predominance of male-owned clubs seems to have arisen simply because men had more control over land—they could set aside a place to build a club, whereas women could not. It seems possible also that men received a degree of preference in the issuing of licenses.

In Tukuyu Town, the monopoly of the government club ended in 1955, and there was a steady growth in the number of clubs in the township, which slowly drew business away from the government club. The owners of these new clubs were almost always men who were not themselves involved in making or selling beer. They simply paid license fees and collected rent from the sellers who used the premises. However, in urban clubs women were not displaced from retailing.

Later, in the 1960s, the development of the clubs took a new turn, with increasing authority and responsibility given to village governments in the political dispensation of independent Tanzania. In many cases villages established their own clubs, and by the mid-1970s there were few clubs in private ownership outside the main towns of Tukuyu and Kyela.[30] In 1976, at a time when all forms of private enterprise were discouraged (Maliyamkono and Bagachwa 1990), it became policy that the ruling (and only) national political party decided how many clubs were required, and where, and seemingly individually owned clubs then disappeared entirely except in the towns.[31] Every village soon had at least one and sometimes two or more clubs, owned by the village.

This shift had several effects. Few women sold beer in the village-owned clubs. Instead, men, and often young men, sold beer in the clubs and paid a rent to the village government. These young men collected beer from brewers and sold it at a profit, allegedly enhanced by watering the beer down so that they could sell 22 or 23 liters for every 20 liters they bought. Only after they had retailed the beer did the brewers receive payment. So both local government and retailers came to take a share of the earnings from beer, while the women brewers bore the risks if the beer was not sold.

The village clubs exacerbated the problem of bad debts, which women had hoped to end by setting up the first clubs in the 1950s. Debts grew worse when the women were not selling their own beer. "There came this new practice of the youths, when you brew he takes the beer without paying, and says: 'I'll sell it for you.' Then when he sells it he doesn't pay you."[32] Women who sold for themselves had some discretion over who they sold to and could use this to limit debts, but they had no control over who the club retailers sold to. A club vendor could simply delay payment for a brew indefinitely by saying that he was waiting for a customer's payment. Women had no effective recourse to law in these circumstances.

Around 1980, an alternative to the clubs emerged with the development of *vikao*, which were in effect little unlicensed drinking groups without any physical premises that met daily and had regular arrangements to buy beer from certain brewers. These *vikao* were a form of tax evasion, as well as a way of cutting out middlemen, and they offered women more control over their earnings from brewing. Although technically illegal, *vikao* became widely established, especially in Kyela.

Technical changes to brewing during this period took advantage of economies of scale. From the mid-1950s oil drums became more easily available, allowing the preparation of a larger volume of beer than did any earthenware pot, and reducing the firewood needed to boil up copious amounts of liquid. These changes were particularly important for the making of "watery" beers, which require much more cooking than the traditional *kimpumu*. The availability of smaller aluminum containers for mixing and, later, large plastic sheets for cooling and drying, further eased the burdensome work of making the watery beer. From the early 1980s, Tanzania's economic problems made sugar a scarce commodity, leading to declining production of *kangara* and market domination of the watery beers.

Returns to women brewers in this period remained stagnant. The technical changes in brewing worked in their favor, but changes in the organization of beer selling worked against them. The urban brewers of Tukuyu still managed to support themselves, mostly without husbands, but by the late 1960s it would seem that the kind of investment in property that had been possible for these women fifteen years earlier was no longer feasible.

Outside the towns, the sharp drop in male migrancy rates during the 1960s meant that most married women now had a husband in residence. Figures show that earnings from beer were an important part of household income, but the principal sources of cash income derived from agricultural exports were still in men's hands (Luning 1969). Men continued to make the major investment decisions.

Education was now even more a route for women to invest in children and in their own future security. With independence, schooling became, in theory, free and much more widespread, but there were still cash costs involved in the provision of books and clothes for school, as well as the opportunity cost of allowing children to study rather than keeping them at home to help with the domestic workload. Earnings from brewing were increasingly limited and gave women little opportunity to accumulate, but did allow some investment for their children's welfare.

SCHOOL FEES AND FOOD: BREWING AND DRINKING IN THE LATE 1990s

The two most striking features of commercial brewing among the Nyakyusa now are ubiquity and marginality. I undertook a small survey in 1997 that revealed that of 37 women surveyed, 26 had at some time brewed beer to sell and that 11 were doing so regularly.[33] Very few relied on this as a sole source of income, but it was the single most important source of income for women. Significantly, it was the principal way in which women obtained money from men, with most of the other sources of women's income relying on selling small foodstuff items to other women. Almost all women insisted that the income from brewing was entirely theirs to spend as they wished.

The pattern of women's involvement in brewing hints at the marginal returns and risky nature of this pursuit. A number of the women surveyed had brewed for a while and then had stopped doing so. The usual reason for this seemed to be a lack of capital. Frequently a domestic crisis, such as illness, consumed all the earnings from a brew so that a woman might not have even the little amount of money needed to make another brew. Several said that they would resume brewing when they had secured enough capital.

Women's accounts of their earnings from brewing also suggest marginality. The relative price of beer has declined since the 1930s. A 20-liter container of beer costs around Tsh 1,700 wholesale or Tsh 2,000 retail, and a sack of maize costs around Tsh 7,000. A rural teacher earns around Tsh 47,000 a month. In the 1930s, a 20-liter container of beer cost 20 percent of a teacher's salary, but by 1997 it was down to only 5 percent despite a steady decline in the value of official wages since the 1970s.

Brewing is small-scale. I neither met nor heard of any woman who brewed more than the 140–160 liters that a single oil drum would hold. Nor did I come across any woman who hired labor to brew. All relied on their own labor and that of their daughters, with occasional help from a female relative or neighbor should this be necessary.

At first glance, the profits from a brew seem reasonable, if not remarkable. Women's estimates of the costs and inputs of their beer varied considerably, depending on where they bought the ingredients and where they sold the beer. They vary from Tsh 2,500 to Tsh 4,450 (between US$4 and US$7). In the group surveyed, the mean estimate of earnings from a brew was US$6. For those women who brew twice a week, as some do (especially around Tukuyu and Kyela), it is possible to earn a monthly income of between Tsh 20,000 and Tsh 36,000 (US$32–US$58). This is a considerable income in a country where the official minimum wage is Tsh 30,000 a month. Many unskilled workers actually earn between Tsh 10,000 and Tsh 20,000 a month, and a casual agricultural laborer may earn only Tsh 800 a day.

There are, however, a number of factors that can reduce the actual income. Brews sometimes go wrong. This may be caused by temperature fluctuations, or by the introduction of alkaline agents to the brew, or by undermodification of the grain. An experienced brewer is less likely to have such problems, but failed brews are by no means uncommon and involve a near-complete loss of investment. Sometimes the failed brew is salvaged by distilling it to produce the illegal drink called *gongo*, but this may involve the extra costs of borrowing equipment and bribing officials to turn a blind eye.

Bad debts due to customers' nonpayment rather than technical hitches are the greatest pitfall, and some women have been driven out of brewing by them. At other times, beer may simply go unsold. The "sale or return" system on which the clubs operate means that women bear all the risks, because beer that is not sold within a day is spoilt. There are also capital costs. An oil drum, a plastic sheet for cooling and a set of containers may cost as much as Tsh 39,000 (US$63). Those who do not possess these items rent them from others at a cost of Tsh 500–1,000 for each brew. All these factors, unpredictably and sometimes disastrously, conspire to reduce brewers' real earnings.

While women control the income from brewing, the uses to which they put it are limited. In the survey, only two had used income from brewing for capital investment purposes, one to set herself up as a fish hawker, the other to buy some land for her son, who hoped to marry and anticipated no land inheritance from his father. All others said that the profits from brewing were spent on food, clothes and other items for themselves and their children. One man said simply of his wife's brewing earnings, "She pays school fees and sometimes she buys food."[34] Investment in the health and education of children was a common theme in the accounts of these women brewers. Men still control the major sources of "lump sum" income—coffee in Rungwe, cocoa and most of the rice crop in Kyela—and consequently take the major investment decisions in terms of land, livestock and buildings. The costs involved in health care and education for children have risen markedly as state provision has shrunk in recent years, but the small amounts women bring in from brewing allow them to meet these costs. Women continue to invest in their children with the proceeds of their beer trade.

Male retailers do rather better out of beer than female brewers. The arrangements under which they work vary from village to village, but these young men earn around Tsh 600 (almost US$1) for every 20 liters of beer they sell; and they can often expect to sell about 60 liters in a day. Usually they have to pay at least Tsh 100 a day to the village to be allowed to sell in the club, but this still leaves them with around Tsh 1,700 each day. Unlike the brewers, they face no risks, as the burden of spoiled beer or bad debts is borne by the brewer, not the retailer. They do, however, have various capital costs—providing a shelter (usually of bamboo and grass thatch) and some aged and remarkably grubby plastic receptacles from which the beer is drunk. In Tukuyu and Kyela towns, the club owners, who tend not to be brewers or retailers themselves, make a limited profit. They simply rent out space in their clubs to women who sell beer. The women usually pay around Tsh 200 per day for a room. Urban clubs vary in size from three to seven rooms, and the income from a club can therefore be between Tsh 600 and Tsh 1,400 a day. In fact, club owners often rent rather than own the club premises. The only club in Tukuyu Town that shows real evidence of prosperity, with smartly painted walls and a roof that does not leak, is owned by a man who makes and sells the banana beer called *mbege*. He combines the roles of owner, brewer and retailer, and evidently derives a good income from the trade.

The village governments receive considerable revenue from selling beer. They generally charge each retailer Tsh 100 a day. A club usually has three or four retailers, and a large village will have two or three clubs. In villages where a regular market is held there may be seven or eight clubs. A village government will thus earn at least Tsh 800 a day from clubs, with some earning twice as much. Legally, this revenue is supposed to be shared with the district council, because the village should take out a license costing Tsh 12,000 for six months. In practice, hardly any village does so. There are 140 villages in Rungwe District, each with at least one club, and there are fifteen clubs in the town; but only seventeen licenses were taken out in the period April–October 1997. Almost all village governments simply keep their beer revenue. From their accounting systems it is not entirely clear what happens to this money, which, at a conservative estimate, must run to over Tsh 30,000,000 (almost US$50,000) each year in Rungwe District. Officeholders in village governments, who are usually men, are apparently the most obvious beneficiaries of brewing among the Nyakyusa at present.

CONCLUSION: BROUGHT UP BY BEER

Brewing beer has become a vital source of cash income for rural and urban Nyakyusa women over the last 60 years even though, as elsewhere in Africa, profits are unpredictable and returns have tended to decline in the last few decades (Saul 1981; Colson and Scudder 1988). It is difficult on the evidence from this area to agree with the assertion that "[i]n the long run women don't profit from beer" (Beckman 1988).

Brewing, however, has hardly been the easy ride to women's financial independence suggested by some of the alternative literature. Only in certain limited circumstances has the result of brewing for sale led to a great increase in female autonomy, with women running their own households and controlling major financial decisions. Men's control over land, over other productive resources, and over the structures of state, local and village government has created a situation in which women earn through brewing the steady trickle of money a household needs, while men control the larger sums that are used to buy land or livestock, pay bridewealth, build a house or shop, or buy a vehicle. Much of the income from beer brewing disappears in the purchase of petty commodities. "If I am out of salt, I brew beer to get money. For buying sugar, or what, salt, soap, cooking oil. So I get money."[35] But brewing for sale has given Nyakyusa women power in one key area of investment. It has brought about some change in the terms of the perennial conflict in Nyakyusa society over the access sons have to the investable resources of the household: women use their brewing earnings to care for and educate their children, especially their sons, investing in them in a way that would not otherwise be possible. As the commercial availability of beer undermined the prerogatives of age, and cash subverted the authority of older men, so cash earnings from beer have allowed women to partly side-step older men's economic control. Brewing has not liberated women economically. It is hard work, with small and unreliable rewards, but as one woman told me, "It [beer] has helped us. Though the Christians say 'Do not drink,' that [beer] brought us up."[36]

NOTES

This chapter is the result of research carried out for the African Studies Centre, University of Cambridge, with the support of the Economic and Social Research Council (ESRC) of the United Kingdom and the British Institute in Eastern Africa. In addition to archival work, interviews were carried out in the Rungwe and Kyela Districts of Tanzania. These interviews are referred to as "Int Nya," followed by a number (identifying the informant) and a lowercase letter (which indicates the interview cited). Translations of interviews will be deposited with the ESRC Data Archive.

1. There have been few attempts to study the actual detail of economics: see Saul 1981 and Carlson 1989.
2. Int Nya16b.
3. Int Nya17a.
4. German East Africa was the site of a fierce military campaign between British and German forces (Monica Wilson Papers, University of Cape Town, BC 880 E, Book I, 39).
5. Barter was still common in 1935 (Wilson notebooks, BC880, Book XIII, 6).
6. There is a description of the making of millet beer in the Wilson notebooks (BC 880 E, Book III, 103–05).
7. Int Nya5b.
8. The demand for foodstuffs for Chunya was noted as early as 1927 (Iringa Province Annual Report, 1927, in Tanzania National Archives [TNA] SMP 11677, I. See also Bryceson 1990: 106–07).
9. Rungwe District Annual Report, 1934, TNA 77/1/57.
10. Int Nya4b.
11. *Kangara* was known and banned in nearby Mbeya by 1931 (Provincial Commissioner, Iringa to District Officer, Mbeya, 25 November 1931, TNA 157/A2/8).
12. Int Nya23a.
13. District Officer Rungwe to Provincial Commissioner, Southern Highlands Province, 21 June 1940, TNA 157/A2/8.

14. TNA 18/T2/6.

15. Wilson notebooks, BC880 E, Book I, 65 and Book IV, 2–3.

16. Wilson notebooks, BC880 E, Book I, 65 and Book XV, 1.

17. Int Nya18b.

18. Int Nya42a.

19. Int Nya5b.

20. Int Nya4b.

21. Sala binti Said to District Commissioner, Rungwe, 1954, TNA 18/T2/6.

22. Int Nya14c.

23. Ndemele binti Said et al. to District Commissioner, Rungwe, 21 August 1952, TNA 18/T2/6.

24. Ints Nya31a, Nya31b.

25 For government enforcement of the club monopoly see District Commissioner, Rungwe to Secretary, Ukukwe Rural Council, 12 April 1951, TNA 18/T2/6.

26. Int Nya31a.

27. Int Nya3a.

28. Int Nya3a and Int Nya40a, with a magistrate, stresses the importance of revenue in the issuing of club licenses.

29. Secretary Ukukwe Rural Council to District Commissioner, Rungwe, 27 April 1951, TNA 18/T2/6.

30. There is a list of the clubs of Suma Ward in Katibu Kata (Suma to Mkurugenzi wa Maendeleo, 4 September 1974, Rungwe District Archive, L3/2).

31. Katibu wa TANU wa Wilaya to Makatibu Tarafa Wote, 16 January 1976, Rungwe District Archive, L3/2.

32. Int Nya19a.

33. A questionnaire was applied to all persons over the age of sixteen in ten households in the village of Ilange and fifteen households in the village of Ilenga. The households were selected randomly by ballot from a list of households.

34. Int Nya3a.

35. Int Nya2a.

36. Int Nya31b.

REFERENCES

Akyeampong, E. 1996. *Drink, Power and Cultural Change: A Social History of Alcohol in Ghana c. 1980 to Recent Times*. Oxford: James Currey.

Beckman, V. 1988. *Alcohol: Another Trap for Africa*. Sweden: Orebro.

Bonner, P. 1992. "Backs to the Fence: Law, Liquor and the Search for Social Control in an East Rand Town, 1929–42." In J. Crush and C.H. Ambler, *Liquor and Labor in Southern Africa*, Athens: Ohio University Press, 269–308.

Bradford, H. 1992. "'We Women Will Show Them': Beer Protests in the Natal Countryside, 1929." In J. Crush and C.H. Ambler, *Liquor and Labor in Southern Africa*. Athens: Ohio University Press, 208–34.

Bryceson, D.F. 1990. *Food Insecurity and the Social Division of Labor, 1919–1985.* Basingstoke: Macmillan.

Carlson, R.G. 1989. "Haya Worldview and Ethos: An Ethnography of Alcohol Production and Consumption in Buhaya, Tanzania." Ph.D. thesis, University of Illinois.

Charsley, S.R. 1969. *The Princes of Nyakyusa*. Nairobi: East African Publishing House.

Colson, E., and T. Scudder. 1988. *For Prayer and Profit: The Ritual, Economic and Social Importance of Beer in Gwembe District, Zambia, 1950–82.* Stanford: Stanford University Press.

Haggblade, S. 1992. "The Shebeen Queen and the Evolution of Botswana's Sorghum Beer Industry." In J. Crush and C.H. Ambler, *Liquor and Labor in Southern Africa.* Athens: Ohio University Press, 395–412.

Harries, P. 1994. *Work, Culture and Identity: Migrant Laborers in Mozambique and South Africa, c. 1860–1910.* London: James Currey.

Luning, H. 1969. *A Farm Economic Survey of Rungwe.* Leiden: African Studies Centre.

Maliyamkono, T., and M. Bagachwa. 1990. *The Second Economy in Tanzania.* Athens: Ohio University Press.

Nelson, N. 1982. "'Women Must Help Each Other': The Operation of Personal Networks among Buzaa Beer Brewers." In P. Caplan and J. Bujra (eds.), *Women United, Women Divided.* Bloomington: Indiana University Press.

Redding, S. 1992. "Beer Brewing in Umtata: Women, Migrant Labor and Social Control in a Rural Town." In J. Crush and C.H. Ambler, *Liquor and Labor in Southern Africa.* Athens: Ohio University Press, 235–51.

Saul, M. 1981. "Beer, Sorghum and Women: Production for the Market in Rural Upper Volta." *Africa* 51: 746–64.

Wilson, M. 1957. *Rituals of Kinship among the Nyakyusa*. London: Oxford University Press.

———. 1959. *Communal Rituals of the Nyakyusa.* London: International African Institute.

———. 1963. *Good Company: A Study of Nyakyusa Age-Villages.* London: Oxford University Press.

———. 1977. *For Men and Elders: Change in the Relations of Generations and of Men and Women among the Nyakyusa-Ngonde People, 1875–1971.* London: International African Institute.

Wright, M. 1972. "Nyakyusa Cults and Politics in the Later Nineteenth Century." In T. Ranger and I. Kimambo, *The Historical Study of African Religion.* London: Heinemann, 153–71.

4

Liquid Gold of a Lost Kingdom

The Rise of *Waragi* Production in Kibaale District, Uganda

Nite Baza Tanzarn

Uganda is one of the world's poorest countries, and Kibaale District is one of the most impoverished districts within Uganda. This was not always the case. The area that now comprises Kibaale has had an illustrious history as an integral part of Bunyoro, Uganda's ancient kingdom. Bunyoro, one of the intralacustrine Bantu kingdoms of Central Africa renowned for the degree of political centralization and economic development it achieved in precolonial times, paid a heavy price for flaunting its political strength to the British colonial state. Wave after wave of political upheaval has chipped away at Bunyoro's once thriving peasant economy. This chapter tells the story of how the people of the area have regained a measure of economic viability by establishing a new export commodity that enjoys seemingly unlimited demand. The commodity is ideal in the sense that it is based on local value-added processing of a plant that thrives in the area. Furthermore, its production and sale are relatively accessible to all sectors of the local society. A development success story—or is it? While there is no doubt that banana beer and its distilled variant, *waragi*, represent a vital economic enterprise to the people of Kibaale, there are drawbacks. This chapter provides historical background about Kibaale and the Bunyoro Kingdom before examining the centrality of banana production in Kibaale and the associated *waragi* trade. The trade's social and economic impact on household welfare is considered, followed by concluding remarks about the *waragi* trade's overall significance in Kibaale.

FROM RICHES TO RAGS: KIBAALE DISTRICT'S DOWNWARD DESCENT

Kibaale District, with a total land area of 4,400 square kilometers, lies in the extreme west of Uganda, bordering Lake Albert and the Democratic Republic of Congo. It forms part of the Western Rift Valley and enjoys agricultural and pastoral land of reasonably high potential. Nonetheless, Kibaale District's social indicators are poor, as it has high infant mortality, low life expectancy and high fertility rates. The district's infrastructure is extremely scanty, with little access to safe water and only 500 kilometers of unpaved gravel roads that are seasonably impassable (Baza 1998). In 1995 Kibaale had a human development index of 0.35, ranking it in 24th position out of Uganda's 39 districts. On the income index, it ranked 35th countrywide (United Nations Development Program [UNDP] 1997).

Formerly, the famous Bunyoro-Kitara Empire covered much of southern Uganda and northwest Tanzania. The empire started losing territory to smaller offshoot kingdoms such as Buganda, Ankole, Toro and Karagwe in the nineteenth century, but at the time of British colonial intervention in the late nineteenth century, it was still a strong and proud kingdom such that the ruler of Bunyoro, Mukama Kabarega II, had the audacity to resist British rule. His neighboring rival, the Kabaka of Buganda, adopted the opposite strategy and ingratiated himself with his new colonial overlords. In 1897 the British crushingly defeated Bunyoro's ruler. A great deal of Bunyoro territory, including what is now Kibaale District, was awarded to Buganda by the British, leading to a subsequent bitter row between the two kingdoms over the "lost counties." The Buganda Kingdom enjoyed a favored status throughout the colonial period, in stark contrast to Bunyoro. Treated as a conquered territory, its monarchy was restored in 1933, but the lost counties continued to be occupied by Buganda until the post-independence era, totaling 68 years of humiliating political subjugation by a rival kingdom.

The Baganda rulers tried to assert their influence in the area through oppression that included bars on speaking the indigenous language, Runyoro, and on other activities that might highlight Banyoro identity. Significantly, they denied the Banyoro[1] access to land. Buganda chiefs, as part of their elevated colonial position, were awarded the freehold title to a great deal of Bunyoro land. This land expropriation and a general lack of development of the area relegated the Banyoro to a perpetually poor and submissive position and forced some of the population to leave and settle elsewhere.

From 1921, pressure groups demanding fair treatment of the Banyoro and a return of the two counties to Bunyoro started to emerge, and by 1950 these pressure groups, especially the Mubende Banyoro Committee, had mobilized the Banyoro masses almost to a point of revolt. Violent incidents involving the destruction of Baganda chiefs' crops and houses became common. Most of the nonruling Baganda were effectively driven out of the counties to settle in Mubende and elsewhere. In essence, there was net migration from the two counties for almost a century as a result of political upheaval.

After national independence, the lost counties were finally returned to Bunyoro following a referendum in 1964. The reunification of the kingdom was short-lived, since Uganda's traditional kingdoms were abolished under President Milton Obote's modernization scheme in 1967. Bunyoro Kingdom became the District of Bunyoro, which was further split into two parts, south and north Bunyoro, in the early 1970s and later, in 1979, renamed after their respective administrative headquarters, Masindi and Hoima. However, some parts of Hoima District were isolated from the headquarters and lagged behind in development, and Hoima District was thus split up into the present Hoima and Kibaale Districts in 1991 (Bishop and Baza 1998).

Even after the referendum that returned the counties to Bunyoro in 1964, most exiled Banyoro could not return to their home areas. Most of their land had been divided up and given to the Baganda chiefs who migrated with the certificates of title back to Buganda after 1964. In most cases, they were not willing to sell the land to the Banyoro. A large amount of the land in Kibaale District is still owned by these absentee landlords, some of whom have died leaving no heirs. The recently enacted Land Law (1998) has addressed this problem, but it has yet to take full effect. The land issue has been an ongoing dilemma. The Banyoro are a highly land-conscious society in which property has always been a major criterion for distinguishing social status. Given the agricultural foundation of the society, land is an asset of central economic importance (Nzita and Mbaga-Niwampa 1993).

"GOING BANANAS" IN AN AGRARIAN ECONOMY

Agriculture is the basis of Uganda's economy. In Kibaale District, more than 80 percent of the population are engaged in smallholder peasant agriculture, producing both their household's food supply and commercial crops for sale. Roughly 2 percent of the district's population are large-scale commercial farmers, and a further 5 percent are formally employed. The rest have specialized in formal and petty trading, and cottage industries (Uganda Ministry of Finance and Economic Planning [MoFEP] 1992; Uganda Statistics Department, Ministry of Finance and Economic Planning [MoPED] 1998).

Only 12 percent of the district's arable land is utilized. Most of the district's resident peasant farmers live in scattered homesteads with average holdings of about 2.5 acres. The low arable land utilization is due to the district's history as a "lost county" and to land tenure constraints connected with the Baganda chiefs' former monopoly on land, as well as the Banyoro farmers' low level of agricultural technology and labor shortages.

Traditionally, the main cash crops of the area were Arabica coffee, cotton and tobacco. Food production was entirely for subsistence, and virtually everyone grew their own food. However, like other parts of Uganda, Kibaale District has experienced considerable changes in agricultural conditions in the postcolonial period. During the 1970s and 1980s, coffee and cotton gradually lost value largely because of the poor marketing infrastructure that prevailed while the country was in the throes of civil upheaval and war. Most farmers neglected their coffee plantations and cotton fields and took up alternative crops for cash. Cotton virtually disappeared and very few farmers have shown any interest in resuming its production.

The production of newer, "nontraditional" export cash crops like maize, beans, groundnut, sesame and sunflower has been encouraged by government policy. Beer banana, cassava, maize and coffee have taken over the former cotton areas as the district's main cash crops (Baza 1998). Nowadays, a typical farm holding comprises some perennial crops like coffee and beer banana, fruits like jack fruit and papaya, and some shade trees, usually grown in the area immediately adjoining the homestead. The rest of the land is under various annual and perennial crops or elephant grass and thickets. Most farmers intercrop in order to maximize their output per farmland unit.

The main food crop in Bunyoro was traditionally millet. Maize was grown in small quantities. Beans and peas were widely grown and were dried and stored for use in the dry season, when they were soaked in cold water and then boiled (Roscoe 1923). Nowadays, sweet potatoes and cassava have replaced millet as the staples because growing and processing millet is labor-intensive and time-consuming. Although bananas have always been grown, it has been on a small scale because they were considered less well suited to the district in comparison with other areas.

Three kinds of banana were traditionally grown: *enkonje*, baked by the women for the men to eat when drinking beer; *ikamba* (Luganda: *mbide*), the so-called male highland beer banana; and *enyamunyu*. The latter type, also known as the "female" highland cooking banana, was cooked as a vegetable and was not grown to any great extent (Roscoe 1923).[2] Usually, each year a few new banana suckers were planted, while those that no longer produced well were abandoned.

Currently, two types of bananas are grown in the district: beer and cooking bananas. The beer type is estimated to cover about 90 percent of the total banana acreage and is extensively used for the production of liquor.

The beer banana variety called *musa*[3] was probably introduced at the beginning of the twentieth century by the British to the botanical garden of Entebbe, and then spread further inland thanks to the Baganda, who quickly became aware of its high juice yield (Rossel 1994, 1998). Banana juice may be consumed fresh or used for brewing banana beer, *tonto*, and the latter may be distilled into the strong banana gin called *waragi*. However, as the taste of the juice and the beer is not considered very attractive, the variety is mainly used for the production of *waragi*.

Almost all homesteads now grow *musa*. Its production spread during the 1970s when the political and economic situation in the country started to deteriorate and coffee and cotton's allure as cash earners was being undermined by the economy's downward slide. Payments to smallholder farmers by the Cooperative Unions for their cash crops were low, late, or never forthcoming. The government's deteriorating finances were revealed in the totally impassable state of the district's roads. Farmers lost the incentive to grow export crops. They restricted production to what their households needed for their own consumption. However, the production of beer banana steadily increased. This could be partly attributed to the fact that the plants of the *musa* variety thrive even in poor soils. They are more resistant to common banana pests and diseases now infesting Uganda's banana stands, such as banana weevil, nematodes and Black Sigatoka. They also require little labor: weeding is not vital, slashing is the only maintenance they need, and they have a ready market throughout Uganda and in neighboring countries. They are easily transportable in a processed or semiprocessed form, whereas this is not the case for other banana varieties.

The sale of bananas represents the most important source of income for over a quarter of the farmers in Uganda's major banana-growing areas (Kyamuhangire 1990). However, since they are sold fresh, they are prone to damage during post-harvest handling, transport and processing. After harvest, the bananas are either loaded onto trucks, carried on bicycles or head loaded to nearby collecting centers. The mode of transport to the market depends on how many bunches a farmer is able to harvest at a time and the accessibility of a farm. A harvested bunch can keep on average a maximum of four to six days before it starts ripening. Kibaale District's poor transport infrastructure and the distance from the main market in Kampala have precluded the district's success as a banana-producing area. No such drawbacks were associated with the production and distribution of beer banana products. Over the past 30 years of civil strife in Uganda, during which the marketing of traditional cash crops became increasingly difficult, the production and trade of banana beer made *musa* Kibaale District's crop of last resort and then first preference.

THE TRADE IN "LIQUID GOLD"

Beer bananas were used traditionally for brewing *tonto* banana beer. Originally, brewing was not commercially oriented. It was a community-centered activity for purposes of entertaining, celebrating harvests, dowry settlement, marriages and deaths, as well as payment in kind for labor services (Koponen 1988; Rutabajuka 1992; McCall 1996). With the introduction of the cash economy in the twentieth century, brewing also became a commercial activity. People started producing alcohol for sale to be able to meet tax obligations, and later cash became increasingly necessary to pay for education, health and transport services.

Formerly, *ikamba*, the so-called male banana, was used for making beer (Masefield 1938). The fruit was cut when about to ripen, put into pots and covered with leaves. Sometimes it was spread over a fire on a frame and arranged so that it got thoroughly heated by the fire without being baked. Grass was heaped over it to keep the heat in and hasten ripening. When it became pulpy it was peeled, and the pulp was thrown into a large wooden trough in which it was reduced to a watery paste either by working with the hand or by treading on it. This paste was then strained, the sieves being merely bundles of grass shaped into a sort of pocket. The first extract was juice, which was usually for domestic consumption or for sale to the local school or parish priest. If a lot of juice was left over, it would be brewed into local beer for serving at social events. To make *tonto* banana beer after the liquid had filtered through the grass, water was added and sometimes a little grain to make it ferment. The alcohol content of *tonto* beer is low, usually 2–5 percent (Davies 1990).[4]

According to local informants, the technique of distilling the beer to make *waragi* gin was introduced into the area during World War II. Some attribute this innovation to Buganda settlers, while others suggest that the technique came from Kenya (Nout 1979). Many Ugandans believe that *waragi* was introduced in the 1940s. This is when it became common, but its introduction came earlier and was associated with the ethnically mixed remnants of Gordon's Sudanese soldiers who were transplanted to Uganda at the turn of the century. They are believed to be the first to have distilled alcohol in Uganda. As they were employed in marginal trade and had no land to cultivate, distilling became their illicit source of income. By the 1950s, *waragi* production was an established part of the informal economy in Buganda, and it had acquired a Ganda name, although the colonialists insisted that it was Nubian gin (Obbo and Willis personal communications, 2000).

Waragi, as a distilled drink, is far stronger than banana beer. Gotanègre (1983) records an alcoholic content of up to 68 percent. It is commonly claimed by local producers and consumers to be almost 100 percent alcohol. Having realized that *waragi* is more alcoholic and has a longer shelf-life compared to the fresh juice's one day and local beer's five days, people experimented with *waragi* production using 20-liter tins (tins in which paraffin was sold in those days) for making the new drink. With the onset of economic and political upheaval in the country, people increasingly fermented the beer banana for longer periods to make *waragi*.

Waragi can be produced from most crops that have a high percentage of carbohydrates, for example, banana, sugarcane/molasses, maize and rice. It is made exclusively from bananas in Kibaale. Originally, the process of beverage production started with the harvesting of the *ikamba* type of beer bananas. Harvested bananas at different levels of maturity were ripened by either burying them in a pit or hanging them above the hearth for several days. Their juice was extracted and brewed into beer that was then distilled to make *waragi*. Given the paraffin tins' 20-liter capacity, only small quantities could be produced at any one time. The pipe taking the distillate was cooled down in a large container whose water contents had to be frequently changed.

During the regime of Idi Amin in the 1970s, *waragi* production escalated. Amin's Islamic leanings did not prevent people from using alcohol as a source of income and psychological escape. *Waragi* producers switched from using 20-liter tins to 200-liter drums and adopted *musa* bananas with higher juice productivity. The process, known as *kibaku*, required large amounts of water to control the pressure because of the volumes involved.[5] The whole process was therefore moved away from homesteads to flowing streams where the pipe could be immersed. Kibaale has numerous streams, with almost 5 percent of the district being swampy or under water.

In the last ten years, however, the *kibaku* method has been replaced by a new technique. Ripe bananas are placed in a container or in a depression made in the ground lined with polythene sheets. The bananas are then mashed with one's feet and left to ferment for five to seven days. During this time the fermenting mash is mixed once a day and left exposed to the sun during the day and covered at night. The fermented juice is subsequently separated from the pulp by putting the mixture in a polypropylene bag and squeezing the juice, using one's hands to apply pressure. Rather than adding sorghum to facilitate fermentation, the extract is distilled and the condensate collected.

Waragi has gained fame internationally as Uganda's national drink. After independence, the International Distillers of Uganda factory was established in Luzira. Licensed home distillation was legalized, but the produce had to be sold to the government factory (Robbins 1979).[6] The industrially produced *waragi* consists of distilled banana beer and sugar molasses with a 40 percent alcohol content compared to the even higher content of locally produced *waragi*. This bottled drink produced in hygienic factory conditions has been approved by the U.S. Food and Drug Administration. Most of the factory's output is consumed in Uganda by relatively wealthy urban-based consumers, with small amounts exported annually.

Local cottage brewing and distilling of alcohol operates on a far larger scale, holding a prime position in the circulation of money in the rural economy (McCall 1996). Kibaale District is believed to be the second largest producer of *waragi* after Kabarole District. However, the quality of Kibaale's *waragi* is said to be the best according to traders based at Kiwunya, the country's main collection center in Kampala.

The *waragi* trade has local, national and international circuits. Within the district, small-scale female *waragi* dealers usually buy to sell locally from their houses. A jerry can of *waragi* is sold for between US$8 and US$10 and can be bought by the liter for about US$1. In Kampala, a jerry can of *waragi* costs US$20. The *waragi* trade provides employment for many urban women, especially slum dwellers, who sell from their one-room apartments. They deal in small quantities, usually not selling more than five liters a day.

Some traders are authorized to collect locally produced *waragi* from the farmers that they are then obliged to sell to the International Distillers of Uganda in Luzira. However, local traders complain that the price that the International Distillers offer for their crude *waragi* is exploitative. The high quality *waragi* that the distillers are now willing to buy has production costs of between US$24 and $32 per 20 liters in Kibaale, whereas the traders are paid only US$14 at the distillery. Not surprisingly, producers and traders have shunned supplying *waragi* to the factory and instead engage in the informal production and sale of *waragi*, which is by far the largest part of the national market.

The biggest *waragi* collecting-center in Kibaale is Mabale, followed by Nyamarunda. For onward sale to distribution centers in Kampala, Gulu, Masaka, Arua and Moroto, *waragi* is taken to Kampala and Hoima en route to the north. It is difficult to trace the growth of the informal *waragi* trade over time, not only in Kibaale but in Uganda as a whole, because it is a business fraught with risks. Most of the *waragi* dealers are unlicensed and do not pay tax. When transporting *waragi*, traders travel at night to evade law enforcement agencies. In Karuguza, Kibaale District, almost all the wholesale traders come from Kampala, with the majority being women. About 25,000 liters are collected from the center weekly. Traders take the *waragi* to distribution centers in Kampala for onward sale to up-country destinations in the central and eastern parts of Uganda and sometimes to Kenya. A few traders take the *waragi* across national borders to the Sudan, Congo and Rwanda, but this is very risky and logistically difficult.

However, the risks of *waragi* production and distribution have decreased during the 1990s. Under economic liberalization, the ban on *waragi* production and trade is no longer heavily enforced and people are not threatened with arrest for its distillation. The Enguli Act of 1964 (Government of Uganda 1966), which made the production of *waragi* illegal unless one had a license from the Enguli Board, is still on the books, but ironically the board is no longer in existence.[7] Nowadays, *waragi* producers can obtain a license from the district authorities and pay a minimal fee for ownership of the large drums used for brewing. Most people are still not licensed and are producing and trading in *waragi* illegally as a result of this outdated law. There is need to update the law and streamline official control of this lucrative activity in order to generate more revenue for both the government and the producers. In addition, some of the negative social effects of *waragi* could be addressed if its production and trade were legalized. The additives that some distillers use to make their product more potent are a public health concern.

It is now a generally held view that Kibaale District and the nation benefit from an expanding informal trade in *waragi*. Many households, both rural and urban, are engaged in either its production or trade, with it often being their primary or only source of income. However, there is no way of monitoring production or of knowing how much money people are earning from the *waragi* trade. District annual production is estimated at roughly 12 million liters, of which over 95 percent is thought to be sold outside the district. Local farmers earn an estimated 12 billion Ugandan shillings from the liquor industry annually (Uganda, Kibaale District 1998).

Waragi production is not an indigenous economic activity in Bunyoro, but *waragi* has gradually asserted itself as one of the district's most important products. District statistics on volume and value of production output have to be treated with caution. They are at best guesstimates. Officially, coffee is the district's main earner. However, casual observation and farmers' acreage allocation to coffee and beer banana suggest that beer banana is the district's most important crop. Certainly in terms of government revenue, beer banana has made its mark. Karuguza is one of the oldest trading centers of the district. The trading center contributes about two-thirds of Kibaale Town Council's revenue from licenses and permits. Karuguza market contributes the biggest percentage of revenue collected (36 percent), followed by shops (26 percent). *Waragi* contributes by far the biggest share of market fees (40 percent), followed by the trade in used clothes and fish, each accounting for 4 percent of the total. In the trading center, rich people are categorized as those who have businesses. The majority are *waragi* traders (Baza 1998).

Compared with the district's agricultural crops, which are seasonal and offer people a chance to earn cash only once or twice a year, beer bananas can be harvested in all seasons, and well-to-do farmers with more than three acres can afford to produce *waragi* on a monthly basis. Smaller-scale farmers have been equally eager to become involved in *waragi* production. During the past two decades of economic crisis, *waragi* has become a vital source of income for "consumption smoothing," meaning households are availed of a more continuous or regular supply of cash needed for necessary consumption (Ellis 1998; Bryceson 1999). The harvesting and ripening of the bananas and the fermenting of beer and distilling of *waragi* take about two weeks. Rich farmers can afford to distill *waragi* twice a month. In Kibaale District at least, this sets the stage for *waragi* production. An indication of the central importance of *waragi* production to the district's population was revealed in 1998 during participatory wealth-ranking exercises within various local communities. People were asked to devise their own measurements of wealth and poverty. Tellingly, they defined the very poorest members of the locality as those who did not own beer banana plantations or those who produced only four jerry cans of *waragi* a month (Baza 1998).

In Kibaale, *waragi* production has helped to overcome the district's former remoteness and inaccessibility. Previously, very few traders dared to venture into the district for fear of being stuck for weeks on end because of the heavily rutted roads and mud. Traders could not risk trading in perishable produce like tomatoes, cassava and sweet potatoes. *Waragi*, on the other hand, is nonperishable, with a long and perhaps endless shelf life. Some people actually argue that its quality improves with time. *Waragi* converts highly perishable bananas into an easily exportable product. Local *waragi* producers never lack a market, because even if outside traders do not come to the district to buy their product, it can always be consumed locally. *Waragi* production and trade have flourished despite the district's poor roads and rampant poverty and the backdrop of national civil upheaval. Not surprisingly, *waragi* has gained the nickname "liquid gold" in Kibaale.

NOT ALL THAT GLITTERS IS GOLD: SOME SOCIAL SETBACKS

The economic fortunes of Kibaale District have taken a turn for the better over the last decade. Many farmers are now able to pay school fees for their children from the income generated from the sale of *waragi*. Others have erected iron-roofed as opposed to grass-thatched houses or have bought bicycles or even mopeds. Although rising incomes have helped make previously unobtainable consumer goods, services and household items affordable, there is concern that the *waragi* trade is ruining the lives of many people.

Commercialization of alcohol production has resulted not only in increased production but also in increased consumption of alcohol. In the homes where brewing is a major activity, children, especially young girls, are extensively involved, leading to their missing classes and eventually dropping out of school. Parents who are heavy drinkers also divert income to alcohol at the expense of other needs. People have reported for work drunk. In school, this has affected the performance of teachers and students negatively. In households where *waragi* is brewed, household members, including children, are likely to drink it. Given its potency, it takes only small quantities for one to get drunk.

Some families take the *waragi* as a drug, using it to treat all types of ailments, even in infants. Some local people argue that if you drink *waragi* you will never suffer from the common cold, but those who use *waragi* as a cure for colds and other illnesses often find they are far worse off.

Although very little research has been published in Uganda about the chemical effects of *waragi* on the body, it may in fact be reducing the body's immunity to illness.

Thus, the transformation of local brewing for social occasions to the district's major export industry is an economic success story with a few murky subplots. By exporting *waragi*, the district has imported social tensions that can and do undermine economic advance and social harmony for various sectors of the population. *Waragi* producers and traders are farmers who have in effect diversified out of strictly subsistence production. The diversification process began decades ago during the colonial period with the introduction of coffee as a cash crop. At the time, colonial officials were concerned about getting a good balance between food and cash crops such that farmers would not experience food insecurity. Later, with the progressive adoption of beer bananas in the postcolonial era, local government officials had the same worry. It was felt that farmers were sacrificing too much food crop land to beer bananas and that too much time was being devoted to harvesting and brewing beer bananas and finally to drinking at the expense of other activities. Furthermore, the brewing of bananas into beer is nutritionally very wasteful, resulting in the loss of 40 to 70 percent of the bananas' calories (Kangasniemi 1996). Distillation of *waragi* causes even more loss of nutritive value.

Traditionally, the subsistence ethic of the people dictated that everyone was expected to produce all their own food needs. There is no culture of buying food. Purchasing food is considered a terrible waste of hard-earned cash, so even if people obtain earnings from the sale of *waragi*, they may not spend that income on food. Most of the people experience periods of hunger lasting about six months per year when they have to survive primarily on cassava (Baza 1998). At any given time of the year, some people are experiencing a lack of adequate food intake such that government officials believe that food shortages are a permanent feature of the district.[8]

Efuransi's case study reveals some of the tensions. Efuransi is married with grown-up children and grandchildren. By village standards, theirs is a well-to-do family. Her husband owns ten acres of land, five of which are under beer banana. Another three acres are under coffee, leaving only two acres for food crops for a family of twelve people. The couple lives with one of their children and nine grandchildren. Originally, half of their land was under food crops, one acre was under beer banana, and three under coffee. Those, Efuransi recalls, were the good old days when there was enough food on their table.[9]

The testimony of the polygamist Jonas confirms the extent of beer banana plantings within households and the need for cross-subsidies of food between polygamist households to rectify the effect of overplanting beer bananas at the expense of sufficient food crop farming.

I am married to two wives. In my second home, I have seven acres under beer bananas and about 0.2 acres of eating bananas. In this homestead, beer bananas are well looked after. In my first home, I have a larger plantation (two acres) of *matoke* [cooking bananas] that is well looked after and about one acre of beer bananas. In my first home, we have no food problems and sometimes I get food to feed my second family from my first home. My second wife has a small plot of about 0.5 acres of beer bananas, which is for her "personal" use. She spends the money on the household, health care and school materials for her children who benefit from the Government's universal primary education.[10]

As in all areas of rural work, activities involved in *waragi* production are divided along gender lines. Traditionally, fruit juice and local beer production were on a small scale. Activities like banana and sorghum production, cutting bananas, cutting grass, fetching water, making juice, yeasting, sieving and the collection of firewood were a female preserve because they were tasks related to women's domestic work. Men and boys extracted juice by trampling on the bananas, which, as a heavy task, was considered best performed by men. Furthermore, men used to brew because it was taboo for a woman to do so. The little alcohol that was sold could be marketed by either women or men. As Rutabajuka (1992) observes, beer banana production was the speciality of women, while the brewing and consumption of beer was a male liberty.

The commercialization of beer and *waragi* production has substantially altered gender relations through the increased incorporation of female labor at different stages of production (Mugabi 1998). Because production is now on a larger scale, these activities are more intense, and thus the women's workload has increased without an accompanying increase in the benefits necessarily accruing to the household. Not unlike other crops, preparation for planting beer bananas usually involves men clearing the land. Planting is done by both men and women. Women continued to perform the tasks related to their routine work, such as growing the bananas, fetching water, collecting firewood and arranging for distillation equipment. Slashing is performed by men, and although both men and women provide the labor for harvesting, the women do most of the work. The whole family and sometimes neighbors help in carrying the bananas from the field to the streams, where all the brewing and distilling activities are performed. When beer plantations are very distant, men transport the bananas by bicycle. Ripening is usually a male responsibility, whereas peeling is done by women and children. Fermenting, if any, and extraction are done by men because women are culturally forbidden to participate in these processes. It is interesting to note that in some communities similar tasks are performed by either men or women, depending on the purpose. For instance, it is common to find women collecting firewood for domestic purposes and men involved in brewing.

Power relations that traditionally favored men are now being contested as the trade in *waragi* has surged forward. Both men and women are currently growing beer bananas, but, like all cash crops, it is viewed as a male crop. However, increasingly women circumvent this view and the demands on their labor time as family workers on their husbands' beer banana plantations and become owners of beer banana plantations in their own right. In this way they control the labor process and cash proceeds. In addition, many women are nowadays found drinking beer and *waragi* publicly.

These female incursions into male activities have created tension between men and women. Men feel that their cash-earning role within the household is being usurped. In retaliation, once a man learns that a woman is earning money, then the chances are high that he will leave the household provisioning to her. So although a woman is free to use the money as she wishes, she often spends most of it on the home and on school and medical fees for the children. Men's income is usually spent on leisure pursuits and objects of status. One male interviewee claimed that whenever he makes a good sale, he marries another woman, but he confided that these marriages do not necessarily last very long (Baza 1998). They are simply flings to be enjoyed while flush with cash. As offhand as this may sound, marital unions in these rural societies have become increasingly loose over recent decades (Southall 1998). The role of alcohol in this process can only be surmised.

CONCLUSION

During the last hundred years, the people of Kibaale District have faced a great number of political upheavals with respect to their Banyoro identity as well as in the larger national context of civil war, which have tended to erode rather than build the economic potential of their home area. Currently Uganda's Museveni government recognizes the Banyoro monarchy as a cultural institution obliged to remain apolitical. However, the Bunyoro Kingdom has never regained its former glory, either politically or economically. It is in this context that increasing cultivation of beer bananas and *waragi* production have arisen.

In effect, the agriculture and trading activities surrounding local *waragi* production have provided a lifeline to the district's population. The local economy has become far more outward oriented, with most of its production being exported to other districts, the capital city, and even to neighboring countries. In the process, the district's agricultural economy has been restructured and gender relations within peasant household production units have been altered.

Local people have known enormous hardship during the past 30 years, and *waragi* production and consumption have both provided some solace. On balance, people see the *waragi* trade as highly beneficial, but there is a general appreciation of its drawbacks. As an export industry, *waragi* offers considerable economic opportunity. The state has yet to fully harness the potential, because there is no effective legislation in place to register and tax traders. Furthermore, at household level, there is more than a little temptation to consume considerable quantities of readily available *waragi*. This occupational hazard can easily undermine household and district welfare. Kibaale District's league table standing tells the story. It remains a very poor and underresourced area within Uganda. The district's "liquid gold" becomes fools' gold for those who do not realize its seductive powers, leading to alcohol dependence.

NOTES

This chapter has benefited from the expert advice of Dr. Gerda Rossel of Leiden University and Dr. Gabriel Rugalema of Wageningen University, the Netherlands.

1. The people of Bunyoro are known as the Banyoro.

2. This male and female distinction is considered to be largely a socially constructed classification that reflects gender roles in the banana-based agricultural system (Gabriel Rugalema, personal communication, 12 October 1999).

3. *Musa* is in fact the botanical name for all banana plants. Its usage to denote a particular banana variety reflects the assimilation of a scientific plant name into the local language, and usually refers to hybrid banana varieties introduced from the 1950s onwards.

4. A stronger beer of 11–15 percent can be made from the fermentation of undiluted banana juice that is considered a delicacy and remains palatable for up to a month (Davies 1990).

5. Accidents as a result of explosions are fortunately rare. They have been minimized by distilling while the drum is on its side as opposed to standing

upright, as was the case in the past. In those days, pressure would build up, usually because of pipe blockages, and the drum would explode, sometimes flying a considerable distance away from the distillation site, causing injuries not only to the brewers but also to other people and their property.

6. Cottage production of distilled alcohol was not legal in most African countries.

7. The 1964 Enguli law was passed to curtail the small producers' market activity and to force them to sell to the factory (Obbo, personal communication, 2000).

8. In the past, people used to have granaries where they could store food, while some foodstuffs like cassava would be stored in the soil. With the introduction of the cash economy, people started selling most of the food they harvested.

9. This is not meant literally, because in Ugandan rural areas, if there is a table at all, it is for the sole use of the man. Other family members have their meals seated on the ground.

10. Since January 1997, the government has offered free primary education for four children per family in preparation for full universal primary education. However, practically all children in rural areas benefit from this scheme.

REFERENCES

Baza, T.N. 1998. *Rehabilitation of Kakumiro-Mubende Trunk Road: Community Mobilisation and Socio Economic Baseline Survey: Inception Report*. Kampala: Barry International.

Bishop, C., and T.N. Baza. 1998. *Irish Aid Contribution to Road Rehabilitation: Feeder Roads and Trunk Road in Kibaale District, Uganda*. Kampala: Irish Aid.

Bryceson, D.F. 1999. "African Rural Labor, Income Diversification and Livelihood Approaches: A Long-Term Development Perspective." *Review of African Political Economy*, no. 80: 171–89.

Davies, G. 1990. "Note on Some Aspects of Domestic Banana-Beer Production in Mpigi District, Uganda." Mimeo, second draft. University of Antwerp, Centre for Development Studies.

Ellis, F. 1998. "Household Strategies and Rural Livelihood Diversification." *Journal of Development Studies* 35 (1): 1–38.

Food and Agriculture Organization (FAO). 1986. *Utilisation of Tropical Foods: Fruits and Leaves*. London: Food and Agriculture Tropical Development and Research Institute.

———. 1994. *Production Yearbook*. Vol. 48. Rome: FAO.

Gotanègre, J.-F. 1983. "La Banane au Rwanda." *Les Cahiers d'Outre-Mer* 35: 313–42.

Kangasniemi, J. 1996. "Bananas in Rwanda: Wasteful Brewing or Food Security for the Poor." Paper presented at the African Local Economy Seminar, University of Helsinki.

Koponen, J. 1988. *People and Production in Late Precolonial Tanzania: History and Structures*. Helsinki: Monographs of the Finnish Society for Development Studies, No. 2.

Kyamuhangire, W. 1990. "Banana Juice Extraction and Processing." M.Sc. thesis, University of New South Wales, Kensington.

Masefield, G.B. 1938. "The Production of Native Beer in Uganda." *East African Agricultural Journal*, March: 362–64.

McCall, M. 1996. "Rural Brewing, Exclusion and Development Policy Making." In C. Swetrion (ed.), *Women, Employment and Exclusion*. Oxford: Oxfam.

Mugabi, E. 1998. "The Gender Implications of Commercialisation of Local Alcohol Production: A Case Study of Ngogwe Sub County, Mukono District." M.A. thesis, Makerere University, Kampala.

Nout, M.J.R. 1979. "Aspects of the Manufacture and Consumption of Kenyan Traditional Fermented Beverages." Ph.D. dissertation, University of Nairobi.

Nzita, R., and M. Mbaga-Niwampa. 1993. *Peoples and Cultures of Uganda*. Kampala: Fountain Publishers.

Robbins, M.C. 1979. "Problem Drinking and the Integration of Alcohol in Rural Buganda." In M. Marshall (ed.), *Beliefs, Behaviours and Alcoholic Beverages: A Cross-Cultural Survey*. Ann Arbor: University of Michigan Press.

Roscoe, J. 1923. *The Bakitara or Banyoro: The First Part of the Report of the Mackie Ethnological Expedition to Central Africa*. Cambridge: Cambridge University Press.

Rossel, B. 1994. "*Musa* and *Ensete* in Africa: Taxonomy, Nomenclature and Uses." *Azania* 29–30: 130–46.

———. 1998. "Taxonomic-Linguistic Study of Plantain in Africa." Ph.D. dissertation, Wageningen University, Leiden, Centre for Non-Western Studies.

Rubaihayo, P.R. (ed.). 1991. "Banana Based Cropping Systems Research." *A Report of a Rapid Rural Appraisal of Banana Production*, Bulletin No. 2.

Rutabajuka, S. 1992. *Alcoholism among the Peasants in Itojo Village, Rwampara County, Mbarara District*. Kampala: Centre for Basic Research.

Southall, A. 1998. "Uganda: Peoples and Cultures." In J. Middleton (ed.), *Encyclopaedia of Africa South of the Sahara*. Vol. 4. 307–09. New York: Charles Scribner's Sons.

Uganda, Government of. 1966. *Statutes Enacted during 1965 and up to 15th April 1966*. Kampala: Government Printer.

———. 1998. *Kibaale District Production Statistics*. Kibaale District.

Uganda, Ministry of Finance and Economic Planning (MoFEP). 1992. *The 1991 Population and Housing Census, Kibaale District*. Entebbe: MoFEP.

Uganda, Statistics Department, Ministry of Finance and Economic Planning. 1998. *Background to the Budget 1998/99 and Medium Term Development Strategy*. Kampala: MoPED.

United Nations Development Programme (UNDP). 1997. *Uganda Human Development Report 1997*. Kampala: UNDP.

5

Brewers, Woodfuel, and Donors

An Awkward Silence as the Fires Blaze

Michael K. McCall

There are two stark realities about the brewing of beer[1] in Sub-Saharan Africa that inform this chapter and that link brewers, fuel and donors. First, small-scale brewing is an economic activity overwhelmingly dominated by women in rural and many urban areas of Africa. Second, beer brewing has an insatiable appetite for fuel, which in all but exceptional cases is provided by vast quantities of firewood.

Over the past three decades, innumerable development projects, whether interventionist or participatory, have aimed to improve the economic lot as well as the sociocultural status of women in rural Africa. As is the nature of small-scale enterprises, the technology employed in local beer brewing is quite basic, and both the inputs and skills deployed are local. Beer brewing and the issue of its firewood consumption embody a number of developmental concerns, namely, local employment, appropriate technology, gender, and environmental conservation, yet curiously it is an area that donors and African governments have studiously avoided. While the significance of brewing for women in terms of social and cultural relationships is sometimes accepted, the environmental implications of the enormous market for locally made beer and the women's role in its supply are rarely examined.

This chapter explores the paradox. The first section highlights the significance of women's artisanal brewing because of its absolute scale as a household business and because it remains almost unique as an enterprise primarily controlled by women. The second through fourth sections examine some of the empirical findings on African woodfuel usage connected with local beer production, describe the craft techniques employed in beer brewing, and discuss the implications of low efficiency of woodfuel usage connected with women's existing beer-brewing technology. The next sections reflect on the combination of reasons behind the willful ignorance of projects in this key area of women's livelihood and the environment, and pose possible future scenarios for women's local beer brewing. Will women's artisanal brewing disappear? This might ease pressure on woodland stocks, but at the expense of women's small-scale enterprises.

BREWING IS WOMEN'S BUSINESS

Small-scale beer brewing is primarily women's business and a household-based business in Sub-Saharan Africa. Brewing is an income-generating activity that rural women have been widely involved in for decades. While women's income-generating activities tend to be considered small-scale and petty in nature, it is important to stress that their beer brewing is by no means a minor enterprise (see Table 5.1). In aggregate, beer brewing is a major element of the rural economy and in many individual cases, a relative business success for the women involved. This does not imply that village brewing is a money-spinner: microeconomic studies usually show that the financial returns on women's labor are poor, but that is true for most rural women's enterprises in Africa. The heavy labor inputs and the relatively high risk of product failure are key factors in determining the nature of this rural industry.

Local beer accounts for a very large portion of intravillage money flows, and particularly of transgender cash flows between men and women (McCall 1996; Nkhoma-Wamunza 1992; Gattegno 1987). Although a considerable proportion of women drink, the customers are primarily men, including the brewers' own husbands. Female village-scale brewing is vital to a woman's function in the rural economy and society.[2]

The brewing economy has economic multiplier effects by providing opportunities for women and increasingly men to be employed by the female brewers in activities such as cutting and transporting firewood or the arduous job of carrying water. Wage jobs also include *askaris* (guards) for the equipment and the brew during the lengthy brewing period (e.g., Nkhoma-Wamunza 1992; Willis, Chapter 3). Sales of malted grain may be important for poorer female farmers who cannot afford to brew due to lack of capital for equipment or bigger grain stocks. Other elements of

Table 5.1
Survey Findings on the Extent and Importance of Beer Brewing in Sub-Saharan Africa

Country/ Finding	Survey location/ Coverage	Year
Burkina Faso		
• 3rd highest household income source (after farm sales and wage labor)	sample survey	1990
Tanzania		
• 73% of women brew at some time	national survey	1983
• 75% state it is the main source of women's income	national survey	1983
• 25% of households brew regularly	FAO survey	1984
• 75% state it is the main source of income in a survey of female brewers	Usangu	1992
• 2nd highest source of household income (after agriculture as a whole)	Tanga Region	1994
Zambia		
• 60% of households brew regularly	Northern Province	1985
• most common income source for women	Northern Province	1985
• 77% of respondents state it is the 1st or 2nd main source of women's income	Luapula	1985
• 25% of female-headed households brew	Chipata District	1985
• women's main cash source (ahead of wage labor & charcoal)	Mkushi District	1990
Botswana		
• 20% - 50% of households brew 1-7 times/week	5 villages	1985
• in top 4 household income sources	5 villages	1985
• by far the highest income source for women	sample villages	1990
• 2nd highest household income source (after cattle sales)	sample village	1990

Sources: Mascarenhas 1983; FAO 1984; ERL 1985; Geisler et al. 1985; Feldstein and Poats 1990; Nkhoma-Wamunza 1992; Fischer and Mshana 1994.

brewing through which women are drawn into the monetary economy are the licenses or brewing fees to be paid to village governments or market authorities.

CONFLAGRATION OF FIREWOOD

Both rural and small-scale urban brewing constitute a massive demand for firewood in Sub-Saharan Africa for several reasons: first, the consumption of local brew in rural areas is very high, a common figure given in eastern and southern Africa being one-half to one liter of brew per adult per day.[3] Second, the brewing devices and process are very fuel-inefficient, a South African Development Community (SADC) rule of thumb being that the average amount of woodfuel used to produce one liter of local beer is reckoned at between one and two kilograms (Kaale 1990). Variations in fuel consumption depend on the different types of brew and the fuel used, and thus the technology in use. But even a rough working estimate raises concerns. Approximately 5 percent to over 30 percent of total

Table 5.2
Estimates of Fuelwood Consumption for Brewing

Location	Source
Ouagadougou, Burkina Faso	
• 20% of urban fuelwood consumption	Sulilatu 1986
Mufindi, Tanzania	
• 25% of fuelwood consumption (2 highland villages)	Kikula & Nilsson 1982
Central Tanzania	
• 10 - 50% of wood consumption (15 villages)	FAO 1984
• 15% of fuelwood consumption (18 villages)	Skutsch 1983
Zambia	
• 25% of national fuelwood consumption (410,000 m^3)	Chisanga 1989
Zimbabwe	
• 10% of national fuelwood consumption	Makoni 1989

annual wood consumption in a typical Sub-Saharan village is used for brewing beer. This estimate includes brewing for home use and ceremonies as well as larger-scale brewing for sale in village bars.

A crude estimate for a typical rural village of, for example, 400 households in eastern Africa is that 300–800 cubic meters (m^3) of fuelwood per village per annum are used in beer brewing. Continuing with very rough typical figures for the MAI (mean annual increment) of woody biomass growth in a dry woodland ecosystem, the maximum area needed to provide sufficient woodfuel can be determined. The calculated source area for the necessary firewood would be 150 to 400 hectares per village, *on a sustainable basis*, meaning that natural woodland regeneration would provide a long-term supply mix of trunks, branches and smaller materials for fuelwood.

The proportion of villagers actually brewing is difficult to generalize, depending to a large extent on cultural and especially religious traditions, as well as the resource base. A figure for Zimbabwe is that a typical rural small-scale brewer accounts for three tonnes of wood per annum. West African studies also suggest extremely high figures. For example, about 20 percent of total woodfuel consumption in Ouagadougou is for brewing (Sulilatu 1986). Even two decades ago, Saul (1981) estimated that Ouagadougou alone used 10,000 tons of firewood per annum for brewing 4,300 tons of red sorghum.

There can be no doubt about the general importance of brewing as a fuel user, as shown by various micro studies of the brewing sector (Table 5.2). To understand the reasons for this massive use—or misuse—of woodfuel, some technical elements of the brewing process need to be described.

WOMEN'S ARTISANAL BREWING SKILLS AND BREWING LOSSES

There is no single brewing recipe. Indeed, there are wide variations even within a particular crop region or farming system because an important determinant of the brewing method, and thus the fuel required, is the source material. *Mbege*, banana beer, for instance, from Kilimanjaro or Rwanda requires bananas to be boiled for five to six hours but uses much less wood than sorghum beer.

The basic technique of brewing beer is characterized by three stages: malting, brewing and fermentation. Normally, all three stages are completed in a week to ten days, from first preparations to drinking. Thus in many cultures, local sorghum beer is called "seven-day brew." Water is needed for the first two stages, but the high levels of firewood use are in the brewing.[4]

Procedures during each stage involve continuous care and skilled management because the technical processes are not as simple as they might appear to the casual observer. Artisanal beer brewing is an inherently risky operation. Some argue that this is one reason that even in male-dominated societies it has been left as a women's enterprise. The risks are great: losses can easily be up to 90 percent or even 100 percent, usually due to overfermentation or to no fermentation at all.

First Stage: Malting (Four to Seven Days)

In the first stage, grain is converted into malt through germination. The grain is soaked and left to germinate in drums or large vessels for up to seven or eight days. The malting has to be carefully controlled to balance quality against malt volume. Malting (soaking) the grain requires 3 to 3.5 liters of water per kilogram of grain, which can cause transport and labor problems. It is important to check the degree of germination in the early stages because later the malt may not ferment properly, affecting the final alcohol content and the acidity.

Second Stage: Brewing (Approximately Three Days)

This stage of brewing or mashing creates the maximum demand on fuelwood supplies. The germinated grain is dried, usually by solar heating, and the dried sprouted grains are ground into coarse flour. The quality of the mash will be affected by how finely or coarsely the grain is ground and/or sieved. A mash is then prepared by adding water and sometimes substances such as gelatinous barks or plant saps in order to avoid curdling. The mash is usually mixed with a "starter" made earlier and heated. The starter may be grains like sorghum, millet or maize, or could be some other produce like bananas. This first cooking period is relatively short in most situations. For example, in Ouagadougou it averages about four hours.

The mixture is then cooled and it is usually filtered. After this, the mixture is heated to evaporate the surplus water, concentrating the unfermented beer, and the important sugar content increases. Souring also takes place as bacteria operate on some of the sugars to make lactic acid. The second cooking period is very long: eight to nine hours on average, and maximum twelve hours. The product at this stage is a thin sweet gruel and low in alcohol ("sweet wort"), but it contains vitamin B and may be fed to children.

Too little mash leads to thin beer with a poor taste and low alcohol content, while too much produces a brew heavy to drink, again with insufficient alcohol. The beer can also burn, giving it a taste and smell unacceptable to the consumer, but the brewer equally has to avoid undercooked beer.

Third Stage: Fermentation (One or Two Days)

The product needs to cool before the final stage of fermentation. It may generate enough of its own yeast, or additional yeast is added, and fermentation continues. The maltose sugars are now converted into alcohol and carbon dioxide, and proteins, B vitamins and more lactic acid are produced. The characteristic dense, milky beer is the result of all the suspended particles of grain, malt, yeast and starch.

Fermentation may happen overnight, or over two nights. Overnight fermentations can be speeded up by heating the mash or mash *nshima* mix. The alcoholic strength of the beer will be low from slow fermentation or if insufficient malt has been used. On the other hand, too much malt leads to overfermentation and a brew that is too acidic. Brewers must watch against souring during fermentation because the acetic acid-producing bacteria can turn the brew into sour vinegar.

Of the few technical writings on brewing techniques, only Nyabeze (1994) describes the indicators and the warning signals of bad brews. But customers can readily identify a bad brew by its poor taste and the hangovers or upset digestion it causes.

Detailed studies of the brewing process show that quality depends on a fine balance of craftsmanship at most brewing stages, and the (female) brewers need all the skills they can acquire to be brewmasters. "Insurance" against losses is common. For example, female members of beer-brewing clubs in Zimbabwe brewed in turn and the rest of the club paid into a common purse against a spoilt brew (Lue-Mbizvo 1991).

GOING UP IN SMOKE?

The striking woodfuel consumption levels are determined by an overall high level of demand, a lack of alternative beverages (i.e., bottled beer) in low-access villages, and the absolute deficiencies in brewing technologies leading to very poor energy efficiency of the brewing process, and high levels of waste and lost brews.

Some rough field figures for the Uluguru Mountains in Tanzania are that five bundles of firewood (approx. 0.5 m^3) were needed per 44-gallon (200-liter) drum of brew (Amiri 1983). Nkonoki (1983) calculated a figure as high as 720 m^3 of wood per village per year, although for *mbege* (banana) beer in Kilimanjaro his estimate was down to 300 m^3 per village. A more detailed and probably more accurate study for FAO of fifteen villages in Tanzania found lower wood requirements of 0.1–0.3 m^3 per 200-liter drum. Nevertheless, the median consumption of wood for brewing averaged over all households in these villages was 0.1 m^3 per year (FAO 1984).

Comparable data for Zimbabwe gave fuelwood consumption at 50 kilograms for a 200-liter drum (MacGarry 1987), and another estimate for Zimbabwe suggested up to 3.2 tonnes per small-scale brewer per year (Lue-Mbizvo 1991). Interestingly, surveys show that modern large-scale commercial brewing makes remarkably little difference to the total energy consumed. Only the form of energy usage is different, being electricity, oil or gas. (See Table 5.3.)

The first determinant of woodfuel requirements is the choice of raw material for the malt, and thus the brewing technology process used. For example, *mbege* requires less fuel and maybe very little firewood, as it can utilize banana waste and scraps as fuel. A second factor, related to the type of brewing process, is the specific technology in use. The containers themselves affect cooking efficiency and thus fuel consumption. Most brewers nowadays make use of 44-gallon (200-liter) petrol drums made of steel, which transmit heat quickly and effectively. The metal is tempered and thick enough to sustain the heat and can survive months of use before needing replacement. Willis (Chapter 3) contrasts this with the small clay pots recorded by Monica Wilson in the 1930s in Unyakyusa. These pots only held about 20 liters, and the thick clay walls were too good an insulation for heat transmission, requiring more time and more firewood. Clay pots are also more vulnerable to breakage.

Variations in the scale of production affect the type of fuel required. Small-scale home brewers may use the same (though a bigger) fire when they are simultaneously brewing and cooking, whereas large-scale brewers use separate fires (as reported in Botswana by ERL 1985). It is questionable, however, whether the scale efficiencies associated with bulk brewing are sufficient to counter the better fuel management associated with small-scale cooks and brewers. Stove-efficiency studies in the laboratory and the field have shown that real-time management of the fire affects

Table 5.3
Fuelwood Efficiencies in Brewing (Cubic Meters per 200-Liter Drum)

Location	Type of brew	Fuelwood consumption (m^3/drum)	Original source
Usambara, Tanzania	*puya* (sugarcane) brew + concentrate	0.600	Hakizumwami 1995
Dodoma, Tanzania	*kangala* (sorghum)	0.500	Nkonoki 1983
Uluguru, Tanzania	*pombe* (maize)	0.210 - 0.350	Amiri 1983
Mufindi, Tanzania	*kangara* /*pombe* (maize)	0.340 - 0.480	Kikula and Nilsson 1982
Kilimanjaro, Tanzania	*mbege* (banana + finger millet)	0.320	Nkonoki 1983
Central Tanzania	*pombe* (maize)	0.100 - 0.300	FAO 1984
Tanzania, 8 regions	*pombe* (various)	0.045	ZERO 1998
Kilimanjaro, Tanzania	*mbege* (pre-cooked)	0.045 - 0.070	Luukkanen 1991
Ouagadougou, urban Burkina Faso	*dolo* (sorghum)	0.075 - 0.084	Sulilatu 1986
Zimbabwe	7 days (maize, sorghum and *rapoko* millet)	0.070	MacGarry 1987
Mozambique	fermented beer	0.005 - 0.016	ZERO 1998
Commercial brewers such as Heineken or Carlsberg	bottled beer	approx. equivalent to 0.035 - 0.050 m^3 wood/200 l.	based on 8.5 - 13 kWh, plus 120 - 180 mJ heat per hectoliter

fuel efficiency relatively more than the technical design of the stove. For example, a well-managed "three stone" or open fire can achieve a higher heat efficiency than a poorly managed "improved stove" (Bussman 1984).

Improved fire management in reality demands a high degree of skill and multitasking: controlling fire draft, preparing and selecting the sizes of fuel pieces, feeding the fire and moving burning sticks, moving the pot, stirring, mixing, and retaining embers. It is necessary to maintain intense heat and low flames and to minimize smoke, in addition to enforcing any childcare or safety imperatives. Of course this is all at the expense of women's time. The brewer can save fuel by focusing the maximum heat at the base of the drum rather than up the sides, but this requires careful management of drum stability; moreover, excessive heat on the base raises the danger of metal failure.

The characteristics of the fuels are equally pertinent. As with domestic cooking fires, dry woodfuel is preferred; the wetter the wood, the more heat energy is used to vaporize the water. Effective drying and storage of firewood are thus important, but covered storage requires space and capital. The optimal fuelwood species are those giving medium flames, intense heat and long-lasting embers. Lower quality fuels (non-fuelwood species, small sticks, scraps, shavings, green wood, etc.) will always require more management and time than quality fuels. Smokiness is a nuisance, but relatively less so for brewing, which is normally done outdoors, compared to indoor cooking fires.

The demand for fuel in the brewing process is almost entirely met by firewood. There are very few places where alternative fuels are available or used. Although coal has been proposed in Zimbabwe, it is not yet a feasible alternative. Thus, as with fuels for domestic cooking fires, the types and sources of wood are very significant. The critical factor, however, is that unlike wood used for household cooking, which is normally small pieces (twigs, broken branches, crop residues) of dead wood collected by the women and children of the household, wood for brewing large quantities (i.e., 44 gallons) needs to be large logs for sustained cooking over many hours. Therefore, wood for brewing is usually live wood deliberately cut as felled branches or whole trees.

Current environmental dogma is that rural firewood consumption is not a cause of deforestation because it is only dead wood and off-cuts that are collected by rural women. They do not usually possess the cutting or transport technology for felling whole trees for fuel, in addition to the culture-specific restrictions on women cutting down trees due to customary tenurial and property rights associated with trees and their control by adult men.

Additional gender-specific arguments are sometimes put forward that women are innately less prone to destroy trees by chopping them down because they have a natural stewardship stance resulting from their reproductive and nurturing life cycle (e.g., the eco-feminist reasoning of Vandana Shiva and others). Given these restrictions on resource access and technology, as well as the domestic time priorities of most rural women, large quantities of bulky woodfuel are more likely to be purchased from professional woodcutters and traders than directly cut by female brewers. It would be unusual to find women employed as woodcutters on this scale, and the larger transporters are also likely to be men. Women are commonly headloaders of marketed firewood, but not for the logs or large branches needed for brewing fires. The transport of firewood by headloading, or more often by bicycle, wheelbarrow, scotch cart or other animal carts, must also be organized and paid for.

In many African rural areas, wood for brewing has become a monetized commodity, unlike the majority of woodfuel used by rural households in villages. Woodfuel supply problems and increasing prices for fuelwood have pushed many families out of brewing as an income generator, as well as raising the price of the final beer (Kaale 1990). In addition it impinges on woodfuel availability for domestic needs provisioned by rural women who must forage for firewood in their home localities. In doing so, market demand for woodfuel for brewing is generating potential conflict within households and between women of different socioeconomic profiles.

THE BURNING SILENCE IN THE GENDER, TECHNOLOGY DEVELOPMENT, AND ENVIRONMENTAL LITERATURE

Whether approached from the more ideological stances of "gender and development" (GAD) and "gender and environment," or from specific studies of the rural social economy (labor or environment studies, or resource-use surveys), there is a general lack of recognition of Sub-Saharan African women's beer brewing and trading.

A survey of influential books on the topics of women and development or the environment shows that they totally ignore the prime significance of brewing in women's economic activities. Typically illustrative of the lacuna are Adepoju and Oppong (1994), Bryceson (1995), Leach and Mearns (1996), MacDonald (1994), Øostergaard (1992) or Wallace and March (1991). Stamp's (1990) comprehensive review of gender issues and development interventions in Africa has nothing on beer except for a mention in a brief labor summary.

These books reflect differing degrees of feminism, socialism, Fabianism or market liberalism, and they can be taken to generally represent the viewpoints of a number of major players in the bilateral and multilateral aid business, among them, the European Union (EU), International Development Research Center (IDRC), International Labor Office (ILO), Intermediate Technology Development Group (ITDG), OXFAM, UN-NGO Group and UNIFEM. The ILO, for instance, which has invested much concern in gender and development issues, does not seem to recognize how so many African women actually spend their time and earn some income; see, for example, Ahmed (1985), ILO (1989) and Dixon-Mueller and Anker (1993).

This is also true of many "gender-aware" case studies of village resource management. Two examples from Tanzania suffice: Lema's (1995) detailed account of gender relations in agriculture and natural resource management on Mount Kilimanjaro simply bypasses the key activity of *pombe* brewing and its significance for women's income and labor time, resource use (bananas, finger millet and woodfuel) and environmental impacts. Holmboe-Ottesen and Wandel's (1991) interesting Rukwa field study has a title directly referring to local brewing and provides detailed data demonstrating women's primacy in brewing. Nevertheless, there is no discussion of the actual brewing process and its resource allocation.

Broader economic studies likewise measure the realities of brewing without apparently recognizing its significance. The Tanzania Gender Network Programme's (TGNP) analysis of the women's informal sector in Tanzania finds "homebrew beer manufacturing and sale" to be bigger than trade, food preparation and sales, domestic employment and prostitution, but the editors write nothing further on the brewing issue (Tanzania Gender Network Programme 1993).

Literature examining potential technology development for women—whether exclusively for women or opening avenues into male-dominated technologies—similarly barely touches on women's brewing activities. This is not for want of knowing, because when women engaged in the business are given the opportunity to express their priorities in open fora, such as that of the Zimbabwe Environmental Research Organization (ZERO), they articulate their need for better brewing devices.

Notwithstanding its long interest in improved technologies for women, the ILO has not turned its expertise to brewing. Ahmed's (1985) review of "technologies for rural women" in West Africa and Kenya mentions brewing, but there is no case study in the book or in the ILO's 1990 village technology manual.

Despite ITDG's years of effort in the fuels of appropriate technology, the organization has barely broached the topic of women's brewing activities. Sandhu and Sandler's (1986) compilation, *The Tech and Tools Book* for women, and Baud and de Bruijne's (1993) review of small-scale industries for women both considered many food-processing businesses, but not brewing. ITDG's latest technical guide to small-scale food processing has a small section on banana-beer beverages, but it is by no means a full-blown handbook tackling technical problems or an endorsement of brewing's importance (Azam-Ali et al. 1998).

At a broad level, the World Bank reviewed the "women and energy" field in 1990 and examined the policies and practices of fifteen UN organs and donor agencies in this area and another fifteen nongovernmental organizations (NGOs) working in rural development. The survey found many technology and enterprise projects for women, but none of the agencies, nor the Bank's own reviewers, showed any recognition of this single most important market activity. Of all the agencies reviewed at that time, only ALTERSIAL (Alternatives Techniques sur les Systèmes Alimentaires) in Burkina Faso and Côte d'Ivoire, supported by the French agency GRET/GERES, were making an effort to solve brewing problems (Gattegno 1987).

In the 1980s, technical research on *dolo* stove improvements was conducted in West Africa by TNO (the Dutch applied scientific research unit) and the (Dutch) Woodburning Stoves Group with the support of GTZ, the German aid organization. The primary motivation of TNO scientists was to reduce overall wood consumption, though secondary considerations were to save women's cooking times, to keep down investment and production costs, and to promote local products instead of imported beer (Bussmann 1984; Sulilatu 1986). Their work has now stopped, but the improved designs of TNO were based on technical and economic needs that included improving heat transfer to the earthenware *dolo* cookers, keeping the costs of the cookers down despite technical advances, and extending the working life of the cooking jars.

More recently, ZERO has shown interest in production and technological problems. Their 1991 workshop identified priority areas that included the lack of energy-efficient and low-maintenance methods of cooking beer, the potential for coal to replace woodfuel, the need for hygienic handling and storage of beer, maintenance problems, and research into the nutritional content of beers. ZERO has produced a training manual for brewers that reviews some of these problems, though the actual technology design issues have yet to be resolved (Nyabeze 1994).

No doubt, if 15 to 20 percent of village woodfuel went into bread baking or heating livestock feed, there would be numerous appropriate technology and income-generating programs directed at research and funding for women's efforts. Women's rural brewing businesses, on the other hand, are excluded or relegated to a mere annex in studies of gender, the rural economy and resource management. As a result, interventions in women's brewing businesses have surfaced in less than a handful of development programs. Projects directed at improving small industries and women-oriented development programs in resource utilization, credit, business training or technology development all overlook women's brewing activities.

Why is this the norm and why is it so widespread? There is indeed some difficulty in getting precise data on brewing (but that is a circular reasoning) connected with brewers' reluctance to impart information to officials, as well as cultural and social prejudice on the part of researchers to even contemplate the business. Partly it is a case of overlooking the obvious, as was the case with women's unpaid domestic labor, ignored by researchers for so long. But primarily the oversight reflects a dubious marriage of the sets of biases of two unlikely partners: donors and foreign NGOs on the one hand, and government agencies on the other. Often government officials perceive "local brew" as unhygienic, backward and primitive. The state is concerned with "modernization," and civil servants and policy makers drink Heineken, Carlsberg or Castle in the bars of Africa's cities.

The fact that the local brewing business is still dominated by women strongly reinforces this. In the deconstructionist analysis of "development," a conceptual equivalence is formulated between underdevelopment and the traditionally female livelihood activities of household reproduction (Scott 1995). Policies toward local brewing illustrate that aptly, in the same way that earlier generations of nationalistic male elites hijacked arguments against the promotion of "appropriate technology." Tautologically, it is argued that if it is a home-based business, it is outside the "recognized" economy because it is women's unwaged labor, technologically undeveloped by definition—and therefore primitive and dispensable. The denigration may be further rationalized by persecuting local brewing for leading to food shortages and distorting the grain market, or for fostering cholera or other diseases caused by lack of hygiene.

Improvement-minded NGOs and donor agencies meanwhile seem to be implicitly adopting a righteous bias against the "demon in drink," perhaps out of avoidance of charges of misuse of funds entrusted to them by the public. Thus they avoid expending funds on assisting women to conserve fuel, save time, or reduce the drudgery in the service of making alcohol—"the poor ought not to be so profligate as to spend any of their money on liquor." Informally, responsible people in donor agencies and NGOs are willing to say that there is an implicit position against anything to do with intoxicants, partly if not largely from their nonconformist and Fabian socialist inheritance. But any commitment to teetotalism is unspoken; it is not explicitly on the GAD or any other development agenda.

The failure to include brewing as a development activity is directly related to moral objections concerned with the production and consumption of alcohol. The strength of both Islam and Protestant Christianity in many areas of Sub-Saharan Africa contributes a moral dimension to the secular disapproval. For example, an Islamic government recently requested that a Western bilateral agency remove a cover photo of brewing from its report on small-scale industries in West Africa. The agency complied. For an extreme case, see van Dijk (Chapter 13).

There is, of course, a well-founded position here. Alcoholism is a significant health concern, as well as being a household economic issue in many countries, notably the migrant labor zones of southern Africa and Zambia. Moreover, alcohol abuse is a gender issue because it is axiomatic that the effects of excessive male, or female, alcoholism fall primarily on women and children. In some countries, women's movements as well as religious groups have campaigned against the sources of alcoholic abuse.

This is less evident in other parts of Sub-Saharan Africa, although alcohol production and consumption is frequently raised as a community issue. For example, in Sumbawanga, Tanzania, during the early 1990s, village authorities were reportedly very concerned about resource problems resulting from beer drinking, namely, the depletion of staple food reserves due to the use of "huge amounts of firewood," and a serious water shortage, as well as moral issues with too much drinking in the village reducing labor efficiency. The Village Council finally proposed arrangements to limit brewing to six drums per day (Mohamed et al. 1993).[5]

Arguments that brewing provides women with a survival strategy and potentially increases their opportunities for economic participation can thus be countered by arguments emphasizing the detrimental effects of alcohol on society, the family, and the health of individuals, as well as the destination of resources. But the donor and NGO stances also reflect a benevolent and "protecting" paternalism, the same as is seen in the reluctance to support rural women's enterprises in "nonproductive," frivolous activities, say, sweet-making or hairdressing. Interestingly, donor finance for smallholder tobacco exports has been a different matter!

The transition from "women in development" to "gender and development" strategies has not been positive for small-scale brewing either, as efforts have switched away from women-specific, project-focused support and toward mainstream agenda-setting and institutional development. Expressly because of the general negative image or invisibility of the brewing business, no agencies have included it in their "big picture" agendas and integrationist programs. An examination of thirteen bilateral and multilateral donors' interests in "Gender in Energy" by Skutsch (1995) found no interest by funders and policy makers in brewing, or in its resource and income implications. Having taken their stance against brewing mainly on moral grounds, donors and most NGOs simply overlook its socioeconomic importance and empowerment potential for women, and are similarly blind to any technical interventions that could make marginal improvements, whatever the gender and environmental stakes.

ARE THERE BRIGHT SCENARIOS FOR WOMEN BEER BREWERS?

If local institutions and supporting foreign agencies continue to disregard women's small-scale brewing, the sector could very soon be absorbed by advantaged and better-positioned corporate or *male* small-scale interests. Having said this, any interventions to sustain women as small commercial brewers must recognize that, if and when the business is legitimized and entrepreneurized, all the familiar institutional barriers against the expansion of scale of female enterprises are likely to surface. These range from employment rights, to informal restrictions on licensing, to recognition of collateral and breaking into monopolized markets, all barriers that may be reinforced by local officialdom on a sexist basis.

Although demand for beer is always high, the entry conditions are low, and new female brewers can easily start up, so the market becomes saturated. A development policy for rural women would have to trade off easy entry, which allows women to brew when their particular resource conditions are right, against a framework of instruments to support continuity and stability for producers to expand in the system.

A significant technical advantage for the small producer has always been that local brew cannot be stored and must be consumed quickly, which precludes an extensive distribution system from a central brewery, and partly explains why there have been so few attempts at commercialization. Only in the big urban markets of southern and eastern Africa is grain beer (*chibuku*) brewed with large-scale modern equipment by big commercial breweries. Notable are TBI (Traditional Beer Investments) belonging to the giant transnational South African Breweries (SAB), which markets *Chibuku* and *Elephant* ("More Malt, More Life") brands; Chibuku Breweries in Zimbabwe (of which SAB is a major shareholder); National Breweries and Shaky Shaky Enterprises (*Mnanti*) in Zambia; Darbrew in Tanzania (*Kwa Nguvu na Furaha*); and National Sorghum Breweries, relatively small, but one of the biggest black-owned companies in South Africa.[6] Chibuku Breweries is also producing in Mozambique and enjoying a monthly growth in sales of 25 percent. A second brewery in Mozambique and one in Zambia's Copperbelt are planned soon.

As these large-scale industrial brewery investments take place in urban areas, other technological developments have far-reaching implications for rural women brewers throughout Africa. The Council for Scientific and Industrial Research (CSIR) in South Africa has developed three stable sorghum beer products, including a wort concentrate that can be later diluted and fermented to make beer. All three are safe to transport over long distances and to keep in storage (NRC 1996).[7]

National Sorghum Breweries' (NSB) long-term strategy is another force to contend with, and likely to countervail efforts to promote women's brewing cooperatives. NSB uses the African "shebeen" system to market its sorghum beer and rewards the women who form its primary sales force by encouraging them to become shareholders in the company; and thousands have. The downside is that township women who formerly were brewers are becoming retailers, albeit also shareholders, rather than producers.

A factor largely unexplored in the commercial world is the persistence of the widespread taste preference for local brew over bottled beers, in part due to the distinctive lactic acid taste and the thicker texture, despite intensive advertising persuasion toward modern products. The key, therefore, to increasing the scale and value-added of brewing is to provide it with cultural and commercial "legitimization."

Local brews have to regain their status within an already modernizing consumer market. They are unlikely to be marketed in smart packaging, although they may already have glitzy topical names. Something could be learned from the sustained marketing achievements of real ales in Britain, with the intention of co-opting a popular modern image for the traditional brew. Real-ale marketing in Britain, as with monastery beers in Belgium, the Netherlands and elsewhere, aims for the market dimension of unique taste and *quality*, and does not strive for *quantity* sales. Focusing on smaller market niches, specific to a locality and to the clientele's special tastes for ingredients, flavors and brewing idiosyncrasies would have the serious advantage of avoiding direct competition with the likes of TBI and NSB.

Moreover, it might be mutually beneficial to couple the point of sale of local brews with that of popular mass consumer goods, for example, by linking quality-licensed women's brewing cooperatives with "respectable" Pepsi/Coke retail outlets. If further cultural legitimization is needed, is it too far-fetched to visualize the marriage of the vernacular culture of *pombe* or *dolo* with the contemporary music and song of, say, Mali or Congo, thus combining the apparently global appeal of youth imagery with the cultural heritage of rural women brewmasters?

CONCLUSION

Women's beer brewing has been sidelined in development efforts despite the fact that the issues of women and development, and the environment, both favorite themes of donors, are an integral part of African beer brewing. While support for the improvement of brewing facilities may place government agencies, NGOs and bilateral and multilateral foreign donors in a difficult position, the arguments for bringing beer onto their agendas should overwhelm any moral qualms or social sensitivities. Small-scale brewing is central to women's livelihood and is a potential key to their economic empowerment, yet in its current condition it is environmentally damaging as well as technically and commercially underdeveloped because it is being undervalued, if not deliberately scorned.

The future of women's brewing businesses is uncertain. Internal competition is fierce, and externally manufactured "local" beers are appearing on the horizon. It is time for innovative thinking on the part of women brewers, governments and donors. At the very least, a proportionate share of GAD attention needs to be focused on brewing as a livelihood support for rural women through cooperatives or small-scale entrepreneurs. The neglect until now has meant stagnation while SAB/TBI and other corporate giants are mopping up the very evident demand.

To encourage women's enterprises and empowerment, and to retain their competitiveness in the face of competition from manufactured local beers, the unique taste and special quality of women's beer products should be developed both in actual production and in marketing terms. In other words, by imaginatively seeking expansion on an entrepreneurial and technical scale, women beer brewers have a more promising future grounded in comparative advantage and a marriage of their artisanal production with modern marketing.

In the area of woodfuel resources and environmental degradation, research and development on improved technologies in fuel preparation and in brewing processes, as well as in local brew storage, have received some limited attention in the past as cited in this chapter. But that flame has mostly been allowed to burn out, and the brewing fires have been permitted to blaze unchecked while government agencies and NGOs fiddle. Environmental concerns ring hollow in the face of this neglect.

NOTES

1. A wide variety of indigenous grains and other foods are traditionally used for beer brewing in Sub-Saharan Africa, though sorghum and millet are most common. For convenience, this chapter usually takes the names commonly used for these beers in large parts of East and West Africa, *pombe* (Kiswahili), or *dolo* (Bambara).

2. Very typical is an offhand comment from a Kenyan Master of Science student in the Netherlands in 1998: "[W]ithout my mother brewing, I would not have gone through primary school."

3. The numbers are obviously a crude generalization that could be modified by localized sociocultural factors, especially the dominant religion.

4. Some descriptions of the technical process place very little emphasis on the cooking and therefore overlook fuel consumption, e.g., Feldstein and Poats 1990 in Zambia.

5. This is still 1,200 liters per day for a population of 2,800.

6. A counter example is provided by Nigeria, where the Federal Institute of Industrial Research developed large-scale *funi* (sorghum beer) brewing technology, but the giant modern beer brewers, Guinness and Nigerian Breweries, both rejected it as not meeting their market.

7. CPC Tongaat Foods is already marketing Funa Beer Powder, made of maize grits, sorghum malt and yeast. Warm water added to a 25-kilogram sack and fermented for a day makes a drum's worth of sorghum brew (CPC Tongaat 1998). Furthermore, SAB is introducing this product into East Africa via its Tanzanian subsidiary.

REFERENCES

Adepoju, A., and C. Oppong (eds.). 1994. *Gender, Work and Population in SubSaharan Africa*. London: James Currey.

Ahmed, I. (ed.). 1985. *Technology and Rural Women: Conceptual and Empirical Issues.* London: George Allen & Unwin for ILO.

Amiri, T. 1983. "The Socio-Economic Impact of Local Beer Brewing in Morogoro District." B.A. thesis, University of Dar es Salaam, Department of Geography.

Azam-Ali, S., M. Battcock and P. Fellows. 1998. *More Traditional Foods: Processing for Profit*. London: Intermediate Technology.

Baud, I.S.A., and G.A. de Bruijne. 1993. *Gender, Small-Scale Industry and Development Policy*. London: Intermediate Technology.

Bryceson, D.F. (ed.). 1995. *Women Wielding the Hoe: Lessons from Rural Africa for Feminist Theory and Development Practice*. Oxford: Berg.

Bussmann, P. (ed.). 1984. "Field Studies: Woodburning Cookstoves; Upper Volta, Nepal, Kenya." Eindhoven, the Netherlands: Eindhoven University of Technology, Department of Applied Physics, Woodburning Stove Group Report.

Chisanga, E.C. 1989. *Wood-Based Energy Systems in Rural Industries and Village Applications in Zambia*. Ndola: Forestry Department.

CPC Tongaat. 1998. www.cpctongaat.co.za/products/traditional.html.

Dixon-Mueller, R., and R. Anker. 1993. "Assessing Women's Economic Contributions to Development." Geneva: ILO, Background Papers for Training in Population, Human Resources and Development Planning No. 6.

ERL (Energy Resources Ltd.). 1985. "A Study of Energy Utilisation and Requirements in the Rural Sector of Botswana." London: Energy Resources for Overseas Development Administration and Botswana Ministry of Mineral Resources and Water Affairs.

FAO (Food and Agriculture Organization). 1984. *Tanzania: Fuelwood Consumption and Supply in Semi-Arid Areas*. Rome: FAO.

Feldstein, H.S., and S. Poats (eds.). 1990. *Working Together: Gender Analysis in Agriculture*. Vol. 1. *Case Studies*. Vol. 2. *Teaching Notes*. West Hartford, CT: Kumarian.

Fischer, R., and J.S. Mshana. 1994. "Inventory of Income-Generating Activities." Main Report. Tanga, Tanzania: Tanga Region, Village Development Programme.

Gattegno, I. 1987. "Woodfuel and Small-Scale Food Processing." Massy: ALTERSIAL.

Geisler, G., B. Keller and P. Chuzu. 1985. "The Needs of Rural Women in Northern Province: Analysis and Recommendations." Lusaka: National Commission for Development Planning.

Hakizumwami, E. 1995. "Field Notes on *Boha* Brewing from Sugarcane, East Usambaras, Tanzania." Enschede, the Netherlands: ITC.

Holmboe-Ottesen, G., and M. Wandel. 1991. "'Wife, Today I Only Had Money for Pombe.' Gender and Food: Women's Bargaining Power and Agricultural Change in a Tanzanian Community." In K.A. Stelen and M. Vaa (eds.), *Gender and Change in Developing Countries*. Oslo: Norwegian University Press, 93–119.

ILO (International Labor Organization). 1989. *Rural Development and Women in Africa*. Geneva: ILO.

———. 1990, *Improved Village Technology for Women's Activities: A Manual for West Africa*. Geneva: ILO.

Kaale, B.K. 1990. "Women Dominate Rural Industries in the SADC Region." *SADC Energy* 8 (22): 53–57.

Kikula, I., and P. Nilsson. 1982. "Trees for Fuel and Building: A Preliminary Assessment in Two Villages Adjacent to the Southern Pulp and Paper Mill." Dar es Salaam: University of Dar es Salaam, Institute of Resource Assessment, BRALUP Research Report (N.S.) No. 51.

Leach, M., and R. Mearns (eds.). 1996. *The Lie of the Land: Challenging Received Wisdom on the African Environment*. Oxford: James Currey for International African Institute.

Lema, A.J. 1995. "Gender Roles in Lyamungo Villages, Tanzania." In A. Sigot, L.A. Thrupp and J. Green (eds.), *Toward Common Ground: Gender and Natural Resource Management in Africa*. Nairobi: ACTS (African Centre for Technology Studies); Washington, DC: World Resources Institute, 65–79.

Lewenhak, S. 1992. *The Revaluation of Women's Work*. London, Earthscan.

Lue-Mbizvo, C. 1991. "The Role of Women in Small-Scale Bread, Brick and Beer Industries in Rural Zimbabwe." Harare: Zimbabwe Environmental Research Organisation (ZERO), Working Paper No. 30.

Luukkanen, J. 1991. "Energy Planning at the Village Level." In J. Luukkanen (ed.), *Energy Use and Planning in Tanzania*. Tampere: University of Tampere, Unit of Peace Research and Development Studies, Research and Training Programme on Energy, Environment and Development Report, 168–80.

MacDonald, M. (ed.). 1994. *Gender Planning in Development Agencies: Meeting the Challenges*. Oxford: Oxfam.

MacGarry, B. 1987. "Biomass Resource Assessment: Measuring Family Fuelwood Consumption in Zimbabwe." London: Commonwealth Science Council, Technical Publication No. 217.

Makoni, T. 1989. "Wood-Based Energy Systems in Rural Industries and Village Applications in Zimbabwe." Harare: Forestry Commission.

Mascarenhas, O. 1983. "Rural Women under Rapid Industrialization in Tanzania." Dar es Salaam: UDSM, Bureau of Resource Assessment and Land Use Planning, BRALUP Research Paper No. 78.

McCall, M. 1996. "Rural Brewing, Exclusion and Development Policy-Making." *Gender and Development* 4 (3): 29–38.

Mohamed, S.A., A.S. Kauzeni, and J.G. Lyimo. 1993. "Resource Assessment for Land Use Planning at Village Level: The Case of Mtimbwa Village, Sumbawanga Urban District, Rukwa Region, Tanzania." Dar es Salaam: University of Dar es Salaam Institute of Resource Assessment, IRA Research Report No. 86.

Nkhoma-Wamunza, A. 1992. "The Informal Sector: A Strategy for Survival in Tanzania." In D.R.F. Taylor and F. MacKenzie (eds.), *Development from Within: Survival in Rural Africa*. London: Routledge, 197–213.

Nkonoki, S.R. 1983. "The Poor Man's Energy Crisis." Dar es Salaam: University of Dar es Salaam, Institute of Development Studies, Tanzania Rural Energy Consumption Survey, Research Report.

NRC (National Research Council). 1996. *Lost Crops of Africa*. Vol. 1. *Grains*. Washington, DC: National Academy Press for BOSTID, National Research Council.

Nyabeze, W. 1994. "Beer Brewing: Improvements to Existing Technologies for Beer Brewing Industries in Zimbabwe." Training Manual. Edited by C. Mbizvo. Harare: Zimbabwe Environmental Research Organisation.

Øostergaard, L. (ed.). 1992. *Gender and Development. A Practical Guide*. London: Routledge for EC-DG for Development.

Sandhu, R., and J. Sandler (comps.). 1986. *The Tech and Tools Book: A Guide to Technologies Women Are Using Worldwide*. London: Intermediate Technology.

Saul, M. 1981. "Beer, Sorghum and Women: Production for the Market in Rural Upper Volta." *Africa* 51 (3): 746–64.

Scott, C.V. 1995. *Gender and Development: Rethinking Modernization and Dependency Theory*. Boulder, CO: Lynne Rienner.

Skutsch, M.M. 1983. "Why People Don't Plant Trees: The Socio-Economic Impacts of Existing Woodfuel Programs. Village Case Studies, Tanzania." Washington, DC: Resources for the Future, Center for Energy Policy Research, Discussion Paper D-73P.

———. 1995. "Gender in Energy: How Some Major Donors See It." Enschede: Twente University, Technology and Development Group, Working Paper No. 71.

Stamp, P. 1990. "Technology, Gender and Power in Africa." 2nd ed. Ottawa: IDRC, Technical Study No. 63.

Sulilatu, W.F. 1986. "Etude sur l'amélioration des fourneaux à Dolo au Burkina Faso." Report for GTZ. Apeldoorn, the Netherlands: TNO, Division of Technology for Society, TNO Ref. 96-096.

Tanzania Gender Network Programme. 1993. "Gender Profile of Tanzania." Dar es Salaam: TGNP.

Wallace, T., with C. March (eds.). 1991, *Changing Perceptions: Writings on Gender and Development*. Oxford: Oxfam.

ZERO. 1998. "Energy and Sustainable Rural Industries: Issues from Pilot Studies in Tanzania, Zambia, Mozambique and Zimbabwe." Comp. H. Chigudu and W. Tichagwa. Harare: ZERO Regional Environment Organisation.

PART III
Political Contests

6

Diluting Drinks and Deepening Discontent

Colonial Liquor Controls and Public Resistance in Windhoek, Namibia

Jan-Bart Gewald

The colonial conquest of Namibia was extremely brutal. Repressive controls continued in the decades that followed as exemplified by the South African colonial administration's regulation of the production and consumption of alcohol by the territory's black African inhabitants. Nonetheless, the colonial state's policies were inconsistent and vigorously opposed at every turn by differing sections of the black population. In this chapter, the unlikely alliance of two of the territory's Herero urban groups, the *Otruppe*, otherwise known as the *Truppenspieler* or "soldier players," and the female *khari* beer brewers, is examined. During the 1920s and 1930s, they faced the colonial state's attempts to undercut and ultimately eradicate the illicit production of alcohol. In so doing, they were pitted against the colonial state and a newly emerging Herero political elite.

Official attitudes to alcohol consumption in southern Africa have changed over time. Colonial administrations were not averse to alcohol per se, particularly on account of the substantial revenues that could be generated through the sale of drink (van Onselen 1982). Regardless of colonial sanctions or moral condemnation, alcohol, as an addictive substance, has always been in demand. The selective provision of alcohol is a powerful political tool, and the degree to which colonial agents controlled and regulated access to it is a good indicator of their power and political acumen. In turn, the urban population, denied access to alcohol, used this as an issue around which to mobilize their political aspirations. There has been much debate about the political nature of struggles over alcohol. As Harries (1994) argues, the mere inebriation of colonial subjects does not constitute anticolonial resistance. On the other hand, an examination of changing patterns of leisure time and the consumption of alcohol in southern Africa can provide insights into the political and social transformation of the region, as this chapter demonstrates for Windhoek in Namibia.

In the first section, brief historical background will be provided, followed by a description of how missionaries perceived African alcohol usage. The remainder of the chapter chronicles the struggle over liquor controls between the colonial state and the black political elite on the one hand, and the powerless women beer brewers and the young male *Otruppe* on the other.

CONQUEST OF THE HERERO BY SUCCESSIVE COLONIAL REGIMES

During the Scramble for Africa, Namibia was declared a German protectorate in 1884. Twenty years later, the Herero, who bore the brunt of the colonial presence, became involved in a genocidal war with Imperial Germany. Following a conscious policy of annihilation, the German military sought out, ran down and executed those Herero who had survived the fighting and had fled into the *omaheke* (coarse sand desert) that lies between present-day Namibia and Botswana. In the face of missionary protests and metropolitan censure, Herero were rounded up, put into camps, and set to work as forced laborers throughout central Namibia. Over four years an estimated 80 percent of the Herero people died. The majority of those who survived were women and children.

In 1908, when the camps were finally abolished, legislation was passed whereby all Herero over the age of eight had to wear a copper disk embossed with the Kaiser's crown, a number, and the magisterial district in which they resided. In addition, Herero were prohibited from owning stock or land, or from practicing any form of non-Christian ritual (Pool 1979; Bridgman 1981; Gewald 1995, 1996). Germany's colonial mission was "to divest the Herero as far as possible of their national characteristics and gradually to merge them with the other native groups into a single colored working-class" (Bley 1996). However, even in the face of such extreme "social engineering," Herero began reestablishing forms of social cohesion little anticipated by the colonial administration.

In 1915 South African armies invaded German South West Africa. In a short, sharp campaign, the once proud and seemingly invincible *Schutztruppe* were defeated. In the aftermath, the Herero believed that better times were upon them. As the South African forces advanced, Herero at all levels of society deserted their erstwhile employers to reoccupy some of their former lands and reestablish Herero leadership in the urban centers of Namibia. In addition, the Herero attempted to establish themselves independently of the ideological institutions associated with the settlers. The South African administration was forced to deal with Herero who were far removed from the shackled, numbered and controlled mass that had emerged at the end of the Herero-German war.

WINDHOEK SURFACING FROM THE RAVAGES OF WAR

The urban Herero population that developed in Windhoek was characterized by one particular aspect: women outnumbered men by about two to one. In contrast to the men, the majority of these women remained staunch Christians associated with the mission church. Herero men, who for their part largely turned their backs on the church, could be divided into two broad categories: a mission-educated literate elite employed in local government and businesses as clerks, drivers, messengers and policemen, or self-employed as small traders; and a second group who were employed as day laborers, herdsmen, gardeners, railway men and factory workers.

During the 1920s and through the introduction of a "Location Advisory Board," the South African administration sought to extend and strengthen its control over the town's black African population. Only literate men were eligible to sit on the board, and board members were either appointed by the colonial administration or voted in by annual elections open only to men (Gewald 1996). Herero women, even though they outnumbered men, were cut off from any formal means of influencing the colonial administration. To a far lesser extent, the same held true for the majority of the illiterate Herero men who lived in the town, and who formed the basis of the *Otruppe*.

The origins of the *Otruppe* can be traced back to the advent of German colonialism in Namibia, when many Herero were employed as auxiliaries in the German army, and Herero military units fought alongside German forces. Following the Herero-German war, Herero orphans and children were captured and adopted, initially as mascots and servants, and later as soldiers for the German army. These young men grew up and were socialized in the confines of the military. With the defeat of the German forces in 1915, they were left leaderless. Their structures of social organization had collapsed, and from having been powerful functionaries of the colonial state, they became young uninitiated men. They sought to maintain and re-create the structures that had given their lives meaning and social standing. As young men with no property and employed as wage laborers in towns and on Namibian farms, they came together to reestablish their power. They appropriated the names and titles of their former commanders and sent hand-written telegrams in German to one another. They issued military passes, pay books and commands to each another. And on moonlit nights they gathered together, to march, talk and dream of the power that could be theirs (Gewald 1996). Effectively, by copying the structures and images of the German military, young Herero men had set up their own countrywide support and information network.

Ideas within the administration were divided with regard to the *Otruppe*, and ranged from outright rejection and demands for the banning of the movement to benevolent mocking. The administration was clearly worried by the sight of black Africans in uniforms.

As the process of social stratification increased within Herero society during the 1920s, urban Herero women increasingly came to be allied to Herero men similarly denied formal access to power. The issue around which these two groups were to mobilize their discontent against the established order was that of the manufacture and provision of alcohol.

THE COLONIAL STATE AND "KAFFIR BEER"

Traditionally *khari* had been a highly nutritional beer of low alcoholic content made of grain. In the immediate aftermath of the South African invasion of Namibia, the newly appointed public health and Native Affairs officials were all for the continuation of the brewing of "native kaffir beer." It was thought that this could help reduce the high incidence of scurvy found among migrant laborers. Detailed step-by-step instructions on its brewing were distributed among the territory's Native Affairs officials.[1] Thus, in the late 1910s, under government sanction, the brewing of beer was placed under the control of men well versed in the fine art of brewing. As the Acting Director of Railways reported: "Kaffir Beer prepared to your recipe (enclosed) is being issued to natives by the Railway compound Managers in daily rations. The difficulty experienced at certain depots has now been overcome by your providing us with Ovambo Foremen who know how to brew this beer."[2]

In 1921 legal responsibility for Windhoek's "locations" (black residential areas) was transferred to the municipality, and a plethora of legislation followed seeking to control every aspect of African life in the territory (Gordon 1998). The issue of urban areas and alcohol was of particular importance in the Natives (Urban Areas) Proclamation (34/1924), and was based on the act of the same name in the Union of South Africa. Essentially a piece of legislation that sought to control the movement of Africans to and from urban areas, the proclamation contained specific reference to alcohol. On account of the substantial revenues received from beer halls in Natal province, where the administration held and enforced a monopoly in beer production, the idea of the beer hall as a money-spinning venture was included in the act (la Hausse 1992). Windhoek's African inhabitants were thus not legally entitled to produce or consume alcohol, but the Urban Areas proclamation held within it the possibility of the provision of beer under the monopoly of the colonial administration. The ambiguity of conflicting legislation and overlapping government regulatory agencies would underpin the colonial state's vacillating policy over the next three decades.

Initially, the government took a hard line. By 1919, with Namibia having been established as a class C mandate to be administered by South Africa, the production of alcohol and its distribution to and consumption in any form by the territory's black African population was prohibited. With the effective banning of grain beer, *khari* soon developed into a low volume yet highly potent alcoholic drink.

Previously *khari* had been brewed solely using grains such as sorghum and millet. The grain was soaked and then germinated, before being dried and ground, and thereafter added to water and allowed to ferment for one to two days. The alcoholic content of the resulting brew was very low, whereas its nutritional value was high. But in a process that had already started in the early 1900s, brewers started adding yeast and refined sugar to speed up the fermentation and to increase the alcoholic content of the brew. As the demand for alcohol, or rather inebriation as opposed to nutrition, grew, brewers left out the grain altogether and used cheaper forms of carbohydrates such as dried peas, beans, maize, stale bread and potatoes. They produced these brews in the hills around Windhoek, where they could be fairly certain that their activities would not be discovered by the authorities.[3] Brewers often buried their wares in the deep, dry riverbeds in the vicinity. The bulky transport of low percentage alcohol and the concomitant risks of being discovered encouraged an increase in the alcoholic content of *khari*.

In Windhoek in the 1920s and 1930s, the brewing of *khari* was almost wholly in the hands of Herero women who refused to be drawn into the demeaning category of domestic labor that had been reserved for them by the colonial state. Following the establishment of Herero reserves in the early 1920s, the urban areas, and Windhoek in particular, became safe havens for

Herero women seeking to escape poverty, polygamous marriages and patriarchal authorities. The brewers of *khari* emerged from among these women (Krueger and Henrichsen 1998; Gewald 2000). Most were in the paradoxical position of being devout Christians defying the moral dictates of their clergy, and consequently they found themselves facing a moral barrage.

CULTURAL COMBAT OF MISSION TEACHINGS

Though the colonial state and the mission did not often see eye to eye, the one issue on which they almost always agreed was drink, or rather what they both construed as "native abuse of drink." They viewed the consumption of alcohol by Namibia's indigenous population as an evil to be vigorously combated at every opportunity. Along with many other missionary movements, the Rhenish Mission wanted to bring about temperance in Namibia. The mission had attempted to prevent the consumption of alcohol at its various stations in the country, and it was supported by some of the chiefs, whose followers tried to seize and destroy the liquor stocks of those who sought to trade alcohol.

Mission Christianity demanded specific behavior in all manner of social contexts, and the mission was anxious to create what it believed was the correct demeanor in church and in everyday life. Thus there was to be no excessive expression of emotion such as laughing or crying. Mission Christians were even expected to refrain from crying at funerals.

Clearly, alcohol, with its tendency to dispel inhibitions, was exactly what missionaries wanted their congregations to avoid. In their eyes, the consumption of alcohol led to licentiousness and bacchanal scenes of carnal delight. Writing in 1921, missionary Kuhlmann let his imagination flow when he wrote:

> When the moon returns with its full yet so subtle light, and spreads its lightly spun silver sheen over the wide African expanse . . . then it is done with the youth, no power can hold them back and prevent them from immersing themselves in the sensual temptations of the night, they flirt, they dance into the bright morning, and as Bacchus was accompanied by Venus, so the temptation is doubly big. The results are a wrecked youth and a shaky adulthood. These orgies usually take place on Saturday.[4]

The consumption, let alone abuse, of alcohol was not something that the missionaries were prepared to tolerate, least of all in church. In the 1920s missionaries reported that church attendance had become an activity almost solely confined to Herero women, and that Herero men, when they did attend services, were invariably drunk. According to the missionaries, Saturdays were spent carousing, and Sundays were spent recovering for the coming working week. As missionary Schmitz observed:

There are more than a few faithful churchgoers among the Herero women, but the men's section of the church is nearly always empty. The few Ovambo, who are employed in the town, sit on the benches of the Herero, and apart from a few evangelists of the community I hardly have any Herero men as listeners. Recently, among the few who did come, there were a few drunks.[5]

In the 1920s, the consumption of alcohol was associated with virile masculine behavior, fitting for those men who were involved in the *Otruppe* movement of the Herero. Writing at the time, Missionary Kühhirt complained, "Most of the youths are totally occupied with playing soldiers [*Soldatenspielen*] and drinking, because their fathers have given them the example."[6]

In the same way that the hard-drinking and swearing soldiers of the German Kaiser had attended church services on special occasions, so too the Herero soldiers of the *Otruppe* occasionally entered church to attend services at, for example, Christmas. In so doing, they unsettled the missionaries, as recorded by Missionary Rethmeijer: "In the Church the troops always bring about a certain amount of disquiet, as they consist of Christians expelled from the community as well as heathens, particularly youths."[7]

Drinking was not confined only to men. Missionaries were puzzled as to why Herero women, whom they generally respected on account of their correct Christian demeanor and attitudes, seemed to be engaging in drinking binges that ran counter to their professed faith. A good example is the account of a missionary stationed in Karibib during the 1920s, who noted that

the thirst for drink [*Trunkzucht*] is increasing as never before. Even those women who remained faithful to the church drink, one can observe how they are degenerating internally as well as externally. On account of the drink, their vision is clouded, they no longer comprehend why one should struggle against their sins.[8]

Particularly disconcerting for the mission were those instances when they were confronted with women wanting to pay their churchly dues with money they had earned from beer brewing. More often than not, brewing was a way in which women could keep their families fed, and certainly did not immediately imply lax moral standing. A perfect example was a single mother who did not drink herself, and who sought to pay not only her own churchly dues, but also those of her daughter. The woman was informed that she could no longer pay her dues with such money.[9]

Over time, the mission intensified its campaign against the consumption of alcohol. In the middle of the Great Depression, at the annual conference of the Rhenish missionary evangelists, various participants presented stirring diatribes against the evils of drink. Indeed, whole days were devoted to the theme of "The Struggle Against Drunkenness," at which sessions entitled "Our Battle Against Sugar Beer" featured prominently.[10] The activities of the mission, coupled with those of the state, led to the development of a culture of mistrust, with informants, spies and vigilantes taking the law into their own hands and spilling beer. The accusation, false or otherwise, of being in possession of alcohol was used by community members to intimidate and defeat the aims and activities of others. Certainly, urban inhabitants saw each and every beer raid as a conscious betrayal by specific persons intent on creating havoc.

BOWKER'S TEMPERANCE CRUSADE

During the night of 16 August 1924, South African police, who had been called in by G.O. Bowker, superintendent of the Windhoek locations, conducted a surprise raid. Records indicate that absolute pandemonium ensued. Panic-stricken, undoubtedly with all too vivid memories of the past, women and children fled into the bush, only emerging days later when hunger and thirst drove them to return. Bowker claimed that he had ordered the raid on account of tax defaulters, incompetent headmen, and illegal alcohol consumption and possession: "You were going from bad to worse and something had to be done, and someone had to act. I say therefore the blame for any stern measures adopted by me should attach to your headmen and not to me."[11]

Captain Octavus George Bowker, descended from 1820 settler stock in South Africa's Eastern Cape, arrived in Namibia in 1915 as part of the invading South African army. Between 1915 and 1920 he headed the Windhoek District Native Affairs Department (NAD), which, like all the branches of government at the time, was run by the military. Following his resignation from the NAD, he was employed by the municipality of Windhoek as superintendent of the city's locations. Bowker retired from this position in 1946, but for thirty years he was the principal figure through which Windhoek's African population came into contact with government policy. In effect, Bowker came to personify colonial rule in Windhoek's locations, with location policemen even being referred to as "Bowkers." Bowker himself viewed the locations and their inhabitants as his personal fiefdom.

Inspired by the manner in which locations were administered in South Africa, Bowker appointed a number of "headmen" whom he believed would assist him in governing. However, these appointed headmen did not see themselves as agents of control, but thought of themselves as representatives and spokesmen for the inhabitants of the locations. In 1919 Bowker defined the role of headmen thus:

> [T]hey are called upon to see that all tax payers fulfill their obligations . . . they are expected to assist in tracing deserters . . . they are held responsible for the proper conduct of the sanitary scheme and maintenance of hygienic conditions in the Locations and . . . they are looked to for the maintenance of order generally among their people.[12]

In part it was the contrasting views of headmen as purveyors or enforcers of the government's wishes that led to conflicts over the production, distribution and consumption of alcohol within the locations. In 1924 those Bowker had appointed as headmen of the locations were men who were in no position either in terms of social standing or power, let alone inclination, to inform Bowker on the production of alcohol. They were not directly engaged in brewing, but they were certainly among those who consumed illicit stocks of grain beer in the Windhoek locations.

Following the raid of 1924, a commission of enquiry into the course of events was held, the results of which make interesting reading. The headmen of Windhoek locations were assaulted by the location dwellers and labeled colonial informers, while the police looked on. Uncomfortably wedged between the colonial government and his own people, Herero headman Constantine Muatie pleaded for the colonial government to clear him of the people's charge that he was a colonial informer: "Please say who told the Police that kaffir beer was being made in the location, because the people say that I and headman David gave them away."[13]

Drew, the officer in charge of Native Affairs Windhoek, reacted angrily by telling Muatie that he was a paid headman whose duty it was to inform Superintendent Bowker on the brewing of beer. Muatie felt that the headmen had a less confrontational way of controlling beer production:

> Last year and this year we seized all kaffir beer and threw it out. We want to be informed by the Superintendent in future of any proposed raid for kaffir beer by police. We are headmen and consider that we should be informed. Had we been

informed of last Saturday's raid we would have seen that there would have been no row. We would have kept order. The people are still of the opinion that we headmen are responsible for this raid, whereas we knew nothing about it.[14]

Bowker, unapologetic as ever, went out of his way to cultivate an image of himself as totally ruthless with "the natives."

I did burn your huts at Orumbo in 1918
I have sold your huts in the location
I have caused you to go to gaol
I have been the cause of your being fined
I have caused police raids on the location for beer drinking
I am appointed Superintendent to place a check on your lawless proclivities, and I have tried for two years to rule you with kind words and you are today more lawless and drunkenness is more rife among you than at any previous time.[15]

Bowker did not stop there and lashed out against his headmen:

Constantine Muatie informed the commission yesterday that he could not understand why the police were called in on account of beer drinking without the knowledge of the headmen; that he and other headmen never failed to report drunkenness and the presence of beer in the location . . . I accuse Constantine of uttering a deliberate falsehood. I have been two years at the head of the location. During that period there is not an instance on record where any of my 13 headmen have reported a case of drunkenness or the presence of beer in any hut in the location.[16]

The event clearly demonstrates how the control of alcohol was used to confirm the black population's colonial subservience. Bowker's raid, or rather the reaction engendered by the raid, initiated the only protest that ever seriously threatened Bowker's seemingly unassailable position. In the aftermath of the raid, the position of headman was abolished.

The raid also reveals the role of up-and-coming Herero and nationalist politicians, the most prominent of whom was Hoseah Kutako. Two months after Bowker's fateful raid, Hoseah Kutako organized a petition calling for Bowker's removal from office, claiming, "I am speaking for the people." Characteristic of his consummate political style, Hoseah wasted no time in drawing attention to the double standards of racial prejudice, pointing to the role of Windhoek's white inhabitants in the lucrative trade in alcohol:

Why should the location be raided for liquor? In March and April I reported to Mr Wilmot that there was drinking in the location and that I had seized and thrown out liquor, that liquor was brewed (obtainable) at Gamams River by Europeans and conveyed into the location. Mr Wilmot said he was a newcomer, but would enquire from others and send for me later. Mr Wilmot also told me of the ill effects liquor was having on people in the Union. Mr Wilmot never sent for me.[17]

Possibly on account of his background as a missionary evangelist, Hoseah echoed the colonial state's policies regarding alcohol and the black population, yet at the same time he used these very issues to draw attention to the hypocrisy of the colonial authorities. Hoseah indicated that it had been on his initiative, and not that of the colonial state, that action was undertaken against brewers "when too much beer was being brewed."[18]

Doubtless affected by the vehemence of the reaction to his raid of 1924, Bowker avoided initiating another raid for at least another four years. This provided ample ammunition for those in the Native Affairs Department who saw Bowker and the Windhoek municipality as a rival to their hegemony. In an attempt to bring Bowker down to size, Cope, the NAD officer in Windhoek, noted, "I assumed Office shortly after the Location was handed over to the Municipality [and thus under the authority of Bowker] and wish to place on record, that loafers, the excessive brewing of liquor and its attendant drunkenness, were not so prevalent as at the present time and there was decidedly better control."[19]

Cope's report indicated that Bowker and the system that he had tried to establish in the locations had failed to control the production, distribution and consumption of alcohol by black Africans. Apart from demonstrating his dislike for Bowker, Cope's report also indicated that the production of *khari* had grown beyond the colonial administration's capacity to control. There was simply too much demand to ever ensure its effective prohibition.

Police figures indicated that although there was a steady increase in the number of people being tried, the production of illicit alcohol continued unabated. Interestingly, the production of illicit beer appeared to be almost entirely in the hands of women. Indeed, 80 percent of those being tried under laws relating to the production and sale of illicit alcohol were women.

There were good profits to be made from the trade, something that had become apparent to many more people in the lower strata of urban colonial life. The commander summed up the colonial state's predicament in the following manner:

We are . . . faced with a position . . . that the Natives, by utilizing the ordinary means of sustenance [mealie meal, potatoes, sugar, peas and old bread] are able to manufacture an intoxicating beverage. . . . I submit that if consumption of Kaffir beer on the premises, in properly controlled canteens, is legalized provided illicit possession is punishable by imprisonment without the option of a fine, considerable improvement will be brought about.[20]

THE DEPRESSION AND "BOWKER'S BREW"

On the eve of the Great Depression, unable to prevent the consumption of alcohol, the colonial authorities in central Namibia had reached the stage where they were willing to countenance the regulated distribution of alcohol to the territory's inhabitants. However, on account of the sudden transformation of urban life that took place during the Depression, the matter went no further and was dropped from all official discussions. During the Depression, with less money all round, the city's black urban inhabitants found themselves retrenched and with less cash to spend on alcohol, while the colonial authorities had no resources to initiate an alcohol-control program either.

Elsewhere in southern Africa research has indicated that during the Depression, women continued to make ends meet precisely because they were engaged in the brewing of beer. For example, women, and the lower strata of society, were dependent upon the brewing of beer in Natal, South Africa. In 1929, when the authorities in Natal attempted to ban the commercial brewing of beer by women and extend government-regulated beer halls, women, supported by young men of the Industrial and Commercial Workers' Union, donned male military uniforms and staged protests (Bradford 1987). Bowker's call for a municipal beer hall in Windhoek the following year brought a swift preemptory response from his rival, Cope, in the Native Affairs Department: "This is a matter which would require the most careful consideration in view of recent events in Natal."[21] The image of social mayhem and the dented confidence of the colonial administration in Natal were enough to ensure that the authorities turned a blind eye to women brewing beer in Windhoek during the Great Depression.

In seeking to strengthen his administration and control over the black urban population of Windhoek, Bowker established a location police force in 1926, and later tried to create an air of consensus with the establishment of the Location Advisory Board. The board consisted of twelve members, six of whom were elected and six of whom were appointed by Bowker. Bowker acted as chairman of the board, and his wife, Sybil, served as secretary. Elections and appointments to the Advisory Board took place annually. Only adult male residents of the locations who had paid their taxes were allowed to vote. Board members had to be literate, and almost without exception they were location notables and businessmen who had developed under Bowker's wing. In one way or another, these men were dependent on Bowker for their livelihoods, since Bowker issued the licenses and permits necessary for any form of economic enterprise in the locations.

The Advisory Board had no legislative powers and was used primarily as the administration's sounding board. Needless to say, this led to extreme frustration among some of the board members (Emmett 1986). One such man, Aaron Mungunda, led the Windhoek branch of the Universal Negro Improvement Association and voiced his frustration as follows:

> We have met here today to appoint a new board. What is the use of doing so? The Council and the Administration treat members of the board as if they were a lot of children. Time after time we make representations through our board minutes and ask that this and that be done or granted us but we never receive proper replies to these representations and questions.[22]

The board did manage to some extent to voice the prejudices and concerns of certain sections of the location, but generally the board represented the newly emergent black elite of Windhoek, whose interests were closely aligned to those of the colonial state. Two of its longest serving members, Kapuuo and Schimming, were Herero businessmen who had annual turnovers "running into four figures."[23]

It was not until toward the end of the Great Depression in 1934 that the issue of illicit alcohol production in the Windhoek locations once again became a topic of official discussion. In what must surely rank as one of the finest examples of racist paternalism, Bowker took it upon himself to brew a sample of grain beer that he, using the Zulu term *utshwala*, referred to as *tjwala*.[24] Bowker's brew was presented to the appointed members of the Location Advisory Board as a sample of the brew that would, in the event of regulated provision, be provided to the male inhabitants of the locations for consumption. Clearly Bowker's brewing skills were not up to the discerning taste and standards of the audience whom he had sought to impress. The Assistant Native Commissioner backed up Bowker's efforts.

> The Government will authorize the Municipality to make native (grain) beer for you but will not hear of any kind of European liquor being allowed you. As you know, Captain Bowker made some of this grain beer to taste; it may be that this sample was not quite right and not as good as it can be made. This native beer is

> the universal beer of Union natives and Ovomboland [*sic*]. You have turned it down and say you don't like it. You say you want stronger liquor. *So far as liquor is concerned you will get this grain beer or nothing*. My advice to you is to give this beer a trial for 12 months, then if you still don't like it come and say so. *Get one thing into your heads: you will get no liquor other than native grain beer*.[25]

This strongly worded recommendation regarding beer consumption was then backed by threats aimed at women brewers. Bowker enlisted Magistrate Ahrens to issue the warning: "I notice that four women who were recently in possession of *khari* have been ordered to leave the location. This will happen to others in similar cases . . . accept our beer or drink water, I don't mean fire water."[26]

The Advisory Board members who supported Bowker's *tjwala* beer were placing themselves in direct opposition to the women brewers, as well as the militarily attired, beer-drinking *Otruppe*. In stark contrast to the public outcry and headmen's protests over the beer raids ten years earlier, by 1934 the Advisory Board was almost wholly staffed by representatives of the locations' economic and political elite who clearly no longer identified with, or were intimidated by, the disempowered population of Windhoek's locations.

It is clear, however, that Bowker's otherwise compliant Advisory Board members were not overly impressed with his brewing skills. With this in mind, the municipality approached the Windhoek breweries with a request for what was euphemistically referred to as "a different class of beer." A batch of 1,000 liters was brewed and supplied to Bowker and the Location Advisory Board for tasting and comments. At the Advisory Board meeting held to discuss the qualities of the brew, Corporal Petrus, a municipal policeman and active *Otruppe* member but not an Advisory Board member, was asked to present his views. After having asked Bowker whether he could speak openly, Corporal Petrus announced:

> The beer is very clean and pure, just as clean and pure as the water in the tanks and has the same strength. If the Government offered me a pair of trousers surely they would not give me a pair made from paper. The Government says our *khari* is poison and we must have something wholesome. We agree but let the Council make a stronger beer. If the people drink too much and get drunk, the police and the law are there to deal with them. . . . I know what liquor is and the beer supplied is no stronger than water.[27]

In the months that followed, with great pomp and ceremony, further casks of beer were supplied for tasting, until eventually in late 1934 a brew acceptable to both the colonial authorities and members of the Location Advisory Board was chosen. Immediately thereafter, urban opposition to the Advisory Board, spearheaded by the *Otruppe*, came to the fore as polling for seats on Windhoek's Location Advisory Board got under way. During the nomination for candidates, the *Otruppe* took a leading stance to get their men into office. Crowds tried to storm Bowker's office and arrests were made.

Women who brewed beer and those most directly affected by the decisions of the Location Advisory Board were not enfranchised. These women sought to influence the outcome of the vote by allying themselves with the *Otruppe.* Bowker and the Advisory Board were alarmed. Their very existence was at stake, and they became focused on rooting out the *Otruppe* movement on moral grounds. Legal proceedings were instituted to remove Festus Katura, the self-confessed leader of the territory's *Otruppe,* from Windhoek and to relocate him to one of the Herero reserves, while board members unanimously voted in favor of the following motion: "This meeting is of the opinion that the organization known as the *Truppenspielers* is harmful to the morals of the young men of the location and that it [is] hostile to the properly constituted government of the locations. For these reasons the meeting asks the authorities to put a stop to the movement entirely."[28]

In the same month, Bowker moved against the women brewers by starting construction of a municipal beer hall for the locations. The *Otruppe* rallied behind the women brewers, as noted by the Assistant Native Commissioner for Windhoek: "The *Truppenspielers* are actually in a minority—but they are an active and vocal minority. They appear to be definitely opposed to the location administration—more especially in regard to the new Municipal beer venture."[29]

The Windhoek locations' municipal beer hall was officially opened on 28 February 1936, and a little less than a month later, the Location Advisory Board met to discuss "Bowker's baby."[30] The proceedings of this meeting clearly reveal the Advisory Board's subservient position vis-à-vis the state. Advisory Board member Kapuuo expressed his thanks to Bowker effusively:

> I never believed that the authorities would be able to provide us with the privileges which [we] are now enjoying. They are privileges which have hitherto been strictly prohibited to natives, and I feel that it is my duty to say that we are pleased to be recognized at last as human beings and as such deserving of the privileges granted.[31]

Bowker saw the beer hall as an exercise in "civilizing the native," a site where social drinkers could set themselves apart from the degenerate, shifty wretches who continued to seek solace in the drink of the illegal brewers. Bowker's ideas and sentiments were clearly modeled on attitudes he and his fellow administrators shared regarding social time, recreation and leisure. For them the beer hall was to develop into what must surely be one of the most well known of British cultural icons, the pub. The aspirations appear in the administration's annual report, which paints an idealized picture of women drinking at the beer hall in the company of men:

> The normal day of a native female living, say, in the Windhoek location . . . would be somewhat as follows: She would rise so as to be at her employer's residence—some two miles distant—by 7.30 a.m. There she would be employed on the ordinary household duties till 2 p.m. . . . when . . . she would be permitted to return to the location where she would proceed to tidy up her hut, undertake the washing and repair of her garments and prepare the evening meal for herself and her husband if she were married. Possibly on her husband's return home she would accompany him to the Native beer hall for a glass of [*sic*] two of beer. If she were religiously inclined she would, after supper, attend a prayer meeting on two or three evenings of the week. Otherwise she would in all probability put in an appearance at the Municipal Dance Hall.[32]

Despite the Advisory Board's vocal praise of the initiative, there was still the nagging matter of the brew's alcoholic quality. Indeed, Advisory Board member Kapuuo, unconsciously echoing Corporal Petrus's criticism, noted:

> It is a clean beer, it is a wholesome beer and it has a very good taste. But from what I have gathered from the talk of the people it is still too weak in alcohol. It is through this beer that we are trying to stop the people drinking the illicit and unwholesome liquor hitherto brewed by the natives known as *khari*. . . . In order to fight this *khari* I would propose that the authorities consider the matter of adding a little more alcohol to our beer.[33]

Other Advisory Board members recommended provision of a "weekend beer," because they were well aware of the location inhabitants' preference for alcohol over colored fizzy water. They needed the physiological effect offered by drinking alcohol. Without it, there would be little reason for people to bother drinking the municipal beer. Added to this, they knew that as long as the physiological effect of inebriation was missing, drinkers would continue to patronize the *khari* brewers. Mungunda ventured to observe, "People who work in bars say European beer makes them feel heady while our beer does not."[34]

In response, Bowker left the Advisory Board in no doubt as to his intentions to eliminate all alcohol other than his brew from the locations, and explained that until now

> [t]he authorities have never really had their hearts in their campaign against illicit brewing of liquor in my locations . . . the Government will not tolerate much longer the defiant attitude being taken up especially by the Herero. Yesterday my police destroyed 76 cans of *khari* representing 300 gallons. I do not wish to threaten people, merely to give them a friendly warning. The Government is strong enough to kill *khari* and it will kill it. If it cannot be done any other way it will be done by the simple process of elimination. That is to say people found in possession of *khari* will be sent away from the location and this can continue until there are no more *khari* brewers left here. Tell your people not to drive the Government to these lengths but rather to submit to an all-powerful government before it is too late. I do not want to see such a law introduced but nor do I want to see my beer hall, which is my baby, killed before it is grown up.[35]

KHARI BREWERS AND THE *OTRUPPE* STANDING FIRM FOR THE RIGHT TO URBAN LIVELIHOOD AND LEISURE

In April 1936, men described as being "members or sympathizers of the *Truppenspieler* movement" and as "the main antagonists of the municipal beer scheme" to whom "most of the women *khari*-vendors belong" engaged the services of an attorney to submit an eight-point written list of their grievances.[36] Apart from protesting about the Advisory Board, the system of hut tax, the expulsion of wrongdoers (the majority of whom had been convicted of alcohol offenses) and other subjects, the petitioners had as their fourth point of complaint "kaffir beer." In the words of Trollope, the Assistant Native Commissioner, "They object to the native police being allowed at night to search their huts without warrants or while dressed in mufti as their women are surprised while naked."[37]

In submitting the petition to his superiors, Trollope commented, "For 'while naked' read 'while in possession of *khari*' and the complaint will be more honest." Bowker's municipal policemen had the right to search any person's premises at any time of the day, while either in or out of uniform. In other words, the system was wide open to abuse. Off-duty policemen could, at their whim and fancy, break into any person's lodgings on the pretext of searching for illicit alcohol. Herero women were outraged and looked to the *Otruppe* to defend their rights. Trollope, municipal authorities and the black African elite saw removal of the women from the locations as the only way to break the deadlock.

> In the location there are 332 Herero men as against 518 Herero women, a great number of the latter being illicit liquor brewers. In March 1929, Hoseah on his own initiative called a meeting in the location and "passed" laws in an endeavor to combat the menace. . . . Last year again Hoseah saw me personally and requested me to take steps to restrict the large number of Herero women flocking into the location. The necessary steps were taken—but it is difficult to get those women who are already here, away. Although the Beer hall has been opened and is being very well patronized, the Herero are standing aloof and there appears little diminution of their *khari*-brewing.[38]

Herero women in Windhoek had fled the strict patriarchal confines of the reserves, where they faced the prospect of being forced into unwanted polygamous marriages, for the comparative freedom, independence in choice of partners, and income in the city. In attempting to make a living through the brewing of beer, these women were naturally averse to any laws or institutions that threatened their livelihood. The Herero men of the *Otruppe*, who were cut off from formal power, knew that apart from themselves, the most powerful social grouping in the locations were the *khari* brewers, who were similarly denied formal power. *Khari* formed the basis around which the *Otruppe* and the women could cooperate and exert pressure on the administration and its allies. Together, they were a formidable force. The *khari* vendors were also able to count on the continued support and patronage of their clients. Six months after the opening of the beer hall, Bowker complained: "Unless illicit Kaffir Beer is kept down, the sale of Municipal Beer and profits there from are adversely affected and, that drunkenness occurs at the Beer Hall, not from over indulgence there, but as a result of natives, already the worse for liquor, making a practice of coming to the Hall to 'top off.'"[39]

Even with a battery of legislation that allowed for the random searches by his policemen, Bowker was unable to eradicate the brewing of *khari*. He failed to bring developments in the locations under control. According to oral testimony, the locations' policemen, the "Bowkers," were corrupt. Bowker, a self-proclaimed expert on native affairs and a firm disciplinarian, was reduced to the indignity of having to request assistance from the regular police to try to control the situation. The addition of regular police did little to diminish the *khari* trade. Indeed, writing six months after the regular police began assisting Bowker, Major du Preez of the South West African police noted, "The illicit liquor had not decreased since the Beer hall was opened. The Herero were boycotting the Beer Hall and their women are still the chief culprits in the illicit *khari* trade."[40]

CONCLUSION

Despite its unpopularity, Bowker's beer hall remained an integral part of the location for almost twenty-five years. It was finally torn down, along with the rest of the location, following the shootings and the subsequent forced removal of people in connection with the Group Areas Act, as "grand apartheid" bulldozed its way through the social fabric of southern Africa (Ridgeway et al. 1991).

In terms of the apartheid regime's Urban Areas Act of 1951, black urban residences had to be established at a minimum distance of five miles from any white residential area. Integral to the new location bearing the name Katatura ("we will not move") was the beer hall. In contrast to Bowker's ideal British pub version of a beer hall, the new beer hall consisted merely of cement tables and benches where black urban residents were allowed to drink. The Katatura beer hall persisted until the repeal of a number of apartheid laws in 1977 when the black population was, once again, permitted to drink what they wanted in places of their own choice.

In summary, this chapter has traced the development of the illicit production and provision of alcohol in Windhoek locations during the 1920s and 1930s, documenting how the provision of illicit alcohol came to be almost wholly within the hands of Herero women. The colonial administration's attempt to eradicate the illicit production and provision of alcohol through the establishment of a Location Advisory Board co-opted a large section of the newly emerging Herero economic and political elite. In response, Herero women allied themselves to those who were similarly cut off from access to formal political power, the young men who constituted the core of the *Otruppe*. These angry young men and the Herero women brewers proved to be an invincible alliance that managed to evade colonial regulations on alcohol.

The South African colonial administration used the selective provision of alcohol as an instrument to control its subjects, presenting a striking example of the extreme colonial paternalism and racist denial that existed in Namibia at the time. The effects have almost certainly been carried over into the present. Past official sanctions against the consumption of alcohol have molded a culture in which the consumption of alcoholic beverages for inebriation has become the norm.

NOTES

1. Namibian National Archives Windhoek (NNAW), South West Africa Administration (SWAA) 1681. SWAA A 324/3, Public Health Scurvy South African Railways (SAR) Employees "Recipe for the Manufacture of Kaffir Beer."

2. NNAW, SWAA 1681, 27/12/16 P.E. Potter, Acting Director of Railways to Secretary for the Protectorate.

3. NNAW, Magistrate Windhoek (MWI) 36/1/37 v. 14, Location Annual Report 1936.

4. Vereinte Evangelische Missions Archive (VEMA) 2514 b Omaruru, 30/9/21, Kuhlmann, Halbjahrsbericht (Vom 1 April bis 30 September). J.B. Gewald's translation.

5. VEMA 2503, Schmitz, Grootfontein Halbjahrsbericht, 30/9/27. J.B. Gewald's translation.

6. VEMA, Rheinische Missions Gesellschaft (RMG) 2533 c, Windhoek 1929–1945, 1/10/29–31/3/30, Halbjahrsbericht, Kühhirt, Windhoek. J.B. Gewald's translation.

7. VEMA 2510, Dreivierteljahrbericht, der Station Okahandja vom 1/4/1930–31/12/1930, H. Rethmeijer. J.B. Gewald's translation.

8. VEMA 2619, Missonarskonferenzen im Hereroland: Protokolle (und Vorstrandssitzungen), 1922–1928 Band 9. Konferenzbericht der Gemeinde Karibib ber die Zeit von März 22–Dez 25. J.B. Gewald's translation.

9. VEMA 2510, Kühhirt, Halbjarsbericht zum 100 Jährigen Jubiläum am 23/9/28.

10. VEMA 1660, Konferenzverhandlungen der Gemeindeältesten und Evangelisten im Augustineum zu Okahandja vom 7–13 Dezember 1930.

11. NNAW, SWAA 66, Statement of the Superintendent of Locations on the Charges brought against him by Natives of the Windhoek Locations, Saturday, 23 August 1924.

12. NNAW, SWAA 66 A13/15, Municipality of Windhoek, Locations Windhoek Klein Windhoek, Native Affairs Windhoek and District, 3 February 1919, the Secretary for the Protectorate Windhoek, Location Affairs.

13. NNAW, SWAA 66, Meeting 22/8/24, Mayor, Town Council, Superintendent, and Officer in Charge Native Affairs Windhoek meet 80 Natives.

14. Ibid.

15. NNAW, SWAA 66, Statement of the Superintendent of Locations on the Charges brought against him by Natives of the Windhoek Locations, Saturday, 23 August 1924.

16. Ibid.

17. NNAW, SWAA 66, 22/10/24, Representatives of Hereros, Damaras and witbooi hottentots, numbering about 50.

18. Ibid.

19. NNAW, SWAA 67, 7/5/26, Native Locations Windhoek report by Cope Native Affairs Department.

20. NNAW, SWAA 67, 16/10/28, Memorandum Brewing of Kaffir Beer, Native Location, Windhoek.

21. NNAW, SWAA 67, Officer in Charge of Native Affairs, Windhoek, 27 May 1930, to the Native Commissioner Windhoek: Location Annual Report.

22. NNAW, Native Affairs Windhoek (NAW) 29, Advisory Board election and minutes, Minutes, 29/12/30, Bowker, Harasemab, Gawachab, Jantse, Etope, Kandjou, Kapuuo and Mungunda.

23. NNAW, NAW 31, Annual reports 1939.

24. By brewing "kaffir beer," Bowker was also indicating and emphasizing his position as an expert on all things related to the "Native."

25. NNAW, NAW 29, Minutes of Advisory Board Meeting of 8 March 1934, p. 4. (Italics consistent with the original.)

26. Magistrate Ahrens, cited in NNAW, NAW 29, Minutes of Advisory Board Meeting of 8 March 1934, p. 4.

27. NNAW, NAW 29, Minutes of Advisory Board Meeting 12/8/34.

28. NNAW, SWAA 432, Assistant Native Commissioner in Windhoek, 13/12/35, to Chief Native Commissioner.

29. NNAW, SWAA 432, Assistant Native Commissioner in Windhoek, 20/1/36, to Chief Native Commissioner.

30. Bowker's own term when referring to the beer hall. NNAW, NAW 29, Minutes of Advisory Board, 27/3/36.

31. NNAW, NAW 29, Minutes of Advisory Board, 27/3/36.

32. South Africa, Annual Report 1939, p. 141 (Wallace 1997).

33. NNAW, NAW 29, Minutes of Advisory Board, 27/3/36.

34. Ibid.

35. Ibid.

36. NNAW, SWAA 67, Memorandum in regard to the section of the Herero tribe who are making complaints: L. Trollope, Assistant Native Commissioner; Windhoek, 27 April 1936.

37. NNAW, SWAA 67, Office of the Assistant Native Commissioner, L. Trollope, Windhoek, 15/5/36 to the Chief Native Commissioner. Windhoek Location Administration. List of grievances handed in by a section of the Herero through Attorney M. Fraser.

38. Ibid.

39. NNAW, SWAA 67, District Commandant, Police District No. 1, Windhoek, 30 June 1936. The Commissioner, SWA Police, Windhoek; Police arrangements, Windhoek Native Location.

40. NNAW, SWAA 67, Resolutions passed at conference on Native Affairs Matters, 23/11/36.

REFERENCES

Bley, H. 1996. *South-West Africa under German Rule*, 1894–1914. Windhoek: Namibia Scientific Society.

Bradford, H. 1987. "'We Are Now the Men': Women's Beer Protests in the Natal

Countryside, 1929." In B. Bozzoli (ed.), *Class, Community and Conflict*. Johannesburg: Ravan Press, 292–323.

Bridgman, J.M. 1981. *The Revolt of the Hereros*. Berkeley and Los Angeles: University of California Press.

Emmett, T. 1986. "Popular Resistance in Namibia, 1920–1925." In T. Lodge (ed.), *Resistance and Ideology in Settler Societies*. Johannesburg: Ravan Press, 6–48.

Gewald, J.B. 1995. "The Issue of Forced Labor in the *Onjembo*, German South West Africa, 1904–1908." *Itinirario*, 19 (1): 97–104.

———. 1996. *Towards Redemption: A Socio-Political History of the Herero of Namibia Between 1890 and 1923*. Leiden: Centre for Non-Western Studies, Vol. 47.

———. 2000. *We Thought We Would Be Free: A Socio-Cultural History of the Herero of Namibia, 1920 –1940*. Cologne: Rudiger Köppe Verlag.

Gordon, R. 1998. "Vagrancy, Law and 'Shadow Knowledge': The Internal Pacification of Colonial Namibia, 1915–1939." In P. Hayes, J. Silvester, M. Wallace and W. Hartmann (eds.), *Namibia under South African Rule: Mobility and Containment, 1915–1946*. Oxford: James Currey, 51–76.

Harries, P. 1994. *Work, Culture and Identity: Migrant Laborers in Mozambique and South Africa c. 1860–1910*. Oxford: James Currey.

Hausse, P. la. 1992. "Drink and Cultural Innovation in Durban: The Origins of the Beerhall in South Africa, 1902–1916." In J. Crush and C.H. Ambler (eds.), *Liquor and Labor in Southern Africa*. Athens: Ohio University Press.

Krueger, G., and D. Henrichsen. 1998. "'We Have Been Captives Long Enough, We Want to Be Free': Land, Uniforms and Politics in the History of the Herero in the Interwar Period." In P. Hayes, J. Silvester, M. Wallace and W. Hartmann (eds.), *Namibia under South African Rule: Mobility and Containment, 1915–1946*. Oxford: James Currey, 149–74.

Onselen, C. van. 1982. *New Nineveh: Studies in the Social and Economic History of the Witwatersrand, 1886–1914*. Johannesburg: Ravan Press.

Pool, G. 1979. *Die Herero-Opstand 1904–1907*. Cape Town: Haum.

Ridgeway, D., et al. 1991. *An Investigation of the Shooting at the Old Location on 10 December 1959*. Windhoek: National Archives of Namibia.

Wallace, M. 1997. "Health and Society in Windhoek, Namibia, 1915–1945." Ph.D. dissertation, University of London.

Werner, W. 1990. "'Playing Soldiers': The *Truppenspieler* Movement among the Herero of Namibia, 1915 to c. 1945." *Journal of Southern African Studies* 16 (3): 476–502.

7

Living on the Proceeds of a Grog Shop

Liquor Revenue in Nigeria

Simon Heap

We import Spirits for the purposes of Revenue. How is the Railway being built? By Gin. How was the Carter-Denton Bridge built? By Gin. How is the Town lighted? By Gin. And now if it be asked, how is the Town to be drained, or how are we to secure a good supply of good clean water? The answer is with Gin.[1]

Nigerians have practiced the art of manufacturing low-alcoholic drinks for ages. Liquor consumption has always been a multifaceted affair, mixing concerns on personal, communal and ritual levels throughout the life cycle of the individual with the village context: from naming ceremonies, entertaining guests at weddings, chieftaincy installments and funeral obsequies to pouring libations to the ancestors. Despite the huge variety of indigenous liquors, precolonial Nigerians did not brew lager beer or distill spirits. Their expertise was restricted to tapping palm wine or fermenting grain beers. The Atlantic slave trade, which encouraged the purchase of slaves with rum and whisky, fostered the habit of importing liquor. The more potent imported alcohol symbolized a greater spiritual strength and became a socially prestigious commodity. There were also economic uses for liquor: as a transitional currency and as a powerful catalyst for trade. When the slave trade ended, the liquor trade continued, reaching large volumes in the second half of the nineteenth century.

The demand for imported liquor in Nigeria grew in tandem with the growth and expansion of British control over the territory from the 1860s onwards. First, there was the Colony of Lagos, established by the British in 1861, which gradually extended a little way into the immediate hinterland. Meanwhile, in the east of the country, at about the same time, a British consul administered the Oil Rivers Protectorate. Eventually a more effective British presence was established in the protectorate in the mid-1880s. The area of the Oil Rivers Protectorate included all the rivers from Benin to Calabar, with the sole exception being the main River Niger outlet and the hinterland above a given point. These were under the control of the River Niger Company, a private mercantile company charged with protecting the British sphere of influence against French interference in the area. The Oil Rivers Protectorate was renamed the Niger Coast Protectorate in 1893. When the British government revoked the Royal Niger Company's charter in 1900, the Lower Niger was merged with the Niger Coast Protectorate to form the Protectorate of Southern Nigeria. Then, on 1 May 1906, the Protectorate of Southern Nigeria and the Colony of Lagos amalgamated and became the Colony and Protectorate of Southern Nigeria. In the north, meanwhile, the ending of the Royal Niger Company's charter led to the direct British takeover of Northern Nigeria on 1 January 1900. These arrangements lasted until January 1914, when Southern and Northern Nigeria merged to form the Colony and Protectorate of Nigeria. The Federal Republic of Nigeria achieved independence in October 1960.

Liquor was the most significant import in terms of volume and value in the British colonies of Lagos, Oil Rivers Protectorate, Niger Coast Protectorate and Southern Nigeria, all of which were eventually integrated into the Southern Provinces of Nigeria in 1914. At that time, Nigeria imported over 4 million gallons of alcoholic beverages, chiefly German and Dutch schnapps (Heap 1995).

PAVING THE WAY: LIQUOR CUSTOMS DUTIES IN SOUTHERN NIGERIA

Prior to colonial intervention, the south, in parts of what is now known as Nigeria, had various types of palm wine, and cereals provided the basic ingredient for various foodlike brews fermented without yeast in the north. Guinea corn was also brewed into *pito* (*peto*), *oti baba*, *jego* or *burukutu*. The women crushed, soaked and boiled it and left it to ferment in large storage jars. The production process from harvesting to drinking took five days. Millet made a beverage stronger in alcoholic content than guinea corn but took a day longer to prepare. Brewing maize produced *ghia* (*giya*), *oti-oka, oti agbado, yangan* or *shekete* by fermenting the maize starch into sugar and then into carbonic acid and alcohol. This simple fermentation process, similar to English cider making, worked equally well with local fruits such as overripe plantain (*oti ogede* or *agadagidi*).

Imported drinks did not displace local beverages. Rather, they coexisted, complemented and competed with each other. Yet to some colonial commentators there was too much consumer choice: "The African has his palm wine and corn beer. To him spirituous liquor is a superfluous and dangerous luxury. He does not want it, he needs it no more than a cat needs two tails" (*Lagos Standard* 10 March 1909, p. 2). But there was no going back, as imported liquor spread inland through the new transport networks and an ever-growing number of Nigerians experienced greater choice and availability of alcohol. Joyce Cary was a Northern Nigeria colonial officer and novelist whose book *Mister Johnson* sang of the sounds and products traveling along the newly opened road: "Here come the motor, foot, foot, whang, Full of beer and salt" (Cary 1939, p. 187).

Gin and rum had stronger intoxicating effects than palm wine or grain beer, a fact that critics of the liquor trade continually reminded their opponents of as imported alcohol pushed into the Nigerian hinterland. A drinker could get drunk on a small amount of imported spirits, but could make up for the weakness of local liquor by imbibing more of it: "A pound's worth of *Fada* (corn) beer is equivalent to a hundred gallons of strong beer. Among forty men it is enough for a two day's party and a week's headache" (Cary 1939, p. 187). Describing concerns over rising palm wine consumption as "very much like ignoring the camel and trembling at the gnat" (*Lagos Weekly Record* 18 December 1909, pp. 2–3), critics of the liquor trade argued that the taste for alcohol was already in place in Nigeria and that the much higher potency of imported spirits could wreak widespread drunkenness and destruction on the population in the near future (Heap 1999).

The Nigerian imported liquor trade provoked fierce debate: was it advancing development or fashioning an economy based on the economically unproductive consumption of alcohol? The liquor trade was caught between two opposing colonial perspectives on African economic development: the paternalist principle that Western civilizations had a duty to protect Africans from bad external economic influences, and the civilize-through-trade concept seeking to modernize Africans by enticing the population into the cash economy. Here, humanitarian concerns and economic interests became entangled. Positive views of the liquor trade claimed its necessity in developing the Nigerian economy. Some admitted that the trade formed a necessary evil, but did not fail to emphasize its role as a transitional currency and promoter of cash crops for export, by virtue of providing motivation for earning cash. Merchants saw commerce as a great civilizing agent, with the liquor trade as its most important constituent, since alcohol was a desirable commodity among those with money to spend. On the other hand, liquor trade critics used the temperance equation to further their cause: drinking alcohol was bad, abstinence was good. Arguing that the imposition of "a Rum and Gin Civilization" would be "a hydra that devours the natives," halting useful commerce and hindering economic development, they agitated for Prohibition and a complete restructuring of the colonial economy along alcohol-free lines (Heap 1994–95).

Ironically, the one group in Nigeria who never questioned the morality or utility of the liquor trade was the colonial administration. Unable to call on metropolitan taxpayers to fund colonial government, the Colonial Secretary, Earl Grey, observed that "the surest test of the soundness of measures for the improvement of an uncivilized people is that they should be self-supporting" (Grey 1852). Self-sufficiency of the administration meant the colonial government had to generate enough revenue to cover administrative expenditure. This lasted for most of the colonial era (Kilby 1969; Liedholm 1970). The taxing of the trade in imported liquor by specific customs duties proved a major source of revenue. Imported liquor served the interests of the colonial state, which manipulated the tariff regime to maximize revenue collection. The liquor trade was ideally suited to government taxation given the constraints of smuggling bulky, breakable bottles across land or through ocean surf, with products of the trade landed at a small number of southern coastal ports in standard cases of bottles and demijohns which could be counted quickly. Thus, the tapping of Nigerian desires for imported alcohol proved an ideal, cost-efficient method of revenue generation. Bishop Herbert Tugwell, one of the liquor trade's fiercest critics, admitted as much:

> It is a very easy and cheap way of raising revenue. A vessel comes into Lagos and deposits 10,000 cases on a wharf. . . . All that the Government has to do is to send down a clerk and have the cases counted, and on each case to charge five shillings, which practically means realizing £2,500. (*Lagos Weekly Record*, 27 May 1911, p. 3)

Within months of its foundation, the Colony of Lagos imposed a tariff on imported liquor, realizing half the total revenue of £6,000. When the government saw the benefits of heavily taxing liquor more than other trades, it singled it out for special taxation. While other goods were subject to a 3 percent *ad valorem* duty, spirits faced a much heavier duty of 30 percent. Soon afterwards specific customs duties were imposed: brandy and wines at 1 shilling a gallon, and other spirits at 4.5 pence a gallon. Beer received a 9 pence duty per dozen bottles, with casked beer at half that rate. The government raised duties on gin, rum and whisky to 6 pence in 1872. These levies appear relatively light when compared to other British West African colonies. The Gold Coast and Sierra Leone charged one and two shillings on spirits, respectively. Mindful of bordering a low-tariff French colony, however, Lagos had to consider the risk of the legal liquor trade switching to nearby Porto Novo. Its close proximity also provided Lagos with a constant problem over the different spirit customs duties existing in the two ports, fearing that wide duty differentials would lead to "an enormous smuggling trade."[2] Porto Novo's very low rates kept a tight rein on the raising of rates in Lagos. The government constantly reminded critics of the consequent boost it would give to smuggling and how it would offset any revenue rise by the need to recruit extra police and customs staff to counteract it.

With customs duties providing around 85 percent of the total revenue of Lagos in the 1880s, and the tax on spirits forming the bulk of such duties, the colonial government's fiscal base largely depended on the number of liquor bottles imported each year. Critics condemned this: "Is it creditable to any Government, and particularly a Christian Government, that any portion of its revenue, not to speak of the largest, is raised from such a fearfully destructive source?" (*Lagos Echo* 1 December 1894, p. 2). Even the Colonial Office felt uneasy about liquor revenue, but to rid itself of the opprobrium would have resulted in "a complete dislocation of its finances."[3] In colonial eyes, the economic concern for a source of revenue had to override any moral consideration. Colonial infrastructural building targets gave ends precedence over means. For example, in 1886, Governor George Denton stated bluntly: "There is need for Lagos to have a really good harbor: I will say that, whilst the duty on spirits is six pence, the Government will not have to look far for a source from which to derive the sum that would be required" (*Lagos Annual Report* 1886, p. 10). When Governor Gilbert Carter reiterated the government's need for liquor revenue, knowing of "no more satisfactory means of obtaining money than by a duty on spirits," the *Lagos Standard* called Carter "a champion of the bottle" (3 July 1895, p. 2).

Frederick Lugard and Mary Kingsley entered the debate over liquor revenue. Lugard thought it "a scandal in the eyes of civilization when the administration of a British Colony has become almost wholly dependent for revenue on the sale of intoxicating drink," while Kingsley found no objection to "living on the proceeds of a grog shop," and if a colonial official did not like the system he should "try and get an appointment in a Colony whose revenue depended on the export of farinaceous food-stuffs or wool" (Kingsley 1898). But alternative revenue sources did not appear politically appealing or potentially revenue-rewarding. Export duties were out of the question given the need to nurture such strong local production during initial forays into world markets. So too was a poll tax, especially given the previous years' Sierra Leonean Hut Tax War and protests in Lagos against property taxes and town rates: "The native has almost unreasonable and unreasoning dread of such a [hut] tax. He looks upon his house as part of himself and would just as soon a tax was levied on one of his limbs."[4]

Electricity came to Lagos in 1895. With the alternative source of money to pay for it being an unpopular property tax, the doubling of spirit duty to two shillings got "the unqualified approval and appreciation of the community as a whole" (*Lagos Weekly Record* 17 June 1895, p. 2). But in the short term, the liquor trade stagnated, causing a running-down of existing stocks held by Nigerian middlemen and a noticeable long-term decline in the volume of spirits imported. The same downward pressure on liquor volumes occurred when the duty rose to three shillings. Nevertheless, in the decade up to 1902 the loss in volume did not translate into a loss of government revenue. While spirit duty trebled, liquor revenues rose one-and-a-half fold. These trends were exactly what the government found most useful: a rise in its income from liquor without any corresponding increase in liquor consumption and so a trend to fight off the arguments of the prohibitionists. (See Table 7.1.)

Sir William MacGregor was newly installed governor of Lagos in 1899. His having presided over a highly prohibitive spirit duty in his previous post in British New Guinea gave hope to the anti-liquor lobby. But once in Lagos, MacGregor realized that the limit of liquor duty increases was being reached. A further rise in the tariff would cause both volume and revenue to decline, and "would lead this Colony in[to] bankruptcy and completely damage its administrative machinery."[5] A *Lagos Weekly Record* (17 June 1899) editorial agreed: to overstretch the liquor trade's ability to absorb increasing duties might "put on the last straw which will break the camel's back."

The Niger Coast Protectorate illustrates the limits of milking the liquor trade. Niger Coast Protectorate Governor Claude MacDonald expressed

Table 7.1
Liquor Revenue, Niger Coast Protectorate, Lagos and Southern Nigeria (in £s and selected octennial periods)

Year	Volume of spirit imports (gallons)	Spirit duty	Total customs Duties	Spirit duty to total customs duties (%)	Total revenue	Spirit duty to total revenue (%)
Niger Coast Protectorate						
1891/2	900,501	58,546	87,695	66.8	89,448 a	65.5 a
1892/3	1,397,158	66,442	96,692	68.7	98,626 a	67.4 a
1893/4	2,647,476	115,768	127,352	90.9	173,606	66.7
1894/5	1,798,523	91,926	117,423	78.3	127,353	72.2
1895/6	2,108,498	116,320	150,106	77.5	153,013	76.0
1896/7	896,420	83,287	109,101	76.3	112,440	74.1
1897/8	1,171,408	116,917	145,542	80.3	153,568	76.3
1898/9	1,348,353	132,854	160,670	82.7	169,568	78.4
Lagos						
1893	1,393,215	70,238	104,203	67.4	115,317	60.9
1894	1,674,868	83,893	119,794	70.0	137,317	61.2
1895	1,746,946	91,432	128,794	71.2	142,049	64.4
1896	1,245, 621	121,582	162,515	74.8	179,745	67.6
1897	1,242,326	121,900	159,819	76.3	177,421	68.7
1898	1,379,816	135,458	179,792	75.3	206,444	65.6
1899	1,060,045	131,531	175,697	74.9	192,792	68.2
1900	919,725	133,835	193,924	69.0	211,467	63.3
Southern Nigeria						
1906	3,321,902	600,784	885,858	67.8	1,088,717	55.2
1907	4,055,024	806,942	1,178,193	68.5	1,459,554	55.3
1908	3,235,669	691,190	1,014,583	68.1	1,387,975	49.8
1909	2,950,111	639,503	987,571	64.8	1,361,891	47.0
1910	4,748,139	999,823	1,440,284	69.4	1,933,235	51.7
1911	4,835,363	975,557	1,439,386	67.8	1,956,176	49.9
1912	4,450,196	1,013,807	1,569,290	64.6	2,235,412	45.4
1913	4,635,273	1,138,305	1,772,619	64.2	2,668,198	42.7

Sources: Niger Coast Protectorate Annual Reports, 1894–1899; *Lagos Blue Books of Statistics*, 1893–1900; *Southern Nigeria Blue Books of Statistics*, 1906–1913.
Note: (a) approximately

sentiments similar to those of Lagos Governors Denton and Carter about liquor revenue:

> [A] strong and independent Administration is requisite; to maintain that Administration a revenue is necessary; could the liquor traffic be entirely and immediately done away with, and a sufficient revenue be obtained from other sources I for one would be very glad. This much-to-be-desired end is at present I regret to say, not feasible. (Niger Coast Protectorate Annual Report [NCPAR] 1894–95, p. 3)

Throughout the 1890s, the duties collected on liquor formed around three-quarters of the total duties collected by the customs service, and, as a proportion, almost as much of the total revenue. MacDonald wanted a slow rise in duties to bring down the volume of the liquor trade while not affecting this crucial source of revenue for the colony's coffers. The colonial government originally set a one shilling per gallon spirit tariff, with an extra penny for every degree over proof strength. In 1895 the spirit duty doubled to two shillings a gallon, leading to a decline in spirit imports of 836,817 gallons when compared to the previous year, and representing a loss of £41,841 in revenue to the Treasury (NCPAR 1891–95). In other words, the change in duty materially decreased the liquor trade without bringing any benefits to the government's revenue. Of course, critics of the trade welcomed the massive decreases recorded in the import and consumption of liquor. But the loss in revenue and the ensuing economic chaos taught the government a hard lesson in liquor trade economics.

By contrast, in 1906 Southern Nigeria became the first West African colony to earn a million pounds in revenue, the majority from liquor duties. It contributed two-thirds of customs duties, which in turn represented around half of the colony's total revenue. Only in two years did revenue fail to exceed expenditure (Olurunfemi 1984; Carland 1985). Liquor revenue alone averaged over 1 million pounds a year between 1910 and 1913. Governor Walter Egerton repeated what he saw as the benevolent relationship between liquor revenue and colonial rule, using a moral justification based on protection of Africans: "Without the revenue good Government cannot be maintained; without it law and order cannot be established; and without it the old West African practices of slave dealing, human sacrifice, trial by ordeal, cannot be effectively prevented."[6]

Yet as time went by, the Southern Nigerian colonial government found itself ensnared in the need to perpetually tax the trade to an ever greater extent. The overwhelming lure of liquor money proved hard to resist, since "it gives money for their schemes good or bad as they may be, but it binds the future government in golden fetters" (Davidson Papers 1907). Critics disagreed, suggesting that other taxes could replace the liquor levy. Bishop Tugwell argued for direct taxation and liquor prohibition. But with Tugwell building a church in Lagos out of a colonial grant, campaigner Edmund Morel attacked him for his hypocrisy: "Southern Nigeria is a wicked administration because it derives its revenues from body-and-soul-destroying drink, but it is right and proper to build a church out of those same revenues" (Morel 1910). Morel himself ruled out both a metropolitan grant as unjustifiable and forced labor in forest products because of the Belgian Congo's ugly precedent. For him and ex-colonial governor Sir Harry Johnston, the only alternative to liquor money was direct taxation, but not immediately. To institute direct taxation on Nigerians straightaway might provoke armed resistance like that seen in Sierra Leone a decade earlier.

The colonial government received valuable support for its liquor policy from an unusual source. In an extensive newspaper article, nationalist Herbert Macaulay pointed out that liquor taxation was not that bad; after all, it supplied one-third of Britain's total revenue. As a lifelong abstainer from alcohol, and with no economic interest in the liquor trade, Macaulay traveled around the western part of the Southern Nigeria hinterland enthusiastically explaining the evil nature of direct taxes when compared with the existing system of liquor taxation. To scare his audience, Macaulay listed the potential types of direct taxation possible in Southern Nigeria: "It means Hut Tax, Land Tax, Income Tax, Poll Tax or Capitation Tax, Export Tax" (*Nigerian Chronicle* 2 April 1909, supplement). Such inflammatory propaganda at once tarred the anti-liquor lobby's calls for liquor prohibition with the brush of direct taxation, and alienated many people previously sympathetic to their cause. The disarming effect of Macaulay's work can be judged by the fact that one of the most powerful chiefs, the Alake of Abeokuta, urged his subjects to end their boycott of the liquor trade or else face direct taxation.

The Southern Nigeria government added another shilling to its four shilling duty in January 1909. It levied an extra 2.5 pence on every degree above fifty degrees in strength and a 1.25 pence reduction on every degree below the standard strength. The government tactics deliberately encouraged the trend to weaker spirits by penalizing over-proof alcohol and making it more economic to import spirits at, or close to, forty degrees in strength. In fact, only a small proportion of spirits paid the full five shillings a gallon duty, as most of the imported alcohol was forty degrees in strength or less and so also attracted the minimum duty of four shillings (Heap 1999).

Heavy spirit duties (196 and 312 percent on the declared value of gin and rum, respectively, by 1909) meant that the main part of a drinker's expenditure consisted of the customs duty, not the actual cost of the liquid contents. Charles Strachey of the Colonial Office liked "the beauty of the system by which the consumers of the spirits are made to contribute more than anyone else to the cost of governing the country."[7] Heavy tariffs on spirits were also part of a wider policy to help place many imports vital to the construction of a colonial economy on the free list: railway materials, bicycles, boats, provisions, coal, bags, cooper stores, building and roofing materials, machinery and agricultural implements. Such imports totaled more than £529,000 in 1910, all duty-free. To compensate, the customs revenue concentrated on four items: spirits, cotton goods, tobacco and gunpowder. Between 1906 and 1913, the former dominated by providing two-thirds of the total collected; in comparison, cotton goods contributed only 8–11 percent annually to total customs duties, tobacco 7–11 percent, and gunpowder 1–3 percent (*Southern Nigeria Blue Books* 1906–1913).

In contrast to the south, Northern Nigeria had a revenue problem because it derived little money from liquor duties and was less attractive to traders but still needed to maintain a large military force. In July 1886, three weeks after the issue of its charter, the Royal Niger Company imposed a two shilling per gallon spirit duty irrespective of strength, the highest customs duties on imported spirits anywhere in West Africa (Flint 1960). Then imperial paternalism, pushed by metropolitan liquor prohibition groups, succeeded in getting the Brussels Conference of 1890 to declare large parts of Africa, including Northern Nigeria, prohibited to the import of liquor because the inhabitants were mostly Muslims and their religion banned the use of alcohol.

FROM BLIND EYE TO WARY EYE: THE BRITISH COLONIAL GOVERNMENT'S LIQUOR REVENUE POLICY IN NORTHERN NIGERIA

Colonial concern about imported liquor began as soon as the British took over formal control from the Royal Niger Company at the end of the nineteenth century. They divided Nigeria into two administrative parts—Southern and Northern Nigeria (later, provinces of amalgamated Nigeria)—and in terms of alcohol a similar division occurred, with licensing in the south and prohibition in the north. But while imported liquor was banned in theory, the provision of adequate supplies of alcohol was crucial to the smooth running of the colonial administration. The government implemented prohibition among the indigenous peoples of the north and restricted drinking among its administrative staff. "Prohibited natives," born and raised in Northern Nigeria, could not import, sell or possess imported liquor. "Non-natives," born outside the region but living there, could buy liquor on a controlled basis (Olukoju 1991, 1996; Heap 1998). Liquor policy and practice in Northern Nigeria were therefore full of internal contradictions. These same conveniences of administration occurred in the contrast between Britain's self-portrayal as a pioneer in slavery abolition and its active preservation of that institution until the 1930s (Lovejoy and Hogendorn 1995).

Before colonial rule, the manufacture and sale of indigenous liquor were strictly forbidden by Muslim rulers, with transgressors liable to be punished by public flogging; but non-Muslims were left to drink their own liquors.[8] In their turn, the British placed no restrictions on rural brewing: any attempt would have needed the support of the Native Administration and influential people in the community, but they were some of the biggest drinkers of alcohol. With such a poor revenue base, the British licensed urban local liquor as much for money as "to check the control to some extent of the production and sale of intoxicating liquors in native towns."[9] With few men on the ground to effect the license system, the colonialists sought "the cordial cooperation of the Emirs and Chiefs of the large Mohammedan centres in enforcing this Proclamation, since indulgence in fermented drinks is opposed to the law of the Koran."[10]

Table 7.2 traces liquor revenue in relation to overall colonial revenue generation in Northern Nigeria as the region moved from being reliant on imperial subsidy to relative self-sufficiency. In so doing, the British government's compromised position in controlling a substance while backing the claims of Muslims to be abstinent comes to the fore: "It appears that Government recognizes and protects, in exchange for the fee, a traffic that is prohibited by Native Law and which is still reproved of by thinking and educated portions of the community."[11] The British colonial administration's need for more revenue in Northern Nigeria led to the morally questionable business of licensing manufacturers and sellers of indigenous liquor. However, the low value of the goods and difficulties of revenue collection made it an inferior revenue source compared to that of customs duties on imported alcohol in Southern Nigeria.

All northbound imported liquor went through Southern Nigeria customs stations, with the duties transferred northwards later, but this amounted to just a few thousand pounds annually (Heap 2000). The government boasted that the colony's imports were "exclusively of a useful kind" that "do not include liquor, which is a foreign article largely transported in foreign ships and adds nothing to the progress of the people" (*Northern Nigeria Annual Report* [NNAR] 1902). But rueful statements about the absence of such a lucrative generator of revenue were also made: "Were they (trade spirits) to be imported (which I trust will never be), the revenues of Northern Nigeria would, doubtless, increase more than a hundred

Table 7.2
Revenue Sources, Northern Nigeria, 1900–1913 (in £s)

Year	Indigenous liquor licences	Imported liquor licences	Imported liquor duties (a)	Other local revenue	Imperial Grant-in-Aid	Southern Nigeria	Grand total
1900	0	13	n.a.	2,167 (a)	88,800	44,750	135,730
1901	0	144	506	3,724	280,000	34,000	318,424
1902	0	75	1,009	15,232	290,000	50,693	357,009
1903	0	75	n.a.	53,652 (a)	405,000	50,000	508,727
1904	294	200	n.a.	94,032 (a)	405,500	60,000	559,526
1905	1,081	125	n.a.	109,339 (a)	320,000	75,000	505,545
1906	1,007	125	1,255 (b)	139,700	315,000	75,000	532,087
1907	456	125	2,906	139,518	295,000	70,000	508,005
1908	390	225	3,100	174,730	290,000	70,000	538,445
1909	381	250	4,049	208,756	237,000	70,000	520,436
1910	423	225	4,790	269,551	275,000	70,000	619,989
1911	569	300	3,621	540,801	347,000	70,000	962,291
1912	69	475	3,408	472,541	95,000	52,500	623,993
1913	24	725	n.a.	657,560 (a)	136,000	0	794,309

Sources: Northern Nigeria Blue Books of Statistics, 1900–1913; *Northern Nigeria Annual Reports*, 1901–1913.
Notes:
(a) approximately
(b) July–December 1906 only

fold" (NNAR 1901). Instead, the vast majority of its revenue came from an imperial grant-in-aid, despite Earl Grey's "self-supporting" colonial fiscal discipline (Grey 1852). Unhappy at "unfair" subventions to its poorer northern neighbor, Southern Nigeria's High Commissioner suggested setting the north's import liquor tax at six shillings a gallon.[12] Needless to say, this received no support, given Britain's international obligations to keep the area free from liquor. The only direct revenue from alcohol came from licensing imported liquor sellers, but this remained a meager source of revenue. It was only the implementation of a land tax near the end of the colony's history that began to tackle the problem of balancing the books. Indeed, behind the idea of amalgamating Northern and Southern Nigeria into one colony lay the need to return to Grey's maxim of fiscal self-sufficiency by welding a nation composed of regions representing widely different tax-generation capabilities (Heap 1998). Strangely, this regional imbalance has remained embedded in the Nigerian nation-state to the present day, with oil replacing alcohol as the source of imbalance.

CHANGING TAX REGIME: OSCILLATING ALCOHOL IMPORT DUTIES AND THE GRADUAL INTRODUCTION OF DIRECT TAXATION

Nigeria's Governor-General Lugard spoke of his long-held dislike of the liquor trade just before the outbreak of World War I, commenting, "I should welcome a decrease in its volume even at the cost of a sacrifice of Revenue."[13] Wartime shipping space shortages did indeed bring about "a wholly new and artificial dislocation of the entire fiscal system."[14] Spirit imports collapsed from over 4.64 million gallons, valued at £1.59 million in 1913, to under 160,000 gallons, worth less than £100,000 in 1919. For the first time, in 1915 duty on other articles exceeded that collected from spirits. Yet despite this, 1919's revenue recorded its highest level. Nigeria seemed to have outgrown its overwhelming reliance on liquor import duties. A large increase in the railways' earnings (£3,634,875 more in 1918 than in 1913) and the introduction of export duties (realizing £3,490,917 in 1918) replaced the lost liquor revenue.[15] This latter tax, resisted previously as being too potentially dangerous to the fledgling agricultural export sector of the economy, was imposed on cocoa, palm oil and palm kernels in 1916. Cocoa paid an export duty of nearly two pounds seven shillings per ton, while palm oil and kernels paid just over a pound per ton. It was extended in the following years to groundnuts and hides and skins.[16] Groundnuts paid ten shillings a ton duty. In February 1920, with the post-war boom at its height, the government raised taxes further to one, two and three pounds per ton on, in turn, groundnuts, palm kernels and palm oil (Olukoju 1997).

When peace came, the Nigerian colonial government saw "the crying need" to catch up with extending the rail and road networks deferred due to war, but with high interest rates it was "desirable to pay for such works out of revenue as far as possible."[17] The question was how. In 1917 revenue from spirits was down by £1,052,000 compared with 1913, whereas the gain from other dutiable goods amounted to only £170,000. So for Governor-General Lugard, direct taxation was "a necessary concomitant of the cessation of the spirit traffic."[18] He preferred a mixture of personal taxation and export duties to cover the revenue lost from the liquor trade. As regards the former idea, Oyo Province adopted a poll tax system in 1918, which spread in the next few years to most of southwestern Nigeria. Nigerian taxpayers found highly visible direct taxation far more burdensome than invisible indirect liquor customs duties, and they staged protests throughout large parts of the south, in Egbaland in 1918, in Owo,

Warri and Kwale in 1927, and, most disastrously, in Aba, Owerri, Opobo and Calabar in 1929.

Nonetheless, the Nigerian government held firm. More widely, there was a growing movement to curb liquor volumes and increase quality by banning cheap trade spirits and putting up liquor prices across Africa enshrined in the 1919 Convention of St.-Germain-en-Laye. In line with this, the Nigerian government's spirit duty rose by 50 percent, to fifteen shillings per gallon, which one commentator saw as "a case of Morality impinging on Finance" (McPhee 1926). Governor Hugh Clifford reckoned that his administration went without 2 million pounds of revenue annually from the disappearance of trade spirits (Osuntokun 1973). Foregoing this huge amount of money was discomforting for some sections of officialdom, especially given the development projects under way to extend the road and rail network and to expand the agricultural export sector of the economy. The Colonial Office did not share the moral concern underlying the Convention of St.-Germain-en-Laye, dismissing the notion that there was something immoral in collecting customs revenue from spirits as old-fashioned and "an idea directly opposed to practice at home, where such duties are considered to be the ideal way of raising money for the state."[19] If London did not see anything wrong in raising revenue from liquor, then why should Lagos? Nonetheless, Governor Clifford warned the Legislative Council to oppose the temptation: "Unless we out here take a firm and united stand against it, we may have the evil back again before long."[20]

However, despite high customs duties, drinking and alcohol as a source of revenue were increasing again with the postwar prosperity of the 1920s. In April 1921 the government hiked the spirit duty to 25 shillings per gallon, fulfilling the Colonial Office's aspirations to bring all four British West African colonies' spirit duties in line with one another. From its wartime trough, liquor revenue rose sharply in the 1920s to provide a significant proportion of the total import duties collected. With the continued social use of liquor, and with very high rates of duty and volumes picking up, the government found taxing the liquor trade very lucrative once again, reaching an interwar high point of £720,577 in 1928. Although less than before, liquor revenue continued to fund colonial rule.

When the world depression hit Nigeria, imported liquor, being a luxury consumer item, again lost its premier place as regards import duties. Liquor revenue declined dramatically, losing half its value between 1930 and 1931, and reaching a low point in 1934 of only 18 percent of the peak figure of 1928. Cheaper homemade spirits were replacing expensive imports, spurred by local technological development. In the 1930s, local alcohol distillation swept the colony in the form of illicit gin or *ogogoro* making. Simple distillation equipment of a kerosene tin, a water pot and a straight or spiral metal pipe with watertight joints produced five bottles of raw alcohol daily. Palm wine and sugar formed the basic ingredients for "those that are cooking the gins."[21] Distillers tapped their own palm trees or bought the sap for a few pence a gallon. Fresh palm wine was alcohol-free, but if left to stand for up to three days its own internal fermentation produced alcohol. By distilling off 50 percent of the mash each time and then redistilling the distillate, increases in alcoholic strength were attained, eventually producing half a pint of spirit comparable in strength to imported brands and without the added inconvenience of paying 18 pence duty. The lasting popularity of *ogogoro* lay mainly in its price because "it could be produced for pence against shillings charged by the firms."[22] Burdened by heavy customs duties and the high cost of retail licenses, imported liquor was dear: the cheapest imported gin was about five and a half times as expensive as *ogogoro.* To many Nigerian drinkers, brought up in the days of cheaper spirits, alcohol of the homemade variety meant the return of affordable drinking. As a consequence, imported gin slid down the list of the most important items that the government could tax.

Untaxed domestic alcohol distillation imposed a double burden on the colonial state. While revenue from legal liquor imports diminished, the detection and control of the illicit locally made alcohol required enormous expenditure to bolster the police service. With the impossibility of stopping an industry built on simple apparatus, easily acquired ingredients and high profits, the only method open to the British was to wage a relentless campaign against distillers and impose severe penalties on lawbreakers. The colonial authorities wanted to stop an illegal, untaxed business and force people to buy legal, taxed, imported alcoholic products. Illicit distillation was the biggest public order menace of the decade. Illicit gin was an unnerving challenge to colonial authority, as distillation called into question fundamental aspects of colonialism: the strong law and order regime, the ability of the government to regulate economic affairs, and the revenue generation of the state. Local commentators like Sylvester Madu of Aba observed that "male and female distillers in Southern Nigeria are very very great which helps to make the Revenue of Nigeria to come down."[23] Despite the novelty and low price of locally prepared alcohol, when purchasing power recovered after the Depression, consumer demand for imported alcohol resurged. By the latter part of the decade the highly buoyant imported liquor trade supported a spirit duty of almost two pounds a gallon.

The oscillating rhythm of imported liquor consumption and taxation in line with economic booms and busts came to an end in the 1940s. World War II instigated new consumer demands and attitudes. Government concerns over liquor revenue were overtaken by liquor supply ones. With foreign soldiers swelling the local demand for beer just as imported supplies faltered, the war revealed the folly of Nigeria's reliance on imports from Europe. The troops were thirsty. Bureaucratic files full of unfulfilled requests from Nigerian colonial officials for beer supplies for their Congolese, Gold Coast and South African soldiers pointed to the shortcomings of reliance on imported supplies of bottled spirits and the lack of local industrial production. Up to this time, the colonial government had not accorded any attention to national industrial planning, but change was afoot, spurred by Keynesian economic thinking and the new developmental focus of the 1940 Colonial Development and Welfare Act.

FROM DOCKSIDE TO FACTORY SITE: IMPORT SUBSTITUTION OF LAGER BEER

In postwar Nigeria, British colonial policy moved toward a wholly positive frame of mind on industrialization, as evidenced by the Ten-Year Development Plan and the orientation of the Department of Commerce and Industries. To achieve development and relieve dependence on external sources for consumer goods more quickly, the switch from commerce to industrialization was formulated in terms of import substitution (Kilby 1969). Alcohol was an ideal commodity for import substitution, given its assured consumer demand and its not overly demanding technical production requirements. Unhesitatingly, the government permitted the construction of Nigeria's first modern brewery.

Lager beer production in Nigeria was initiated by foreign merchant firms to protect and promote their interest in the growing domestic market. Those that came together under the title of the Nigeria Brewery Limited (NBL) in November 1946 read like a list of beer importers: UAC (United Africa Company), John Holt's, G.B. Ollivant's, PZ (Paterson Zochonis), UTC (Union Trading Company), CFAO (Compagnie Française de l'Afrique Occidentale) and SCOA (Société Commerciale de l'Ouest Africain). The Dutch firm of Heineken acted as brewing advisor. These trading companies clearly saw that the only profitable long-term future lay in domestic production rather than in continuing imports. On 14 July 1949 the Nigerian Brewery Limited (NBL) started manufacturing its Star lager beer at Iganmu, Lagos.

Lager beer became very fashionable after the war, and consumption boomed. If cheap local beverages represented a somewhat old-fashioned and rural way of life, Western-style lager beers catered for a burgeoning market of urban consumers seeking a progressive "modern" lifestyle. Without home production, Nigeria would have imported over 10 million gallons of beer by the late 1950s. Instead, the local brewery promoted a good quality beer and gained an increasing share of the market. NBL then spread geographically with the opening of two other brewing plants, one at Aba in the east (1957) and the other at Kaduna in the north (1963). NBL's local monopoly was then broken: by Guinness stout brewed in Lagos, by the Independence Brewery at Umuahia making both Golden Guinea lager and Eagle stout, and by West African Breweries producing Top lager at Abeokuta. By 1966 the 3,000 employees of these companies brewed virtually all the beer consumed in Nigeria.

The breweries satisfied the fiscal requirements of both the colonial and postcolonial government and its independent successor by more than replacing import duties with excise and corporation taxes. Finance Minister Festus Sam Okotie-Eboh echoed the colonial mentality of revenue self-sufficiency when he acknowledged the fiscal value of beer import substitution: "The revenue which will be derived from all the excisable projects will be considerable and will further strengthen our foreign exchange position."[24]

From the collection of £1.19 million in liquor import duties in 1948, the government received £3.4 million from the combination of alcohol import duties and excise duties in 1960. As the rising demand for beer was met by the increased capacity of more breweries, imports declined. But falling imports were more than compensated for by excise duties. The government reaped a total liquor revenue of £4.9 million in 1966 and £7.9 million in 1970, of which all but £23,000 came from Nigeria's flourishing beer-brewing industrial sector. Overshadowed in importance by oil revenues in the 1970s, the excise tax on beer has nonetheless proved to be a steady revenue generator. In 1964, 36 percent of NBL's income went on excise tax. Exactly thirty years later NBL alone paid several hundred millions of Naira to government coffers. Nigerian breweries collectively spent 45 percent of their disposable income on excise and corporation taxes, making the brewing sector a crucial source of non-oil revenue for the government throughout the postcolonial economy's booms and busts (Heap 1996).

CONCLUSION

Revenue from the liquor trade was a major prop of British colonial administrations in Nigeria, which consciously fashioned customs duties to extract maximum revenue from the trade. Customs duties formed the most lucrative source of revenue, with the bulk collected from alcohol. It averaged three-quarters of total annual revenues in the Niger Coast Protectorate, two-thirds in Lagos, and half in Southern Nigeria, and continued to contribute to revenue generation under colonial and postcolonial Nigerian regimes. For Lugard, Governor-General of Nigeria from 1914 to 1919, such a state of affairs shamed him; he called it "a disgrace," but the allure of the liquor trade as a source of revenue for the colonial government proved overpowering (Lugard 1919). Import duties collected by customs, of which those from spirits proved the greatest until the 1930s, formed a vital source of revenue. Therefore the tariff regime was a matter of great significance and debate. Given the overwhelming dominance of German and Dutch spirit imports into Lagos, the irony of taxing the liquor trade to supply the financial foundation of British colonial rule should not be forgotten. No governor found an easy alternative to liquor revenue. Similarly, all felt less concern over the volume of the trade than over the loss of the revenue derived from that source. Rising duties restricted the volume of imports, and it was claimed that they were keeping the liquor trade under firm control. So morally and financially, the restrictionist policy adopted by the use of tariffs was the most attractive option for the government. The setting of the rate of liquor duty gave the government a certain degree of control over the trade and a good deal of money for its administration.

Prior to World War II, the colonial government of Nigeria, like its counterparts elsewhere in much of Africa, was not prepared to become involved in the active promotion of industry by means of subsidies or tariff protection. The liquor trade highlights the conservative nature of colonial economics: the government was content to tax an import trade to pay for its administration, while the idea of developing a modern economy founded on home production rather than an imported trade hardly entered their commerce-based economic thinking. It would take the drastic supply shortages experienced during World War II for far more positive colonial policies on the advantages to be gained by encouraging an alcohol import-substitution industry. Such infant import-substituting industries as breweries had to stand on their feet unaided, robust enough to withstand the competition from direct liquor imports, and yet operating in a way designed not to disrupt the existing fiscal and commercial context of colonialism. Postcolonial governments not surprisingly followed an essentially similar line, aiding a local industry and reaping the rewards of liquor revenue through excise duties on domestic alcohol production.

NOTES

1. Public Record Office, London (PRO), Colonial Office, London (CO) 147/157, H. Tugwell, CMS Bishop of Western Equatorial Africa, *Proceedings of the Lagos Institute*, 1901, p. 29.

2. PRO, CO 520/10, Sir R.D.R. Moor, High Commissioner, Southern Nigeria, to J. Chamberlain, Secretary of State for the Colonies, Britain, 4 December 1901.

3. PRO, CO 444/3, Minute by R.L. Antrobus, Under-Secretary of State for the Colonies, Britain, 3 November 1899.

4. PRO, CO 444/3, Sir W. MacGregor, Governor, Lagos, to Chamberlain, 27 December 1899; *Ilorin Town Annual Report*, 1901–02, p. 2.

5. PRO, CO 444/3, MacGregor to Chamberlain, 27 December 1899.

6. PRO, CO 520/62, Sir W. Egerton, Governor, Southern Nigeria, to Lord Crewe, Secretary of State for the Colonies, Britain, 6 July 1908.

7. PRO, CO 520/62, Minute by C. Strachey, Colonial Office, London, 5 August 1908, on Egerton to Crewe, 6 July 1908. Nigeria was much more dependent on liquor revenue than Ghana (38–39% annually, 1910–13) (Akyeampong 1996: 81).

8. National Archives, Kaduna (NAK), Secretary, Northern Provinces (SNP) 8/5/4/1918, H.S. Goldsmith, Lieutenant-Governor, Northern Provinces, to F.D. Lugard, Governor-General, Nigeria, 31 December 1917.

9. PRO, CO 446/30, Lugard, High Commissioner, Northern Nigeria, to Chamberlain, 13 January 1903.

10. Ibid.

11. NAK, SNP 8/5/4/1918, F.H. Ruxton, Resident, Muri, to C.L. Temple, Secretary, Northern Provinces, 4 July 1910.

12. National Archives, Ibadan (NAI), Chief Secretary's Office, Lagos (CSO) 1/15/5, Egerton, High Commissioner, Southern Nigeria, to A. Lyttleton, Secretary of State for the Colonies, Britain, 5 November 1904.

13. NAI, CSO 1/32/8, Lugard to L.V. Harcourt, Secretary of State for the Colonies, Britain, 25 May 1914.

14. PRO, CO 657/19, *Governor Clifford's Address to the Legislative Council*, 26 February 1923, p. 20.

15. Nigeria Annual Report, 1918, p. 2.

16. Nigeria Ordinance no. 46 of 1916. The Customs Tariff (Export) Ordinance: PRO, Co 657/5, Nigeria Customs Annual Report, 1917, p. 6: PRO, CO 583/78, Sir H.C. Clifford, Governor, Nigeria, to A. Milner, Secretary of State for the Colonies, Britain, 31 October 1919.

17. NAI, CSO 1/36/5, A.G. Boyle, Acting Governor, Nigeria, to A. Milner, 21 January 1919; PRO, CO 583/67, W.H. Long, Secretary of State for the Colonies, Britain, to Lugard, 10 October 1918.

18. NAI, CSO 19/5/N.1676/1917, Lugard, *Memorandum on Taxation* (July 1917), pp. 3–4.

19. PRO, CO 583/65, Minute by Strachey, 28 May 1918, on Lugard to Long, 26 March 1918.

20 PRO, CO 657/19, *Governor Clifford's Address*, 6 February 1925, p. 148.

21. National Archives, Enugu (NAE), Brass District Office (BRASSDIST) 10/1/80, A. Omekwe, Brass, to A.F.F.P. Newns, Assistant District Officer, Brass, 13 November 1933.

22. NAE, Itu District Office (ITUDIST) 2/1/13, G.H. Findlay, Resident, Calabar, to E.J. Price, District Officer, Itu, 3 July 1931.

23. NAE, Aba District Office (ABADIST) 14/1/169, S.T. Madu to C.J. Pleass, District Officer, Aba, 8 December 1932.

24. "Budget speech, 1964," in *Nigeria Estimates*, 1964–65, p. 319.

REFERENCES

Akyeampong, E. 1996. *Drink, Power and Cultural Change: A Social History of Alcohol in Ghana, c. 1800 to Recent Times*. Oxford: James Currey.

Carland, J.M. 1985. *The Colonial Office and Nigeria, 1898–1914*. London: Macmillan.

Cary, A.J.L. 1939. *Mister Johnson*. London: Victor Gollancz.

Davidson, Randall, Archbishop of Canterbury. Papers. Lambeth Palace Library, London.

Flint, J. 1960. *Sir George Goldie and the Making of Nigeria*. London: Oxford University Press.

Grey, H. 1852. *The Colonial Policy of Lord John Russell's Administration*. Vol. 2. London: Richard Bentley.

Heap, S.D.H. 1994–95. "Alcohol in Africa: A Supplementary List of Post-1875 Literature." *A Current Bibliography on African Affairs*. 26 (1): 1–14.

———. 1995. "The Liquor Trade and the Nigerian Economy, 1880–1939." Ph.D. dissertation, University of Ibadan.

———. 1996. "Before *Star*: The Import Substitution of Western-Style Alcohol in Nigeria, 1870–1970." *African Economic History* 24: 69–89.

———. 1998. "'We Think Prohibition Is a Farce': Drinking in the Alcohol-Prohibited Zone of Colonial Northern Nigeria." *International Journal of African Historical Studies* 31 (1): 23–51.

———. 1999. "The Quality of Liquor in Nigeria during the Colonial Era." *Itinerario* 23 (2): 29–47.

———. 2000. "Transport and Liquor in Colonial Nigeria." *Journal of Transport History* 21 (1): 28–53.

Kilby, P. 1969. *Industrialization in an Open Economy, Nigeria, 1945–66*. Cambridge: Cambridge University Press.
Kingsley, M.H. 1898. "The Liquor Traffic with West Africa." *Fortnightly Review* 69 (April): 537–60.
Liedholm, C. 1970. "The Influence of Colonial Policy on the Growth and Development of Nigeria's Industrial Sector." In C.K. Eicher and C. Liedholm (eds.), *Growth and Development of the Nigerian Economy*. East Lansing: Michigan State University Press, 52–61.
Lovejoy, P.E., and J.S. Hogendorn. 1995. *Slow Death for Slavery: The Course of Abolition in Northern Nigeria, 1897–1936*. Cambridge: Cambridge University Press.
Lugard, F.D. 1919. Report by Sir F.D. Lugard on the Amalgamation of Northern and Southern Nigeria, 1912–1919. Command Paper 468. London: His Majesty's Stationery Office.
McPhee, A. 1926. *The Economic Revolution in British West Africa*. London: Routledge.
Morel, E.D. 1910. *The Attack upon the Commission of Inquiry into the Spirit Trade in Southern Nigeria*. Liverpool: John Richardson.
Olukoju, A. 1991. "Prohibition and Paternalism: The State and the Clandestine Liquor Traffic in Northern Nigeria, 1898–1918." *International Journal of African Historical Studies* 24 (2): 349–68.
———. 1996. "Race and Access to Liquor: Prohibition as Colonial Policy in Northern Nigeria, 1919–45." *Journal of Imperial and Commonwealth History* 24 (2): 218–43.
———. 1997. "Rotgut and Revenue: Fiscal Aspects of the Liquor Trade in Southern Nigeria, 1890–1919." *Itinerario* 21 (2): 66–81.
Olurunfemi, A. 1984. "The Liquor Traffic in British West Africa: The Southern Nigeria Example, 1895–1918." *International Journal of African Historical Studies* 17 (2): 229–41.
Osuntokun, J. 1973. "Post-First World War Economic and Administrative Problems in Nigeria and the Response of the Clifford Administration." *Journal of the Historical Society of Nigeria* 7 (1): 35–48.

8

Drinking, Prestige, and Power

Alcohol and Cultural Hegemony in Maji, Southern Ethiopia

Jon Abbink

The sociohistorical study of alcohol use in the context of power relations and public policy has markedly increased in recent years, although much of it has focused on cross-cultural varieties of alcohol abuse or delinquency (cf. Molamu and Manyeneng 1988; Molamu and Kebede 1988) and on ritual contexts (Karp 1980; Rekdal 1996). Predictably, the broad field of alcohol studies emerging since the early twentieth century is grounded in the idea that alcohol use is inherently problematic, as something associated with lack of self-control, unpredictable behavior and violence (Heath 1987). Such qualifications are often part of a social process of ranking and distancing, and often applied by people to some other group than their own. Alcohol, apart from its potential for "generating trouble," can be used as a theme to belittle, patronize and differentiate people, often in subtle ways. This happens especially when different kinds of beverages are accorded a different status across social and ethnic groups in society.[1]

The Ethiopian case study presented in this chapter highlights cultural aspects of social inequality and ethnic stratification by tracing the ambivalent connections among alcohol, power and cultural dominance. The Maji region of southern Ethiopia is a culturally diverse society, which offers a fruitful setting to analyze such phenomena. Its "drinking situation" reflects the area's history of divergent ethnocultural traditions and exposure of people to state narratives of civilization and governance.

KATIKALA'S APPEARANCE IN THE PROCEEDINGS OF MAJI LOCAL GOVERNMENT

The Maji region is a politically and economically marginalized area where various ethnic groups meet. Local indigenous people have witnessed the influx of settlers from Ethiopia's northern highlands, notably the Amhara, Tigrinya and Oromo-speaking settlers of mainly Christian belief,[2] who came as traders, farmers, soldiers and administrators. The latter are located in villages founded about a century ago. Historically, the local people, among them the Dizi, Me'en and Suri, were deemed politically and culturally less civilized by the central state and the northern immigrants. The Suri people, as agro-pastoralist lowlanders, were considered especially coarse and unrefined in their mannerisms and livelihood pursuits.

Under Ethiopia's new federal state instituted after May 1991, these local groups were given a measure of local autonomy, with corresponding cultural rights and a political voice, at least in name. A new local self-government unit, the Surma Local Council, was instituted for the Suri people. This Council, formed in 1994, is a body of about eleven Suri men, assisted by a few other Ethiopians sent by the Zone, the higher administrative unit, and the regional state government. It is designated as the main administrative body of the new Surma *woreda* (district), which has within its borders almost all Suri-speaking people. Befitting their status and responsibilities, the Council members are paid a government salary, which is an entirely new phenomenon for the Suri. With this regular cash income, Council members can buy presents for family and friends, acquire extra cattle, and, as I observed in 1995–96 during fieldwork, procure almost daily deliveries of strong liquor, called *katikala*, from Maji village.

Katikala is not a traditional drink for the Suri. A relatively recent import, it is consumed in substantial quantities. Allegedly intoxication is a frequent phenomenon within the Council premises, leading to fights and occasional shootings. The record of the Council is said to be dismal. Alcohol (ab)use is explained by many non-Suri northerners in the neighboring villages as another example of the Suri's still uncivilized or "backward" social behavior—they "cannot deal with strong liquor." It is said that their problems will only be remedied with time, when they gain literacy and education and become sedentarized.

This chapter explores the basis of such remarks and what they reveal about hegemonic relations and group prestige. The next section provides background on the geopolitics and economy of the area. The different types of alcohol that are produced and consumed by the area's various ethnic groups are then reviewed before examining the alcohol economy and its prestige rankings in more detail. The conclusion compares *gèso*-beer drinking and *katikala*-drinking as cultural-political statements.

THE MAJI AREA: ETHNIC INTERACTION AND STATE AUTHORITY

The Maji area is a fertile but economically underdeveloped area comprising two main ecological zones: (1) a highland range (at places up to 2600 meters) inhabited by indigenous agriculturalists with an ancient history (the Dizi people) and descendants of northern immigrants of mixed origin; and (2) a surrounding savannah lowland, inhabited by Suri and Me'en agro-pastoralists. The region's economic role in southern Ethiopia is limited, due to its remoteness, lack of transport facilities (only one precarious dry-season motor road for big trucks), and relative lack of natural resources and export crop production. The only products that are sold to outside agents on a small scale are coffee, honey and, since about 1990, alluvial gold.

Gold is panned in the various rivers of the area by indigenous people (mostly Suri) and immigrants from the North, who have flocked to one especially promising location just north of the Maji area. Here, Dima, a new frontier town with some 3,000 inhabitants of very diverse origins, has emerged on the banks of the Akobo River in the last ten years. The Suri are frequent visitors to this new town and sell their gold to traders with connections in the capital.

Though there are notable differences in ecology, economic activities, language and culture between the highlanders and lowlanders in Maji, they are dependent on each other for the exchange of food products, utensils and livestock. There are six small villages-*cum*-towns in this region, of which Maji and Tum are the administrative centers. The population of these six towns (less than 10,000 people combined) consists largely of state-employed officials, teachers, administrators, traders, barkeepers, police or militia, and local people who work as domestics, beer brewers and builders. Among town-dwellers Amhara are predominant, but their actual "ethnic profile" is hard to characterize because they represent a complex ethnic mixture, with about 60 percent hailing from the Amharic-speaking Shewa, Gojjam and Wollo regions, whereas the others originate from ethnolinguistic groups, such as Kaficho, Gurage, Oromo and Tigrawi.

Before the inclusion of the Maji area in the Ethiopian state in the late nineteenth century, the local people were politically autonomous. The Dizi people (some 26,000) settled on the mountain ranges were organized in several chiefdoms, based on mixed agriculture, beekeeping and forestry. The Suri (about 28,000 people) and Me'en (about 65,000) were autonomous agro-pastoralists grazing their herds in the lowlands but also practicing shifting cultivation of maize and especially sorghum, and hunting and gathering. To this day, very few Me'en and Suri have settled in the small towns and villages, which has contributed to the ethnocultural divide along ecological and altitudinal lines that is typical of southern Ethiopia.

The gradual expansion of village society and the cultural models—among them Christianity—brought by the northerners, many of whom were state representatives, led to a system of cultural ranking in which the customs and traditions of the local people were considered uncivilized. Beginning in the days of the Ethiopian revolution from 1974 onwards, many were declared to be "harmful customs" (Amharic: *yegodjee bahil*). These included people's "lack of" clothing, certain rituals of cattle sacrifice, body scarifications, and specific food habits, as well as the consumption of certain types of alcohol.

Since the toppling of the Mengistu regime in 1991 and the establishment of the EPRDF regime,[3] Ethiopia has entered a new political phase, in which ethnicity and cultural difference are explicitly recognized. The country's administrative map has been redefined, largely along ethnolinguistic lines, and the officially stated policy aim is to avoid political hegemonism of one "ethnic group," notably the Amharic-speaking, predominantly Christian highlanders, as was the case in the past according to the perception of the present EPRDF leadership. Sovereignty in the new "ethno-federal" system is constitutionally vested in the "nations, nationalities and peoples" of the country (Cohen 1994; Abbink 1997). The political organization of Ethiopia as an ethno-regional federation is a very significant departure from the past and is at present redefining group relations and national identity. Nonetheless, while cultural differences are now officially acknowledged and sanctioned, the traditional civilizational images of highlanders (who still dominate the present government)[4] toward the local population remain in force and have political implications. At the local level, distancing and ethnic ranking persist.

Cultural ranking has not, of course, prohibited contacts between groups. Economic, social, sexual and marital relations have led to partial assimilation, yet cultural ranking remains. Alcohol is one element that has become emblematic of group distance and civilizational images that people have of each other, even if they are blurred in actual social practice.[5]

ALCOHOLIC BEVERAGES IN SOUTHERN ETHIOPIA

Among the indigenous people of Maji region (Me'en, Dizi and Suri), the only alcoholic drink before the arrival of the northerners some hundred years ago was the local maize-sorghum beer. There are reports that Me'en and Suri people had their own honey wine, called *boké*, somewhat similar to the highlander drink *t'ädj* (see below), but it is difficult to say whether it was made independently or derived from the example of *t'ädj*.

In the second half of the twentieth century, alcoholic drinks from the highland culture began to be available. These various beverages spread to Maji and within Ethiopia in general, by the processes of group contact and migration of mostly Christian highlanders. The alcoholic drinks in the area under discussion may be categorized into three main types.

The first are *t'älla* and *t'ädj*,[6] the "good ones," considered to be harmless social drinks consumed mainly during communal and family gatherings. The *t'älla* beer is of low alcohol content (ca. 6 to 7 percent)[7] and has a somewhat smoky taste. It is usually made by women, but men also prepare it in monasteries and church compounds. The production of this beer demands considerable skill, and a good brew is a source of pride. It takes more than a week to produce *t'älla* and several weeks for *t'ädj*, not counting the gathering of the ingredients. The *t'älla* beer is almost never produced or sold in bars.[8] It is a mainly a beverage for family occasions and Christian religious days and is very popular and highly valued.[9] *T'älla* is not generally considered a beer on which people get drunk, although this is often more a prescriptive norm than reality. Even Orthodox priests are alleged to get drunk on *t'älla* during religious festivals.

The *t'ädj* is the typical Ethiopian honey wine or mead, made of water, honey or occasionally sugar in the cruder blends, and crushed buckthorn[10] leaves as a fermenting agent. Formerly, it was drunk mostly by the upper classes, but it is now widespread among all social groups, drunk on secular holidays and weddings, and served in bars and small cafés all over Ethiopia.[11] These places owe their name to the drink: *t'ädj-bet*, house of the *t'ädj*, whereas there are only very few *t'älla bet*s. Traditionally it was largely ceremonial and not a beer to get drunk on, but now *t'ädj* is often sold in bars in a diluted form using sugar instead of honey as its base and has lost some of its prestige. The alcohol content of *t'ädj* can vary from 8 to 14 percent.[12] It has become the main drink of most Ethiopians not only in the towns, but also in the southern countryside bars. The *t'ädj-bet*s are places where people tend to drink and get drunk and spend a considerable amount of money. On market days in the South, a significant portion of the cash that the rural sellers in the market acquire from village dwellers for their foodstuffs and other products is converted back again into the village economy through drink sales.

The second genre of alcohol is that of the "local beers," subsumed under the name *bordé*. These are made from fermented maize, sorghum and sometimes barley or a mixture thereof and are typical for southwestern Ethiopia. *Bordé* is a thick and heavy beer, almost a fluid porridge that can serve as a meal in itself. The Suri term for their own beer similar to *bordé* is *gèso*.[13] The production of these traditional beers is always by women and is a laborious process, taking from eight to ten days. The alcohol content has not been measured scientifically, but is estimated to be around 6 to 9 percent.

Among the Suri, there are four kinds of *gèso*, according to quality and alcoholic content: first, the *jendáy*, a warm, very fine filtered beer and the strongest and most alcoholic variety; second, *nyána gid'anga*, and second in alcohol content; third, the *chállá*; and fourth, the *b'oru*. These traditional beers have low prestige in the eyes of the village and small-town people and of the people connected with the state administration. When they visit the lowlands they are jokingly advised by the others to take their own *t'ädj* or *katikala* and not to drink much *gèso*.[14] This attitude of mild disdain or scorn implies that "civilized people," that is, those in the village and connected with the wider Ethiopian culture,[15] should not drink this beer, at least not in large quantities and not too publicly. Only on a long walking journey in the countryside for trade or other purposes would one drink it for lack of other food and drink. Here again the ambivalent attitude toward these "native beers" surfaces. They are drunk when there is no choice, but ridiculed when one is back in one's town or village. Nevertheless, for the Suri the consumption of *gèso* was and continues to be a social activity par excellence, and an example of what Mary Douglas (1987) called "constructive drinking," to be detailed below.

The third and more problematic drink is the local *araqé*, or *katikala*, a homemade distilled drink originating from the highland areas, and now also found in the Maji area. It is made from germinated grains, especially maize (*Zea mays*) or finger millet (*Eleusine coracana*), sometimes mixed with wheat (*Hordeum vulgare*) with added agents like sugar and the leaf *kosso* (*Hagenia abyssinica*) (see Ethiopian Nutrition Institute 1980 for a traditional recipe). It can have an alcohol content in the range of 30 to almost 50 percent.[16] There are imported and factory-produced varieties, but these are not considered as good as the homemade ones.

Other strong drinks available in some bars in the villages in the Maji area are imported whisky and Ethiopian-produced gin, ouzo and cognac, drinks for the elite that are not popular among the rural people in Maji. *Araqé* and *katikala* are more expensive than any beer, and seen as very strong and challenging to the drinker. The best *araqé*s are reputed to be the *mar araqé* (made on a basis of honey) from the Debre Berhan area and *dagim araqé* from the Gojjam region (Central Highlands). While the real *araqé* from these areas is seen as a real treat and to be consumed with care and enjoyment, the related *katikala* is viewed more ambivalently. Even though it is accepted and widespread among the rural highland societies, it has the aura of being dangerous, a sure and quick way to drunkenness, and a cause of violent, uninhibited behavior. In contrast to *t'älla* and *t'ädj*, it is a "bad drink," moreover considered by the people themselves to be highly addictive: an example of destructive, not constructive, drinking. *Katikala* is nevertheless popular all over the Ethiopian countryside, and its alcohol content there can be estimated at some 35 to 40 percent.

Its production requires special equipment and skills, usually possessed by Christian village women living in the Maji area. The Suri and other people of the Maji countryside do not know how to produce it. But they all buy *katikala* in the village bars and transport it to their distant home areas in bottles owned by the village producers.

THE ECONOMICS OF LOCAL BEER PRODUCTION AND CONSUMPTION

The production of alcoholic drinks in this area of Ethiopia is situated within a local economy where market exchange is not widely prevalent and many activities are based on the direct appropriation of natural resources. There is still no problem of land and firewood scarcity in the Maji area. All farmers of any of the groups mentioned can get sufficient land for cultivation. Even returning soldiers from the former army of the Mengistu regime could easily start farming in the Maji area in 1991–1992, unlike most other areas of Ethiopia. Suri and other groups maintain the fertility of their land by rotating crops and shifting cultivation.

Nonetheless, poverty is rampant, and due to pressure by the state for tax payments in cash, there has been a growing demand for money over the past thirty years. Up to the mid-1960s, tribute was often paid in kind (cattle, grain, livestock, honey, etc.) or in labor services. In the later years of the Mengistu regime (1980s), the taxes increased significantly. After Mengistu's fall they were abolished for a few years in 1991–1993, but they are now back again in full force under the new federal government.

In order to pay taxes the local people often sold their livestock during Emperor Haile Selassie's time up to 1969, but at present the state administration has not been able to effectively enforce taxation. Tax collection is hampered by the lack of an appropriate infrastructure of roads and government services in the area, difficulties of transport, the remoteness of the lowland areas, feared because of malaria and other diseases, and the lack of food supplies there. Furthermore, Suri are often on the move and difficult to track down, especially when they hear that government administrators or soldiers are arriving. Among the Suri, strong pressure to find alternative sources of rural income outside the agricultural or agro-pastoral economy has yet to surface.

Since the 1940s, when economic and market integration of the Ethiopian southwest started, there has been an expansion of beer brewing and alcohol sale as a business on which the producers can sustain themselves, but *only* in the region's six small market towns. Beer brewing was never a source of cash for rural people. In virtually every Suri household, the women now and then make *gèso*, but only for ritual purposes or to lubricate work parties when beer is exchanged for labor. Households are "self-sufficient" most of the time, and the noncommercial production and consumption of local beer for limited social or ritual reasons within Suri society short-circuits the local market for alcohol.

Transport problems also militate against the commercialization of local beer, as carrying the big clay beer jugs to places of demand is virtually impossible. The few smaller calabashes that are brought to the market towns by some Dizi women (never Suri) yield on average no more than about fifty to eighty Ethiopian *birr* profit per market day.[17] In any case, Suri (and Me'en and Dizi) beer brewing has not yet become a commercial business that could provide a source of income for women beer brewers. Women dominate beer brewing and the production of other drinks, not unlike in other East African countries. However, the big difference in the Ethiopian situation is that the alcohol sales in the small market towns, where thousands of people of various groups gather twice a week, are controlled by village women who are descendants from earlier migrants from the highland north, and not by those from indigenous groups of the area. Local Suri and Me'en women never own bars.

In the town of Maji, with a population of only 1,617 people (Central Statistical Authority 1996), there are at least twelve *t'ädj-bets* and two *bordé* sorghum beer cafés. Whether the bars are supplied on a particular day can easily be recognized by a tree trunk or stool placed outside on the path, on which an empty can (meaning *bordé*), a small cup (*katikala*) or a bottle (*t'ädj*) is placed. In Maji town, only one of the bars (for *bordé*) is run by a Dizi woman and is patronized by Dizi people. The rest are operated by others, mostly of northern or mixed descent, who are, however, considered to be locals rather than immigrants. The clientele they serve are from the surrounding countryside, the population of which is estimated at 30,000, of which perhaps one-third are adults. On market days twice a week, every bar is full throughout the day, and the profits can be substantial. It is an economy of drinking which thrives on the clientele of the local rural population, but which nevertheless remains confined to the small market towns and villages in the area and does not spread beyond.

SOCIAL ASPECTS AND ASPIRATIONS EMBEDDED IN ALCOHOL CONSUMPTION

What *t'älla* and, to a lesser extent, *t'ädj* are for the Amhara and other highlanders, *gèso* is for the Suri people, perhaps even in a deeper sense: a social drink celebrating commensality on occasions calling for coming together. *Gèso* drinking in itself signifies relaxed social relations and peaceful or conciliatory intentions. It is always drunk in a group and in public, rather than being consumed like food in silence and solitude in the family hut. It is always drunk while seated, never when standing. Men and women drink it together.

Its most frequent and obligatory use is during agricultural work parties called *gasa*. The Suri practice hoe rather than plough agriculture, and such collective work parties are an essential part of the work process, especially in the heavy stages of clearing a field and harvesting. *Gèso* has a high nutritional value and is usually taken as the lunch meal. Any person, male or female, who decides to clear and cultivate a piece of land must first prepare beer, spread the word, and then be ready for a big turnout of laborers. Among the Suri the rule is where there is no beer, there is no work. A Suri work party starts about 8:30 A.M. and goes on until about 10:00–10:45 A.M. Then there is a break for drinking *gèso*, after which they return to work until 3:00 P.M., whereupon the remaining beer is drunk.

The farmer's mother or wife (and in the case of a female farmer her mother or sisters) sits together with other women, chatting and joking while the men do the work, impervious to the men's calls for refreshments until a substantial amount of work has been completed.[18] Women often serve themselves before serving the men. They also decide who gets any *gèso*, because the beer drunk during a work party implicitly stands for the recognition of the mutual dependence of households, especially of and through women, who organize the work parties and make the beer. Even though there may be conflicts and arguments during the consumption of the *gèso* beer (among the Suri certainly), it always brings people together. The ritual leader of the Suri (the *komoru*) is invited to all work parties in the neighborhood.

It is noteworthy that in the other main branch of Suri economic life, the herding of livestock, beer was not traditionally drunk. The Suri have cattle camps that are located at some distance, often about a day's walk, from their villages and hamlets, and while the young men take food with them, they only rarely take *gèso* beer. Beer is solidly associated, both economically and symbolically, with agricultural, that is, female, activities. In the cattle camps, the young men drink blood and milk from their animals.

Hence, the *gèso* beer can be seen indeed as one of the fuels of the rural economy, but not for the purpose of earning money. Only in the last four to five years have some Suri women started to sell *gèso* in their own compounds, but irregularly, and with very marginal profits. If beer is left over from the above-mentioned work parties, the women may decide to sell it to other people.

Gèso beer is drunk at all festive occasions, the main ones being a name-giving, the conclusion of a day of ceremonial dueling, the inauguration of a new field for crop cultivation, weddings, and the initiation of an age-group. This points to its use as a ritual drink. Its social significance is further underlined by its use in reconciliation. After a dispute is resolved, the mediators, who are of another clan or family group, have to bring local beer to seal the reconciliation. The two opponents have to drink it cheek to cheek from one calabash.[19] This is never done with *katikala.*

Tellingly, at several important political occasions in Suri society, such as public debates, divination from intestines, funerals, and during homicide compensation talks, beer is never drunk (Abbink 1998). Therefore, one can note many sociocultural restrictions on the actual use of *gèso* beer, which refutes the ideas that it was drunk "all day by almost everybody," as some northerners claim.

Katikala, however, is changing the picture, due to its extraneous origin and functions. It is becoming the new status drink among the Suri and other indigenous people in the Maji area. People say they simply like it because of its physical effect: giving a feeling of warmth and strength, at least initially. They often take it before traveling, which usually means a long walking journey back to their home area. Undoubtedly, other familiar reasons apply here: suppressing hunger, forgetting immediate worries, group pressure, and so on. But social reasons are also relevant. First, *katikala* is expensive, and thus a drink given as a present by people to important friends and guests denotes status. To give a good bottle of *katikala* is a sign of generosity and/or wealth, and is highly esteemed by the receiver. Second, in local rural society, it is a drink located outside familiar social categories, originating from the sphere of trade objects and commerce. It is neutral and objectified. This contrasts markedly with the status of local beer.

In Suri society, *gèso* beer served as compensation for participation in agricultural work parties and was never sold until recently. It functioned as an incentive for the Suri, who had no other means of labor recruitment in a labor-scarce society. The increased acceptance of *katikala* reflects the expanding monetization and market integration of the Suri economy into the wider regional economy. In this sense, the introduction of this hard liquor has signified the coming of modernity. *Katikala* drinking has become a habit throughout rural Ethiopia, predictably connected to emerging notions of strength and masculinity (cf. Heald 1986), although Suri women also enjoy the drink.

Katikala drinking is developing alongside rather than in place of the traditional *gèso* beer drinking in Suri social life. Still largely uncommercialized, it will continue to function as a socializing agent and as compensation for agricultural work. *Gèso* is associated with food, life and procreation, while *katikala* is not. *Katikala* has no positive qualities yet, apart from its physical effect of warmth and excitement. It is surrounded by ambivalence. *Katikala* appears mostly in social contexts that are structurally located outside the local moral economy, at informal meetings of male friends in small groups visiting the villages, and also in the cattle camps, but never at work parties or at rituals.

It can be said that in the period before the import of new alcoholic drinks, the number of drunks in the Suri or Me'en communities was not socially significant. All my informants from the Suri, Me'en and Dizi agree that constant problems of drunkenness and even of liver disease started only in the last fifteen to twenty years. For the Suri the phenomenon is even more recent, dating back to around 1989, when *katikala* production and consumption increased markedly. This may be a biased view on the part of the Suri people, the majority of whom came into close contact with the highland town culture only in the last decade. However, the records of the local health clinic in Maji over the past decades confirm it.

For the Suri, unlike *gèso, katikala* has no traditional, spiritual or social meaning. It is still unclear in what terms they will ultimately incorporate *katikala* in their drinking culture. While it is now indeed a prestige object given and shared between people as a sign of respect, wealth or virility, it may be that people, especially women, will not remain impervious to its negative side-effects, not least being the frequent state of male drunkenness and its expense, which drains household cash reserves, and the inevitable brawls and physical violence.

Alcohol abuse is associated with the increased consumption of *katikala,* both by the Suri and by the town people who sell it to them, but who also blame them for drinking too fast and too much. This brings us back to the different, and partly paradoxical, valuations of alcohol and its use between the local population groups of the Maji area.

GÈSO AND *KATIKALA* CONSUMPTION AS CULTURAL-POLITICAL STATEMENTS

The Suri's changing alcohol use and its valuation in many respects mirror the experience of groups in other parts of Ethiopia and East Africa (e.g., Rekdal 1996). Ethiopia is interesting in that there is no direct colonial legacy and corresponding alcohol policy with which people have had to deal; nonetheless, there are oppositions, often imagined, between several kinds of groups. The most salient is that between the culturally dominant Christian highlanders and other local, indigenous groups of various ethnic or social backgrounds. Southwest Ethiopia was only included in the Ethiopian empire in 1898 and has, in political and economic terms remained marginal, though not isolated, ever since.

A moral rejection of the local population's alcohol use by colonial or settler elites is not uncommon in Africa (cf. Partanen 1991; Crush and Ambler 1992; Diduk 1993; Siiskonen 1994; Akyeampong 1996). At the same time these elites tend to show a laissez-faire attitude toward use and abuse, because such alcohol usage allowed them to further ground their hegemony in a civilizing narrative and to expand their economic influence over people, especially through the import of new kinds of drink. Recent studies have also noted the interrelations between changing political and economic conditions and ideas and attitudes about indigenous beer and its cultural referents (Colson and Scudder 1988; Hutchinson 1996). Hence, alongside economic mechanisms, we simultaneously see ideological ones at work. Clearly, alcohol is always embedded in relations of valuation: economic, but even more significantly, political and moral-cultural. Viewed in this light, there is no such thing as a history of alcohol in Africa. Alcohol's existence and use cannot be separated, not even analytically, from its social conditions and "constructions."

In Ethiopia there is no government policy restricting or regulating the import or consumption of alcoholic beverages except with respect to taxation. Regardless of the federal government's policy of ethno-federalism, which is intended to promote ethnic parity, the expansion and inclusion of alcoholic beverages in a local pattern of cultural valuation have served to rank drinks and drinkers along old political fracture lines of highlander and lowlander. Drinking patterns are perceived as the measure of "being civilized," whether or not this is matched in actual behavior.

In the Maji area, ethnic hierarchies structure alcoholic hegemonism. The culturally dominant townspeople, largely of northern descent, want to have the best of both worlds. Their types of alcoholic drinks, so they say, are the best, and they think they know how to use and not abuse them. In their view the Suri are still caught in their traditional drinking habits of their local *gèso* beer and cannot handle the greater alcoholic strength of *katikala*.

It is in this vein that they comment on the inefficient and sometimes chaotic Surma Council, where heavy drinking inhibits serious policy-making. That the townspeople themselves have commercially introduced *katikala*, supplying it to the Suri, is not mentioned, or at least it does not make them feel in any way responsible for the trouble. They have succeeded in spreading the consumption of the new alcoholic drinks (*t'ädj* and *katikala*) and derive substantial economic gain from it.

This attitude is, as such, an unwitting part of the expanding domain of the state and of the wider Ethiopian society, which still tends to devalue local traditions, including local types of alcohol like the "crude *gèso* beer." Tolerated as part of "Suri culture," *gèso* drinking is looked down upon, ridiculed, and seen as the root cause of alcoholism, despite the fact that it represents a tradition of moderate socially constructed alcohol usage. Suri interpersonal violence is often explained by reference to "their habit of always drinking too much beer." When villagers see the Suri drink there, they often say that "too much money is thrown away again by these people," suggesting that, in contrast to themselves, the Suri cannot drink in a controlled, civilized manner. But Suri beer drinking is not a social pathology, at least no more so than among any other group in the Maji area. What the townspeople do when they speak with disdain about *gèso* beer is make a statement about difference, about social prestige, about the Suri way of life and their solid group behavior.

The introduction of *katikala* has led to a new form of drunkenness and uncontrolled behavior in settings where tensions may easily be triggered. At funerals and dueling places, and also at collective gatherings such as the meeting of the Surma Council, *katikala* is becoming more common, and according to both Suri and other informants leads to heated verbal exchanges and even physical conflicts.

Views on heavy drinking at Surma Council meetings differ. Townspeople see a dereliction of public office in the councilors' regular drinking on the job, whereas in Suri eyes the Surma Council and *katikala* are both northern imports to the area and part and parcel of the town culture that they now engage in politically as well as economically. *Katikala* drinking and council meetings are culturally entwined.

For the townspeople, the Suri's failure to distinguish the demarcation of work and leisure, and public responsibility and social enjoyment, provides all the more evidence that the project of political, and especially cultural, integration of people like the Suri is far from complete. As for the Suri, their enjoyment of alcohol in the Surma Council represents political and cultural integration in Ethiopia's new ethno-federal system.

NOTES

I am very grateful to the bar owners and customers of Maji town and to the Suri women beer producers for their hospitality and willingness to answer questions over the years (1991–1999). I also thank the editors of the journal *Northeast African Studies* for permission to use material from an article published in 1999 as the basis for this chapter.

1. A pioneering collection in this field is Gordon 1978.
2. Muslims are a minority in this area.
3. The Ethiopian People's Revolutionary Democratic Front, which took over power in Ethiopia in May 1991, having emerged from the insurgent movement, the Tigray People's Liberation Front.
4. People from the historic core region of Tigray dominate the present government and are self-conscious about their civilizational status. The program of the EPRDF has also inherited much of the social-revolutionary outlook and rhetoric of the Socialist regime (1974–1991) in matters of "national progress," development and the removal of "harmful customs."
5. In recent years, another party has also presented itself in the local moral discourse on alcohol. Since 1991 Christian missionaries of a Protestant denomination, with both foreign and Ethiopian backgrounds, have settled in the Suri area, where

they have established a school, a medical post and a church and where they do language research and Bible translation. The missionaries reject all forms of alcohol, including the Suri *gèso* beer. Even the socioeconomic role of *gèso* parties in the agricultural process is devalued and rejected, and no Suri or other local person who drinks alcohol may work for them.

6. Amharic terms with no equivalent English words.

7. In the research of Belachew Desta (1977) an average of 6.07 ethyl alcohol percentage was found.

8. Although some restaurants in Addis Ababa have started to serve it.

9. Imported beer or bottled beer from factories elsewhere in Ethiopia is scarce and only available in some bars. It is drunk by the political, educational and civil servant elite only.

10. Locally known as gesho (*Rhamnus prinoides* L'Hérit).

11. When the drink is not yet fermented, it is called *birz*, a kind of honey lemonade.

12. Desta (1977) gives an average alcohol percentage of 13.36.

13. The Dizi term is *muugu*, the Me'en term *sholu*. They refer to the same thick and strong brewed sorghum-maize beer.

14. However, beers somewhat similar to *bordé* or *gèso* are found in the Northern and Central Highlands as well. Among them are *korefé* in the Gondar area, made from barley, and *shaméta* in the Gurage area, which is, however, lighter in alcohol content, made from roasted barley. A nonfermented grain drink is *buk'r*, in the north Shewa, Gondar and Gojjam areas, which has virtually no alcoholic content but is produced from barley, and drunk during religious holidays. These beers are not drunk as food, unlike the *bordé* in Southwest Ethiopia.

15. Which basically refers to being Christian or Muslim.

16. In Belachew Desta's research, the average alcohol percentages of *t'erra-araqé* and the *dagim araqé* were found to be 34 and 47 percent, respectively (Desta 1977).

17. In 1994–95 this was about US$9–11, in 1999 US$6–8.

18. On these occasions the women can sit back, having already done most of the weeding and other work between the work of preparing the fields and harvesting.

19. The same is true for the local *sholu* beer among the related Me'en people (cf. a similar custom among the Iraqw, Rekdal 1996).

REFERENCES

Abbink, J. 1997. "Ethnicity and Constitutionalism in Contemporary Ethiopia." *Journal of African Law* 41 (2): 159–74.

———. 1998. "Violence and Political Discourse among the Chai Suri." In G.J. Dimmendaal (ed.), *Surmic Languages and Cultures*. Cologne: R. Köppe Verlag, 321–44.

Akyeampong, E.K. 1996. *Drink, Power and Cultural Change: A Social History of Alcohol in Ghana, c. 1800 to Recent Times*. Oxford: James Currey; Portsmouth, NH: Heinemann.

Ambler, C.H. 1987. *Alcohol and Disorder in Precolonial Africa*. Working Papers in African Studies, No. 126. Boston: African Studies Center, Boston University.

Cohen, J.M. 1994. "'Ethnic Federalism' in Ethiopia." *Northeast African Studies* N.S. 2 (2): 157–88.

Colson, E., and T. Scudder. 1988. *For Prayer and Profit: The Ritual, Economic and Social Importance of Beer in Gwembe District, Zambia, 1959–1982*. Stanford, CA: Stanford University Press.

Crush, J., and C.H. Ambler. 1992. *Liquor and Labor in Southern Africa*. Athens: Ohio University Press.

Desta, B. 1977. "A Survey of the Alcoholic Content of Traditional Beverages." *Ethiopian Medical Journal* 15: 65–68.

Diduk, S. 1993. "European Alcohol, History and the State in Cameroon." *African Studies Review* 36 (1): 1–42.

Douglas, M. (ed.). 1987. *Constructive Drinking: Perspectives on Drink from Anthropology*. Cambridge: Cambridge University Press.

Ethiopia. Central Statistical Authority. 1996. *The 1994 Population and Housing Census of Ethiopia: Results for Southern Nations, Nationalities and Peoples*. Vol. 1. Statistical Report, Part 1. Addis Ababa: CSA.

———. Ethiopian Nutrition Institute. 1980. *Ethiopian Traditional Recipes*. Addis Ababa: ENI.

Glazer, I.M. 1997. "Alcohol and Politics in Urban Zambia: The Intersection of Gender and Class." In G. Mikell (ed.), *African Feminism: The Politics of Survival in Sub-Saharan Africa*. Philadelphia: University of Pennsylvania Press, 142–58.

Gordon, A.B. (ed.). 1978. *Ethnicity and Alcohol*. Special issue of *Medical Anthropology* 2 (4): 1–155.

Heald, S. 1986. "Mafias in Africa: The Rise of Drinking Companies and Vigilante Groups in Bugisu District, Uganda." *Africa* 56 (4): 446–67.

Heath, D.B. 1987. "Ethnicity and Alcohol Use." *Medical Anthropology* 2 (4): 1–155.

Hutchinson, S.E. 1996. *Nuer Dilemmas: Coping with Money, War and the State*. Berkeley and Los Angeles: University of California Press.

Karp, I. 1980. "Beer Drinking and Social Experience in an African Society: An Essay in Formal Sociology." In I. Karp and C.S. Bird (eds.), *Explorations in African Systems of Thought*. Bloomington: Indiana University Press, 83–119.

Molamu, L., and Kebede Gessesse. 1988. *Alcohol and Alcoholism in Africa: A Bibliography*. Gaborone: University College of Botswana, National Institute of Development Research and Documentation Unit (NIR).

Molamu, L., and W.G. Manyeneng. 1988. *Alcohol Use and Abuse in Botswana: Report of a Study*. Gaborone: Health Education Unit.

Partanen, J. 1991. *Sociability and Intoxication: Alcohol and Drinking in Kenya, Africa and the Modern World*. Helsinki: Finnish Foundation for Alcohol Studies.

Rekdal, O.B. 1996. "Money, Milk and Sorghum Beer: Change and Continuity among the Iraqw of Tanzania." *Africa* 66: 367–85.

Rocha-Silva, L., S. de Miranda, and R. Erasmus. 1996. *Alcohol, Tobacco and Other Drug Use among Black Youth*. Pretoria: HSRC, 1996.

Siiskonen, H. 1994. "Namibia and the Heritage of Colonial Alcohol Policy." *Nordic Journal of African Studies* 3 (1): 77–87.

9

Democracy's Heady Brew

Cashew Wine and the Authority of the Elders among the Balanta in Guinea-Bissau

Roy van der Drift

Guinea-Bissau is a small country[1] on the West African Upper-Guinea coast that gained its independence from Portugal in 1974. It is now considered one of the poorest countries in the world, with an estimated 87 percent of the population having access to less than US$1 per day.[2] After independence, Guinea-Bissau's export production performance has been disappointing, measuring only 25 percent of the value of its imports between 1975 and 1980 (Poelhekke 1980). During colonialism, groundnuts were the major export crop, but they gradually lost their potential due to, among other factors, soil erosion.

Since the mid-1980s, however, a new export product has made spectacular gains. Between 1986 and 1996, cashew nut exports increased from 200 tons to 26,500 tons annually, and the new cashew plantations have yet to mature to reach their maximum productivity.[3] Currently cashew nuts comprise 85 percent of Guinea-Bissau's total exports. The country ranks third among the world's cashew producers after India and Brazil and is the prime exporter of raw cashew nuts. Cashew planting is expanding yearly by 22 percent. In 1996, 25 percent of the total area (103,000 hectares) used for agriculture was occupied by cashew plantations. Most cashews are grown by small farmers (88,000 hectares), whereas the relatively large-scale plantations run by *ponteiros* (registered agricultural entrepreneurs) comprise only 15,000 hectares.

Apart from the commercial value of cashew nuts, the cashew tree produces a small pear-shaped fruit that can be used for making alcoholic beverages, both fermented wine and distilled liquor. In Guinea-Bissau, the expansion of cashew nut production has been accompanied by a more or less parallel increase in alcohol production.[4] This alcohol is mainly sold on the domestic market, and the country has seen a significant increase in domestic alcohol consumption.

My hypothesis is that the alcohol by-product is a main stimulus for cashew expansion. Alcohol is a product with considerable value in various local societies within Guinea-Bissau. Its increased consumption as a societal phenomenon in Guinea-Bissau should not be mistaken for a sign of misery, poverty or anomie.[5] It is related to a social order that is adapting to various changes, not least its success on the world market.

This chapter presents a case study of Balanta society.[6] The Balanta constitute one of the largest ethnic groups in Guinea-Bissau, accounting for 25 percent of the national population. Of old, they were known as mangrove rice farmers, producing surpluses for export in colonial times. From the 1960s onwards, many Balanta engaged in new activities outside their villages. Balanta constituted the majority of the people who joined the *Luta de Libertação,* the armed struggle, led by the PAIGC,[7] against Portuguese colonialism (1962–1974). After the war, urban migration, petty trade and, since the mid-1980s, cashew production have become important "modern" economic activities.

Along with these changes, local power relations shifted. Male elders continued to dominate traditional mangrove rice farming at a village and family level, whereas other economic activities were pursued primarily by youth and women. Through labor migration and petty trade, many of the youth reached a certain economic autonomy vis-à-vis their elders.

Nonetheless, Balanta villages and extended families still have a very high degree of internal cohesion, and elders occupy an important position. In the wider context of Guinea-Bissau, the Balanta are perceived to be conservative and closed to external influences, maintaining their traditions in various domains. This is a group of people who are creatively combining being successful on the world market with maintaining their local identity and customs. This chapter considers the important role alcohol is playing in this dynamic process.

I wish to distance myself from pejorative images, as well as from moralistic judgments, which are too often and too easily related to alcohol consumption. Any reader who wishes to draw observations or conclusions of this kind does so on his or her own responsibility. Cheers!

EARLY IN THE MORNING . . .

Tchosso Sanya, born in the village of Foia,[8] is twenty years old. Foia is a large village, situated in an impressive forest on a plateau surrounded by extended *bolanhas* (rice paddies) in the southern region of Quinará. Tchosso is the only salaried worker in the village; he works in the small *taberna* (shop) of Bian Blatta, the local trader. Tchosso is living on his father's compound. In the dark, just before dawn, some men have gathered in front of the door of his bedroom. They are somewhat tipsy. Starting at around four o'clock that morning, these men met to discuss a wedding that would take place within the next month. The future groom brought five liters of *cana de bordão*[9] to the family of his promised one. *"Tchosso, binte! Winni sida!"* ("Tchosso, come out, give us liquor"). Reluctantly, Tchosso appears and makes his way to Bian's shop. The shop, consisting of one room with a small counter, exudes the heavy alcoholic smell of *cana*, stored in 200-liter oil drums. The counter is filled with small glasses, funnels and measuring cups. On a shelf some boxes of matches, cigarettes, and bottles of vegetable oil represent the rest of the shop's merchandise. After buying a liter of *cana de bordão*, the men sit comfortably on the grass underneath a huge *poilão* (silk-cotton tree) outside Bian's compound. I am invited to join them. Inhaling the fresh, tickling morning air, I sit down, knowing what is about to happen. . . .

Selu, a younger man who appears to be the one who bought the *cana*, is appointed to be distributor. Our one and only glass consists of an empty tomato-paste tin. Against our western protocols, Selu is the first to drink, which is called *tira colaude* ("draw out death"), to show that the liquor he offers will not harm anyone. Then, he fills the small tin carefully and, following the hierarchy of age, starts to serve every man in turn. Every time, the tin is carefully presented with the right hand accompanied by some fingers of the left hand, while Selu bows slightly to the older men. The recipient accepts the tin with a serious nod, and purposely spills some drops on the ground "for the ancestors." Another man puts some drops of *cana* on the amulet he is wearing around his neck. The tin is generally emptied in one sip, with a serious expression on the face, followed by a groan and loud spitting on the ground. In spite of the relaxed situation we are in, drinking is a highly serious matter that needs a "strong head." Unlike youth, older people are generally considered to have "strong heads" such that they have a leadership and perhaps even a guardian role in the proceedings of these drinking sessions.

After the first liter, the morning freshness is gradually substituted for a blurring haze. *"Roy, winni sida"* ("give us liquor"). For the older men it is totally acceptable to insist that a young person (I was thirty years old, which is considered very junior by Balanta standards) arrange the procurement of more liquor.

After the third liter, the conversation is lively. A standard joke is pretending to have had enough to drink. In the end, everyone reaches a consumption level of about one liter per capita, resulting in a condition which the Balanta call *momsida*, literally "full with liquor." Some of the old men fall asleep in the grass. With glazed eyes, I stare at the colorful motion-picture I find myself in. . . .

OLD MEN

Balanta society is organized on the basis of patrilineality and virilocality, yet it has often been characterized as egalitarian, horizontal and even anarchistic. The Balanta are considered to be a difficult group to approach by outsiders because they do not have visible well-marked leadership. In colonial times, this resulted in the installation of artificial paramount chiefs by the Portuguese administration.

Contrary to appearances, leadership and authority are very much present and sometimes even quite rigid in Balanta social structure. The main basis for leadership and hierarchy is age. Age is defined in terms of membership in socially constructed age-groups instead of chronological years. Both men and women have their subsequent age categories. Giving birth to their first child, rather than marriage per se, confers an adult status on women. Men reach their adult status after the male circumcision initiation *fô* or *fanado*.[10] Until now, the *fô* has been considered to be the main ritual in Balanta society. It is organized every eight to nine years at a village level, but certain relatives from outside are also allowed to participate. The initiates are men of approximately thirty to thirty-five years of age, who are circumcised, then isolated for a period of over two months and given numerous lessons and secrets by the oldest men. After the *fô*, a man is considered a *lante n'dang*, an adult man, and he is allowed to wear the *bareta vermelha*, a red hood,[11] which is proudly used when men are traveling and during important ceremonies.

Within the general category of *belante bindang*, age-groups are divided on the basis of initiation cohorts. Members of the oldest living initiation cohort are the real elders, in charge of public authority. Older women, although excluded from the political meetings of the men, notably exercise a kind of hidden power, which may be even more decisive than male authority, especially in times of crisis, as illustrated by the example of the *yangue yangue*, discussed later in this chapter. Their power is exerted in intimate rather than public spheres and mainly through silence rather than words. Nonetheless, the old men are considered to wield the levers of economic and ritual power within an agrarian pattern of livelihood.

MANAGERS OF PRODUCTION

Traditionally, the Balanta in Guinea-Bissau were known as rice producers.[12] They grew rice in paddies, situated in mangrove areas. During the rainy season (June–September, with an average rainfall of between 1,500 and 2,500 mm), the fields were prepared and rice was sown and subsequently transplanted. Construction and maintenance of dams and dikes, often near the sea or brackish estuaries and creeks, was a complex and essential aspect of this system. Mangrove rice farming was particularly productive and ecologically sustainable, requiring specialized knowledge and experience, as well as strict organization and intensive mobilization of labor at temporary intervals. Moreover, various agricultural activities, notably ploughing and harvesting, were considered to be hard physical work.

The village served as a more or less autonomous organizational unit.[13] The first clearing and construction of the main dike, a *bolanha*, was organized at the village level under the authority of the male elders. Public authority was in the hands of male family elders who made up the council of village elders.

A Balanta village generally consists of a number of patrilineal family compounds, *moranças*, which can consist of up to ten or even twenty houses. Formally, the male *morança* elder was in charge of most socioeconomic and religious affairs. Rice production was organized on a *morança* level in terms of land distribution, labor mobilization, production and harvest management. The male elders of the *morança* kept the rice in huge clay pots and were in charge of its distribution according to daily consumption needs as well as ritual obligations.

In the past, the Balanta were known to exchange or sell their surplus in rice or other food crops to neighboring groups and traders. Mangrove rice farming went through a huge expansion at the end of the nineteenth century. This was instigated by massive migration of Balanta to the southern regions of Quinará and Tombali, which offered agriculturally suitable mangrove areas that had not been previously exploited. The Balanta migration was stimulated by entrepreneurs, *ponteiros*.[14] From the 1930s up to the late 1950s, the *arroz de bolanha*[15] of the Balanta was exported.[16] Thus during the colonial period, mangrove rice farming was based on tight local organization, while at the same time being connected to the outside world. Family and village elders managed commercial contacts, as they were in charge of the land, labor, harvest and stocks.

For several reasons, the mangrove rice system in Guinea-Bissau declined rapidly from the 1960s onwards, and the country turned from being a rice exporter to increasing dependence on rice imports. A number of social and political factors contributed to the "mangrove crisis." The Liberation War against Portuguese colonialism from 1962 to 1974 played a major part. The extensive guerrilla war reduced the agricultural labor force. The Portuguese strategically destroyed *bolanha* infrastructure of dikes and dams. In the process, producers ran out of stocks such as seeds. Apart from the war there were forces arising from the government's changing economic policy, starting in colonial days, when the degraded administration began to replace "free" *ponteiros* with state-controlled *centros comerciais*. After independence, the Guinean government continued the state control of marketing.

At the same time, important changes were taking place within the local organization of mangrove rice farming. The village and extended family (*morança*) gradually lost their importance as production units. Younger adult men, women and youngsters achieved greater freedom of economic movement, not only as individual rice farmers, but also through engaging in new activities involving labor migration, petty trade and the production of other crops. This had negative consequences for the organization of labor in mangrove rice farming and helps to explain why numerous development projects in the late 1970s and 1980s directed at reconstructing dams and dikes in *bolanhas* never had any positive impact.[17]

The dramatic decrease in rice production was interpreted by outsiders as an illustration of the fact that Balanta society was falling apart and that they could not live without their *bolanha.*[18] At the same time, however, the Balanta were actively participating in the spectacular increase of agricultural production that, since the second half of the 1980s, has taken the form of cashew production. A closer look at Balanta society shows that it is as coherent as ever, indeed maybe even more so.

THE CASHEW BONANZA: SELLING YOUR CROP AND DRINKING IT TOO

The village of Foia is situated in a splendid environment, a lush forest of enormous trees, such as the silk-cotton tree and the baobab. Nowadays, planted within the natural flora are numerous cultivated fruit trees, notably mango and cashew. They are situated in small concentrations within the *hortas* (plantations). During the period from March to June, most of the women spend their time picking cashew and squeezing the fruits. The massive presence of cashew trees and the wealth of nuts, representing the money and rice they can purchase, and juice for making alcohol are striking to older people in Foia, who contrast the situation with the old days when they used to live on what the forest offered them.

Cashew is believed to have been introduced into Guinea-Bissau by Portuguese traders and agricultural entrepreneurs during the 1930s. Until independence in 1974, cashew planting was relatively rare and limited to private plantations. In a village like Foia, the majority of the Balanta had neither access to nor interest in cashew. Some entrepreneurs, representing other ethnic groups, had their *hortas* in the village. After independence, the majority of the agricultural entrepreneurs lost their positions and/or abandoned trading because of the socialist economic model the Guinean government adopted. The PAIGC administration stimulated cashew planting, for commercial reasons as well as for soil regeneration (Cornelis 1997).

From the second half of the 1980s onwards, cashew development expanded rapidly, on the basis of economic liberalization policies. The Guinea-Bissau government, confident of its cashew exporting capability, entered into a contract with India for the exchange of cashew for rice. Between 1985 and 1996, the area occupied by cashew increased by 22 percent annually. The expectations for the near future are that production will continue to rise in the same striking manner.

Cashew has become extremely attractive for traders, who invade the countryside during the months of March, April and May—the *campanha do cajú*—for the purchase of cashew nuts, which they very often exchange for imported rice.[19] The market greatly favors the cashew producers, who can sell their produce practically on their doorstep.

A cashew nut grows within a fruit. The nut/fruit weight ratio is one to nine. The fruit is very tasty and has a high vitamin C content.[20] Every 100 kilograms of fruits can be turned into 65 liters of juice, and within two days the alcohol content of the fermented juice is 6 percent. Two hundred liters of cashew juice can be distilled into 30–35 liters of *cana* (with a 30 percent alcohol content).

Meanwhile, the attraction of cashew juice and its transformation into alcoholic beverages became integral to local Balanta communities. Traditionally the Balanta were not involved in any alcohol production. The only authentic alcoholic beverage among them is fermented honey. It was women and young men, especially migrants or petty traders, who introduced the techniques of fermenting, conserving and distilling cashew wine and liquor that they had gained familiarity with elsewhere.

The actual production of cashew fruits is spectacular, totaling an estimated 360,000 metric tons per annum, a national average of 250 kilograms per capita. In turn the fruit is transformed into an estimated 130 million liters of juice.[21] During the cashew season from March to June, village life is characterized by vast consumption of fruits, juice and wine. Women with containers[22] tend to stock as much as they can, with a major objective being to transform it into *cana*. Young men do the cashew distilling, for which they use two old oil drums and a copper tube. This *cana* is sold at markets, inside and outside the village. In Foia, the major part of the *cana* does not leave the village. In addition to being sold, it is used to hire labor and, last but not least, it is kept for ritual purposes.

Cashew is an "easy" crop. After clearing a plot and planting cashew, it requires little care. The canopy of cashew leaves is so thick that grasses and weeds hardly sprout beneath a cashew tree. Harvesting is a matter of simply picking up the fruit and nuts that have fallen from the trees. The bulk of the labor invested in cashew production (58 percent) consists of squeezing the fruit. Cashew is the highest yielding crop in terms of a day's earnings. Women who harvest and squeeze fruits have an average daily earning of CFA Franc 1,956.[23] The daily income in terms of nuts is estimated at CFA Franc 5,860. In comparison, the value of a day's work on the *bolanha* is estimated at CFA Franc 1,140 (Camara and Vayssié 1996; Cornelis 1997).

Cashew liquor is often bartered for hiring labor, notably for rice production. But beyond monetary valuation and trade, these alcoholic beverages are considered a vital component for all kinds of social occasions and meetings and for the reception of guests. *Cana* also has an extremely important ritual value.

The economic impact of cashew production is profound. New forms of income generation and a new division of income have been introduced. Men, who are generally the owners of the cashew trees, receive the nuts. Most are exchanged for rice and consumed by the household. Women have obtained a new and important source of income through the production of cashew wine and *cana*. A significant part of this income source ends up being consumed locally.

LORDS OF CONSUMPTION

During my fieldwork in 1988–1990,[24] I was initially struck by the fact that old men were complaining that their children no longer respected their authority and did not contribute to work on the family *bolanha*. At the same time, I did not notice any visible conflict. The old men generally were not wealthy and some appeared very poor, but, nonetheless, they seemed to be quite satisfied. I found an answer to these contradictory observations in the execution of their *ritual* power.

The principle of ritual power among the Balanta is that elders, both male and female, have exclusive access to and communication with the ancestral spirits (*wule*). Ancestral spirits are considered to be protectors, but at the same time they need to be respected, otherwise they may turn against living persons. As such, the elders have the keys to protection, but also have the potential to bend the ancestors' supernatural powers to produce a negative or even lethal outcome.

The major part of ceremonies is related to assuaging ancestors, and it is the task of the living elders to supervise all ceremonies in order to safeguard a proper execution, not only in terms of ritual procedures, but also, and especially, in terms of material investments.

Six-thirty in the morning. The entire night, the *bombolong*[25] has sounded from the *morança* of the Amara family. The oldest man of the family died late in the afternoon, and today the funeral will take place. I arrive in the compound and see the villagers, who are already present in considerable numbers. They are grouped according to age and gender. The male elders sit together near the house of the deceased. One of their responsibilities is to construct the stretcher used to carry the corpse later in the afternoon to the burial site.

My assistant explains that the *belante bindang* are waiting for a first "payment" before doing this job. Soon, a son of the deceased appears with a liter of *cana*. The old men look critically at the bottle and one of them checks its quality. After his approval, the *cana* is quickly consumed. During that morning it appears that this "payment" is part of a huge quantity of *cana* brought by numerous relatives and neighbors. The elders supervise, control, criticize, taste and divide all alcoholic contributions brought in. As is usual, cows and pigs are slaughtered as well, and a huge quantity of rice is prepared. But, as someone tells me during this occasion, "It is as if alcohol has become the main item in our ceremonies."

Alcohol has always played a very important role in Balanta ritual life. It was one of the standard items in the ritual "package," together with rice, meat, loincloths and tobacco. Traditionally, however, alcohol for ritual purposes was mainly exchanged or bought, as local alcohol production hardly existed. There are four main differences between what my informants called the old days and the current situation. First, alcohol has become extremely important in a *quantitative* sense. Second, an increasing part of the alcohol is produced by the people themselves. Third, those who contribute are younger men and women following their elders' directives. Finally, drinking is no longer taboo for young people.[26] Nowadays, everybody is entitled to drink, whereas before consumption was restricted to a small, privileged group of old people. There is a happy coincidence in the fact that the traditional season for organized ceremonies, such as weddings, initiations and mourning ceremonies (May–June), coincides with the cashew harvest (March–June) so that the financial and alcoholic requirements to meet ritual expenditures are on hand.

What is most significant about the changes over time is that the elders, who formerly produced rice surpluses needed for ceremonies, are now managing the ritual investment (and consumption) of the produce of others, thereby obliging women and younger men to invest their income, or the concrete source of their income, that is, liquor. They formulate and reformulate rules and tariffs, and if necessary force people to meet their ritual obligations.

One morning I was called by Péu, a forty-five-year-old man, whom I considered one of my friends in the village. Just the day before, Péu had organized the funeral and mourning ceremony for the oldest man of his compound. It was a ceremony like many I had already witnessed involving a huge potlatch of cattle, rice and alcohol, consumed by a large number of people. The *belante bindang* had occupied their usual position in the "midfield," closely observing everything that happened. The next morning, Péu stood trembling before me. "The *belante bindang* are threatening me. Yesterday, they insisted that more *cana* was offered, but we had completely run out of stock. I told them that this was all we had. We served 200 liters I had gathered with the women of our *morança*, and I borrowed an additional 30 liters from some of my aunts! At night, demons were flying through my bedroom. I know they were sent by the old men. They are actually killing me!" He was looking for money right now and needed about US$200 for a very important protection ritual. It would be performed by a Fula *muru* (an Islamic healer) in the capital, Bissau, who dispensed a *mezinhu* (amulet). I knew Péu quite well and I was convinced that he did not have any intention of manipulating me for financial gain. Later on, Péu eventually bought his amulet and was greatly relieved. Two years later he died and people in the village, remembering the incident, remarked that Péu had been unable to resist the "power of the ancestors."

A man in the village of Foia, commenting on the authority of the elders, once told me, "*Unicu cusa cu ilis ta manda nel, i so cusa di cume.*" This translates as "The only thing they rule is consumption." In effect, the elders were no longer seen as "managers of production" but as "lords of consumption," with a certain negative connotation.

In the Balanta perception of life, it is totally acceptable, even desirable, to ostentatiously display, destroy or consume one's wealth during a mourning ceremony, especially when the deceased in question is an elder. This is in marked distinction from "normal life," when it is considered dangerous to reveal your wealth. In this respect, the Balanta are highly egalitarian. A person who has enriched him/herself individually should hide this wealth, otherwise s/he can be forced to share it or may become a victim of witchcraft. The Balanta generally hide their savings or invest them in prestige goods that do not serve as an individual indulgence. This is the case with cattle. There is a heavy taboo on selling cattle. Individual cattle owners pool their cattle at the level of the *morança*, for big mourning ceremonies. Family and even clan elders supervise the cattle and make sure that no one removes a cow for individual use.

Bringing family wealth out into the open, for example for a mourning ceremony, is considered to be a *legitimate* demonstration of the *faye*, that is, the labor power of the family. Such displays do not result in jealousy because after the display of family wealth everybody joins in consuming it. As such, a potlatch of this kind serves the *witma*, that is, the reputation of the family, as well as appeasing the spiritual world of the deceased.

But the social balance of egalitarianism may be becoming destabilized, tipping in favor of the elders at the expense of more youthful members of the Balanta society. The ritual investment of alcohol has increased and is still increasing. The source of this investment is the labor of younger men and women who are producing alcohol from cashew, and who are obliged to follow rigid rules related to the consumption of alcohol at funerals and mourning ceremonies. The increasing engagement in cashew production has a very significant commercial dimension, in effect an obligation to produce for ritual investment. During my research it became abundantly clear that alcohol plays an extremely important role in the maintenance of family relations and community networks. In the process of the continuous reinforcement of alcoholic obligations with the growth of cashew production, the elders are putting escalating strain on the producers.

The tragic case of Péu demonstrates that elders can use their ritual power, that is, their access to ancestral spirits, to coerce others. The negative use of ancestral spirits may be called witchcraft or, in Crioulo, *contrato cu irão* (a contract with a spirit). The Balanta notion of witchcraft can be literally translated as "eating one's soul," or "eating your companion," implying that the person who has closed the contract with the spirit is getting stronger at the expense of the contractee. Resentment and criticism are beginning to surface. The "lords of consumption" may be pushing their luck.[27]

A FEMALE RESPONSE TO THE RITUAL POWER OF THE ELDERS

In 1984 a young Balanta woman near the southern regional capital of Catió revealed that she was called by God, referred to as N'Ghala in Balanta.[28] Within a short period of time, this woman amassed a huge following of Balanta women. They were called *Yangue yangue.*[29] During the first phase of this spontaneous movement, it was unclear to nonfollowers inside and outside Balanta society what was going on. The "white women," so-called because of the dress they adopted, were insular in manner and were believed to be possessed by N'Ghala. They spoke an inaccessible language and started writing in an Arabic-like script. At the same time, their mounting numbers, which had started to include young men as well, began to worry the national government, which feared an ethnic uprising.[30]

Over time, instead of being a threat to national security, *Yangue yangue* followers started to express a high degree of discontent about their own Balanta society. At first this took a spontaneous form, gradually becoming a well-enunciated reform program. The *Yangue yangue* opposed the authority of the elders in various ways. Ancestral shrines were violently attacked, Balanta elders were accused of witchcraft, and a number of criticisms were leveled against the ritual power of the elders by N'Tombikte, the founder of *Yangue yangue,* which culminated in the formulation of fifteen commandments. These included calls for all ancestral spirits and shrines to be abolished; all practices connected with witchcraft to be stopped; people to stop slaughtering all the cows of a deceased person; slit-drums to remain silent during a mourning ceremony; no red clothes to be worn or red foods to be eaten; and the prohibition of pork and alcohol consumption at funerals.

Women and young men were openly demonstrating their discontent and making efforts, maybe not to topple the elders, but to "soften" their powerful influence. The presence of ancestral shrines as such was not criticized; rather it was the way they were misused and their links to witchcraft that were rejected.

What the *Yangue yangue* attacked was the elders' shift of power from production to ceremony, from working to eating and, increasingly, drinking. The major threat that the *Yangue yangue* highlighted was the consumptive way that this ritual power was being maintained by means of "eating one's companion," consuming his/her income.

More than ten years after the rise of *Yangue yangue*, it appears that the movement has failed to abolish alcohol and expensive ceremonies. On the other hand, *Yangue yangue*, as an expression of discontent, had a liberating effect, sparking group solidarity among women and youth, in an ongoing process of democratization.

DEMOCRATIZATION AND THE FREEDOM TO DRINK

After independence, Guinea-Bissau was ruled by the sole and legitimate party, the PAIGC, the former liberation movement. In 1994 the country held its first multiparty elections, which did not overturn the existing order. The PAIGC and President João Bernardo "Nino" Vieira were popularly elected to remain in power. The word "democracy" entered the Guinean grammar, both at official national and local village levels.

Terms like "democracy" and especially "multiparty system" were legitimized and ceased to be synonymous with "subversion." The word "democracy" was absorbed into the local vocabulary, used to denote new developments within the village which had become accepted, as opposed to previously being socially disapproved. Generally, this has to do with today's youth, who are claiming and achieving a higher degree of freedom of movement and new habits.

When I did my fieldwork in 1988–1992, I heard old men in Foia complain about their sons, who were not willing to help them in the rice fields. However, very few conflicts arose. They feared the encroaching new world popularly known as "democracy," but at the same time reluctantly admitted that it was *bon ton* to accept it.

More recently (1996–1998), I paid several visits to my former research area in Quinar, often for special occasions like funerals and mourning ceremonies. The amounts of alcohol distributed and consumed during these occasions were even more excessive than during my earlier residence in the area. Strikingly, the young men and women were much more involved in the festivities. Young people had clearly obtained the right to participate in a less subordinate way. They brought their own food and drinks and behaved as they liked. This included being dressed in fancy, erotic clothes, and dancing to modern and very loud music from boom boxes. This behavior was accepted by elders, sometimes with a certain fatalism:

> It's a new world coming in. This is normal for every young generation. But today's youth are getting too loose, and they are supported by democracy. We know that their heads are still too weak to cope with it. But what can we do? You are a white man, you seem to know the advantages of democracy.

The democracy dilemma came to a dramatic climax at the national level on June 7, 1998, when a group of soldiers, mostly *antigos combatentes* associated with the country's earlier liberation war, led by the former head of the armed forces, Brigdeiro Ansumane Mane, took over the main military bases in the capital of Bissau. Known as the *Junta Militar*, they accused President Vieira of abusing power and of corruption, and demanded a fair system or at least fair functioning of the system. In one of their radio communiqués, they stated: "*Camarada* Presidente Nino was our brother during the Liberation War. Since he was democratically elected, he is no longer the good old Nino we knew. He has become a dictator."

The Vieira administration reacted furiously, stating, "We are democratically elected." The government's refusal to negotiate with "bandits" and the junta's determination to bring about change with their slogan, *hora tchiga* (the time has come), led to fierce conflict, with tens of thousands of people fleeing the capital, massive physical destruction, and an unknown number of fatalities. The international community supported the "democratic" government by sending troops to fight an enemy which, within a week, consisted of almost the entire Guinean army largely supported by the population.

At one level, these violent events markedly contrast with the convivial village drinking events I have described above. At another level both are riddled with ambiguous, layered meaning that is difficult to interpret. Changing rules and habits concerning alcohol consumption in Balanta society, as I have argued, demonstrate local dynamics that represent and facilitate integration of various categories of people within a local community embedded in wider global processes. The resultant drinking patterns may be understood as the "fuel" for maintaining social relations in a local, cohesive, agrarian community successfully competing on the world market, rather than as a manifestation of a disoriented rural society that has lost its way in a globalizing world.[31] On the other hand, current alcohol consumption is seen by some as excessive and a point of contestation with "oppressive" forces within Balanta society.

Certainly, in several respects, the "democratization" of alcohol consumption parallels the "democracy dilemma" so vividly displayed in the recent coup. Older people return to the basic idea behind the traditional taboo on alcohol consumption: drinking needs a "strong head," meaning one has to be aware of one's responsibilities. The same counts for having the right to express one's opinions. More and more people in Balanta society state that democracy easily leads to "confusion," and the word itself has gained this connotation. The opponents of the Vieira administration go further and state that "democracy" leads to dictatorship.

As such, local Balanta notions of power, democracy and alcohol show striking similarity. As concepts, they are all under continuous reevaluation in this period of rapid change. Currently, there is a growing consensus in which they are seen as privileges that are better handled by people who know how to deal with them, those who know not only their rights—like the "dictator" who shouts, "I am democratically elected!"—but also their responsibilities.

NOTES

I wish to express my gratitude to Dr. Julieta Barbosa, researcher at the National Research Institute of Guinea-Bissau (INEP), and Jan Cornelis, agronomist, for their constructive comments on this chapter.

1. 36,125 square kilometers.

2. *The Economist*, August 1997. Obviously figures of this nature may only be considered as an indication of the country's economic situation. A great deal of income and consumption is not included in official statistics.

3. All statistics on cashew in this chapter are derived from Camara and Vayssié 1996.

4. In the eastern region of the country, where the population is predominantly Islamic, alcohol production from cashew fruits is marginal. The cashew territory in the east is 23,500 hectares (1996), but has been expanding rapidly since 1985 (34 percent a year).

5. See Douglas (1987). Obviously in Guinea-Bissau, and especially in the capital, Bissau, the alcohol consumption of some people is related to poverty, unemployment and/or plain alcoholism. Until now, hardly any research has been done on this subject. I am examining the wider phenomenon of a general increase in alcohol consumption throughout society.

6. It is partly based on my Ph.D. research (1988–1992) among the Balanta Brassa, the largest subcategory of the Balanta in Guinea-Bissau.

7. *Partido Africano para a Independência da Guinée do Cabo Verde* (African Party for the Independence of [Portuguese] Guinea and Cape Verde).

8. Foia consists of fifty family compounds. The permanent population was estimated at 1,500 people in 1990, with an additional 300 migrants.

9. This distilled drink, made from sugarcane, is considered the "Black Label" of local liquors in Guinea-Bissau.

10. *Fô* is a Balanta Brassa term, otherwise known as *fanado* in Guinea-Bissau's national language of Crioulo.

11. This hood was introduced by the Portuguese, and probably traditionally was used by fishermen. Somewhere in history, the Balanta integrated this item into their tradition as a main sign of male adult status. Hoods are still imported from Portugal.

12. According to Portères (1950), the authentic mangrove rice variety of West Africa (*Oryza glaberrima*) originated from the Senegambia. According to Handem (1986), Balanta, coming from the east, started to inhabit the coastal zone of Guinea-Bissau from the fifteenth century onwards, where they started to produce mangrove rice.

13. It is important to note that certain social relationships pass the geographical limits of the village. This is related to the fact that Balanta villages are exogamous, and to the historical migratory movements, notably migration from the central region of Oio to the southern regions of Quinará and Tombali from the 1890s onward.

14. Generally, a *ponteiro* can be defined as a plantation owner. Historically, *ponteiros* were also traders and, eventually, had their main interest in trade, that is, buying up local produce and selling imported articles. The earliest *ponteiros* were Portuguese or Cape Verdean people who reoriented their interests after the abolition of the slave trade. Later on, their example was followed by Guineans.

15. Rice of the *bolanha* is mangrove rice.

16. It is impossible to find correct or reliable statistics on rice exports during the colonial period because of the competition between official Portuguese trade and private entrepreneurs who found it more profitable to "smuggle" rice to other European traders.

17. Since the early 1990s, an impressive revival of mangrove rice production has been taking place, with new principles of labor organization based on individual entrepreneurs and their employment. Although alcohol plays an important role in the mobilization of wage labor, the space limitations of this chapter do not permit greater elaboration. However, according to official figures, rice production is increasing by 1.4 percent per annum, lagging behind a population growth of 2.3 percent. Moreover, demand for rice is increasing because of the diminishing production of other grains (maize, millet, sorghum) as a result of the territorial expansion of cashew.

18. Various publications from the late colonial period onwards show a tendency to describe the Balanta as conservative, traditional "noble savages" who are intimately, exclusively and definitely linked with their *bolanha*. In my opinion, there have been political and ideological reasons for this false, one-sided picture, among them the fact that the Balanta played, and have continued to play, an important role as the country's main rice producer. Examples of this are Valoura 1970, Hochet 1979, Sidersky 1982, and van der Ploeg and van der Slobbe 1988.

19. It is often said that this cashew-rice trade has had a devastating influence on mangrove rice farming. On the basis of various studies I carried out in Guinea-Bissau, this is contestable (van der Drift 1992; van der Drift and Viegas 1997).

20. 40–600 mg compared to 10–180 mg in mangoes and 35–80 mg in oranges.

21. According to Camara and Vayssié (1996), about 30 percent of the fruit is lost and 5 percent is consumed. Thus, about 65 percent or 216 metric tons remains, on the basis of which 129.6 million liters of juice are made.

22. Generally, 200-liter oil drums are used for this purpose.

23. 100 CFA = 1 French franc.

24. I spent nearly two years in the village of Foia in southern Guinea-Bissau, which allowed me to witness daily life intensively over a long period of time (van der Drift 1992).

25. This is a wooden slit-drum traditionally used by the Balanta as a means of communication. A small version is used for general messages, whereas the bigger model (normally two drums at a time) is used during the *oca tchur*, that is, the mourning ceremony for a relatively old person.

26. In the former perception, one had to be *capable* of drinking, and strong enough to deal with the effects of it. This quality was considered to be "in the head," and thus only old people, who had obtained a "big" or a "strong" head over the years, were considered to be able to drink alcohol. Young people might "lose," "waste" or "open" their "weak" heads by drinking alcohol.

27. Comparable cases of increasing ritual power resulting in rigid control of material resources can be found in Dupré, *Un ordre et sa destruction* (Paris: ORSTOM, 1982), and van der Klei, *De expansie van de Diola* (Amsterdam: Free University, 1994).

28. My discussion of the *Yangue yangue* in this chapter is limited to the theme of alcohol. A wide variety of interesting aspects remain undiscussed.

29. According to N'Tombikte, the founder of the movement, it was N'Ghala (God) who told her to change her name to *Yangue yangue* (the shadow). Later on, this name was given to all her followers (De Jong 1987).

30. The Balanta were the main contributors to the Liberation War, but their contribution was not acknowledged afterwards in terms of political influence and economic investments. The vice-president in that period, a Balanta called Paulo Correira, was sentenced to death and executed in 1986 because of an alleged coup d'état plot.

31. I do not wish to be accused of overlooking the negative aspects of alcohol consumption in Guinea-Bissau in a positive way. It is important to research and develop public policies (van der Drift 1992) regarding

- the medical consequences of alcohol consumption on the countryside, notably in Biombo, the region with the highest production of cashew (alcohol) per capita and a high rate of alcohol consumption (see van der Drift and Mamadú 1997; van der Drift and Viegas 1997);
- the chemical implications of spontaneous and "primitive" liquor distillation;
- hygienic aspects of production and storage of cashew wine in used oil drums;
- alcohol consumption among youth in the rapidly growing but economically stagnating capital of Bissau.

REFERENCES

Camara, M., and J. Vayssié. 1996. *La Filière Anacardier en Guinée-Bissau*. Bissau: Ministério de Desenvolvimento Rural e Agricultura (MDRA).

Cornelis, J. 1997. *Estabelecimento da Cultura de Cajú na Terra e Vida da Guinée-Bissau*. Bissau: SNV Nederlandse Ontwikkelingseorganisatie.

Douglas, M. (ed.). 1987. *Constructive Drinking: Perspectives on Drink from Anthropology*. Cambridge: Cambridge University Press.

Drift, R. van der. 1992. *Arbeid en Alcohol: De Dynamiek van de Rijstverbouw en het Gezag van de Oudste bij de Balanta Brassa in Guinee-Bissau*. Leiden: Centre for Non-Western Studies.

Drift, R. van der, and J. Mamadú. 1997. *Água, Saúde e Saneamento Ambiental. Um Estudo Antropológico Sobre as Etnias Balanta, Fula e Papel*. Bissau: INEP/PROCOFAS.

Drift, R. van der, and C. Viegas, 1997. *Iagu Salgadu mas nós Forte, Suma nô Mindjeres. A Situação da Bolanha e o Género em Biombo*. Bissau: INEP.

Handem, D.L. 1986. *Nature et fonctionnement du pouvoir chez les Balanta Brassa*. Bissau: INEP.

Hochet, A. 1979. *Etudes socio-économiques de bas. Document no. 6: Etudes socio-économiques conduites dans les Régions de Tombali et Buba*. Bissau: CECEP.

Jong, J.T.V.M. de. 1987. *A Descent into African Psychiatry*. Amsterdam: Royal Tropical Institute.

Ploeg, J.D. van der, and L. van Slobbe. 1988. "Sociologie." In *Eindrapportage Tweede Fase Cultuurtechnisch Project Bissassema*. Wageningen: Landbouwuniversiteit.

Poelhekke, F. 1980. *Guinee-Bissau Landendocumentatie*. Amsterdam: Royal Tropical Institute.

Portères, R. 1950. "Vieilles Agricultures de l'Afrique intertropicale: Centre d'origine et de diversifications varietale primaire et berceaux d'agriculture antérieures au XVI siècle." *L'Agronome Tropicale* 9–10: 489–507.

Sidersky, P. 1982. *Approche de la riziculture Balanta (Région de Tombali, Guinée-Bissau)*. Bissau: DEA EMSS.

Valoura, F. 1970. "O Balanta e a Bolanha." *Boletim Cultural da Guinée Portuguesa*, 25 (100).

10

Drinking Mothers Feeding Children

Market Women and Gender Politics in Kilimanjaro, Tanzania

Tuulikki Pietilä

Before traveling to Kilimanjaro, I planned to study the local markets and their impact on the household economy. However, when I arrived there, market activity did not present itself so readily in the categories that I had envisaged. I was surrounded by diverse and controversial discussions about the nature of markets and market women. So vehement were these discussions that they seemed to play as important a part in the construction of the reality of the markets as the concrete economic activities did. Their existence demonstrated that although markets are often considered to be anarchistic places, market behavior is governed by prevailing cultural conventions and social relations, not least by cultural ideas and expectations of gendered behavior and space. Simultaneously, however, markets as spheres outside the domestic realm are places where those conventions are constantly under negotiation and redefinition. It is because of this close relatedness of markets with the surrounding sociocultural world that such simple acts as women's eating and drinking in the market are intensively observed and discussed in Kilimanjaro.

In this chapter I examine two opposing discourses, arguing that they are part of a larger local debate and not just idle talk. Centering on changing gender patterns among the Chagga people of Kilimanjaro, the discourses function to interpret and influence the society's tipping balance of power between the sexes.[1]

WOMEN'S HISTORICAL CLAIMS TO THE MARKETPLACE

Chagga local markets have a long history. The first written records of them date from the 1860s when the first Europeans visited the area (Von der Decken 1871 cited in Moore 1986). There is every reason to believe, however, that their history stretches much further back in time. In the nineteenth century, women gathered in the local markets to exchange their surplus produce. Market trading was part and parcel of a married woman's responsibility to provide sustenance for her family.

Then, as now, Chagga families lived in a *kihamba*, a patrilineally inherited plot of land on which bananas, vegetables and coffee are grown. Many of the expectations and ideas embodied in the gender division of labor of old have prevailed to the present. A husband is responsible for providing the basic means of survival for his family in the form of the *kihamba* and a house. He is also expected to pay for the medicines, clothes and school fees of the children, and to provide meat. This is the only male contribution to the daily diet, because it is the wife's responsibility to provide for all the other basic needs of the family. She is the family's chief food producer, cultivating the *kihamba* and the larger *shamba* (agricultural field), feeding and milking the cows, and engaging in market activities, or nowadays, in some cases, employment.

In the nineteenth century, local markets were strictly women's terrain. Besides bartering, women managed the marketplace, maintaining peace and order. Markets were the first place women appeared virtually after every important life cycle transition, that is, after initiation, marriage, giving birth or following a husband's death. It was totally inappropriate for men to appear there. Markets were described as a female sphere where married women did not hesitate to mock their husbands by publicly recounting their weaknesses to other women (Gutmann 1907; Dundas 1968).

Today the market has lost much of its ritual significance. The church has replaced it as the primary site for the ritual transitions of a girl or a woman. Yet, the market is still an important public place, where the woman appears after each seclusion period connected with her rites of passage through life. To this day, a man will avoid going to the market to buy household necessities, because it is considered a woman's task.

There are now many male traders in the local markets, although women traders are still predominant in number. Men tend to be involved in larger-scale and longer-distance trading. Male traders transport truckloads of different foodstuffs like grain, millet, bananas, vegetables and fruits to or from Kilimanjaro, and many male petty traders and young boys sell goods illegally imported from Kenya. Women are involved in the smaller-scale trading of foodstuffs, although some bigger female traders do exist, as well as male petty traders. Secondhand clothing, a relatively profitable line of business, is pursued by both women and men. Cloth and clothes trading used to be restricted to men. At the end of the 1920s and during the 1930s, Mayanka men started to sell cloth and clothes that they either imported from Kenya or bought from the Indian merchants in Moshi town.[2] According to the female traders, the number of men in the local markets increased during the 1970s and 1980s. Besides the upsurge in male traders, there has been a recent tendency for younger, unmarried women to enter market trading.

Thus, men, boys and girls trade in local markets formerly considered the sphere of adult married women. Simultaneously, due to economic needs, Chagga women's market trading has also intensified. It is not uncommon for women to be involved in trading four or even six days a week. The markets are held twice a week at any one location, and market days of adjacent marketplaces are arranged so that they do not overlap with each other.[3] The furthest markets lie within about twenty to thirty kilometers of practically any homestead. Unlike during the nineteenth century, women rarely sell their own produce now. Instead, they buy articles at one marketplace and sell them in the same or another market. For most, this keen involvement in trading, combined with cultivation, milking and domestic work, provides only the basic necessities (*riziki*). A minority of successful traders, however, are fully occupied with their relatively large trading ventures, while hired hands, children and possibly relatives take care of their cultivation and housework.

The changes in the local economy and markets in Kilimanjaro relate to larger national economic developments. Throughout Tanzania during the 1980s and 1990s, what Smith, Wallerstein et al. (1992) call "peripheral households" have been on the increase. Such households are characterized by their constant need for cash, which forces them to diversify their income-generating activities and sources of livelihood. Tanzanian case studies have documented that in order to reproduce a household, ever more household members have to earn cash. The hardship of declining real wages and employment opportunities combined with trade liberalization has led even more men, women and young people to seek a livelihood in trade.[4] During the past twenty years Tanzania's petty trade sector has proliferated.

Regardless of the long history of Chagga women's marketing, controversial attitudes surround markets and market women in Kilimanjaro in the 1990s. Two major discourses have emerged, that of the market women themselves, and that of their critics. The themes within these discourses and the reasons for their existence are examined in the following sections. Attitudes for and against women's trading derive from the persisting expectation that trading is an organic part of an adult woman's domestic responsibilities. The debate centers on the duties of motherhood, notably a mother's responsibility to feed her children and husband, as opposed to the trader's relative social and economic autonomy, expressed through drinking and eating in bars. These discourses concern the rules and boundaries of gendered behavior, and form a political debate about gender relations and order in contemporary Kilimanjaro.

MARKET WOMEN TRADERS' DISCOURSE: RESPONSIBILITY AND CUNNING

In the course of their working day, market women talk among themselves as well as to a broad spectrum of people they encounter while selling their goods. I spent time with them in the market and observed their market conversations and selling rhetoric. Their discourse was both defensive and proud. It was aimed at preempting outsiders' criticism of their behavior as well as proclaiming ceaseless efforts and the burdens of family provisioning. There were overlapping and sometimes contradictory themes, which are covered in the following subsections.

Motherhood and Feeding

In the market, Chagga women constantly talk about food and feeding rather than prices and profits. Whatever the scale of their trade, the women emphatically deny making any profits (*faida*), maintaining that they are merely earning food (*chakula*) for their children and basic necessities (*riziki*) for their family. Typically, in the course of sales negotiations, both traders and customers make reference to their maternal duties. A customer may try to demand a lower price on the basis of her children's "need to eat," while a trader can refuse the demand on the same grounds. A seller might also appeal to an undecided customer by saying, "Please, kind customer, buy these last bundles of bananas so that I can go home and make food for my children."

In addition to presenting these basic and indisputable needs as the grounds for fixing the price at a certain level, the mother's nurturing role is frequently invoked as proof of the moral respectability of her trading activities. If a customer is being critical of the quality and price of articles, the seller can proudly finish her sales pitch with the assertion, "I foster children" (*Mimi nalea watoto*). It is meant as a final unquestionable guarantee of the quality of her goods and her honest trading.

In addition to reflecting a female trader's responsibilities as mother, motherhood is thus frequently used as a sales strategy in the market. I observed a young man who was deputized by the local government to collect market fees experiencing difficulty with one large-scale female trader. Irritated by the young man's persistence in demanding the tax, she exclaimed, "I am your mother, and don't you dare point your finger at me! I am your mother!" After that she refused to talk to him, let alone pay the tax. Powerless, the young man had to seek the assistance of an older tax collector with whom the woman was used to negotiating the rate of tax she would pay. Eventually she paid less than the official tax.

Market *Ujanja*

Negotiation skills are important for a trader's success in the market. The market women themselves often say that trading requires "mouth" (*mdomo*), "experience" (*uzoefu*), "intelligence" (*akili*), and "cleverness and cunning" (*ujanja*). In practice these qualities demand a certain persuasive way of talking to the customer, which in Kiswahili is called "coaxing" (*kubembeleza*) or "drawing a customer" (*kuvuta mteja*). It also often involves small tricks in the process of the transaction, especially in measuring out the purchased amount for the customer. *Ujanja* is an especially critical but morally controversial attribute that relates to the nature of the marketplace.

Women traders generally regard *ujanja* as a necessary skill required in order to survive in the market's harsh environment. They describe *ujanja* as a calculating capacity that assures the avoidance of loss. The closest English equivalent would be "cunning." Market women maintain that there are two kinds of *ujanja*, good and bad, and that only the negative brand can be equated with craftiness and deception. In doing so they define *ujanja* in more flexible terms than many other people who see it as synonymous with "betrayal and deception."[5]

A trader's *ujanja* is comprised of her behavior, selling techniques and verbal negotiating skills that are central to her economic success. However, her negotiating skills are a central aspect of the suspicion that surrounds women traders (Kapchan 1996). I encountered this at the beginning of my fieldwork, when after explaining to a local man that I had come to Kilimanjaro to study market trading, he curtly observed, "All traders are thieves." It is widely believed that trading women are especially crafty and outdo male traders' cunning.

The cultural meanings attached to market women's negotiating skills stretch further than the purely economic realm of the market. Beyond the negotiation of prices, quantities and profits, the cultural order and gender politics are at stake.

MARKET-WISE AND BEER HAPPY

An important and frequently mentioned feature of the market is that it is a place where different people and genders "mix" (*kuchanganya*) and where information, as well as money and commodities, is exchanged. An employed woman once noted that market women "know the news and information before the radio reports it" (*wanajua habari na taarifa kabla redio*).[6] In addition to the news, because of frequently being "amidst crowds of different kinds of people" (*jumuiya ya watu mbalimbali*), the market women are thought to be accustomed to many different attitudes and ways of life. A nontrading woman once said that a market woman is like a person who "goes to school" (*anayekwenda shuleni*) and becomes "animated" (*mchangamfu*), in contrast to a woman who only stays at home and is like a "dummy" (*mjinga*). In fact, market women use the same word, *mjinga*, to describe any woman who stays at home without work. They explain that such a woman lacks money and is likely to experience "hunger" (*njaa*) and "trouble" (*shida*), because she is solely dependent on her husband's ability to provide for the household. Market women themselves use the school analogy to describe their dedication to work: "a woman trader wakes up in the morning and goes to the market as diligently as children go to school each morning."

Market women are proud of their economic autonomy and the relative freedom it brings. They would frequently express this by saying that they can go and have a beer in a bar without having to ask someone to buy it for them. They carry the school analogy still further by jokingly comparing bars to schools. According to the size of the bar, they are referred to as a "university" (*chuo kikuu*), a "secondary school" (*sekondari*) or a "primary school" (*shule ya msingi*). The sellers in the bars are called "teachers" (*waalimu*), whereas the women themselves as customers are "pupils" and the money to purchase *mbege*[7] is called an "exercise book" (*daftari*). Without an exercise book a pupil naturally cannot go to school. As is the case in many occupations, especially those in which information exchange is critical, chatting over a drink provides an important opportunity to collect market intelligence. Furthermore, it is an expression of the female trader's relative economic and social autonomy and as such of gender politics, as will be discussed below.

In her public person, the woman trader must be market-wise. An important part of the moral dilemma that market women and their behavior raise is their position as intermediaries between the domestic and "village" spheres on the one hand and the wider market economy on the other (Seligmann 1989). Markets, bars and roads are characterized as places where people become informed and advised of the latest news and fashions. As places "outside" the *kihamba,* they are considered to be more appropriately male spaces, yet market women are familiar with both bars and roads and the way of life that is culturally associated with them. Market women's familiarity with these "outside" spheres is demonstrated by their knowledge of "new words" (*maneno mapya*), often disparagingly described as *maneno kihuni kihuni* (vagabond or street language), which they have learned in the market and that other village people are innocently unaware of.[8]

It is worth noting that market trading is not only considered to require certain qualities but that these qualities are thought to increase with the presence and passage of time spent in trading. The women traders are believed to develop *mawazo*, that is, "ideas," referring to a meditative, imaginative and reflective kind of thinking. Fabian (1995) described the semantics of *mawazo* in Zaire (Congo) as "popular thought or popular knowledge" connected to processes of dreaming, remembering, conceiving and elaborating on ideas. Such thinking is challenging and contestable, and extends to the notion that people can think or imagine themselves out of problems and sufferings. According to Fabian (1996), *mawazo* and the verb *kuwaza* are conceptualized as "a purposeful intellectual activity, not a handing-down of something that had been passively received" from authorities such as traditional elders or colonial schoolbooks.

Similarly, in Kilimanjaro, people connect innovative and revolutionary possibilities and impetus to knowledge, intelligence and cleverness.[9] One commonly hears market women and others say that one is able to survive and prosper only by having and using *akili*. The popular association of these qualities with market women, as a category of people, is one crucial reason for the suspicions they raise in their communities. By amassing knowledge and experience of the world, it is widely believed that they can use their imagination in a way that could potentially challenge the existing sociocultural order.

COUNTER DISCOURSE ON MARKET PITFALLS: TEMPTATION OF BEER AND BARS

Straddling domestic and market spaces, a market woman is bound to meet moral censure. The basic social threat embedded in a woman's market activity, as posed by protagonists of this discourse, is that, instead of seeking a livelihood to support her family, she might negate her domestic motives for trading, and lapse into selfish "enjoyment and relaxation" (*kustarehe*). This would take the form of spending her earnings on eating and drinking in the bars around the marketplace, rather than buying food for her family. Sometimes, going to the market is suspected of being a pretext for a woman's "real business" taking place in the surrounding bars and guest houses where she enjoys food and drinks offered by rich men in return for sexual favors.

Sexual innuendo is also included in such expressions of market trading as "to pass to the small paths" (*vichochoroni*), "to go ten ways" (*kwenda njia kumi*), or "to seek dark corners" (*kutafuta makona makona*). Other disparaging expressions used for market trading refer to constant restless motion as well, such as "to keep on passing" (*kupita pita*) or "to keep on jumping" (*kuruka ruka*).[10] All these spatial images express and build on the negation of the cultural ideal of female "settled" attachment to a husband and his patrilineage and *kihamba*.

Some trading women are suspected of becoming so blinded by the monetary prospects of their trading that they do not have time to take care of their children, with the consequence that the children allegedly become undernourished. Or the women are suspected of using birth control and abortion to prevent the nuisance that children would pose for their businesses. In extreme cases, they are believed to have used "medicines" (*dawa*) to "bind" (*kufunga*) and make their husband "stupid" (*mjinga*), so that the wife can move around, make money and meet her boyfriends, while the unsuspecting husband stays at home cultivating and minding the children. Some affluent market women are believed to have reached the point of being "Sugar Mommies," entertaining men in bars, offering them beers and expecting them to supply sexual services in return.

The women's spatial mobility and eating and drinking practices in the market are intensively observed, because they are the most telling acts that are believed to signal either a trader's deference to the domestic values or their violation. Each trader has a regular market spot that has become hers over a period of time and that no other trader is entitled to invade. Ideally a trader keeps to her place for most of the market day and does not wander about. It is considered especially inappropriate for a female trader to eat meat or to drink beer in the surrounding bars during the day. Many women traders spend the whole day in the market without eating anything or only having a couple of doughnuts or some fruit. They might drink a cup of tea or a bottle of lemonade, or share a calabash of *mbege* with the nearby women. After finishing their trading, the women usually go to a bar to drink *mbege*, but it is not considered appropriate to go to one of the bars around the marketplace. First they should return home with their food and baskets, and only later proceed to a bar near their home. This "boundedness" to a certain space is a replication of the cultural practice of "binding" a woman to a certain husband, patrilineage and *kihamba* through marriage (see Pietilä 1999) and simultaneously an expression of the domestic orientation of market trading.

While market women constantly talk about food and the aim of feeding their children, proponents of the counter discourse forcefully link markets with the potential for women to take sexual liberties that are mediated and expressed by the consumption of beer, *mbege* and meat in the bars. Eating and drinking in the market are meaningful because they are interpreted as highly socially related acts. Eating and drinking by necessity involve "feeding"; either the woman herself is being "fed" in the bar or she is "feeding" somebody, and both are considered to deprive her children and husband. The mere act of a woman eating and drinking in a bar at the marketplace readily hints at illicit sex. "Eating" is a very common euphemism for sex in different parts of Africa, but among the Chagga, images of drinking also serve as sexual metaphors. A woman desiring sex is said to be "thirsty" (*ana kiu*). This derives from the Chagga idea that a man "feeds" a woman's vaginal mouth with his semen during intercourse.[11]

Regardless of the charges of selfishness, what is at stake in the counter discourse is not a female trader's individualist aims. Instead, the accusations voice the possibility and threat that market trading fosters a woman's economic strength or her alternative and contestable loyalties, which weaken her relationship to and her dependence on her husband. The politics of the debate become evident when one observes that, in fact, most of the market women are responsible mothers who take good care of their children and would not waste their money on excessive drinking. Despite most market women's abstemious code of daily behavior, the counter discourse criticizing them is vigorous. Market women are pinching a cultural nerve.

RISING GENDER POLITICS AND ECONOMIC HARDSHIP

Why is this critical discourse and perceived threat found among a people who have a long history of female trading? Clearly part of the reason arises from the conception of the market as a special sociocultural space outside the *kihamba* and the domestic sphere. The spatial threat is intertwined with, and intensified by, the present socioeconomic situation in which women's incomes have become ever more important to household survival, but at the same time they are obliged to be away from home far more than in the past.

In rural Kilimanjaro, the economic importance of such male resources as land, cattle, coffee and employment has declined. The number of cattle started to decrease during the first part of the twentieth century as increased coffee cultivation turned former grazing areas into arable fields. By the 1950s, population pressure led to land scarcity in many mountain areas. Increasingly, men sought work in towns and outside the region, either in the form of self-employment or in the administrative and public sector, in which the Chagga have been well represented because of their high level of education. Wives and children were left in the rural area living on the husband's *kihamba.* These *vihamba* grew smaller over time as sons divided the land inherited from their fathers. The existing *vihamba* plots have become too small to secure a livelihood for a family. Meanwhile, the cultivation of coffee, traditionally a male task generating income that had hitherto been an important feature of Kilimanjaro smallholder farms, has been undermined by the steady decline of coffee prices on the world market.

Since the 1980s, wage employment has also declined due to layoffs in government ministries and parastatals. The economic crisis has caused a drastic decrease in real wages such that the wages of the formally employed men can easily be lower than what the wife earns through trading. Increasing differentiation between Chagga men has appeared. Those living in the urban areas in Tanzania or abroad are often much better off than their rural brothers. The wealthy Chagga men resident in towns often have other commitments and relationships that tend to decrease their support to their rural family. Thus, in cases where the husband lacks permanent work or regular income or where he lives and works outside the region, the importance of the wife's cash income and her position in the household economy have tended to rise.[12]

Notions of feeding, eating and drinking form the language with which the contemporary political economic order and gender relations are discussed in Kilimanjaro. When market women state that feeding their family is their aim, this often includes fulfilling traditional male responsibilities of buying clothes, meat and medicines as well as paying the school fees. There are even families where the wife has built the house because the husband could not afford to do so, but this is always a "secret" (*siri*) because such a situation is profoundly shameful to the husband. Thus, in their discourse the market women extend the category of "feeding" to include all the basic necessities of life (*riziki*) and present them as fulfilling their responsibilities.

However, there is a another more structural dimension to the concept. As in many other parts of Africa and South Asia, "feeding" can refer to more than food and the act of giving food. It is a metaphor for taking care of another person in a very broad sense, enabling the establishment and advancement of the other one's social identity and personhood.[13] Consequently, "feeding" creates an emotionally and morally charged expectation of future reciprocity involving transfers from the one fed to his/her feeder.

The market women's emphasis on their responsibilities for feeding their children and their autonomous eating and drinking underscore their importance in the material and social maintenance of Chagga households and society at large. Likewise, the discourse criticizing women's drinking outside their home is concerned with the perceived threat of the declining authority of men in Chagga society. A local priest echoed the anxieties of many when he articulated contemporary domestic problems as the general relegation or "pushing down" of men by women (*wanaume wameshushwa*) while women gain ascendancy (*wanawake wamepanda*), a tendency that he believes will worsen in the years to come. Women traders describe the present situation as "there are no women or men any more; everyone has to scramble for a livelihood" (*Hakuna mwanaume na mwanamke siku hizi; lazima kila mtu akimbie huko na huku*). Other women strike a more triumphant note, however, referring to current gender relations by recourse to national political terms like *mapinduzi* (revolution) or *mageuzi* (change).[14]

It is no coincidence that the critical discourse pays so much attention to women's beer drinking and meat eating in bars. These acts encapsulate the perceived threats of female trading. It is significant that beer and meat are central to this discourse, as both are characteristically male items of consumption and epitomize the way men form and maintain relationships with women, other men and their ancestors. *Mbege* and, nowadays, beer are crucial in the initiation of different male-female relations because they form an essential part of bridewealth negotiations and payments, and the offering of *mbege* or beer in a bar is the quintessential means—and, indeed, also the key metaphor—for initiating or soliciting a commercial and/or occasional sexual relationship.

If a market woman has a beer in a bar at the marketplace, it means that she is either being served by a strange man or that she is buying her drinks herself, and possibly also serving them to other men. In both situations she is understood to be forming a reciprocal relationship with a man other than her husband, and to be betraying her loyalty to her husband. She can be labeled, in the first case, as a "loose" woman (*mhuni*); or as an economically strong autonomous woman who "binds" her husband and possibly other men as well. Both images of a woman "binding" her husband and "feeding" other men in bars are expressions of gender reversal. "Binding" men in sexual, social and spatial terms is tantamount to the feminization of a man by a woman, an action that threatens not only the one particular man but also Chagga patrilineal culture.

Drinking, eating and feeding are intensively observed and debated because they are culturally meaningful and highly gendered practices through which social and gender relations and order are ultimately created. Drinking, eating and feeding are inherently social in that they form or maintain a relationship where the one who offers the food or drink becomes established as the provider, and the one fed becomes dependent and indebted, until the time of reciprocation. For this reason, both the acts and the arguments of feeding, eating and drinking have an important constitutive or contestable political element.

CONCLUSION

Market women's discourse and the opposing discourse form a debate and dialogue in which current gender and political economic orders are being reconstructed. At issue are the relative positions of men and women in Chagga households and in the wider society. A certain degree of male authority is guaranteed by the persistence of land inheritance by males only. The perceived "ascent by women" does not in general mean that women have become affluent; what their intensive economic activities bring is most often the basic necessities for the family. However, these necessities are expanding as women have had to take over several of men's responsibilities for family provisioning.

Discussions among market women interpret and attempt to order contemporary gender relations. Chats about women's drinking and eating habits are not merely about consumption patterns but more broadly about Chagga society, in which women have an ever more important public role. Women emphasize their importance in social reproduction through their constant talk about motherhood and feeding as well as through their pride in being able to buy their own drinks. Beer, meat, sex and bars are the central notions for which market women are criticized. They denote male patterns and spaces of consumption and relating and are thus apt images for gender reversal. Rather than irresponsible mothers, these discourses reveal the fear of women becoming ever more pivotal in Chagga public life.

Regardless of the strong ideological emphasis on patrilineages, it is not too far-fetched to claim that motherhood is the emotional core in Chagga society. Once a man in his mid-fifties explained to me how natural it is that he should love his mother more than his father: "Well, isn't it the mother who has cooked food and fed me?" he said. Due to the centrality of the rural Chagga women's daily economic activities and their cash incomes for the households, the importance of mothers is ever more apparent. Under the circumstances, a drinking mother is the cultural mark of a patrilineal household and a society that is going dangerously astray.

NOTES

The chapter is based on my 1994–1995 fieldwork among the Chagga on eastern Kilimanjaro in an ex-chiefdom that I call Mayanka. My research was funded by the Academy of Finland as part of a project entitled "Gender Relations in Three African Communities," which was based in the Department of Sociology, University of Helsinki, and led by Dr. Karen Armstrong.

1. For studies on how people discursively construct and debate their sociocultural reality and order, see, for example, Cohen and Odhiambo 1989, Kapchan 1996, Malkki 1995, and Werbner 1991.

2. Several Indian traders were in Moshi and Marangu as early as 1898. They recruited petty African itinerant traders to sell cloth and other goods in the surrounding countryside (Koponen 1994).

3. Markets are held every day except Sundays. The most entrepreneurial

women are involved in trading seven days a week, however, for instance by selling from their stores or homes.

4. For case studies, see, for example, Booth et al. 1993; Bryceson 1993, 1994; Mbilinyi 1994; and Tripp 1997. For case studies on the households' sources of income on Kilimanjaro, see Bevan et al. 1989; German Development Institute 1983; Swantz 1985; and Bagachwa 1997.

5. Johnson's dictionary (1939) gives the following definition for the word *ujanja*: craftiness, cunning, roguery, deceit, fraud. The *Kamusi ya Kiswahili Sanifu* dictionary (1988) gives several synonyms for the word, all referring to deception, cunning and slyness.

6. The daily Radio Tanzania news is called *Habari na taarifa*.

7. *Mbege* is a local beer made of bananas and finger millet.

8. A special language is found also among the female vendors in the Kampala night markets (Musisi 1995). In Morocco, market language is referred to as "dirty words" or "street language" (Kapchan 1996). It is pertinent to add that, in general, the old Chagga female traders were far more fluent in Kiswahili than other old women without a trading background who spoke the tribal language Kichagga almost exclusively rather than the national language, Kiswahili. Obviously this difference has to do with both the verbal liveliness and the "mixing" of different peoples in the marketplace.

9. This is shown also by the great efforts and investment the Chagga put into education, for which they are widely known.

10. Interestingly, *kuruka* also means "to pass over or beyond," "overstep," "trespass," referring thus to crossing borders or limits.

11. For the Chagga, see Emanatian 1996 and Moore 1976. For other examples, see Beidelman 1993, Feldman-Savelsberg 1996, Masquelier 1995, and Weiss 1996.

12. The tendency for women to become more prominent in their household's economy, mostly through petty trading and services, has been found in several studies in different parts of Tanzania (Booth et al. 1993; Bryceson 1994; Maula 1997; Tripp 1997).

13. See Carsten (1995) on the creation of kinship and personhood through feeding, co-residing, and eating together in Malaysia.

14. The word *mapinduzi* comes from the name of the governing, and until 1992, Tanzania's only political party, the *Chama Cha Mapinduzi* (CCM), the Revolutionary Party. The word *mageuzi* became a catchword for multiparty politics and the new more liberal political era in the 1990s.

REFERENCES

Bagachwa, M.S.D. 1997. "The Rural Informal Sector in Tanzania." In D.F. Bryceson and V. Jamal (eds.), *Farewell to Farms: De-agrarianisation and Employment in Africa*. Aldershot: Ashgate.

Beidelman, T.O. 1993. *Moral Imagination in Kaguru Modes of Thought*. 2nd ed. Washington, DC: Smithsonian Institution Press.

Bevan, D., P. Collier, and J.W. Gunning. 1989. *Peasants and Governments: An Economic Analysis*. Oxford: Clarendon Press.

Booth, D., et al. 1993. "Social, Economic and Cultural Change in Contemporary Tanzania: A People-Oriented Focus." Report to SIDA, commissioned through Development Studies Unit, Department of Social Anthropology, Stockholm University.

Bryceson, D.F. 1993. *Liberalising Tanzania's Food Trade: Public and Private Faces of Urban Marketing Policy, 1939–1988*. London: James Currey.

———. 1994. "Trade Roots in Tanzania: Evolution of Urban Grain Markets under Structural Adjustment." *Sociologia Ruralis* 34 (1): 13–25.

Carsten, J. 1995. "The Substance of Kinship and the Heat of the Hearth: Feeding, Personhood, and Relatedness among Malays in Pulau Langkawi." *American Ethnologist* 22 (2): 223–24.

Cohen, D., and E.S.A. Odhiambo. 1989. *Siaya: The Historical Anthropology of an African Landscape*. London: James Currey.

Dundas, C. 1968. *Kilimanjaro and Its People*. 2nd ed. London: Frank Cass & Co.

Emanatian, M. 1996. "Everyday Metaphors of Lust and Sex in Chagga." *Ethos* 24 (2): 195–236.

Fabian, J. 1995. "Popular Culture and Local Democratization." Paper presented at the Graduate School of Anthropological and Ethnological Sciences seminar, University of Helsinki.

———. 1996. *Remembering the Present: Painting and Popular History in Zaire*. Berkeley and Los Angeles: University of California Press.

Feldman-Savelsberg, P. 1996. "Cooking Inside: Kinship and Gender in Bangangté Idioms of Marriage and Procreation." In M.J. Maynes, A. Waltner, B. Soland, and Strasser (eds.), *Gender, Kinship, Power: A Comparative and Interdisciplinary History*. New York: Routledge.

German Development Institute (GDI). 1983, *Farmers' Reactions to the Present Economic Situation in Tanzania with Respect to Production and Marketing: A Case Study of Five Villages in the Kilimanjaro Region*. Berlin: GDI.

Gutmann, B. 1907. "Die Frau Bei den Wadschagga." *Globus* 92 (1): 49–51.

———. 1926. *Das Recht der Dschagga*. English translation. New Haven: Human Relations Area Files.

Kapchan, D. 1996. *Gender on the Market: Moroccan Women and the Revoicing of Tradition*. Philadelphia: University of Pennsylvania Press.

Koponen, J. 1994. *Development for Exploitation: German Colonial Policies in Mainland Tanzania, 1884–1914*. Helsinki: Finnish Historical Society.

Malkki, L. 1995. *Purity and Exile: Violence, Memory, and National Cosmology among the Hutu Refugees in Tanzania*. Chicago: University of Chicago Press.

Masquelier, A. 1995. "Consumption, Prostitution, and Reproduction: The Poetics of Sweetness in Bori." *American Ethnologist* 22 (4): 883–906.

Maula, J. 1997. *Small-Scale Production of Food and Traditional Alcoholic Beverages in Benin and Tanzania: Implications for the Promotion of Female Entrepreneurship.* Helsinki: Finnish Foundation for Alcoholic Studies.

Mblinyi, M. 1994. "Gender and Structural Adjustment." Background paper for Symposium on Gender and Structural Adjustment, Tanzania Gender Network Programme, Dar es Salaam.

Moore, S.F. 1976. "The Secret of the Men: A Fiction of Chagga Initiation and Its Relation to the Logic of Chagga Symbolism." *Africa* 46 (4): 357–70.

———. 1986. *Social Facts and Fabrications: "Customary" Law on Kilimanjaro, 1880–1980.* Cambridge: Cambridge University Press.

Musisi, N. 1995. "Baganda Women's Night Market Activities." In B. House-Midamba and F. Ekechi (eds.), *African Market Women and Economic Power: The Role of Women in African Economic Development*. Westport, CT: Greenwood Press.

Pietilä, T. 1999. "The Politics and Rhetorics of Virginity and Motherhood among the Chagga in Kilimanjaro." In K. Armstrong (ed.), *Contested Ground: Changing Gender Relations in Developing Countries*. New York: University Press of America.

Seligmann, L. 1989. "To Be In-Between: The *Cholas* as Market Women." *Comparative Studies in Society and History* 31: 694–721.

Smith, J., I. Wallerstein et al. 1992. *Creating and Transforming Households: The Constraints of the World Economy*. Cambridge: Cambridge University Press.

Swantz, M.-L. 1985. *Women in Development: A Creative Role Denied?* London: St. Martin's Press.

Tripp, A.M. 1997. *Changing the Rules: The Politics of Liberalization and the Urban Informal Economy in Tanzania*. Berkeley and Los Angeles: University of California Press.

Von der Decken, C.C. 1871. *Reise in ost Afrika 1859–1865 Beanbeitet Von Otto Kersten.* 2 vols. Leipzig and Heidelberg: C.F. Wintersche Verlagshandlund.

Weiss, B. 1996. *The Making and Unmaking of the Haya Lived World: Consumption, Commoditization, and Everyday Practice*. Durham: Duke University Press.

Werbner, R. 1991. *Tears of the Dead: The Social Biography of an African Family*. Edinburgh: Edinburgh University Press.

PART IV
Social Comforts and Discomforts

11

Drinking with Friends

Popular Culture, the Working Poor, and Youth Drinking in Independent Ghana

Emmanuel Akyeampong

During my fieldwork in Kumasi in 1992, I conducted a series of interviews with teenagers and youth[1] in the working-class area of Roman Hill on drinking patterns and leisure. I was struck by the celebration of hard drinking among the young, contrary to traditional norms, and this chapter seeks to elucidate reasons for this trend. Roman Hill takes its name from the local Roman Catholic Church of St. Peter, and it borders Kumasi Central Market to the east. The main street in the area descends steeply to intersect with Fuller Street, which runs into Kejetia Circle about 200 meters to the west. Roman Hill is thus situated in the commercial district of Kumasi, and many of its residents earn a livelihood from the Kumasi Central Market or as shop assistants. This chapter situates the drinking patterns among the youth of Roman Hill within the wider historical context of alcohol in southern Ghanaian—especially Akan—cultures. It then draws on the images and import of popular culture to shed light on the connections among drink, friendship and escape among the working poor.

The marketplace (*dwamu*) in Asante has always been an economic, social and religious site. The market in Kumasi was closely supervised by the royal court, and it served as *dwaberem*, the site of major durbars. Significantly, it was also the site for the public drinking sessions of the royal court in precolonial Asante (Bowdich 1966). In precolonial Kumasi, a group of commoners, the *edwibisofo* (indigenes), lived near the market and occupied a unique status. They were seen as autochthonous to the area, and they became a special client group of the Asantehene (King of Asante). They were permitted a distinct social life in which drinking was central.

This chapter argues that youth drinking in contemporary Roman Hill needs to be placed within the broader cultural-historical context of social groups that have lived in proximity to the Kumasi market; the rapid decline of the Ghanaian economy, especially in the post-1970s; and the collapse of the educational system, which has necessitated the early entry of teenagers into the job market. Having been forced into premature adulthood and into being self-sufficient, they have used drink as a balm to soothe the indignities of poverty, unemployment, underemployment and insecurity. In this, interestingly, they share a common trait with Ghanaian adults. When I returned to Roman Hill in 1996, some of my young interviewees from 1992 had become industrious workers and moderate drinkers. Others were still hard drinkers. I offer some thoughts on the different outcomes in the conclusion.

DRINK AND THE DISCOURSE OF POWER IN PRECOLONIAL GHANA

Among the Akan, Ga-Adangme and Ewe of southern Ghana, the history of drink has been closely associated with the culture of power. The peoples of southern Ghana shared a similar worldview in which a Supreme Being (Akan: Onyame; Ga: Nyonmo; Ewe: Mawu), the lesser deities (Akan: *abosom*; Ga: *wodzi*; Ewe: *trowo*), and ancestors (Akan: *nsamanfo*; Ga: *blemabii*; Ewe: *togbewo*) occupied prominent positions. The lesser deities and the ancestors, creations of the Supreme Being, served as intermediaries between humans and the Supreme Being. This was a cosmos in which the natural and the supernatural coexisted in an intimate relationship. In this cultural and historical context, alcohol facilitated communication between humans, their ancestors, the deities and the Supreme Being. Alcohol, a spiritual fluid, was necessary in the rite of libation (prayer), and through libation humans engaged and manipulated the supernatural world in the pursuit of human goals (Kilson 1969).[2]

For chiefs and male elders in precolonial Akan, Ga-Adangme and Ewe societies, who were the living representatives of the ancestors, the ritual use of palm wine—and later European liquor—in communication with the gods and ancestors reinforced their secular power. Male elders incorporated the ritual use of alcoholic drinks into all important social contracts and occasions such as rites of passage and community festivals (Akyeampong 1996a; Dummett 1974). Social drinking also constituted an important recreational activity for male elders. The rural palm-wine bar was a central social institution, and drinking with friends is an image that adequately captured rural socialization. In these societies, where material differentiation had not become a significant avenue for maintaining social control, control over palm wine presented a badge that enhanced the social superiority and identity of male elders. Male elders fastidiously excluded women and "young men" from using alcohol.[3] Male elders forged an indigenous ethic of temperance to strengthen their monopoly over alcohol use and to codify their own temperate use of alcohol. For alcohol to contribute to the power of male elders, its sacred links had to be preserved through moderation in its use. Thus, from early times, the history of drink and the politics of inclusion and exclusion were interconnected. And even in these early times, tension existed between the ritual and the social uses of alcohol. Rules regulated drinking, and men who drank excessively were forced to conform to drinking norms through social ridicule.

The role of alcohol in the culture of power achieved an elaborate form in the centralized state of Asante. Indeed, a Twi proverb ridiculed the poor who could not afford to buy palm wine: *wunni ntramma, na wuse nsa nye de* (when you do not have cowry shells, then you say wine is not sweet). In early nineteenth-century Asante, royal largesse and power were reflected in the generous distribution of alcohol to those who called at the Asantehene's palace. Bowdich observed that, in 1817, forty pots of soup and a *peregwan* (about £8) worth of palm wine were made available at the palace in Kumasi for visitors every day. It was common for children, youth and adults to convene at the palace of the chief they served "for an expected midday meal, as prescribed by tradition, each carrying his or her stool."[4] This was the *adidiye* (communal meal), and it reinforced the image of chiefly generosity and the ethic of reciprocity. To assist a chief in meeting these commitments, particular villages were assigned the task of supplying the palace with foodstuffs, and the occupant of the Derma stool, for example, was the Asantehene's chief hunter (Arhin 1993). Palm-wine tappers in Asante were required to send their chief a pot of palm wine daily (*ahen nsa*—chief's drink) for entertaining his guests (Busia 1968). Drinks and their distribution were so central to political power that this function was accommodated in Asante architecture. In the palace of the Asantehene were a palm-wine house (*sa fie so*) and a place for the distribution of drinks (*pato a yekye mu nsa*) (Arhin and Afari-Gyan 1992).

Bowdich commented on the almost daily ceremony of the Asantehene's court retiring to the marketplace for a public drinking session (*nsadwa*). These were open occasions and every adult male could join the drinking party. The Asantehene drank from a calabash decorated with gold, which underscored his wealth and power (McLeod 1984). Unusual drinking rules structured these sessions. The king and his aristocrats drank first, emphasizing their social ranking. But they spilled more than they drank, and a boy knelt beneath with a gourd to collect the spilled palm wine (Bowdich 1966). The palm wine collected in this way was shared among lower court functionaries (*ahenkwaa*) and commoners who could not drink in the presence of their political superiors and/or could not afford the palm wine.[5] It is noteworthy that the congenial drinking sessions of the royal court provided the most intimate glimpse most commoners had of royal wealth and power. These images of drink, wealth and power would stay with them.

In precolonial Asante, where stringent sumptuary rules regulated the use of clothing, drink, and jewelry and access to women in order to maintain the status quo, an important exception was made for the *edwibisofo*.

> The people who had Kumasi as their only village were a special group in the population, called the *Edwibisofo*. The *Edwibisofo* lived near the main market (near the present Kingsway store), filling their days as butchers, traders, and palm wine sellers. These carefree fortunates were described by informants as having no village but Kumasi and no chief but the Asantehene and as being free to enjoy their palm wine and the favors of local women. (Brown 1972)

During the nineteenth century, the *edwibisofo* became an influential group. As rival claimants contested the position of Asantehene between 1885 and 1888, the Queen Mother of Asante, Yaa Akyiaa, armed the *edwibisofo* with 500 modern rifles purchased by Asantehene Mensa Bonsu (1874–1883). Led by Asamoa Kyekye, the *edwibisofo* became the guardians of Kumasi as Asante plunged into civil war.[6] The unique lifestyle of the *edwibisofo*, and their connection to the Kumasi market, hold important insights for our examination of contemporary drinking patterns in Roman Hill. Colonial rule and an emerging popular culture would expand the uses and meanings of drink.

COLONIALISM, POPULAR CULTURE, AND *AKPETESHIE* (ILLICIT GIN)

The onset of British colonialism in the Gold Coast (1874) and Asante (1896) altered the traditional relations of power, and increased the access of young men or commoners to alcoholic drinks. British political influence and trade had expanded significantly with the Maclean Treaty of

1831, which had recognized the area south of the River Pra as independent from Asante. Several Asante commoners acquired wealth from trading in rubber in the second half of the nineteenth century. The emergence of a cocoa industry in the late nineteenth century and the introduction of mechanized mining and railways expanded economic and wage-labor opportunities and promoted rural-urban migration. Urban life provided exciting opportunities for the fashioning of new social networks and the accumulation of cash. Among young migrants in coastal towns, drinking circles replaced the family and kin networks abandoned in rural areas and provided a platform for demonstrating their newly acquired wealth. Town life presented a novel context for self-redefinition. For young men excluded from alcohol use by rural elders, it was fortuitous that European liquor was one of the cheapest trade items in coastal towns (Akyeampong 1996a). For these young men, drink, independence and empowerment were explicitly linked. As early as the 1860s, the *African Times* reported that a drinking club called the Tiger Club had emerged in the coastal town of Winnebah. Since rum and gin were even cheaper than drinking water, the young men of the Tiger Club indulged themselves in competitive binge drinking. The club was disbanded when two of its members died after a drinking bout.[7]

With the British annexation of Asante in 1896 and the deportation of the reigning Asantehene, Agyeman Prempeh I, the strict sumptuary laws observed in Kumasi collapsed. Indeed, commoners who had amassed wealth through trade (*akonkofo*—rich men) had the audacity to establish a social club around 1900 called the Kumasi Gentlemen. This group was headed by two merchants, Kwame Kyem and Pankroso Kankam. The *akonkofo* usurped aspects of the lifestyle of the traditional political aristocracy; they indulged in conspicuous displays of rich clothes and jewelry as well as the lavish consumption of imported European drinks. To be a wealthy trader became the social aspiration of many Asante in early twentieth-century Kumasi. It is instructive that when the exiled Prempeh I was repatriated in the mid-1920s, one of his first acts as the restored king of Kumasi was the abolition of the Kumasi Gentlemen's Club (Brown 1972). Ostentation among commoners was an anomaly in Asante political culture.

Recreational resorts multiplied as urban life became more elaborate. World War I and the stationing of foreign troops in Gold Coast towns added impetus to urban social formation and the popularity of social drinking. European-style drinking bars mushroomed in large towns (Dummett 1974). Dance bands proliferated, and dances became a key feature of nightlife (Collins 1992). In Adum in central Kumasi, Ellis Bar, run by a Lebanese, was the center of social drinking in the 1920s. More drinking bars were opened in the 1930s: Bridge Bar in Adum and the Railway Bar opposite the station in Bompata.[8] It was in this vibrant social context that popular music ("highlife")[9] and comic opera ("concert")[10] developed as important forms of leisure in an emergent popular culture. Popular culture interpreted the social experience of new urban migrants and mediated the entry of would-be migrants into the urban setting.[11]

Ironically, illicit gin (*akpeteshie*) became popular from 1930 when the colonial government, in response to pressure from indigenous chiefs, increased tariffs on imported European liquor and put it beyond the financial means of commoners. Drink had become central to new forms of leisure, and enterprising Gold Coasters distilled illicit gin to meet rising demand. What distinguished *akpeteshie* at this experimental phase was its cheapness, potency, harsh taste and pungent smell. As its patrons were hounded by the colonial government, *akpeteshie* became a symbol of protest against colonial rule. But it had an important class dimension also, as it was considered the poor person's drink (Akyeampong 1996b). In the postcolonial era, it is the association of *akpeteshie* with the lower classes that has persisted. Highlife songs about poverty often include references to *akpeteshie*. It consoled the poor and provided escape from economic hardship. The decline of Ghana's economy after independence in 1957 enhanced *akpeteshie*'s grip on the poor. Networks of friendship and solidarity among the poor have sprung up around *akpeteshie* bars. I gained access to these drinking worlds of the working poor in central Kumasi through the teenagers of Roman Hill. I was struck by the familiarity with which older men greeted my teenage friends. The tie that bound drinkers here was not age but poverty.

THE DRINKING WORLD OF THE POOR: THE YOUTH OF ROMAN HILL

Akpeteshie gained ground in the lives of the working poor when it was incorporated into marriage and funeral ceremonies in the postcolonial era, especially among coastal fishing communities. It became the drink for all occasions. Rapid political and economic decline since independence has made adulthood, marriage and the family fragile, increasing the lure of cheap hard liquor. Ghana has experienced ten different governments since independence in 1957, five having been ushered in through military coups. A continuous drop since 1958 in the world market price for cocoa—Ghana's leading export—has served as the backdrop for military intrusions. Flight Lieutenant J.J. Rawlings has been the dominant figure in Ghanaian politics since his sudden appearance in a military coup in 1979. He subsequently returned to power in December 1981, when he overthrew the civilian government of the People's National Party. Rawlings successfully transformed himself into a civilian ruler as his National Democratic Congress won general elections in 1992. His party was re-elected in 1996. Ghana's economic recovery program from 1983 onwards was under the auspices of Rawlings. In 1983 the Ghanaian economy ground to a halt and the UN Food and Agriculture Organization reported widespread hunger in Ghana. In that same year, the Rawlings government abandoned its populist stance and called in the World Bank. The resultant structural adjustment program involved major reforms in the socioeconomic system.

Structural adjustment stipulated the trimming of the civil service, for the government has been the largest employer in most Sub-Saharan African countries. Unemployment and underemployment were already rife in Ghana's weakened economy, and the situation had worsened with massive retrenchment in the civil service. The working classes were severely affected by the withdrawal of government subsidies in the health and education sectors required by structural adjustment. By the late 1980s, two images of Ghana's economy emerged: externally, the World Bank claimed Ghana as a model of structural adjustment; and in Ghana, Ghanaians struggled daily to afford one main meal for their families. I conducted several interviews in the summer of 1992 at Green Partition, a popular *akpeteshie* bar in Nima, Accra. The bar was empty on my first visit, and the bartender informed me that the patrons came in around 6:00 A.M. on their way to work and at about 6:00 P.M. as they returned from work. For many workers, drink fortified them for jobs they disliked, and then prepared their reentry into tense domestic situations. Several patrons opted for European lager beer on the day I announced that the drinks were on me. They usually drank *akpeteshie*, not by choice but because of low finances. Ironically, *akpeteshie*—the drink of the poor—reminded its patrons of the poverty they hoped to escape. As the refrain of a popular highlife song by A.B. Crentsil puts it, *Akono bekum hiani* (desire—for better things—will kill the poor person).[12] Poverty was a key theme in various conversations at this bar.

The strong connections among poverty, domestic strife and drinking are revealed in several highlife songs. A classic is Crentsil's *I Go Pay You Tomorrow*.[13]

Akpeteshie seller give me quarter [size][14]
I go pay you tomorrow
Akpeteshie seller give me half
I go pay you moon die [on pay day]
My wife dey shout for money
My children dey cry for chop [food]
So so wahala [trouble] in my house
I go pay you tomorrow.
I want to forget my troubles
I want to forget my sorrows
Life hard for me
I go pay you tomorrow.

Pensive, solitary drinkers were a common sight in drinking bars. They were often struggling with insurmountable problems. I struck up a friendship with Abrokwa at the Green Partition bar. One Saturday in June 1992, I found Abrokwa at Green Partition looking very morose. I sat next to him and enquired about his health. Abrokwa, in his fifties, lived with his wife and grandchild in a compound house in Nima. His landlord had just served him an eviction notice with only a week's grace. The landlord's son had sent money from overseas for the house to be renovated. Abrokwa's meager salary made it difficult for him to move to a new room, as he could not afford the rent advance landlords demanded. The cheapest room he had found required an advance of 35,000 cedis, which he did not have.[15] His employers were unhelpful, and in his distress he had turned to cheap, potent *akpeteshie*.[16] Akans have a saying that *onipa nom nsa a, na ofa adwene* ("a person drinks when he is thoughtful or disturbed"). Rapid urbanization and the growth of individualism have reduced the security value of the kinship network. In towns, misery is often an individual experience, with alcohol as the only loyal companion. A troubled worker may drink with his friends, but their common socioeconomic circumstances dictate that none can offer the other financial relief. Ties of solidarity are essentially moral.

Ghanaian workers are aware of the contradictory consequences of this recourse to liquor as they strain already tense marital relations and low family budgets. These developments often form the themes of comic opera. *Abyssinia*, by the Osofo Dadzie group, is a good illustration. In this play, Donkor, an alcoholic goldsmith, loses his wife in childbirth through his own neglect. While Nana Ama, the wife, was heavily pregnant and weak from malnutrition, Donkor spent his paltry income at *akpeteshie* bars. Nana Ama's ghost decides to wreak vengeance by taking Donkor to the world of the dead. Only Osofo (Priest) Dadzie's timely intervention saves Donkor on the fateful night Nana Ama's ghost appears to collect her debt. Donkor subsequently gives up drinking and vows to be a responsible adult.[17]

Drinking pervades Ghanaian social life, and the youth drink, as one Roman Hill teenager put it, because "when we set out, our elders were drinking so we picked it up."[18] This striving to be an adult is a universal phenomenon. In Ghana the role of a father as the head of a household entitles him to the choicest part of household meals. Children perceive the privileges of adulthood and remain ignorant of its responsibilities. They yearn to be adults. Youthful drinking reflects, in a way, a premature striving for adulthood. The availability of very cheap types of alcohol facilitates the usurpation of this entitlement of adulthood. What is striking about the drinking culture of the youth is the strong association between drink and masculinity. Popular fiction documents this connection. In Duodu's *The Gab Boys* (1967) both the rural and urban youth overindulge in drink. Drinking bestows the aura of toughness and enhances a person's image. The youth at the village of Pusupusu camp in the house of the *akpeteshie* seller whenever they experience a financial windfall.

Not unlike these fictional accounts, several teenagers in Roman Hill have been forced prematurely into the adult world of self-sufficiency, casualties of Ghana's declining educational system and economy.

> Nearly half of all primary school teachers were unqualified in 1982/83, as were about a third of the middle school teachers and a fifth of secondary school teachers. What money was available was spent almost entirely on salaries so that schools were without textbooks, furniture, chalk, paper, and other nonpersonnel inputs; and maintenance of the physical plant of the system was severely neglected, resulting in some classrooms being totally unusable, particularly in inclement weather. (Cobbe 1991)

Educational reform was overdue, and the World Bank's structural adjustment program encouraged this. Reform was launched in 1986, and the old pre-university system, capped by the Ordinary and Advanced Level General Certificate of Education, was replaced with a junior and senior secondary school system. Government subsidies for education were reduced. The goal was to replace the old elitist system of education with a broad-based one that equipped even junior secondary school graduates with marketable technical skills. The reforms were introduced without adequate preparation, and the results were disastrous. Many teenagers in Roman Hill were victims of the educational system in either its unreformed or reformed phase. Out of school and from poor homes, they were compelled to earn a living. They eked out a livelihood running errands for the store owners of Roman Hill and picking up odd jobs in the Kumasi market. My own father had operated a pharmacy in Roman Hill from the 1960s onwards, and this gave me an entry into the community. Two teenagers, Boy Shacki and Osei, became my guides around the drinking world of Roman Hill.

We visited several drinking establishments in June 1992. It was quickly obvious that my guides were also patrons of these bars. The most popular *akpeteshie* spot was Backyard V.C. 10 (alias the Railway Bar). We arrived at the Railway Bar on the evening of 6 June 1992. My teenage friends were treated as "adults" here, and we joined a table with three elderly men, Mr. Ashong, Mr. Mensah and Uncle Otama. I bought drinks for the table, and we were soon immersed in a discussion on alcohol and marriage. The discussion attracted more people to our table, and the consensus among these men was that they would not marry a woman who drank frequently. It was an interesting reflection of the double standards that characterize gender relations in Ghana (Asante-Darko and van der Geest 1983). It was instructive that while we were at this bar, three young men from Boy Shacki's house came to drink. Apparently, most of the patrons knew each other. This was a man's world, a comfortable place of retreat.

My interviews with the teenagers of Roman Hill revealed a strong culture of drinking among the youth. Mastery in different categories of alcoholic drinks was carefully recorded. This implied that one drank with friends in order to have witnesses to one's talent for drinking.

There were three categories in this drinking competition: *odoka* (wine tapped from the raffia palm), *akpeteshie*, and *akpeteshie* strained through ginger (*akikaduro*). Expertise in other types of hard liquor was also noted. In June 1992, Boy Shacki was the recognized champion of *odoka*. He was on record for remaining sober after twenty bottles of *odoka*.[19] Jimmy was the uncrowned king of *akikaduro* after having drunk nine bottles in one day. Osei was the champion of brandy.[20] Boy Shacki was quick to point out to me that these were people who had genuinely developed their tolerance for alcohol, and none used "medicine." It was believed that people from the north possessed medicines for drinking and could drink copious amounts of alcohol without getting drunk.

Akpeteshie was central in the social life of Roman Hill's teenagers because of the uncertainty in their lives. In many ways it was a coping device, a reality underscored by a highlife song called *Akpeteshie Special*.[21]

Se me kae m'asem bi'a	When I remember my plight
Enam awerehoo nti	Because of my sadness
Na ewose me twa kakra o	I am compelled to drink
Nsa yi!	This liquor!
Ewiase abrebrese yi	Life's hardships
Me nni boafo biara	I have no helper
Nti nsa yi mo mma me nom bi o	So let me drink
Se ye de anigyie na enom o	Whether we drink in happiness
Se ye de awerehoo so na enom o	Whether we drink in sadness
Obia so tease (2x)	Everyone understands.
Ewiase amane hunu yi	Life's struggles
Obra akwantuo yi	Life's journey
Obia so ka ho (2x)	Everyone embarks on it
Enye me nko'a na me pe	I'm not the only one who likes it
Akpeteshie ee, o akpeteshie ee	Akpeteshie ee, o akpeteshie ee
Enye me nko'a ne me nom	I'm not the only one who drinks it
Akpeteshie ee, o akpeteshie ee.	Akpeteshie ee, o akpeteshie ee.

Osei, for instance, was orphaned in early childhood, and his life looked very bleak. His relatives ran a chop bar across from my father's pharmacy, so he could count on his lunch and a late afternoon meal from this source. He had a roof over his head but was responsible for his own clothing. Roman Hill was a center for dealers in used clothes, and Osei used some of the money he received for running errands on clothes. Osei was barely literate and was desperately in need of a patron. Boy Shacki was still in school and highly intelligent. How long he could remain in school was, however, uncertain, and he performed several odd jobs to accumulate some savings.

Roman Hill was divided into three distinct parts based on leisure patterns. Those at the bottom of the hill preferred cigarettes; the carpenters, who dominated the middle portion of the hill, smoked marijuana; and those at the top of the hill drank alcohol. In the compound house where Boy Shacki lived there was a competition for the uncrowned "King of Drink."[22] There were reportedly fifteen people in the house who could drink a bottle of *akpeteshie* without getting drunk. I was puzzled and mused over how unemployment and underemployment had created a "leisure" class of people who had time on their hands but little money. What explained the neat delineation into different leisure styles on a hilly street less than 200 meters long? I had lived for years in Kumasi but had encountered nothing like this. It seemed possible that the forces of history and culture were operative here, as well as contemporary socioeconomic pressures.

The *edwibisofo* of precolonial Asante were the quintessential *nkwankwaa* (young men or commoners). Not only were they ineligible for traditional office, but, being Kumasi's autochthones, they had no access to land, an important basis of wealth in Asante. Kumasi was conceived politically as "urban space," and farming within the precincts of the town was illegal.[23] Thus, unlike other Asante commoners resident in Kumasi but whose families owned land in outlying villages or in the other constituent states of the Asante union, the *edwibisofo* could not aspire to own land. In an interview the ethnomusicologist John Collins emphasized how generational conflict over the decades spurred creativity in "popular music." The youth of each generation seeks its distinguishing badge: a way of marking themselves off from their elders. But the popular music of today becomes the traditional music of tomorrow, and the youth of today grow up to become elders in opposition to a newly emerging youth.[24] Without access to traditional office or land, the *edwibisofo* were frozen in a state of "youthfulness" and the celebration of popular culture. Perhaps the lifestyle concessions granted them by the Asantehene were in appreciation of the limitations on their social mobility. The liminality of the *edwibisofo* in the Asante polity was minimized when they were constituted into the royal bodyguard in the 1880s. The celebration of popular culture continues among the contemporary youth of Roman Hill. Immigration by other Asante into the area has probably brought land-owning families, sharpening social distinctions between the landed and the landless. Roman Hill is also bordered by the Muslim *Zongo* (stranger community) and Fanti New Town, a suburb formed by Fanti immigrants from the late nineteenth century. The twentieth century witnessed significant Anlo immigration from southeastern Ghana, and Anloga—on the Kumasi-Accra road—is a vibrant community of Anlo carpenters. The Anlo dominate carpentry in Kumasi, and detailed interviews in the middle section of Roman Hill reveal their presence. The elaboration of leisure styles among the youth of Roman Hill may be an attempt to demarcate ethnic lines. It would then represent an interesting interface between ethnicity and popular culture.

The parallels between the *edwibisofo* of the nineteenth century and contemporary residents of Roman Hill are significant: economic dependence on Kumasi market, residence beside the market, and unique social lifestyles. Roman Hill's teenagers had very traditional aspirations: they hoped to become successful traders. They sought out apprenticeships with merchants in the area that would serve as a stepping-stone to their own careers as independent traders. The strategy itself was very traditional. In precolonial Asante, many commoners or *ahenkwaa* earned their start in trade by acting as carriers for wealthier traders and chiefs in the kola nut trade.[25] But certain developments in independent Ghana had pushed these teenagers toward these traditional options. The collapse of the old educational system, the teething problems of the new junior and secondary schools, and the withdrawal of government subsidies for education eliminated one important escape route from poverty. These teenagers lived in an uncertain world. They indulged in drinking common to teenagers intrigued by adulthood, but they also drank out of a sense of despair driven by poverty and the need to fend for themselves. They had been pushed into an adult world at a very early age, and they had adopted drink as a coping device just as the adults around them had done.

EPILOGUE

The circumstances of Osei and Boy Shacki had improved considerably when I visited Roman Hill in 1996. My younger brother had hired them both. Boy Shacki had completed secondary school and enrolled in a program for training technicians at the Kumasi Polytechnic. He worked at my brother's pharmacy after school, and his honesty had secured him a place in the wholesale division, where he earned commission based on sales. Late in 1996, luck smiled on him and he won the United States visa lottery for immigrants. Boy Shacki had saved the commission he had earned and was able to afford an airline ticket. He now lives in Chicago. Osei worked in the retail part of the pharmacy. His illiteracy remained an obstacle to the responsibilities he could be assigned, but he earned a secure income. Both had exited the hard-drinking scene. Indeed, it was one of the requirements my brother insisted upon as their employer. But entrusted with responsible positions and assured of their livelihood, neither felt the need to pursue their old drinking habits. Today, Boy Shacki represents the success story from that group of teenagers I interviewed in June 1992. Others like Jimmy remain hard drinkers. For them, caught in the adult world of poverty, drink serves as an escape from life's struggles. He lives the life of Kantata's *Akpeteshie Special*.

NOTES

1. "Youth" as defined here refers to unmarried people under twenty-five years old. Traditionally, adulthood is a state marked by marriage and parenthood.

2. Libation is prayer accompanied and punctuated by the pouring of drink. Libation essentially involves three processes: invoking the presence of the Supreme Being, the gods and ancestors; explaining to these supernatural beings the occasion for the human gathering; and supplicating these spirits to grant the assembly success in their endeavors.

3. Traditionally, the "young men" did not constitute an age group, but formed the social category of "commoners." The young men could be in their thirties and forties. On defining young men, see Allman (1990) and Rathbone and Allman (1991).

4. Albert Mawere-Opoku, "Asante Adae and Akwasidae Kesee 1991," undated manuscript, 22.

5. Interview with Albert Mawere-Poku, Accra, 30 April 1992.

6. Prempeh II, "The History of Ashanti," undated manuscript, 352.

7. *African Times*, 23 December 1862, 23 November 1863.

8. Interviews with A. Attakora Gyimah, Kumasi, 11 June 1992, and Osei Assibey Mensah, Kumasi, 7 June 1992.

9. Highlife music resulted from the blending of Akan rhythms and melodies with Western instruments and harmonies. See Collins (1992) and Agovi (1989).

10. Concert gained attention through the drama performances on Empire Day in the early twentieth century. Beginning as an elitist recreation in coastal towns, it acquired popular appeal with the emergence of itinerant actors. Blackface, borrowed from American minstrel shows, became the most striking image in concert performances. See also Collins (1976) and Cole (1996).

11. Popular culture is used here in the sense defined by Fabian (1978). He presents it as an urban mass culture distinct from modern elite culture and traditional rural culture. Unlike Fabian, this chapter posits no inherent tensions between rural and urban culture. Indeed, popular culture has the potential to link or integrate urban and rural social experiences. Popular culture in Ghana encompasses film, soccer, clothing ("dressing up") and other forms of social activity that are not examined here. Music and comic opera were selected for special treatment because they offer social commentary on drinking patterns.

12. A.B. Crentsil, *Akono bekum hiani*, ABO 194 (1994).

13. A.B. Crentsil, *I Go Pay You Tomorrow*, Wazuri Productions, WAZ 101 (1985).

14. *Akpeteshie* is sold in "standard" measures in Ghana. In 1992 a bottle of APC analgesic tablets was used for a 50 cedi measure, a bottle of TCP disinfectant was used for a 100 cedi measure ("quarter"), "half" was a full bottle of Coca-Cola, and "full" (a bottle of beer) sold for 400 cedis.

15. For most of 1992, the cedi maintained an exchange rate of 400 cedis to one U.S. dollar.

16. Personal communication, Accra, 20 June 1992.

17. *Abyssinia* was written by Nana Bosompra around 1980 and was shown several times on Ghana Television by the Osofo Dadzie Drama Group.

18. Interview with Boy Shacki, Roman Hill (Kumasi), 6 June 1992.

19. *Odoka* contains between 3 and 5 percent alcohol by volume.

20. Much of this information was confirmed in conversations with Osei.
21. Kantata, *Akpeteshie Special*, Oval OVLP 508.
22. Interview with Boy Shacki, Roman Hill, 6 June 1992.
23. Prempeh II, "History of Ashanti," 89; Kwame Arhin, "Peasants in 19th Century Asante," *Current Anthropology* 24, no. 4 (1983): 471–79.
24. Interview with John Collins, Ofankor (Accra), 11 January 1997.
25. On social mobility in precolonial Asante see McCaskie (1980) and Wilks (1979).

REFERENCES

Agovi, K.E. 1989. "The Relevance of Ghanaian Highlife Songs since 1957." *Research in African Literatures* 20 (2): 194–201.

Akyeampong, E. 1996a. *Drink, Power and Cultural Change: A Social History of Alcohol in Ghana, c. 1800 to Recent Times*. Portsmouth, NH: Heinemann.

———. 1996b. "What Is in a Drink? Class Struggle, Popular Culture and the Politics of *Akpeteshie* (Local Gin) in Ghana, 1930–1967." *Journal of African History* 37 (2): 215–36.

Allman, J.M. 1990. "The Youngmen and the Porcupine Class, Nationalism and the Asante's Struggle for Self-Determination, 1954–57." *Journal of African History* 31 (2): 263–79.

Arhin, K. 1993. "The Political Economy of a Princely City: The Economy of Kumasi in the Nineteenth Century." *Research Review Supplement*, 5–27.

Arhin K., and K. Afari-Gyan (eds.) 1992. *The City of Kumasi*. Legon: Institute of African Studies, University of Ghana.

Asante-Darko, N., and S. van der Geest. 1983. "Male Chauvinism: Men and Women in Ghanaian Highlife Songs." In C. Oppong (ed.), *Female and Male in West Africa*. London: Allen and Unwin.

Bowdich, T.E. 1966. *Mission from Cape Coast Castle to Ashante*. London: Cass.

Brown, J.W. 1972. "Kumasi, 1896–1923: Urban Africa during the Early Colonial Period." Ph.D. dissertation, University of Wisconsin.

Busia, K.A. 1968. *The Position of the Chief in the Modern Political System of Ashanti*. London: Cass.

Cobbe, J. 1991. "The Political Economy of Education Reform in Ghana." In D. Rothchild (ed.), *Ghana: The Political Economy of Recovery*. Boulder: Lynne Rienner.

Cole, C.M. 1996. "Reading Blackface in West Africa: Wonders Taken for Signs." *Critical Inquiry* 23: 183–215.

Collins, J. 1976. "Comic Opera in Ghana." *African Arts* 9 (2): 50–57.

———. 1992. *West African Pop Roots*. Philadelphia: Temple University Press.

Dummett, R. 1974. "The Social Impact of European Liquor Trade on the Akan of Ghana (Gold Coast and Asante), 1875–1910." *Journal of Interdisciplinary History* 5: 69–101.

Duodu, C. 1967, *The Gab Boys*. Suffolk: Chaucer Press.

Fabian, J. 1978. "Popular Culture in Africa: Findings and Conjectures." *Africa* 48 (4): 315.

Kilson, M. 1969. "Libation in Ga Ritual." *Journal of Religion in Africa* 2 (3): 161–78.

McCaskie, T.C. 1980. "Office, Land and Subjects in the History of the Manwere Fekuo of Kumase: An Essay in the Political Economy of the Asante State." *Journal of African History* 21 (2): 189–208.

McLeod, M.D. 1984. "The Golden Ax of Ashanti." *Natural History* 93: 72.

Rathbone, R., and J.M. Allman. 1991. "Discussion: The Youngmen and the Porcupine." *Journal of African History* 32 (3): 333–38.

Wilks, I. 1979. "The Golden Stool and the Elephant Tail: An Essay on Wealth in Asante." *Research in Economic Anthropology* 2: 1–36.

12

To Drink or Not to Drink

Beer Brewing, Rituals, and Religious Conversion in Maane, Burkina Faso

Sabine Luning

Codes for eating and drinking provide a rich domain for constructing social distinctions (Barthes 1967; Bourdieu 1979; Lévi-Strauss 1968; Douglas 1984). Styles of food consumption help to shape class differences and also relations between religious groups. Conversion to another religion often implies a change in diet. The early Christians' breaking of the Jewish food taboos, for example, was a major move toward universalistic missionary ambitions. Transgressing rules for wining and dining is one way of disassociating from religious practices; abstaining from drinking is another.

The question "to drink or not to drink" is a good starting point for investigating the relations between coexisting religious communities. Beer has always been at the heart of debates about traditional and more recently introduced religious practices in many African societies. Hammond-Tooke (1962: 65) cites a Bhaca song line: "Pagans are people of beer and beer alone." In southern Africa, McAllister (1993: 79) shows that beer was historically associated with pagans in two ways. It was the drink par excellence to be shared with the ancestors, and excessive drunkenness epitomized the moral degradation of heathens. Both reasons incited Christian mission churches to demand that their converts abstain from drinking and move up to a "higher" Christian morality.

This chapter is concerned with the place of beer in the socioreligious life of Maane, a *département* 100 kilometers north of Ouagadougou in Burkina Faso. It deals with the ways in which attitudes toward beer express relations between various religious communities. In this region, beer engenders a local discourse on how to value relations of contiguity with the ancestors, rather than a rating of the moral standards of different religious groups. Converts in Maane do not so much want to avoid alcohol, drunkenness and the company of beer drinkers, but rather they seek to avoid contact with the various exchange partners in "traditional" offerings, the foremost being their ancestors. The question of how (supernatural) recipients of libations are dealt with and talked about is crucial for an understanding of traditional practices as well as for appreciating what is at stake once people choose to dissociate themselves from traditional religious practices. The assessment of attitudes toward beer drinking by members of various religious communities leads to opinions shared by adherents to traditional practices, Muslims, Roman Catholics and Protestants, about what "tradition" is and how it should be dealt with.

The first section of this chapter outlines Maane's rural setting, the social identities of its people and their drinking habits. This is followed by a discussion of the meaning of tradition in Maane and beer brewing in ritual contexts. Differences between ritual and ordinary beer brewing are delineated as a basis for analyzing Christian religious converts' attitudes toward brewing. The chapter concludes with a discussion of the incidence of drinking among Christians.[1]

SOCIAL LIFE IN MAANE

At present, half the population of Burkina Faso, some 4 million people, ethnically identify themselves as Moose.[2] Moose chiefdoms came to dominate the region from the mid-fifteenth century onwards (Izard 1970). In a gradual process of expansion, immigrant Moose obtained political rule over people of different ethnic origins. Nowadays Burkina Faso contains a patchwork of Moose chiefdoms. The French based their colonial rule on the Moose chiefdoms and centered their colonial administrative unit of Haute-Volta in the Moose heartland. The administrative subdivisions in large parts of Burkina Faso are still based on the Moose chiefdoms.

Maane is one of these Moose chiefdoms that currently has the administrative status of a *département*. Mooré speakers[3] constitute over 85 percent of Maane's inhabitants. Among these Moose, a wide range of social identities is found. A substantial group of people claim to be of rulers' descent (*nakombse*). Others consider themselves to be autochthonous "children of the earth" (*tengabiise*), or blacksmiths, weavers, and so on (Izard 1985). Many of these collective identities are distinguished on the basis of common patrilineal descent, but status groups may also comprise various kin groups. This social diversity strongly identifies differences in "traditional" ritual practices. Each group is supposed to have its own "tradition" (*rogem miki*) inherited from, and directed toward, its own ancestors, which explains the diversity in ritual practices and the widespread tolerance of other people's rituals. The enormous variation between different groups may at times confuse the anthropologist, but for people in Maane it is just a matter of "everyone with their own road."

Religious conversion of individual members within a group does not necessarily imply the demise of family rituals. On the contrary, even though Muslims and Roman Catholics abstain from traditional sacrificial tasks, they normally attend and appreciate the goals of their group's ritual practices (e.g., rituals to ensure a good harvest). Only Protestants avoid all contact with tradition, and they often opt for moving away from their kinsmen. Conversion to Islam sometimes implicates whole groups. In those cases traditional practices related to the ancestors or earth shrines are abandoned. According to the national census of 1996, Maane has a total population of about 40,000, with roughly 22,500 classified as *animistes,* 7,000 as *Musulmans,* 5,500 as *Catholiques,* and 4,000 as *Protestants.* Unfortunately, these figures are of limited value, if only because they presuppose mutual exclusion. In practice, people switch religious alliances regularly over time, or they may combine various religions simultaneously.

For all inhabitants of Maane, agriculture is crucial. Everyone farms, often in combination with commercial and craft activities. The conditions for farming are extremely difficult, with irregular rainfall and poor soil making food production haphazard. Scarcity of land and uncertain yields have given tremendous impetus to migration. Economically motivated migration dates back to at least the colonial period and has its origins in the practices of *travail forcé* and heavy tax burdens (Marchal 1986; Cordell and Gregory 1982; Cordell, Gregory and Piché 1996). Migration is a major factor in conversion. In particular, Islam provides migrants with a strong sense of belonging wherever they are.

The rainy season is unpredictable in Maane: red and white sorghum, millet, some peanuts, beans and vegetables are sown and planted in June in the hope of a harvest in October or November. In this situation, labor linked to the harvest takes two forms: work on the land, and ritual activities.

Differences in group identities emerge during the agricultural cycle. At the start of the season specific groups perform rituals to provide the seedlings with a life principle or a "soul" (*siiga*). Without a soul, grains are not considered nutritive. Then, when the crops start to ripen in the fields (September/October), the palace of the chief of Maane becomes a center of ritual activities. These chiefly rituals are said to stimulate the process of ripening. Subsequently, at harvesting time, all but Muslim patrilineal groups perform "first-fruit" ceremonies. Only after the ancestors have been offered drinks and food prepared from the new crops are farmers free to use the new harvest for their own consumption. When new-harvest beer has finally been brewed and libated, the new crops can be sold at the market.

The dry season is a time for leisure and rituals. Beer is important in both. The dry season provides ample opportunities to those who love the taste of a good calabash of beer. The most popular place for people to enjoy beer is the market. Markets have a three-day cycle, which suits the process of beer brewing perfectly. The *département* of Maane has three major villages with markets—Maane, Silmidougou and Zeko—and the system of alternate market days allows notorious drinkers daily attendance at a market during the dry season.

With a three-day cycle, Sunday is market day every third week. This market day is called the "twenty-one," and is larger in terms of goods and beer availability than the weekday markets. This may be indicative of Christian influences. Indeed, a strong Christian influence pervades the market. The majority of professional beer brewers in Maane are Roman Catholic women. Their *dolocabaret*, the common West African term for commercial beer outlets, are visited by Roman Catholics and people adhering to traditional ritual practices. Men are the main customers, but women may, without risk of disapproval, join in. Beer prices run from CFA Franc 50 for a small calabash to CFA Franc 650 for a larger earthenware pot—a *canarie*.[4] The gender bias of the customers belies women's financial constraints. Within limits, drinking at the expense of others is socially accepted, but always hanging around bars in the hope of sponging drinks off others testifies to a lack of shame (*yande*).

The dry season, however, offers regular opportunities for free drinking. In particular, funerary rituals provide occasions for drinking and socializing. After the first-fruit ceremonies, the newly harvested sorghum can be sold at the market, or used for beer brewing connected with funerary rituals, the so-called *kuure*. These rituals, characteristic of West Africa, take place long after the actual burial of the deceased and serve to turn the dead into an ancestor (Goody 1962; Liberski 1991; Bruyer 1987). Two categories of relatives of the deceased brew beer, namely, all the classificatory children of the dead, and the in-laws. Men who are married to a daughter or sister of the house of the deceased bring beer brewed by their wives. In recent times, the children of the dead have started taking great pride in excessive brewing. Funerals have become potlatch—like occasions for gaining individual prestige. Young migrants in particular use their parents' funerary rituals to show off, coming back specifically for the mortuary rituals. After years of absence, they want to advertise their success. Male migrants buy large quantities of red sorghum to facilitate their sisters' extensive brewing. At funerary rituals anyone may come to drink, and there is no limit to the amount one drinks. Drinking continues for three days until the beer has gone off. In a proper funerary ritual large amounts of sour beer are left over.

After a good harvest, beer is abundant in Maane. The markets and the many funerary rituals going on in various villages during the dry season afford those who like beer, and who are not inhibited from drinking for religious reasons, ample opportunities for heavy drinking.

"TRADITION" AND WOMEN'S ROLE IN RITUAL BEER BREWING IN MAANE

People adhering to traditional ritual practices are called *rogem miki-damba,* people of the *rogem miki. Rogem miki is* literally translated as "to have been born" (*rogem*) and "to have found" (*miki*). Francophone Burkinabè generally translate the concept as *la coutume,* and in the French literature a recurring translation is *né-trouver* (Badini 1994: 108; Izard 1992: 125; Pageard 1969: 24). The translation is misleading because it suggests that Mooré speakers see the *rogem miki* as a set of customary rules of a static and unchanging nature.[5]

In the local discourse, the concept of *rogem miki* has a variety of meanings, some of which indicate that the "customs" are intrinsically subject to change. The *rogem miki* is not just a set of rules or the ancestral past; it is synonymous with the ancestors as they live and may act in the present (Badini 1994: 108).[6] Moreover, the ritual acts directed to the ancestors are referred to as *rogem miki.* In Mooré there is no word for "rituals" people just say, "We are going to do the *rogem miki.*" The notion of *rogem miki* indicates the ancestors as well as the ritual acts directed toward them. People stress the burdensome and difficult nature of the customary practices. For ordinary mortals the rules are too difficult to remember, and mistakes and changes are inevitable. Customs are bound to change either through unintentional errors or through skillful adaptation.[7]

This use of the notion "to have been born and to have found" is crucial for understanding ritual practices and their changes, and for the relationship among the various religions people in Maane adhere to. All informants insist that one should be careful with "customary" ritual practices. The *rogem miki*, in its capacity as a living entity composed of all that existed in the world before the present, may act to set limits to manipulations and changes. Prudence characterizes the behavior of people who practice the customs, as well as those who have decided to convert.

In contrast to other West African societies (van Beek 1987), beer brewing in Maane is an exclusively female activity. Even though potentially a very lucrative economic activity, men do not engage in the production or the sale of beer. The process of brewing takes two days and is closely associated with pregnancy and childbirth. A popular drinking song states: *Raam saamba yaa "kagiendi," a mao yaa "kanegekoom." Bamb biga yaa "rayita." Bamb faa sondre yaa "yiimyiire."* (The father of beer is called a "bundle of millet," his mother is "to mix the water." Their child's name is "the day after tomorrow." Their family name: "forget the worries.") Beer brewing is likened to a child about to be born.

The association with fertility is also evident in the stages of brewing the beer. Women brew for rituals in their marital house as wives in virilocal residence, and also in their natal homes as daughters. Most of the beer brewed in the context of annual rituals is prepared by wives, whereas funeral beers demand substantial brewing activity by sisters of the house. In courtyards of every residential unit, large water basins and fireplaces are used for beer brewing. Senior wives and sisters may use these places for ritual brewing or for the commercial preparation of beer.

The distinction between brewing for rituals and for the market is important. Certain procedures and outcomes arising from ritual brewing are deemed out of bounds for "ordinary" beer brewings. To illustrate this, I will first describe the process of beer brewing in general, and then specify the effect of particular ritual contexts in the palace and houses of ordinary people in Maane.

In Maane, beer is made of red sorghum that has been made to sprout by a process of wetting the grains. The germinated grains are crushed to malt at the grinding place. Most beer brewing for ritual purposes has specific rules for grinding. The senior wives responsible for the brewing cannot ask for any help from younger women, and they should not speak loudly at the grinding place. During the course of the day enormous amounts of water are fetched, and the real brewing starts shortly before nightfall. In the large water basins in the courtyard the malt is mixed with water. After the heaviest substances have sunk to the bottom, the surface water (*rakoom* or beer water) is poured into large jars above the fireplace. The mixture is put on the fire for about an hour. Beer that is brewed for rituals often demands an additional gesture: before the beer water can be put on the fire, a libation is required. The brewer throws some of the beer water on the ground for the ancestors present. This never happens when beer is being brewed for commercial reasons.

The result of cooking is called *biiskado* (ripening raw). The mixture has to cool down, and during the night the beer water should turn sour (*mikame*). Good brewers know exactly when to stop the souring process. They stay awake to around 3 A.M. or 4 A.M. to determine the right moment. Again, a heavy sediment settles, leaving the surface water. The surface water in its pot is returned to the fire to make malt beer (*zam*). The curdled sediment is also boiled separately, then filtered[8] and mixed with the malt beer. It will be filtered after cooking, and the filtered beer water is mixed with the malt beer. The resulting mixture is the real malt beer. These two brewing sessions take all day. On the evening of the second brewing day, yeast is thrown into the malt beer. This again demands perfect timing. The process of fermentation will take another night, and by the following morning the beer will be ready for consumption.

The association of beer brewing with childbirth is particularly clear from the names given to the final steps when the yeast is added to the beer. The malt beer starts fizzing after the yeast is added, and the noise is associated with a baby's cry. The more the baby cries, the better the beer will taste. For this reason a beer brewer may ask one of her children with a reputation for being a cry-baby to come to throw the yeast in. The crying capacity of this child will be transmitted to stimulate the fermentation of the beer. That night and the next morning the young beer is called "baby" (*bipelga*). Thereafter, as the beer settles down and starts to turn sour, it "grows older." Beer that is one day old is called "old person" (*nikiema*).

Links between beer brewing and childbirth are very explicit. One morning I heard that my neighbor, a renowned beer brewer, had just given birth to a child, and I went to congratulate her. One of her best friends and a brewing colleague pointed to the child and said, "Last night we did not give birth to beer, but to this [child]!"

BEER IN "CUSTOMARY" RITUALS

Annual and life-cycle rituals form the heart of the "customary" rituals, the *rogem miki*, and beer is never absent from these rituals. Marriages demand the brewing of sweet (happy) beer; mortuary rituals go with bitter (sorrow) beer. Beer is the customary beverage, so crucial that it is simply referred to as "water." Beer's centrality in rituals is most significant in the annual rituals associated with the agrarian calendar. In the context of the ripening and first-fruit ceremonies, the process of beer brewing and the ritual role of female beer brewers are key. Annual rituals at the end of the season involve the ancestors. In the palace, the chief engages in relations with his predecessors, while in the houses of ordinary people the first-fruit ceremonies involve libations to the ancestors of the house.

Both these ritual contexts necessitate the arrival of the ancestors in the houses of the living. The homes of the living are supposed to be situated in the east, whereas the ancestors reside in the west. The east-west axis is important in all rituals relating to the ancestors. In funerary rituals, the ritual performer aims to establish the departure of the spirit of the deceased from the house. He or she has to move toward the west to join the ancestors. Annual rituals imply the return of the ancestors among the living in the east. The movement of the moon signals the passages that can be made between the residence of the ancestors and the houses of the living.[9]

For annual rituals, the first appearance of the new moon and the subsequent fourteen days are crucial. The moon "walks" from west to east, and so do the ancestors. This period is considered to be daytime for the ancestors, whereas they are asleep—and absent from the houses of the living—during the waning moon. Rituals that demand the presence of the ancestors are planned during the waxing moon. Funerary rituals (*kuure*), on the other hand, scheduled years after the actual burial of the deceased, take place in the fourteen days of the waning moon.

The annual rituals of the chief coincide with specific stages in the growth of sorghum. The stages are equated to pregnancy and the birth of a child, and the chief's rituals occur both when the sorghum becomes pregnant and when the eyes open.[10]

At the end of the agricultural season, rituals called "fleeing from the moon" are scheduled for the three subsequent appearances of the new moon.[11] With the arrival of the new moon that comes closest to the phase in which the millet "becomes pregnant," the first "fleeing from the moon" takes place.

I studied these rituals in 1991–92 and 1993–94, but only in the last year did I attend all three successive "fleeings from the moon" (Luning 1997). Each time beer brewing was at the heart of the activities. The arrival of the predecessors constitutes the necessary condition for the senior wives of the chief to start brewing beer. Shortly before the appearance of the new moon, the chief "flees" his palace to the east so that the predecessors may move in from the west. The evening when the moon appears on the western horizon signals the arrival of the predecessors. The names of the founding chiefs of Maane are drummed to confirm their presence in the palace. The beer brewing can then begin.

In the first two "fleeings from the moon" beer is brewed with last year's malt made of red sorghum from the chief's main field. The new crops are still ripening in the field and the beer brewing provides encouragement in these last stages. The process of beer brewing strongly resembles the description given above, though one important gesture is added. Before the brewing starts, the senior wife goes to her main field to fetch some ripening ears of red sorghum. The ears contain similarly pregnant sorghum, and the second time "sorghum with the eyes open." As soon as the beer water boils on the fire, these ears are thrown into the jars. The ears thus go through the whole process of beer brewing, ending with the "birth of a baby." In this manner the beer brewing mimics a process of transition that should also happen to the crops in the field, leading to a complete ripening. The conceptualization of the beer brewing process forms the basis of the efficacy attributed to the two brewing sessions preceding the harvest.

The third "fleeing from the moon" takes place after the harvest and resembles the first-fruit ceremonies in ordinary houses. The beer brewed with new red sorghum makes the harvest available for sale at the market. To accomplish this, the ancestors have come to the houses to join the beer drinking. Consequently, first-fruit ceremonies also coincide with the appearance of the new moon. The preparations for beer brewing help to trigger the arrival of the ancestors, demanding the previously mentioned precautions during the grinding of the sorghum.

In all three "fleeings from the moon" beer brewing establishes ritual effects: before the harvest the brewings stimulate the growth of the crops, and later they encourage the presence of the ancestors.

RITUAL VERSUS ORDINARY BEER BREWING

These examples demonstrate what makes a daily routine activity like beer brewing into a ritual act. Goody (1977) makes the point that general definitions of ritual are not useful. The current tendency in anthropology is to study the specific strategies employed to set certain behavior apart from ordinary social life. Bell (1992) states that ritual is not *a priori* a separate domain of specific social activities. Certain events, like a harvest, demand actions that people formalize and demarcate by procedural rules. Through a negotiating process, certain social activities are ritualized. Which activities are labeled as "ritual" as opposed to "ordinary" is an ongoing question for researchers. This labeling is what Bell, borrowing from Gluckman (1962), calls "ritualization." Too often anthropologists evade the problem related to the term "ritual" by simply referring to types of ritual: marriages, first-fruit ceremonies, sacrifice, and so on. These descriptive typologies appear unproblematic because they concern events and acts that seem inherently ritualistic. Crucial aspects of what ritual is and does extend beyond the scope of anthropological discussion.

In this regard, the case-study material from Maane is revealing. There is nothing inherently "ritualistic" about beer brewing. It may be a strictly income-generating activity, it may be a preliminary act preceding the start of a ritual, and it may also be part of ritual work. If the latter is the case, indeed, as Bell's theory suggests, this can be deduced from specific rules applied to the process of brewing. The rules serve to ritualize beer brewing. Acknowledging this process of ritualization necessitates recognizing the contribution of women. The literature on rituals in Burkina Faso pays a lot of attention to the "big" rituals such as sacrifice.[12] Because these acts of ritual killing are largely the work of men, women's ritual work goes unnoticed. Moreover, blood sacrifices have traditionally drawn more anthropological attention than libations.[13]

The question of when beer brewing is and when it is not ritualized points to a second feature that has so far been ignored in the literature, namely, the relational perspective of ritual work. We have seen that beer brewing in Maane is ritualized when it has to produce certain outcomes, for example, the coming of the ancestors. The nature of this ritual work implies that, even though the ancestors exist at any time, people are not involved in active relationships with them all the time. On the contrary, certain ritualized acts have to first modify these relationships before other ritual goals can be achieved (such as the growth of crops and sharing first fruits). In Maane, quite a sharp distinction is made between ritual and ordinary time. In ordinary times the ancestors are not close to the living—they are away in the west. In order to relate to them, a situation of contiguity has to be created. Beer brewing serves that purpose.

My case study from Maane differs in this respect from those of other regions described by anthropologists and historians. McAllister (1993), for instance, emphasizes that it is difficult to distinguish beer brewed for ritual purposes from that brewed for social purposes. Whenever beer is drunk among the Zulu, the "shades" (ancestors) always take their part. Here, the distinction between ritual and social use of beer is defined in terms of people and other beings being implicated in the relations of commensality. The distinction between ritual and nonritual uses of beer is often determined by the exchange partners involved: is the beer exclusively consumed by human beings, or are supernatural beings involved? Rekdal (1996), like Karp (1980), argues that this boundary is not always very sharply defined. He proposes that this is perhaps the reason why drinking, or not drinking, may reflect important social and religious boundaries. He assumes that Christians and Muslims would decide not to drink because they could not be sure if the ancestors were among their drinking partners.

In Maane, Rekdal's argument would have to be put on its head: the boundaries of drinking, inclusive or exclusive of the ancestors, are quite clear. On ordinary social occasions the ancestors do not take part. For them to participate, they have to be consciously invited during the production process. Beer is the drink par excellence associated with creating contiguity with the ancestors. Thus, the social and religious boundaries related to whether one drinks or not are not so much an outcome of restrictions on the act of beer consumption, but more significantly encompass the way in which beer is produced, that is, whether or not its production is ritualized.

BEER BREWING, DRINKING, AND RELIGIOUS CONVERSION

How do converts relate to the various contexts in which beer is produced and consumed? We have seen that people adhering to traditional ritual practices are called *rogem miki-damba*. It is important to underline that these customs are seen as a living entity: the ancestors as they live, act and receive offerings in the present. Changing religion is to leave the *rogem miki*. People of the *rogem miki*, Muslims (*more*), Protestants and Roman Catholics (*mon père-damba*, "people of *mon père*") all agree that this is a weighty matter. The expression goes, "You can leave the customs, but the customs do not leave you" (*Fo toin n baas rogem miki la rogem miki pa nan baas fo ye*). All three groups of religious converts have their own strategies for severing or preserving relations with the customs. The differences come to the fore in attitudes toward beer.[14]

In Burkina Faso, Protestants are called *mericandamba*. The Assemblée de Dieu is nowadays mainly made up of Burkinabè *pasteurs*, but started in the early 1920s on the initiative of American Baptists (Bonnet 1989: 315). Protestants take great care to stay away from ritual contexts related to the ancestors. Protestant preachers stress the wrath of the ancestors and that any form of contact with them should be categorically avoided. This explains their attitudes toward the drinking of malt. Even though Protestants do not drink beer, they are allowed to consume malt. However, one sort of malt should never be drunk, namely, malt that has been prepared for use in funerary rituals. Consuming this malt could bring the converts into close contact with their ancestors because they are believed to be drinking the same beer simultaneously. The ancestors would use the occasion to kill the Protestants and take revenge for their neglect. This Protestant rule of avoidance confirms the very existence of the ancestors. Obviously, those who leave the *rogem miki* do not simply adopt a new set of moral ideas. The changes they want are inspired by their assessment of the present nature of ritual practices. In doing so, Protestants do not simply acknowledge the existence of the ancestors, they also confirm the importance of the relationship between the ritualized production of beer on the one hand, and the establishment of relations of contiguity with "that which precedes" on the other. Hence, they studiously avoid everything associated with the ritual production of beer.

The attitudes of Roman Catholics in Maane contrast sharply with those of Protestants. Roman Catholics both drink and brew beer. Roman Catholic women are the market's foremost brewers, but they also continue to participate in brewing for ritual purposes. In fact, Roman Catholics in Maane brew up a most interesting mixture of pleasure, blessing and custom adherence. This mixture can be understood in relation to historical developments connected with the Catholic mission.

The activities of Roman Catholic missionaries have been extensively documented in the context of the French colonial regime from the beginning of the twentieth century until 1960 (Skinner 1964; Benoist 1987). Catholic missionaries occupied an ambiguous position vis-à-vis the colonial administration. At various times both the colonial staff and the missionaries of the *Pères Blancs* styled their efforts as a *mission civilisatrice*, blaming each other for their recourse to conservatism and dependency on the hierarchical feudal structures of Moose chiefdoms. After the French administration admitted the failure of its policy of *assimilation*, the mission stressed individualistic values. Accordingly, colonial officers changed the moral discourse to one in which respect for indigenous social structures was proclaimed under the label of *association*. The missionaries posed as a liberating, enlightened force. They offered refuge to girls who wanted to escape arranged marriages and gave protection against so-called feudal chiefly power-holders (Benoist 1987). Despite the slogan "liberty, equality and brotherhood," these power-holders were strengthened in their position by the colonial authorities. In the process, relations between the mission and Moose chiefs were strained. Chiefs accused the missionaries of using the girls who had fled to them as the basis for building their own alternative marriage system: boys who converted would be given a Catholic wife, providing a strong incentive to convert to Catholicism (Skinner 1964).

The antagonism between the Roman Catholic Church and the Moose chiefs intensified during the run-up to national independence. After World War II, the chiefs had to compete for positions of power with new indigenous groups voicing political ambitions. These included *anciens combattants* (young men with an Islamic educational background) and especially young Catholic *séminaristes.* The first president of independent Haute-Volta (the former name of Burkina Faso), Maurice Yameogo, demonstrates the point. Soon after his nomination he declared the chiefs to be his main enemies. So in direct contrast to colonial times, the Roman Catholic Church has, since independence, been strongly associated with the national state and its "*fonctionnaires*."

However, Maane case-study material reveals that the political situation is more complex. At present the Catholic Church operates in a dual fashion. In the towns, Catholic liturgy and teachings have a modern profile. Mass is said in French and the importance of modern values is stressed: monogamous marriage, free choice in partner selection, baptism, and so on. In the villages such as those in Maane, a quite different approach is taken. The local language, Mooré, is the vehicle of communication. In Mass the emphasis is on the value of the belief in God. This is interpreted very liberally and allows converts to pursue their existing lifestyle. The issue of polygamy is never brought up, and the lack of choice for marital partners and marriage practices are also not mentioned. Moreover, Catholic Church teachings stress the compatibility of tradition (*rogem miki*) and conversion. The present strategy of the Roman Catholic Church at a local level can be described as one of *association.*

Local Roman Catholic practices concerning beer production and consumption are similarly laissez-faire. One of the daughters of the chief of Maane is a nun and came back to Maane to preside over Mass one Sunday. Afterwards, a big feast was organized to celebrate her visit. Modern brewed beer was abundant. When I asked if I could photograph her, she walked over to the table and grabbed a bottle of beer with which to be photographed. The message was clear: the Roman Catholic Church does not oppose the drinking of beer.

Roman Catholic women who choose to brew beer for the market do not risk the disapproval of the clergy. Meanwhile, many Catholics in Maane continue to participate actively in customary ritual practices. Roman Catholic women brewers do not fear contact with the ancestors. Many of them are, however, quite explicit: they brew for rituals, and they will drink this beer, but they do not drink the beer in a calabash that is used for libations. Thus, direct communion with the ancestors is avoided. This avoidance is not caused by feelings of fear. Roman Catholics do not consider their conversion to Catholicism as a dangerous break with traditional local customs. They do, however, want to show that they participate in customs as Roman Catholics. The abstinence from traditional communion with the ancestors marks these participants as different, not as dissidents.

The adherence of Roman Catholics to customary practices has recently led to interesting innovations. Most young Roman Catholics have changed their participation in first-fruit ceremonies. The elders of their respective houses still offer their first-fruit beer in accordance with the movement of the moon. These ritual offerings are performed on behalf of the whole household, making it possible for the new harvest of all household members to be sold. The younger Roman Catholic members of the house delay their ritual brewing. They wait until Christmas so as to celebrate a variety of religious beliefs simultaneously. This postponed beer brewing does not aim to have any ritual effect, be it to trigger the arrival of the ancestors, or to make the new harvest available to the living. Rather, it is intended solely for social purposes and marks a big Catholic feast in which good beer contributes to a very merry Christmas.

CONCLUSION

In Maane, beer is central to a set of traditional religious practices as well as to the sociability of work parties and economic objectives at the marketplace. Brewing beer for ritual purposes is different from beer brewing for the market. Specific rules set the ritual activity apart from ordinary beer brewing. In Maane, it is significant that the beer production process can itself be a ritual act with specific goals.

Why beer is the main medium for communicating with the ancestors cannot be understood solely from its use as a beverage for offering. There are other drinks such as flower-water that may be used for this purpose. In addition to beer consumption and exchange patterns, the production side has to be taken into account. In most West African studies, beer is analyzed in terms of its ritual role or as an economic asset. In relation to rituals, beer is seen as a means of communication and exchange with the ancestors. I have argued that the ritual importance of beer in Maane can only be understood in relation to the way beer is produced. The production of beer is not just an act preceding a sacrificial ritual. Beer brewing can be the heart of ritual work, and the brewing process itself embodies the aims of the ritual performers.

Thus, this chapter on beer brewing as effective ritual work contributes to three debates. First, through an analysis of the relation between ritual and brewing it is clear that women are major ritual agents in Maane. Consequently, the rather exclusive emphasis on male activities in descriptions of rituals of a sacrificial nature that appears in the literature can be contested. Second, I revisit the debate on the question of what "ritual behavior" is. Beer brewing in Maane is considered to be a ritual act only in specific cases. Brewing beer for commercial purposes is not. This raises the question of how the distinction between ritual and nonritual brewing arises and what this tells us about the nature of ritual acts. Third, the value of beer production and consumption in ritual contexts has been highlighted to facilitate an understanding of the ways in which converts to other religions opt out of, or keep their distance from, certain customary practices and association with beer as a traditional drink. Roman Catholics have a very liberal attitude toward "traditional" customs, whereas Protestants are more negative. Comparison of their post-conversion attitudes is highly revealing, because their attitudinal differences are related to the distinctions between the production and consumption sides of beer's ritual uses.

The notion of *rogem miki*, "to have been born and to have found," is crucial for an understanding of local tradition and what is at stake once people convert to other religious practices. To protect themselves, Protestants make a severe but decisive break with local customs by avoiding all contact with ritual beer brewing and choosing "not to drink" for fear of their ancestors' wrath. By contrast, Roman Catholics seem at ease in combining traditional and Catholic practices but avoid the most direct forms of communion with the ancestors. In Maane, everyone remains aware of the ancestors, and the production of beer remains at the center of effective ritual practice, but Christians subtly distance themselves to greater or lesser degrees through their drinking habits.

NOTES

1. Islamic attitudes toward drinking have been dealt with in various West African contexts. See, for example, Gaillard 1995.

2. The singular is "Moaga." Mossi is the French version of the ethnonym. The language spoken by Moose is Mooré, a Voltaic language (Manessy 1975).

3. The research was limited to Mooré speakers.

4. These are the prices when red sorghum is at an average price after a relatively good harvest. The preparation of about seventeen *canaries* demands the purchase of five *tines* (the local measure) of sorghum, which may cost CFA Franc 1,750. In addition, one cart of firewood (CFA Franc 3,000) would be needed.

5. Izard writes, for instance, "Ce qu'on est *né-trouver* c'est la coutume envisagée comme un ordre immuable, à propos duquel ne se posent que les questions de sa préservation et de sa transmission" (1992: 125).

6. The expression for libations in Mooré is "We are going to give water to what we found at birth. *Ed nan kot rogem miki koom.*" Water means beer, the most important liquid used in libations.

7. Luning (1997) provides examples of errors and changes in the performance of rituals.

8. The waste product is excellent food for pigs. Therefore most professional brewers keep pigs.

9. During the period called the white moon (*kipeelgo*, indicated by Europeans as a waxing moon), the moon moves from west to east, and during the waning moon from east to west.

10. Depending on the variety, 100 to 135 days elapse between sowing and harvesting sorghum. The midway stage, when the plant does not as yet have grains at the top, is called "maiden" (*kipoaka*) sorghum (*ki* is the generic word for varieties of sorghum and millet; *poaka* refers to females who are still too young to give birth). Subsequently the leaves at the top start to contain grains: the sorghum "has a belly" (*ki tara poga*) just like a pregnant woman. When the grains start to come out of their envelope of leaves, the sorgho "gets its eyes" (*ki tara nini*). Finally, when the last protective covers drop off the grains, "the eyes open" (*nini pukdame*).

11. *Kiuzoega*: *kiygu* (moon), *zoega* (to run away from).

12. This is exemplified in a whole series on sacrifice in *Systèmes de Pensée en Afrique Noire*, edited by M. Cartry between 1974 and 1983. See also Cartry (ed.) (1987) and de Heusch (1986).

13. This dates from the classical studies by W. Robertson Smith (1894) and Hubert and Mauss (1964).

14. Only Protestants and Roman Catholics are discussed here, as they contrast in their emphasis on the production and consumption of beer within rituals.

REFERENCES

Badini, A. 1994. *Naître et Grandir chez les Moosé Traditionnels*. Paris/Ouagadougou: Sepia- ADDB.

Barthes, R. 1967. *Système de la Mode*. Paris: Editions de Seuil.

Beek, W.E.A. van. 1987. *Bierbrouwers in de Bergen: De Kapsiki en Higi van Noord-Kameroen en Noord-Oost Nigeria*. Utrecht: Instituut voor Culturele Antropologie.

Bell, C. 1992. *Ritual Theory, Ritual Practice*. New York: Oxford University Press.

Benoist, J.R. 1987. *Eglise et Pouvoir Colonial au Soudan Français*. Paris: Harmattan.

Bonnet, D. 1989. "Désordres Psychiques, Etiologies Moose et Changement Social." *Pschychopathologie Africaine 1988–89* 22: 293–325.

Bourdieu, P. 1979. *La Distinction: Critique Sociale du Jugement*. Paris: Editions de Minuit.

Bruyer, A. 1987. *Que Font en Brousse les Enfants du Mort? Morphologie et Rituels chez les Moosi*. Paris: EHESS.

Cartry, M. 1987. "Le Suaire du Chef." In M. Cartry (ed.), *Sous le Masque de l'Animal: Essais sur le Sacrifice en Afrique Noire*. Paris: PUF, Bibliothèque de l'Ecole des Hautes Etudes, Section des Sciences Religieuses, 88: 131–231.

Cordell, D., and J. Gregory. 1982. "Labour Reservoir and Population: French Colonial Strategies in Koudougou, Upper Volta, 1914–1939." *Journal of African History* 23: 205–24.

Cordell, D., J. Gregory, and V. Piché. 1996. *Hoe and Wage: A Social History of a Circular Migration System in West Africa*. Boulder: Westview Press.

Douglas, M. (ed.). 1984. *Constructive Drinking: Perspectives on Drink from Anthropology*. Cambridge: Cambridge University Press.

Gaillard, G. 1995. "Les Yola du Compony: Un Cas de Conversion en Guinée Maritime." *Islam et Sociétés au Sud du Sahara* 9: 5–29.

Gluckman, M. 1962. "Les Rites du Passage." In D. Forde (ed.), *Essays on the Rituals of Social Relations*. Manchester: Manchester University Press, 20–35.

Goody, J. 1962. *Death, Property and the Ancestors*. Stanford: Stanford University Press.

———. 1977. "Against 'Ritual': Loosely Structured Thoughts on a Loosely Defined Topic." In S. Falk Moore and B.G. Myerhoff (eds.), *Secular Rituals*. Assen, The Netherlands: van Gorcum, 25–35.

Hammond-Tooke, W.D. 1962. *Bhaca Society: A People of the Transkeian Uplands, South Africa*. Cape Town: Oxford University Press.

Heusch, L. de. 1986. *Le Sacrifice dans les Religions Africaines*. Paris: Gallimard.

Hubert, H., and M. Mauss. 1964. *Sacrifice, Its Nature and Function*. 1899. Reprint, London: Cohen and West.

Izard, M. 1970. *Introduction à l'Histoire des Royaumes Mossi*. Paris/Ouagadougou: Recherches Voltaïques, 12 and 13.

———. 1985. *Gens du Pouvoir, Gens de la Terre: Les Institutions Politiques de l'Ancien Royaume du Yatenga (Bassin de la Volta Blanche)*. Cambridge: Cambridge University Press.

———. 1992. *L'Odyssée du Pouvoir. Un Royaume Africain: Etat, Société, Destin Individuel*. Paris: EHESS, Bibliothèque de la Maison des Sciences Humaines.

Karp, I. 1980. "Beer Drinking and Social Experience in an African Society: An Essay in Formal Sociology." In I. Karp and C. Bird (eds.), *Explorations in African Systems of Thought*. Washington, DC: Smithsonian Institution Press, 83–119.

Lévi-Strauss, C. 1968. *Origine des Manières de Table*. Paris: Plon.

Liberski, D. 1991. *Les Dieux du Territoire. Unité et Morcellement de l'Espace en Pays Kasena, Burkina Faso*. Paris: EPHE.

Luning, S. 1997. *Het Binnenhalen van de Oogst: Ritueel en Samenleving in Maane, Burkina Faso*. Leiden: Centre for Non-Western Studies.

Manessy, G. 1975. *Les Langues Oti-Volta: Classification Généalogique d'un Groupe de Langues Voltaïques*. Paris: SELAF.

Marchal, J.Y. 1986. "Prémisses d'un Etat Moderne? Les Projets Coloniaux dans le Bassin des Volta, 1897–1960." *Cahiers d'Etudes Africaines* 103 (26): 403–20.

McAllister, P.A. 1993. "Indigenous Beer in Southern Africa: Functions and Fluctuations." *African Studies* 52 (1): 71–88.

Pageard, R. 1969. *Le Droit Privé des Mossi: Tradition et Evolution*. Ouagadougou/Paris: Recherches Voltaïques.

Rekdal, O.B. 1996. "Money, Milk and Sorghum Beer: Change and Continuity among the Iraqw." *Africa* 66 (3): 367–85.

Robertson Smith, W. 1894. *Lectures on the Religion of the Semites*. Edinburgh: Black.

Skinner, E.P. 1964. *The Mossi of the Upper Volta: The Political Development of a Sudanese People*. Stanford: Stanford University Press.

13

Modernity's Limits

Pentecostalism and the Moral Rejection of Alcohol in Malawi

Rijk van Dijk

One bright, sunny afternoon, a large gathering of people assembled at Mpemba, a small village near Blantyre, Malawi's main commercial and industrial city. Addressing them from a platform overlooking the crowd was a young woman dressed in a flowing white robe. Much to the amazement and shock of many, after singing a few Christian songs, the young lady exploded, crying, screaming and stamping her feet. Most insultingly, she pointed her finger at members of her audience, lashing her listeners with one insult after another totally out of keeping for a woman of her age and stature. Calling her audience drunkards more interested in nocturnal orgies where witches (*afiti*) indulge in eating human flesh and enjoy dancing naked (*kutamba*) than in praising God, she angrily rebuked them:

> You, you are clapping your hands (in praise of God) as if you have thorns in your hands! But when we see you in the taverns you are active, clapping your hands with force for the devil. I tell you *dzidakwa* (drunkards): when Jesus comes, some of you will be caught red-handed, spilling *kachasu* (local distillate) from the big bottle to the small cup that you use when drinking! (Linley Mbeta, Mpemba Jama, 8 April 1989)

The crowd's shock turned to hilarity. The young woman's mimicking of the shaky movements of a drunkard trying to fill a cup with the local distillate provoked embarrassment-by-recognition of the effects of alcohol on the body. The laughter ended abruptly when the woman addressed her audience as *nthakati* (experts in sin and malice). Such drinking harms others and disrupts society. Such evil comes from the earth and *za kunthaka* (powers beneath the earth's surface), while redemption from such evil, the woman proclaimed, comes from heaven and from *ku lapa* (repentance to God).

The young woman in question here is Linley Mbeta, the leader-founder of the Redemption Voice Ministry, one of the many born-again Christian fundamentalist groups that have sprung up in Malawi's urban areas since the late 1970s. Linley Mbeta is one of the best-known preachers of the group of thirty that I studied in Blantyre (van Dijk 1994, 1995). She became a national figure, known for her effective anti-witchcraft campaigns following a rebirth she experienced in April 1985. At the time of this sermon she was twenty-three years old. Her group has flourished and, after democratic changes in Malawi dating from 1994, came to be known as the *Dzimvere* (Obedience) Ministry (Kaunda 1995). Like many similar groups, fellowships and emerging churches belonging to this new Pentecostal movement that have swept through the country, its membership is drawn particularly from among the young and in some cases educated urbanites. The striking feature of this born-again charismatic Pentecostalism is its rigid insistence on a strict moral ideology and a denunciation of alcohol. The rejection of alcohol falls within a wider moral spectrum of activities, objects and rituals that these Pentecostal groups denounce while recommending other positively valued activities and rituals.

This chapter investigates the rejection of alcohol in Malawi's Pentecostal moral order from two perspectives: first, against the backdrop of developments in Malawi's Independent Christianity movement, and second, in relation to the modernist debate that this type of Pentecostalism represents. Paradoxically, the rejection of alcohol presents an image of being "modern" and therefore refraining from being a part of "traditional" Malawian culture. In anthropology, the emergence of Pentecostalism is generally believed to represent a specific variety of what generally can be termed "Christian fundamentalism," albeit Pentecostal groups offer extensive room for the expression of religious emotionalism which many other fundamentalist groups lack.

Christian and Muslim fundamentalism is widely explored within the theme of the ever-tightening grip of expansive, modern capitalism (Marty and Scott Appleby 1991; Caplan 1987; Gifford 1991). In anthropology this interpretative framework has been further developed by Taussig (1980) in Latin America and the Comaroffs (1991, 1993) in Africa. Their work has imparted a deeper cultural dimension, demonstrating how local societies interpret and negotiate the encroachment of modern forms, modern market relations, and commodities through the prisms of local representations of fear, danger and anxiety. An extensive anthropological literature has emerged in which local debates about witchcraft, demonic forces, threats and immorality are explored and explained in terms of modernity's malcontents (Comaroff and Comaroff 1993; Fisiy and Geschiere 1991; Geschiere and Fisiy 1994). Several authors—Meyer for Ghana (1995), Marshall for Nigeria (1993) and Maxwell for Zimbabwe (1998)—have situated Africa's new Pentecostal movements within this conceptual framework.

This chapter explores the extent to which Malawi's Pentecostal movements offer individuals the means of coming to terms with modernity and of dealing with its inherent dangers, in this case alcohol, by offering spiritual protection and seclusion. In the first section, the Pentecostal modernist moral order is explored in view of the development of Independent Christianity in Malawi. In the second section, more information is presented about the born-again movement, their ideology and their rejection of alcohol. In the final section, some conclusions are drawn with regard to the central place of this rejection in their ideology. The most important basis for these conclusions will be the acknowledgment of the fight of the born-agains against gerontocratic power structures.

POWERFUL LIQUIDS IN MALAWI'S COLONIAL PAST

The Pentecostal movement is the latest stage in the development of Independent Christianity in Malawi (MacDonald 1970; McCracken 1977; Chakanza 1982; Langworthy 1985; Schoffeleers 1985; van Dijk 1992b). Its moral views on alcohol should therefore be placed in the context of an understanding of how independent churches have developed in Malawi, and more specifically how they have placed themselves between two cosmological orders. One order was that of precolonial, "traditional" cosmology, its symbolism and ritual practice. The other order was that of mission Christianity, which arrived in Malawi in the second half of the nineteenth century. During the 1870s, Scottish missionaries started preaching a moral regime and cultural logic of orderly conduct, containment of body and soul, and abstinence from lustful violations of moral integrity.

Following the work of Akyeampong (1996) on alcohol in Ghana, one can trace the arrival of modernity in Malawi through the missionaries' insistence on a mode of inspection and supervision of what may be called the powerful liquids: blood, alcohol and water. In line with the missionaries' prohibitions against "paganism," indulgence in alcohol was condemned and its ceremonial presence at various "heathen rituals" rejected. Interestingly, the missionaries never denied the relationship between alcohol and the world of the unseen. After all, during Holy Communion, wine symbolizes the relationship among God the Father, Jesus and the Holy Spirit. Instead, in Christian ritual, missionaries introduced a sense of "inspection" of one's internal, moral world before wine, the Blood of Christ, could be consumed.

This relationship between in(tro)spection, alcohol and blood was further developed and represented by colonial medical practice. As Vaughan (1991) argued for Malawi and Zambia, the inspection of an individual patient's blood for the diagnosis of disease echoes local onlookers' understanding of modernity. The missionaries' moral inspection of the person through the doctrinal association between blood and wine bore similarities to the colonial medical practice of treating diseases, disinfecting and cleaning wounds by inspecting blood and administering alcohol. Both symbolized a new, modern notion of embodiment.

Water became a third powerful liquid domain of modernity through Christian baptism. Missionaries introduced water as the *madzi wa moyo*, the water of life, representing a transition from life to death to renewal of life through which eternity could be reached. Writing about the moral politics of water, the Comaroffs quote an early London missionary in Tswana who wrote, "Here vast moral wastes must be watered by the streams of life. Rainmakers are our inveterate enemies, and uniformly oppose the introduction of Christianity amongst their countrymen to the utmost of their power" (Comaroff and Comaroff 1991: 207–08). In time, water would become a major symbolic feature of syncretist and Africanized Christian movements. Baptism demonstrated the power of this liquid, representing the resurrection to life from the deep, dark waters of death. Before any baptism could take place, the person was subjected to inspection and ran the risk of being rejected if he or she had not renounced all heathen activities.

The colonial administrative and medical system introduced techniques for the inspection of water to prevent contamination. Colonial records indeed show how these measures facilitated the separation of black and white residential areas in emerging urban areas such as Blantyre, to prevent "contamination." The regime engaged in a seemingly hopeless battle to convince local populations to use only safe and pure drinking water. As Vaughan (1991) demonstrates with an element of irony, the colonial educational campaigns showed the local populace, on big cinema screens, how germs would multiply in contaminated water. This provoked disgust, anxiety, laughter and, above all, confusion.

In many instances the missionary and colonial ideological orders confronted and encroached upon existing cosmologies in which these three liquids carried deeply rooted symbolic meanings related to rituals of ancestral veneration, life power (*mphamvu*), spiritual forces, healing, and marriage and funerals. Alcohol played and still plays a significant symbolic role in the libation ritual (*nsembe*) whereby the first few drops of an alcoholic drink are poured in honor of ancestors in moments of consultation, rainmaking and secret dances. There are two generic distinctions in alcohol: *mowa* and *kachasu*. The first refers to alcoholic beverages that are beers produced by brewing, while the second refers to distilled beverages, although in both types maize and sugar are the raw materials. *Mowa* generally takes a prominent place in ancestral veneration in this pouring of libation (*ku tsira mowa*). *Kachasu*, on the other hand, is dominant in the strengthening of social relations, for instance between relatives at certain festivities such as marriages. At "beer parties" it is common to see *kachasu* being served, although it is not technically a brew. In general terms, alcohol plays a dominant role in the strengthening of ties with family ancestors and in the creation of mutual ties and obligations within the extended family. It is seen as a substance that binds the person to his family and keeps his identity "dividual," that is, eternally locked in social relations. Alcohol signals the presence of ancestral spirits (*mizimu*), which are mollified to release their benevolent powers onto the life of their descendants. Thus alcohol plays a role in constituting the subject as a dividual rather than an individual, a person whose well-being, protection, healing, future, coming into adulthood, marriage, death and funeral are directly located within the family and its *muzimu*.

INDEPENDENT CHURCHES AND DEMON ALCOHOL

Around the turn of the century independent churches emerged in Malawi presenting a syncretist cosmological order that combined elements from precolonial symbolism and ritual with selected elements from missionary teachings and colonial ideology. Malawi's independent churches evolved under the influence of black American religious communities originating from Illinois, and Pentecostal, Apostolic, Zionist and so-called Ethiopian churches offering religious revivalism, enthusiasm and ecstasy (Chakanza 1983; Fields 1985). These were soon recognized by the local population as places where there was room for acknowledging powers and spiritual experiences that the already established Christian missionary churches denied as mere superstition. Instead of negating the power of evil and ancestral spirits, affliction, and misfortune caused by witchcraft, independent churches incorporated elements of African cosmology, including the means for healing individual and social bodies as well as a toleration of polygamy. From the 1920s onwards, independent churches proliferated into hundreds of different churches usually led by one founding prophet. They occupied the middle ground between a range of traditional religious practices and notions, on the one hand, and the formal but foreign doctrine of missionary Christianity, on the other (Chakanza 1983).

In this middle terrain of independent churches, the moral inspection of individuals by powerful liquids remained a crucial undertaking. Ritual practices of the Zionist independent churches focused on the purifying application of water (Sundkler 1961; Daneel 1974; Kiernan 1981; Comaroff 1985). Holy water, blessed by the healing prophets, could be taken home for the ailing in bottles, and baptisms in streams of water were turned into grand and colorful events.

Representing an extremely wide range of moral programs, the location of alcohol in the independent churches' paradigm of powerful liquids was ambiguous (Schoffeleers 1985). In Zionist churches, for example, alcoholic beverages were strictly prohibited. Their production, however, was not, nor was trading in alcohol or its use in settings that required it to fulfill social obligations, for example at weddings and funerals. Although prophet leaders in these churches would ensure they were personally not involved in practices that would directly require them to apply alcohol, church workers' purposeful avoidance of social obligations where alcohol was involved was virtually impossible.

Most of these churches consisted and still consist primarily of women. Women are central to the production and redistribution of alcohol, and as such play an important role in the social relations that are maintained through its application (Englund 1996). Outright rejection by independent churches like the Zionists of any dealing with alcohol would deprive many committed members of additional income, of arranging social affairs and relational ties, and of structuring the male-female power balance that dictates control over resources commanded through alcohol. A strict prohibition on dealing with alcohol would alienate many women who produce alcohol to earn cash. The membership of independent churches would be jeopardized by a ban on alcohol, thus undermining the stature, influence and efficacy of the church.

The move of many independent churches from rural areas into the cities in conjunction with increasing rural-urban migration in the period just before and after World War II also influenced attitudes toward alcohol. Although Malawi is still one of the least urbanized countries of southern African (11 percent of the total population as opposed to 55 percent in Zambia), its urban areas began to expand rapidly after 1945 (van Binsbergen 1981). Independent churches played an important role in the migration process by providing a "home away from home" for the urban migrant (van Dijk 1998). The churches offered an array of comforting symbols and rituals derived from a rural cosmology.

The urban setting triggered a reorientation of people's leisuretime pursuits. Drinking gained importance as a social pastime because alcohol was more widely available than in rural areas. Factory-produced beer was on hand for those who could afford it, with Carlsberg having one of the biggest beer-producing plants in the region in operation in Blantyre. The informal sector supply of home brews, which dwarfed factory-produced beer, was geared to those with more limited purchasing power.

Most independent churches soon abandoned attempts to prohibit the use of alcohol and adopted an ambiguous position similar to the lukewarm rejection that the missionaries of established churches preached from their pulpits. Only those independent churches such as the Johane Masowe Apostles representing Puritanism in its "pure" form were able to establish closed communities that successfully kept urban life with its beer parties, taverns and pubs at bay (Dillon-Malone 1978).

Other churches faced difficulties supervising alcohol consumption that became more and more Western in style over time. The consumption of industrially produced beer and other alcoholic beverages figured prominently, especially among the young. In the 1980s, young urban couples were eager to indulge in conspicuous consumption at their wedding ceremonies by serving South African champagne. Older people were incredulous at the expense, labeling their behavior "K.T." (*katanghale*). This term refers to the conspicuous consumption of urban businessmen and "wheelers and dealers" that appalled the thrift-conscious first generation of urban migrants. In newspaper cartoons, a "K.T. man" is usually depicted with rows of empty beer bottles around him, indicating a lifestyle of indulgence if not gluttony.

In short, in the context of modern life, the independent churches reenacted rural rituals related to powerful liquids, especially water, but largely sidestepped the issue of alcohol and its association with new social roles, lifestyles and forms of consumption. Urban economic occupations like beer brewing evolved amid a sense of ambiguity about the place of alcohol in the social fabric of relations and balance of power. In urban areas the inspection, supervision and purification of "water" as well as "blood" for healing remained a strong paradigm within these churches. Alcohol, however, slipped beyond their control to lurk as a major source of impurity, defilement and temptation in the minds of the faithful.

BORN-AGAIN RIGIDITY, ALCOHOL, AND GENERATIONAL CONFLICT

In the mid-1970s, teenagers and secondary school and university students suddenly took to the streets of Malawi's main urban areas to proclaim a moral reordering of society based on Christian fundamentalist notions. A whole array of Pentecostal groups and organizations emerged, led by young itinerant preachers varying in age from nine to thirty (van Dijk 1992b, 1992c, 1993). These young people attracted crowds by conducting mass revival meetings with fire and brimstone sermons denouncing the evils of everyday urban life. To a large extent the movement represented a new stage in Malawian Independent Christianity, part of an ongoing process dating back to the first decade of the twentieth century (Schoffeleers 1985). The purpose of their actions was unlike earlier forms of Independent Christianity and certainly did not present a nostalgic retreat into rural romanticism.

The type of Pentecostalism that these young preachers espoused mirrored the "charismatic" Christianity reported recently in many other countries (Gifford 1994; Marshall 1993; Meyer 1997; Maxwell 1998). It exemplified a high level of religious emotion and ecstasy related to the search for healing, protection and fortune. The preachers focused on spirit-healing, prosperity gospel and individual conviction, by "working upon the Holy Spirit" (*Mzimu Woyera*). Their followers rarely embraced first generation rural-urban migrants. Instead, second or third generation urbanites proved to be more receptive to their preachings.

Of the thirty *alaliki* (preachers or literally "sayers") I studied in Malawi, those who were the first to take up their call to preach belonged to an urban class of well-educated college and university students. Their education permitted them to occupy higher-ranking positions in urban society. These preachers can be called "part-timers," because they were, and still are, only involved in preaching in their spare time. Later on, in the early and mid-1980s, a second group of preachers came to the fore, most of whom had no more than a few years of primary schooling and in no way belonged to the young urban elite. They conducted their activities on a full-time basis and, in one way or another, their preaching activities provided them with a livelihood.

In the doctrines they preach, conversion is perceived as a process of dying so that a new person can emerge. At the altar call, the congregation is urged to step forward to receive the "infilling" of the Holy Spirit as a way to become cleansed of worldly, defiling forces. Only after infilling can a person be considered to be born again (*kubadwa mwatsopano*).

This born-again experience takes place in an atmosphere of intense emotionalism and must result in a person's rejection of his/her past life in all social, communal, ritual or cultural respects. Preachers of the *Abadwa Mwatsopano* (Born Again) movement stress the need for the person to reject any immediate social life and call for a rejuvenated morality in which the "satanic habit" of frequenting bars, hotels and discos is condemned, because these are understood to be places of utter moral depravity. As I witnessed many times myself, while the audience is exhorted to sing and dance, sinners are commanded to kneel before the young people, who then insist that all evil objects such as cans of beer (*chibukhu*), knives, tobacco and stolen goods and all esoteric, magical tokens be surrendered.

In addition to breaking with one's immediate social life, the preachers also demand a complete break with the past, which relates to a much deeper understanding of how "immorality" may ruin a person's life (Meyer 1997). Here ties with one's ancestors are considered of tremendous importance, or rather of immediate danger. It is through one's ancestors that magical, esoteric powers are perceived to control a person's life and destiny, which could cause a person to experience misfortune and no advancement of prosperity in ordinary daily existence. These ties are related to the powers of witchcraft (*ufitii*). Evil spirits are perceived to run counter to the benevolent powers of the Holy Spirit, which manifests itself in ecstatic speaking in tongues (*malilime*), whereby people lie groveling on the ground, sweating profusely and shouting incomprehensible sounds.

By being born again, a line is established with benevolent, heavenly powers. In this process *malilime* is the physical sign that superior power is at work protecting one's day-to-day existence and healing any spiritual afflictions, even witchcraft. As one preacher told his audience, the born-again who feels attacked by witches trying to abduct people to nocturnal orgies where human flesh is eaten may counter them through *malilime*. In so doing, witches are trapped and paralyzed at the door of the house. Some born-again preachers even feel empowered to detect witchcraft and related harmful objects, and are convinced that nothing will harm them if they destroy them.

The aim of this inspiration is *kutsirika*, the sealing-off of the person from their immediate social environment and former lifestyle and their ties with the family and its ancestral powers. Conversion narratives of new born-agains emphasize how one's involvement in certain rituals (initiation, healing, funerals, ancestor worship) or in certain kinds of social behavior (drinking, violence, etc.) can be repudiated by becoming a born-again and by speaking in tongues. The individual born-again is protected by being "sealed off" from the outside world, from its bonds and ritual obligations. One way the born-again preachers create a sense of protection is by organizing as many prayer sessions as possible where people are requested to enter into lengthy and highly ecstatic periods of speaking in tongues. The intense involvement in born-again religious occasions minimizes the time one can devote to meeting obligations toward the family, and the authority of its elders. In this way a person gains distance from his or her origins.

The ritual application of the three powerful liquids—alcohol, water and blood—is deeply resisted and condemned by young born-again preachers. Contrary to the practices of most of the independent churches, water is rejected as a means of moral purification of the soul, as a way of consulting the spirits, and as an object in the ritual healing of a person. The young born-again preachers do not engage in baptisms, as there is only "baptism in the Holy Spirit." Openly and mockingly the application of water in other churches is ridiculed and condemned as "superstition which will invoke the powers of Satan." Likewise the symbolic reference to blood as a means of protecting the body and sealing off its porosity from outside malicious influences, as practiced in many Zionist and Apostolic churches, is branded as superstitious, and people are encouraged to hand in their red cords, beads, headbands and the like for destruction by the preachers (van Dijk 1992a).

The same strictness applies to alcohol, which is viewed as a demon in itself. But, like Bacchus, this demon has two faces and combines threats on two accounts. First of all, the rejection of alcohol must be understood as a debate within modernity and as an attempt to establish a moral reordering of present-day society. The line that is established through *malilime* with heavenly powers should not be jeopardized by enticement into modern styles of consumption which "decenter" the person. As a total program, the moral power and authority of this fundamentalism are meant to directly approach the center, the heart of a person, unmediated and undisturbed. Hence alcohol is portrayed as a modern demon luring people into disorderly conduct and threatening the moral order of society.

The born-agains, therefore, resist settings where alcohol is pledged to the ancestors, such as traditional initiation ceremonies at childbirth, coming into adulthood, and marriage, and prefer to target funeral ceremonies in their "crusade" against immorality in society. As a born-again, one is to be sealed off (*kutsirika*) from one's family and bondage with ancestors so that individuality can be constituted. Gerontocratic authority, which is reflected symbolically in the pouring of alcoholic libation (*nsembe*) to the ancestors, is rejected. At a symbolic level, the brewing of beer resembles the process of "ripening," of becoming *kukhwima*, which is acquiring a powerful position in various political, economic and religious dimensions of life. At a social level, born-again ideology directly opposes the authority of older people. Elders are perceived by the born-agains to represent involvement in other lines of power such as ancestral veneration and politics, pursuits that are considered comparable in the degree of evil they involve. They are excluded from positions of authority within the born-again groups, in contrast to the practices of established mission churches and Malawi's urban independent churches. They may not preach, organize meetings or speak in tongues. Preaching to the elders of an independent church in one of the townships of Blantyre, Linley Mbeta reflected on this notion by saying:

> Have you ever seen the injured help the injured? Do injured people help injured people? Do patient and patient inject each other? If it is heard, nowadays, that people are unable to come to Jesus, it is because the Deacons and Elders are also drinkers, Christians who are also drinking! Patients do not help each other! (Linley Mbeta preaching at the African International Church, 18 December 1988)

A hostile tone is adopted toward any inclination to copy behavior from older people as far as religious practice is concerned. Elders are also not considered as role models for how a born-again should behave. This exclusion of older people reaches further to a rejection of symbolics, styles and other phenomena related to "the ritual past." The older generation is being held responsible for sinful symbolic repertoires connected with initiation or dealings with the traditional priests and healers (*asing'anga*). Secrets related to the relatively "hidden" process of initiation (*chinamwhali*) are readily and mockingly disclosed by born-agains. So too are funeral ceremonies targeted by born-again preachers to fulminate against ancestral veneration, the pouring of libations and the use of alcoholic drinks.

Linda Mbeta, for example, has provoked resentment among older people because she openly holds them responsible for the existence and salience of witchcraft in society. At one of her sessions she rebuked them by saying:

> Where do you think you will go to, you fools, with those charms (*zitumwa*) that were left you by your grandparents? You, *you* are learners today. It takes you hours to bewitch somebody, but you still cling to your witchcraft (*ufiti*), just because your forefathers handed the charms down to you. . . . You fools, if these charms were things that could lead someone into the Heavenly Kingdom, I doubt if your grandparents could have left them to you, but because they lead somebody to hell, that's why they handed them over before they died. Only to increase the number of people accompanying them on their way to hell!

Such rejection extends beyond contesting the power of the older generation to an outright rejection of central elements of Malawian cultural traditions. Ruptures with a perceived cultural past generate conflict and tension between relatives, and usually entail the departure of new born-agains from their immediate circle of family members.

It can be concluded here that the rejection of the use of alcohol by the born-again preachers coincides with a deeper generational conflict. This has had ramifications since it emerged in the context of the Banda regime that relied on gerontocratic power structures. In the urban areas where the first born-again groups became active, the salience of this gerontocratic structure was felt on a daily basis as local party chairmen of the sole governing Malawi Congress Party worked hand in hand with elders in their capacity as local chiefs (*mfumu*) and religious authorities. Against this background one can argue that the debate about alcohol was, and still is, a modernist one, a discourse that allows for the moral rejection of things and structures emerging from the impure and threatening "past." According to born-again Christians, the modern moral individual does not indulge in smoking or drinking, or in what the "cultural" or the "traditional" may provide.

ALCOHOL, MORAL REORDERING AND THE UTOPIAN PARADIGM

In the born-again ideology, alcohol has been turned into a site of contestation. Moreover, it pits the power of authorities in the daily existence of young urbanites in Malawi's major cities against each other in a variety of ways. First, the rejection of alcohol turns the ordinary daily life of many urbanites into an area of immorality by prohibiting the common practices of visiting beer halls, beer parties, discos, bars and other public places. In effect, this prohibition serves the purpose of controlling young urbanites' leisure time. Time saved in the evenings and weekends is redirected to born-again meetings, an antidote against the "idleness" of visiting bars and getting drunk. The rejection of one's past lifestyle and social life can be regarded as a profoundly effective form of discipline.

The second area of contestation is that of rejecting the power of other independent churches as the ones who fail to discipline their membership and who hypocritically proclaim that they are against the use of alcohol while not enforcing their teachings. A similar sort of criticism is voiced against the established missionary churches that are considered "lukewarm" in their proclamations against alcohol indulgence. The born-agains stand out in their intolerance of the consumption and local production of alcohol.

At a third and deeper level, where the balance of power between the younger and the older generation is concerned, the rejection of alcohol plays a crucial role for born-agains in severing their links with the past. The born-again discipline entails a rigid rejection of the cultural traditions and practices that would bind the young to the authority of their elders. This is primarily understood as "breaking" with the ties of the past, the threads by which ancestors would be able to hold sway over a person's life. In this perspective, alcohol is seen as the most powerful liquid signaling the presence and continuing importance of ancestor worship. To reject alcohol therefore is to reject one's cultural past. This aspect of the born-again ideology removes the firm believer from the cultural ties with the family and its social and cultural obligations. Furthermore, it precludes the creation of a mnemonic scheme whereby the born-again movement would represent or reflect deeper social and cultural structures.

This process of "de-mnemonization," as I have called it elsewhere, puts the entire born-again movement in a different perspective from the salient political and religious organizations in the urban areas which, through their practices, aim to preserve the moral order of the past (van Dijk 1998). In earlier independent churches, the elderly enjoyed meaningful positions that could then be re-created in an urban setting.

In the born-again ideology, however, this is contrasted with a strong future orientation of religious ideology in the group. The preaching and speaking in tongues are geared to the achievement of an ideal society. Beyond the eschatological doctrine that every sinner will incur the wrath of

God with the imminent return of Jesus Christ and the final Day of Judgment, there is a marked striving toward a perfect reordering of society. The born-agains propose a prognostic program for a thoroughly purified Malawian society. In this utopian imagery, alcohol has become the substance most despised and condemned. Progress (*chitikuko*) can only be attained by the avoidance of the worldly temptation of alcohol and the bondage of a cultural past that alcohol symbolizes.

Focus on the creation of a religious Utopia, purified of all sorts of contaminating evil influences, implies the adoption of an "outsider" identity. Being a born-again necessitates becoming a stranger in one's "home village," to one's immediate relatives, friends and peers. This is accentuated by dress and style; some preachers speak only English at their meetings, which then is translated into Chichewa by an interpreter. Born-again meetings are envisaged as safe havens where the new puritan order is already in effect and where alcohol has no place.

REFERENCES

Akyeampong, E.K. 1996. *Drink, Power and Cultural Change: A Social History of Alcohol in Ghana, c. 1800 to Recent Times*. Oxford: James Currey.

Binsbergen, W. van. 1981. *Religious Change in Zambia: Exploratory Studies*. London: Kegan Paul.

Caplan, L. (ed.). 1987. *Studies in Religious Fundamentalism*. New York: State University of New York Press.

Chakanza, J. 1982. "Towards an Interpretation of Independent Churches in Malawi." *Africa Theological Journal* 11 (2): 133–42.

———. 1983. "An Annotated List of Independent Churches in Malawi." Blantyre: University of Malawi Occasional Paper.

Comaroff, J. 1985. *Body of Power, Spirit of Resistance: The Culture and History of a South African People*. Chicago: University of Chicago Press.

Comaroff, J., and J. Comaroff. 1991. *Of Revelation and Revolution: Christianity, Colonialism and Consciousness in South Africa*. Chicago: University of Chicago Press.

———. 1993. Introduction to J. Comaroff and J. Comaroff (eds.), *Modernity and Its Malcontents: Ritual and Power in Postcolonial Africa*. Chicago: University of Chicago Press.

Daneel, M.L. 1974. *Old and New in Southern Shona Independent Churches*. Vol. 2, *Church Growth, Causative Factors and Recruitment Techniques*. The Hague: Mouton.

Dijk, R.A. van. 1992a. "Van hegemonisch tot demonisch gezag. Jonge Puriteinse predikers en icono-clastisch verzet in Malawi." *Etnofoor* 5 (1–2): 188–212.

———. 1992b. "Young Malawian Puritans: Young Puritan Preachers in a Present-Day African Urban Environment." Ph.D. dissertation, Utrecht University, ISOR.

———. 1992c. "Young Puritan Preachers in Post-Independence Malawi." *Africa* 62 (2): 159–81.

———. 1993. "Young Born-Again Preachers in Malawi: The Significance of an Extraneous Identity." In P. Gifford (ed.), *New Dimensions in African Christianity*. Ibadan: Sefer Books.

———. 1994. "Foucault and the Anti-Witchcraft Movement." *Critique of Anthropology* 14 (4): 429–36.

———. 1995. "Fundamentalism and Its Moral Geography in Malawi: The Representation of the Diasporic and the Diabolical." *Critique of Anthropology* 15 (2): 171–91.

———. 1998. "Pentecostalism, Cultural Memory and the State: Contested Representations of Time in Postcolonial Malawi." In R. Werbner (ed.), *Memory and the Post-Colony*. London: Zed Books.

Dillon-Malone, C.M. 1978. *The Korsten Basketmakers: A Study of the Masowe Apostles: An Indigenous African Religious Movement*. Manchester: Manchester University Press.

Englund, H. 1996. "Witchcraft, Modernity and the Person: The Morality of Accumulation in Central Malawi." *Critique of Anthropology* 16 (3): 257–79.

Fields, K.E. 1985. *Revival and Rebellion in Colonial Central Africa*. Princeton, NJ: Princeton University Press.

Fisiy, C.F., and P. Geschiere. 1991. "Sorcery, Witchcraft and Accumulation: Regional Variations in South and West Cameroon." *Critique of Anthropology* 11 (3): 251–79.

Geschiere, P., and C. Fisiy. 1994. "Domesticating Personal Violence: Witchcraft, Courts and Confessions in Cameroon." *Africa* 64 (3): 323–41.

Gifford, P. 1991. *The New Crusaders: Christianity and the New Right in Southern Africa*. London: Pluto Press.

———. 1994. "Ghana's Charismatic Churches." *Journal of Religion in Africa* 24 (3): 241–65.

Kaunda, J.M. 1995. "Malawi: The Post-Colonial State, Development, and Democracy." *Africa* (M) 3: 305–24.

Kiernan, J.P. 1981. "African Religious Research: Themes and Trends in the Study of Black Religion in Southern Africa." *Journal of Religion in Africa* 12 (2): 136–47.

Langworthy, H.W. 1985. "Charles Domingo, Seventh Day Baptists and Independency." *Journal of Religion in Africa* 15 (2): 96–121.

MacDonald, R.J. 1970. "Religious Independency as a Means of Social Advance in Northern Nyasaland in the 1930s." *Journal of Religion in Africa* 3 (1): 106–29.

Marshall, R. 1993. "Power in the Name of Jesus: Social Transformation and Pentecostalism in Western Nigeria Revisited." In T. Ranger and O. Vaughan (eds.), *Legitimacy and the State in Twentieth Century Africa*. London: Macmillan.

Marty, M., and R. Scott Appleby (eds.). 1991. *Fundamentalism Observed*. Chicago: University of Chicago Press.

Maxwell, D. 1998. "Delivered from the Spirit of Poverty? Pentecostalism, Prosperity and Modernity in Zimbabwe." *Journal of Religion in Africa* 28 (3): 350–73.

McCracken, J.L. 1977. *Politics and Christianity in Malawi, 1875–1940: The Impact of the Livingstonia Mission in the Northern Province*. Cambridge: Cambridge University Press.

Meyer, B. 1995. "Translating the Devil: An African Appropriation of Pietist Protestantism. The Case of the Peki Ewe in South-Eastern Ghana, 1847–1992." Ph.D. dissertation, University of Amsterdam.

———. 1997. "Make a Complete Break with the Past: Time and Modernity in Ghanaian Pentecostalist Discourse." Paper presented at the Thirteenth Satterthwaite Colloquium on African Religion and Ritual, University of Manchester, 19–22 April.

Schoffeleers, J.M. 1985. *Pentecostalism and Neo-Traditionalism: The Religious Polarization of a Rural District in Southern Malawi*. Amsterdam: Free University Press.

———. 1992. *River of Blood: The Genesis of a Martyr Cult in Southern Malawi, c. 1600*. Madison: University of Wisconsin Press.

Sundkler, B.G.M. 1961. *Bantu Prophets in South Africa*. London: Oxford University Press.

Taussig, M. 1980. *The Devil and Commodity Fetishism in South America*. Chapel Hill: University of North Carolina Press.

Vaughan, M. 1991. *Curing Their Ills: Colonial Power and African Illness*. Cambridge: Polity Press.

PART V
Conclusion

14

Pleasure and Pain
The Ambiguity of Alcohol in Africa

Deborah Fahy Bryceson

Focusing on the past two decades, this chapter discusses the darker side of alcohol, alcohol consumption levels and outcomes that are deemed socially undesirable. Highlighting the decline of public alcohol controls amid the widespread informalization of alcohol production, the concept of heavy drinking cultures is introduced and related to deepening processes of impoverishment. Sub-Saharan Africa's immunity or possible vulnerability to the emergence of heavy drinking cultures is examined, before turning to the current ambiguity of alcohol usage in Africa.

FROM WHO DARES TO WHO CARES: NEOLIBERALISM, AFRICAN LABOR REDUNDANCY, AND ALCOHOL DEREGULATION, 1980–2000

Public alcohol control, almost an obsession for many colonial governments as exemplified by Gewald (Chapter 6), is now extremely lax in most parts of Sub-Saharan Africa. Structural adjustment and liberalization policies implemented by African governments at the insistence of international financial institutions have inadvertently accelerated the erosion of local, municipal and national controls on alcohol production within the informal sector (van der Drift, Pietilä and Tanzarn in this volume; Molamu and Manyeneng 1988). In rural communities across the continent, smallholder cashcropping has become less remunerative and farming households have turned to nonagricultural income diversification, notably brewing and distilling, to make up the shortfall (Bryceson 1999). Traditional authority figures who safeguarded community values have been increasingly discredited as the local agrarian order experienced the upheaval of market liberalization.

Van der Drift (Chapter 9) documents a curious inversion of tradition in Guinea-Bissau where male elders encouraged drinking among former nondrinking categories of people. This overturn of the local community's ritual and economic order was termed "democratization" by youthful men who enjoyed greater autonomy and leisure. Tanzarn (Chapter 4) describes a similar process of rural reorientation with the easing of alcohol restrictions in Uganda. Despite laws banning the cottage industry of distilled alcohol, *waragi* became Kibaale District's main export. The administrative laxity of local-level leaders associated with the district's decades of economic hardship meshed with the Ugandan government's implementation of economic liberalization policies nationally. Most distilled drinks in Africa are not traditional drinks subject to community sanctions. Culturally neutral, they are readily accommodated and molded to prevailing economic and social exigencies (Abbink, Chapter 8).

McCall (Chapter 5) raises the environmental implications of the nonenforcement of alcohol control regulations. The expansion of cottage-industry production has had a direct impact on woodfuel supplies and has triggered or exacerbated the threat of deforestation in many rural areas. Local and national governments' as well as donors' circumvention of the issue has served to entrench the problem still further.

The 1980s and 1990s also witnessed the declining importance of measures to curb drinking taken by private employers preoccupied with labor-force restructuring. Blue- and white-collar workers alike experienced widespread retrenchments linked to the implementation of structural adjustment. The vast majority of Sub-Saharan Africa's economically active population became self-employed. Despite continent-wide compliance with international financial institutions' conditionality, direct foreign investment in Sub-Saharan Africa has been woefully lacking given investors' views on the productivity of African labor and their preference for better-educated, "disciplined" Asian labor forces.

Akyeampong (Chapter 11) documents how rising unemployment in the wake of structural adjustment gave many segments of the urban population in Kumasi ample reason to drink. Unemployment contributed to economic hardship and marital instability. Rather than causing a cutback in alcohol consumption, unemployment provided more leisure time for men to drink. They economized by drinking cheaper types of alcohol.

In the face of a contracting formal sector and econo
male family breadwinners, family members flocked to th
work, resulting in a growing proportion of the popula
(Bryceson 1999). With some money in their pockets, albeit s
creasing numbers of people have been at liberty to decide if, when, where and what they drink, and in so doing new social categories of drinkers have emerged. Pietilä (Chapter 10) documents how Chagga women traders sought to relax and have a drink with friends after a long working day. Drinking as a form of conspicuous consumption provides individuals with a subtle way of communicating their newfound economic status.

Over the past two decades the African drinking population has expanded and stronger forms of alcohol have gained popularity. These trends can be related to broader transitional processes connected with the continental experience of structural adjustment and globalization. Amid the decline of peasant farming, urban blue- and white-collar job retrenchments, and decreasing levels of educational attainment, alcohol production has become a substitute economic activity for large numbers of people in both rural and urban areas. African governments and nongovernmental agencies have loosened their control over locally generated supplies. Under economic liberalization and privatization policies, a renewed interest in brewery investment by international corporations is now boosting the availability of bottled drinks.

Meanwhile, public medical services and social welfare departments of national governments have been contracting under the weight of shrinking budgets and understaffing related to the implementation of structural adjustment and the AIDS epidemic. There is no way of knowing the extent of social disruption, ill health and death that excessive alcohol inflicts on people. International agencies monitoring global health and welfare seem largely oblivious to the changing patterns of alcohol consumption, in marked contrast to recent efforts to prevent increasing tobacco usage in developing countries. In view of the inherent risks in this oversight, the next section focuses on characteristics of heavy drinking cultures and their association with historical periods of rapid change and impoverishment.

MARGINALIZATION AND THE MAKING OF HEAVY DRINKING CULTURES

"Heavy drinking cultures" are defined here as the leisure and livelihood patterns of population groups in which sociability is deeply entwined in alcohol consumption. The alcohol preferences of such cultures are neither innately nor culturally preordained. On the contrary, there is evidence to suggest that the heavy drinking cultures that have surfaced in the last two centuries, such as the well-documented Irish, Russian and Navaho drinking cultures, are part and parcel of processes of economic, political and cultural marginalization (Brody 1974; Levy and Kunitz 1974; Stivers 1976; White 1996).

Five main features characterize heavy drinking cultures. First, drinking is accorded a major role in leisure activities. Alcohol consumption is widely sanctioned and encouraged, and drinking opportunities are frequent in festive as well as daily social life.

Second, drinking is used as a means of establishing a collective social identity and demarcating status. One's sense of belonging and status are communicated by the amount and type of drink one consumes. Drinking together imparts a common identity and sense of solidarity, further solidified by a shared favorite drink. For example, the Irish drinking culture has a strong affinity with Guinness and whisky, as has the Russian drinking culture with vodka, and Scandinavia's now largely repressed heavy drinking culture identified with aquavit.

Third, heavy drinking cultures have a social tolerance for frequent or copious drinking and drunkenness. Physiological and cultural factors deeply influence levels of intoxication. Nonetheless, medical opinion views the consumption of 10 cl (3.4 liquid ounces) of pure alcohol per day per person as the cut-off point for moderate intake (Whitehead and Harvey 1974, cited in Heath 1987: 43).[1]

Fourth, there is a higher risk of mortality due to alcohol-related disease and accidents in a heavy drinking culture. Chronic alcohol dependence[2] and cirrhosis of the liver are commonly linked, and diabetes, hypertension and certain forms of cancer are associated with heavy drinking (Room 1968). Furthermore, the influence of alcohol is frequently traceable to the incidence of sexually transmitted diseases, AIDS and unwanted pregnancies as well as traffic and work-related accidents.

Fifth, adverse socioeconomic consequences, including marital discord, family breakup, violence and child welfare problems, are frequent among participants in a heavy drinking culture, and the connection between alcohol and lack of harmony at the level of the household and community is well documented.

Heavy drinking cultures tend to arise in historical contexts of unstable economic and political circumstances, and they generate their own vicious circles of social deprivation. The proximate causes surface readily.

Changing alcohol supply conditions, state and employer policies, alcohol production technology, customary exchange patterns, and livelihood uncertainty all play a part.

Why does alcohol figure so centrally in processes of economic marginalization? Why is alcohol so readily at hand and so malleable in the hands of those gaining as well as those losing? Certainly, the answers to these questions vary from case to case. However, as a highly valued substance with religious, social, economic and political significance, alcohol has virtually universal potential as an object of exchange and leverage. People drink for an array of reasons related to the practical and symbolic value they vest in alcohol. An individual's predisposition to alcohol can be heavily influenced by the cultural coding embedded in alcohol usage, but it is tautological to argue that anyone or any group has a *cultural* predisposition to drink. Alcohol is a historically contextualized cultural artefact. Its place in any culture is not inherent in the culture itself but arises from historical events and processes that are traceable, but never inevitable.

Globally, traditional drinking cultures of hunting and gathering, agrarian and pastoral societies were based on fermented drinks with a low alcohol content, whereas heavy drinking cultures are intimately related to the increasing use of strong distilled or fortified drinks that have appeared over the past four to five centuries. Thus, the formation of a heavy drinking culture is not buried in the mists of time but can be discerned by tracing successive mosaics of livelihood and leisure activities within a society in relation to changing drinking practices. The next section attempts some crystal ball gazing, weighing up some of the more salient material and normative factors that promote or alternatively provide a check on the appearance of heavy drinking cultures in Sub-Saharan African societies.

WET, DRY, OR MODERATELY MOIST? FUTURE DRINKING PATTERNS IN SUB-SAHARAN AFRICA

It was argued in Chapter 2 that supplies of alcohol are generally expanding in both rural and urban areas. Expansion of supply is taking place at a time of rapid social change involving the marginalization of Africa vis-à-vis the world economic order. In rural and urban areas alike, new risks and opportunities are being faced; cherished community-held values are being rejected and new ones embraced as a means of coping with or capitalizing on current circumstances.[3] Leisure pursuits are being restructured and the place of alcohol in society is being reevaluated. The subsections that follow explore the nature of changing alcohol demand, beginning with the social restraints that serve to dampen alcohol consumption on the continent.

Barriers to Formative Drinking Cultures

Abstainers and Religious Restrictions on Alcohol Consumption

Haworth et al.'s (1981) WHO study emphasized the significance of the all-or-none pattern of African drinking in Zambia, where a large portion of the population reported abstaining from alcohol. Survey evidence from various countries indicates that this pattern is common (Botswana: Molamu and Manyeneng 1988; Zambia: Rootman and Moser 1984; Zimbabwe: Reader and May 1971; Wolcott 1974; Tanzania: Njelekela 1978; Kenya: Acuda 1983; Nigeria: Odejide 1986). Measured as a percentage of total respondents, abstinence is higher in urban than in rural areas and among women as opposed to men (Haworth et al. 1981; Partanen 1990).

There is, as is often the case in alcohol surveys, a great deal of ambiguity about what constitutes abstention. Haworth et al. (1981) concluded that abstinence was interpreted liberally by respondents, who were not inferring that they had never taken a drink in their lives or even that they never drank in normal daily life. Similarly, Wolcott's (1974: 181) respondents were highly ambiguous: "Although I come from a Christian home where liquor was not allowed, and I don't drink myself, I sometimes do take sips with my friends. And occasionally I even have one sip too many."

Clearly, drinking is more than just an individual act of alcohol consumption in the minds of these informants. It denotes membership in a social group whose lifestyle accords significance to drinking not only as a pastime but also as a symbol of group identity. Abstainers may drink occasionally but they are not "drinkers" who pursue a drinking lifestyle.[4] This discourse relates to traditionalist-modernist dichotomies that missionaries as well as current donor agencies have deployed in attempts to modify drinking behavior (Gewald and McCall in this volume). As van Dijk (Chapter 13) argues, modernity's adherents construct a strict duality between old agrarian and new urban lifestyles. Drinking habits serve as a critical marker, and religious conversion is a key means of moving from the traditional to the modern (Luning, Chapter 12).

Religion has long been an inhibiting force on alcohol consumption, and religious conversion can provide a transformation of social identity. The interactional effects of these two social processes are complex. Muslim and Christian religions tend to espouse more temperate drinking norms than traditional agrarian communities, but as Luning (Chapter 12) stresses, religions vary in the strength and consistency of their temperance message. It is generally assumed that Muslims are the strictest abstainers. The Koran has injunctions against Muslim involvement in the consumption, production or distribution of alcohol. However, adherence differs widely, with the Sahelian countries and northern Nigeria being known for more stringent controls. Surveys suggest that the incidence of Muslims drinking is low but that Muslims who do drink are prone to heavier than average consumption (Beckman 1988; Yguel et al. 1990; Heap 1998).

Catholics and followers of liberal Protestant religions usually have a higher incidence of drinkers than those from strict Protestant faiths (Haworth et al. 1981; Yguel et al. 1990; Baroin 1996). Luning (Chapter 12) explores the differences among Protestant, Catholic and animist attitudes to alcohol, showing how Catholics in Burkina Faso are not only far more liberal in their drinking habits but have also managed to bridge the discursive dichotomy between traditional drinking and modern abstinence. Sidestepping the issue of consumption, they have constructed a distinction between traditional and secular beer-brewing techniques that disassociates them from traditional allegiance to the realm of the ancestors. The rural Sahelian situation that Luning describes is one of surprising cosmopolitan tolerance. Differing drinking styles associated with religious affiliation are not viewed as a source of tension but rather as "everyone with their own road," with the possibility that an individual's chosen road may alter as life circumstances change. Van Dijk's (Chapter 13) case study of Christian fundamentalists in Malawi provides vivid contrast. The Pentecostal movement demands an individual's exclusive commitment to a new religious and social identity, with alcohol abstention as the litmus test of one's faith. Nonbelievers, including one's family, are seen as sources of temptation that Pentecostal followers must seek to avoid. Instead, emphasis is placed on current rewards, namely, believers' acquisition of modernity and economic advance.[5] The growing popularity of Christian fundamentalist religions has been an inhibiting influence on the incidence of drinking among adherents.

Youth's Disdain of or Indifference to Alcohol

Youth, regardless of religion, have surprisingly been perceived as a social category who are disinclined to heavy drinking in specific settings. For example, the 1976 Soweto uprising in South Africa witnessed youth's vehement protest against alcohol. While ransacking beer halls and bottle-stores, the Soweto Students' Representative Council called for change: "We can no longer tolerate seeing our fathers' pay packets emptied on drink" (la Hausse 1988: 1). In this highly politicized context, youth were disassociating themselves from the alcohol consumption patterns of their parents' generation.

Less dramatically, urban youth cultures in many African countries have sought to set themselves apart from earlier generations by gravitating toward recreational drug use in preference to alcohol consumption (Ghana: Yangyuoru 1987; Nigeria: Said and Last 1991; Adejunmobi 1992; Obot 1990). Nontraditional drug-taking affords a distinct identity that is not restricted solely to urban youth. Beckerleg (1995) records the use of heroin among rural youth in Watamu, a Muslim village on the Kenyan coast visited by foreign tourists. In far more remote Sahelian villages, returning migrants from Europe have been known to introduce amphetamine use.[6] The allure of drugs in the first instance tends to be the income-earning potential of drug-dealing. Certainly the up-country Sahelian amphetamine trade is seen as highly lucrative because amphetamines are easy to transport and hide during police border checks. It may be significant that both examples represent Muslim contexts, in which drugs are not tagged with the same moral injunctions as alcohol. In South Africa, the role of drugs in the urban political economy is increasingly grabbing the spotlight (du Toit 1991; Tayob 1996).

However, there is no overall indication in the literature that African youth are rejecting alcohol in preference for drugs. Survey findings suggest that alcohol consumption among girls and boys is still more common than drug-taking and that boys are especially liable to start drinking in their teens (Akyeampong, Chapter 11).[7] African urban youth, as elsewhere in the world, experiment with both alcohol and drugs, tending to drink in groups, while taking drugs on a more individual basis.[8]

Connoisseur Tastes

Based on the principle of substituting quality for quantity, connoisseur tastes distinguish alcoholic drinks as well as drinkers, because status is asserted by being seen to be drinking a specific type of alcoholic beverage (Douglas 1987). The discriminating palate does not necessarily require a wide range of drinks. The rural Lele of the Kasai region in Congo, whose only alcoholic beverage was palm wine, distinguished twelve different variants of palm wine, derived from two types of palm trees, related to tree maturity and the age and flavor of the wine itself (Ngokwey 1987). Certain categories of people drank specific types of palm wine chosen on the basis of the occasion.

In precolonial and more subsistence-based societies of today, connoisseur tastes tend to be well established for traditional drinks. Consumers' appreciation and producers' standards are reinforced by the physical presence of the producer at the drinking occasion, where s/he often receives direct praise or criticism of the drink's quality. As alcoholic drinks become more commoditized, these social feedback mechanisms can be stymied. Producers are less likely to have face-to-face contact with consumers. Their brewing objective is to earn income such that they may resort to watering down or adulterating their brews to enhance monetary profit or drink potency to attract customers. Producers and distributors try to maximize sales, and quantity, not quality, is being marketed.

During the 1980s connoisseur consumption contracted in the face of a severe decline in purchasing power. Fierce competition among cottage-industry producers was directed at low-cost methods as well as pleasing consumers with ever more potent drinks, often by using additives of a suspect nature.[9]

The 1990s witnessed the resurgence of expensive, standardized bottled beer and other alcoholic drinks more likely to lend themselves to connoisseur appreciation. As McCall (Chapter 5) comments, it remains to be seen whether the producers of local brews can establish niche markets in urban areas for quality traditional beer. As craft brewmasters, some women could possibly find escape from the treadmill of overcompetition and put a check on the public health hazard frequently associated with cottage-industry output. In so doing, quality may be substituted for quantity of alcohol consumption.

General Unease with Levels of Drinking in Society

One continuing check on alcohol intake remains public approbation. As community sanctions break down, sanctions on the drinking habits of certain social categories, especially women and youth, remain.

Men in a wide range of African societies are apt to express strong distaste for women drinking, while they themselves may be heavy drinkers (e.g., Botswana: Molamu and Manyeneng 1988; Zimbabwe: Ambler 1990; Nigeria: Obot 1993). Traditional and missionaries' sanctions against women drinking have lessened, but a male double standard nonetheless prevails. In Tanzania and Ghana, for example, men's attitudes toward female drinking are entwined with discomfort over women's increasing financial self-reliance during the past two decades of economic crisis (Pietilä and Akyeampong in this volume; Diduk 1993; Akyeampong 1996). Members of the youthful male drinking group that Akyeampong (Chapter 11) describes were averse to marrying women who drank.

Haworth et al. (1981) observed a similar disdain for youthful drinkers in Zambia. Despite heavy drinking among the adult population, there was a strong consensus that young people should not drink at all. In Cameroon, a growing generational gulf, exacerbated by the financial constrictions of the economic crisis, was attributed to increased drinking on the part of young men. The Kedjom people of rural northwest Cameroon talked about alcohol "spoiling the country" and the social relations in their ethnic group. In the cities, civil servants jokingly referred to Cameroon as "a country of drunkards" (Diduk 1993: 19–20).

Various overt forms of opposition to the expansion and entrenchment of heavy drinking in the social fabric of local communities and nation-states became salient during the 1980s and 1990s. Van der Drift (Chapter 9) documents the appearance of the *Yangue yangue* in 1984, a spontaneous movement of Balanta women in Guinea-Bissau that opposed the authority of the elders for, among other things, allowing heavy drinking at traditional events like funerals. Secular, as opposed to religious, community sanctions may increasingly come to bear on heavy drinking segments of local populations in settings where there is growing concern about the adverse social or health effects of heavy drinking.

Snapping Out of It: Self-Restraint Challenging Theories of Addictive Drinking

There is evidence that some heavy drinkers in Africa can turn their backs on alcohol with relatively little difficulty. This may be due to the prevalence of binge patterns of drinking that differ from Western-style alcoholism, which tends to be associated with continual daily dependence on alcohol consumption (Haworth, quoted in Beckman 1988: 138).

In Ghana, Akyeampong (1996) witnessed cases of heavy drinkers who simply cured themselves, unaware of the medical belief that alcoholics cannot stop drinking. One Ghanaian doctor reported having patients who stopped drinking after being informed of the serious health problems of chronic drinking (Akyeampong 1996: 257, citing Adomako 1976). The physiological state of alcohol dependence is culturally contextualized, and may be easier to shirk when it is believed that alcoholism has a supernatural rather than a natural cause. Thus, heavy drinking becomes a pastime in times of pain and woe dictated by supernatural forces, but it can be cast aside as the material and spiritual crisis lifts and the drinker is afforded a better life (Akyeampong 1996). In these cases, a person's decision to give up heavy drinking would depend on the availability of life chances within the local economy, and suggests that exit as well as entry into heavy drinking is entwined in fluctuating processes of inclusion and exclusion.

Bridges to Formative Drinking Cultures

In contrast to these tendencies that may serve to curb alcohol demand, there are several other proximate factors militating for growing demand. Most of these tendencies have well-established historical antecedents that are reinforced by Sub-Saharan Africa's protracted economic crisis and political upheaval.

Existing Heavy Drinking Cultures of Southern Africa

The sheer volume of literature that exists on drinking in southern Africa relative to elsewhere on the continent points to the regional importance of alcohol culturally, economically and politically. As illustrated by several of the preceding chapters, historical circumstances have served to embed alcohol in the national and local cultures of the nation-states of this region. The early introduction of distilled drinks by the Dutch East Indies Company, the use of alcohol as a wage-labor incentive, alcohol's role in the demarcation of work and leisure time in dormitory-based migrant labor forces fostered by the mining industry, and the commercial interests of Portuguese and later South African corporate alcohol manufacturers have all played a part.

Racist labor practices in the region's mines, plantations and settler farms and the legacy of a male barracks subculture have left a deep imprint. Drinking was an escape from the heavy-handed discipline of the workplace and the boredom of the stark, male residential environment (Gewald, Chapter 6). It provided an affordable, shared leisure pastime of beer hall drinking with no holds barred.[10]

Compared to the rest of Sub-Saharan Africa, southern Africa has a more proletarianized and urban history. Its heavy drinking culture has come to be symbolized by shebeens—covert unlicensed drinking places, often fronted by a family house, where alcoholic beverages are dispensed at any time. The shebeen combines notions of cosy surroundings with illicit danger (Malahleha 1985; la Hausse 1988). An early age of drinking as well as heavy adult drinking characterizes the countries of the region. In South Africa, youthful drinking is high by international standards and increases with age and the transition to a married or cohabiting status (Rocha-Silva et al. 1996: 69). As the rest of Africa becomes less rural and more dependent on waged or casual labor forms, will southern Africa's heavy drinking cultures blur into drinking patterns observed elsewhere?

Links Between Drinking and Male Underemployment, Unemployment, and Poverty

Elsewhere in Sub-Saharan Africa, ethnic groups that have been edged out of agrarian livelihoods due to growing landlessness have evidenced early leanings toward alcohol dependence. One such area is Kisii, western Kenya, where high rural population densities and shrinking farm sizes have led to a male livelihood crisis (Silberschmidt 1990). A public health survey recorded alcoholism in 24 and 27 percent of the female and male population, respectively, noting that "the majority of people still drank for a social purpose. But there was a growing number who drank to relieve worries and boredom" (Otieno, Owola and Oduor 1979: 665). A similar heavy alcohol dependence prevailed among the Chagga on the densely populated slopes of Mount Kilimanjaro in Tanzania (Swantz 1985). Mamdani (1984) observed that people trying to eke out a living as casual laborers in a village on the outskirts of Kampala where landlessness was rife sought solace in the local distillate, *waragi*. One of the informants confided, "*Waragi* is my blanket" (Mamdani 1984, quoted in Iliffe 1987: 234).

Prolonged unemployment and urban retrenchment have not surprisingly coincided with the increased demand for alcohol in many places. In the recent massive wave of urban layoffs related to structural adjustment policies, men's loss of earning power has been compounded by the double indignity of women's relatively greater success in the informal sector (Tanzania: Pietilä, Chapter 10; Lesotho: Hall 1999; Cameroon: Diduk 1993; Niger-Thomas 2000). Drinking becomes compensatory, a way to while away free time and forget one's circumstances.

Akyeampong (Chapter 11) demonstrates how certain low-priced local drinks, like the strong gin *akpeteshie* of Ghana, have become associated with poverty. The solidarity of drinking groups composed of impoverished unemployed men supercedes age and ethnic differences. Bound by the common experience of unemployment and marital instability, they have constitute a leisure class with time but very little money.

Expansion of Female Drinking amid Economic and Gender Upheaval

As intra-household relations have shifted and tensions deepened amid economic crisis, women are more likely to be seen drinking publicly (Pietilä, Chapter 10). Heavy drinking on the part of women may also be increasing in frequency, mirroring a phenomenon observed in other parts of the world (Ettore 1997).[11]

In southern Sudan, Huby (1994) described the household gender struggles that arose as women's beer brewing and distilling incomes grew relative to the formal income earnings of men. Husbands drank and initiated quarrels with their wives to divert attention from their unfulfilled obligation to provide money, taking the offensive by claiming authority over them. Women, drinking in reaction to their men's heavy drinking, seized the opportunity to engage in time-out behavior, defying their husbands' authority and pushing behavioral boundaries in their favor. Too many drunken physical confrontations resulted in elders enforcing a ban on the consumption of the strong local black beer, distilled from grain and dates. "Giving up drinking" was synonymous with the avoidance of black beer, whereas the more traditional white beer brewed from sorghum, which has a far lower alcohol content, continued to be consumed.

In southern Africa, wives have long been suspected of drinking at home (Ambler 1990; Glazer 1997). Women's heavy drinking became more widely apparent in reaction to the economic crisis, with men further distancing themselves from participation in household maintenance. In their study of the social ramifications of structural adjustment policies, Moser and Holland (1997: 69) collected case studies of disillusioned women in Zambia:

> Sophie, 27, is single and still living with her parents. She admits to drinking herself and believes that the increase in women drinking arises out of their frustration at not finding men to marry them. Anna, 37, points out that it is often the poorest women who drink, linking female drinking and prostitution. She says, "Yes, women are drinking a lot. The situation has deteriorated. Women are hungry, and since they cannot afford to buy their own beer, they let men pay and sleep with them in return. Some end up drinking while working as prostitutes to get money to feed their families."

During Ghana's recent economic crisis, Akyeampong's (1996) search of hospital records revealed increasing female alcoholism, particularly among women of economically active ages, notably traders and nurses. Juggling busy work lives and raising children, often as single parents, these women experienced alcohol gradually taking over their lives.

Role Model Elites' Heavy Drinking

The rising demand for alcohol is not restricted to those at the lower end of the social scale. Historically, access to alcohol was the right of elders. Powerful rulers such as the Asantehene of Ghana made a display of drinking publicly (Akyeampong, Chapter 11). The British colonial administration in Nigeria considered it futile to place restrictions on rural brewing since enforcement would rely on traditional rulers, who "included some of the biggest drinkers" (Heap 1998: 29). But they were not alone. Colonial officials themselves often drank heavily. In southern Africa, African elites contested their access to so-called European liquor in the run-up to independence, and heavy drinking was noticeable among those later spearheading the anti-apartheid struggle in South Africa (Ambler 1990; Cobley 1994; Mager 1999).

Currently African elites, encompassing urban-based civil servants and the growing ranks of businessmen, show few inhibitions about drinking publicly. Furthermore, they are not subject to the check on drinking that income constraints pose for less affluent drinkers. In Cameroon, only elite men can drink daily, and their beer drinking is a symbol of social prestige and status (Diduk 1993). In Botswana, the incidence of drinking increases as one moves up the occupational ladder.[12] The expansion of multinational corporations' beer brewing, documented in Chapter 2, and the accompanying advertising campaigns that have promoted images of drinking and success, have enticed an already receptive elite clientele to carry on drinking with a strong sense of self-esteem.

Increasing Social Tolerance for Drunkenness in Rural and Urban Settings

Traditional controls on drinking involved strong sanctions against overindulgence and drunkenness (e.g., Carlson 1992). Akyeampong (Chapter 11) relates how excessive drinkers faced ridicule. Community-bound drinking occasions of the Iteso of western Kenya were carefully orchestrated to guard against unruly drunken behavior (Karp 1980). Ngokwey (1987: 118) wrote at length about social disapproval of drunkenness among the Lele in the Congo in former times:

> [Drunkenness] indicates a lack of self-control and an egoistic lack of sharing. . . . The individual who tends to drink too much will be warned by the other members of the group against the negative behavioral disruptions which accompany drunkenness; they will also remind him of his obligation to save some for those who stayed in the village; the elderly, the sick and the women.

Urban migration and mobility connected with income diversification over the past two decades have greatly undermined the sense of community cohesion necessary for the enforcement of local-level sanctions. In fact, the opposite can occur. Changing values may lead to drinking becoming a major social pastime and to getting drunk becoming the shared objective of drinking (van der Drift, Chapter 9). Furthermore, economic hardship may leave individuals with little companionship other than their drinking group and their communal experience of drunkenness (Akyeampong, Chapter 11).

The rising consumption of modernity drinks, often involving stronger distilled alcohol as opposed to traditional brewed beers and tapped palm wine, has accelerated the breakdown of community-based alcohol controls. Not all modernity drinks are factory manufactured. *Cana*, the distilled cashew wine of Guinea-Bissau (van der Drift, Chapter 9), is an example of an ever-widening range of nontraditional drinks made from local ingredients that are not embedded in community-based ritual patterns or carefully calibrated reciprocity. Generally, they are connected with the increasing influence of market exchange and the need to find new sources of income. The popularity of these drinks derives from their ready accessibility and relative cheapness. The dynamics of local drinking groups generate drinking protocols influenced by the political and economic mood of the times. This is illustrated by the new phenomenon of binge drinking in rural Guinea-Bissau, which is collectively rationalized in terms of democratization and empowerment but is viewed by one village elder with a sense of unease: "Today's youth are getting too loose, and they are supported by democracy" (van der Drift, Chapter 9).

Drinking as Proof of Masculinity and Esprit de Corps for Armies

In many parts of Africa, drinking has long been associated with male rites of passage to adulthood (Akyeampong, Chapter 11). Not only was one's first drink a sign of coming of age, but competitive drinking was often considered proof of masculinity.

Gewald (Chapter 6) demonstrates how alcohol was interwoven in the military identity and social life of young men in early twentieth-century

Namibia. The *Truppenspieler* of Nambia defended their access to *khari* beer despite formidable attempts by colonial officialdom to block it. During the same period, in correspondence to Lugard, a commanding officer commented about drunken soldiers in the capital of northern Nigeria whom he described as "a standing disgrace in the eyes of all good class natives of the Northern Provinces . . . many men who have never touched liquor before learn to drink in the regiment . . . we do not wish it to be considered that drink is part of our syllabus of military training" (Heap 1998: 31).

In the early twentieth century, the Asafo of Ghana, a traditional paramilitary institution for young men, saw alcohol as an integral part of warfare. It was believed that alcohol imparted the aggressive disposition and manliness necessary for battle (Nti 1998).[13] The use of alcohol as an important logistic of war continues in West Africa's many military hot spots to the present. In Sierra Leone, the atrocities committed against civilians by Foday Sankoh's army of youth high on cocktails of alcohol and drugs are now legendary. The recent imposition of *sharia* law in northern Nigeria's Niger State has been enforced by an army presence that is, ironically, exempt from the ban on alcohol consumption.[14] More spontaneously, the law enforcement vacuum of one marginalized rural district of strife-torn Uganda during the 1980s was filled by drinking groups of young bachelors-cum–militaristic vigilantes who acted as self-appointed policemen and judges (Heald 1986).

Africa is currently a continent embroiled in armed conflicts, concentrating young men in situations of stress and heavy alcohol usage. Once demobilized, soldiers take their drinking habits home with them as well as leaving drinking legacies behind. The large number of South African troops stationed in Namibia, who were evacuated at independence in 1990, bequeathed a proliferation of "cuca shops" selling an array of alcoholic drinks. Cuca shops have become an entrenched feature of the Namibian rural landscape, fueling the local thirst for alcohol in a period of rising unemployment and uncertainty (Siiskonen 1994).

In summary, this section has reviewed some of the many social, economic and political factors influencing the current demand for alcohol in African countries. As the supply of alcohol has increased and cultural sanctions on drinking by various social categories of people have eased, the urge to drink has strengthened amid deepening poverty and unemployment. This tendency is being countered, however, by the growing popularity of fundamentalist religions advocating temperance and by some youth and elites expressing reservations about drinking locally made alcoholic beverages of mass appeal. Drinking patterns of specific communities vary tremendously, of course, depending on local responses to these broad trends.

If and when heavy drinking cultures do emerge, there are inestimable costs, as demonstrated in southern African communities where heavy drinking is historically entrenched. Besides poor health and the discord that alcoholism creates in homes and society at large, there is a growing public health threat linked to the AIDS epidemic. The relationship between heavy drinking and the incidence of AIDS has received little attention even though average HIV prevalence of 15 percent in Southern Africa supercedes that of the rest of Africa. However, local communities, health authorities and development agencies are now increasingly taking cognizance of the role heavy drinking plays in sexual disinhibition and the spread of AIDS.[15]

International agencies may have an important supportive, possibly catalyzing, role to play in formulating innovative and timely alcohol policy proposals. However, judicious policy deliberation on the part of African governments is most pivotal for the instigation of measures to preempt or curb alcohol excess. Public policy related to alcohol is a sensitive area with a panoply of vested interests, not least the fiscal interests of governments themselves. Vast numbers of occupationally displaced people now generate income from the cottage production of alcohol. Furthermore, international corporate interests have targeted brewery expansion in Africa. Alcohol in Africa mixes business, pleasure and politics in a heady cocktail of public and private affairs. The welfare concerns of individuals, families and communities ordain the need for public debate and the formulation of national and local alcohol policies capable of maximizing the benefits and minimizing the detrimental effects of alcohol consumption.

ALCOHOL'S AMBIGUITY IN AFRICA

This book has been written to draw attention to the multifarious utilities and meanings of alcohol in Africa. While existing literature presents a wealth of detailed anthropological data about alcohol usage in specific local settings, there has been a dearth of information about aggregate economic and social patterns related to alcohol usage. The case studies and schematic picture of major continental trends presented here begin to fill this gap, pointing to the complexity of alcohol in African societies and the need for research and policy consideration, especially at national level.

Over the last twenty years, rapid income differentiation and economic marginalization have spurred production and consumption of alcohol. In many localities, an expanding supply of alcohol has led to drinking patterns that impinge on general social welfare. The widespread incidence of these circumstances coincides with the continent-wide implementation of structural adjustment and economic liberalization policies. Have these policies literally driven people to drink?

In the past, alcohol's destructive powers were recognized and attempts made to contain them ceremonially (Karp 1980). Among the Xhosa of the Transkei, beer has been perceived as morally ambiguous:[16] "beer can be a force for good or for evil, depending on how it is used. . . . On the one hand it is associated with the ancestors, sociability and the building of the homestead; on the other with the effects of drunkenness, which are disorderly and destructive" (McAllister 1986: 188).

Alcohol also enhances sociability and is appreciated as a source of community-shared happiness. Its status as a symbol of the staff of life with power-affirming functions in the domain of male elders has been gradually giving way to a communal leisure pastime. Tensions have surfaced between the maximization of relaxation and pleasure individually experienced on the one hand, and the sociability of the community on the other. In short, drinking for drinking's sake and intoxication interfere with the sociability associated with alcohol consumption. Finding the balance between the pleasant sociability of drinking and the awkward, antisocial state of drunkenness is difficult, especially in view of the multiple layers of ambiguity in alcohol's usage.

The theme of social solidarity has dominated the African alcohol literature. Is conviviality now being subverted by economic duress and occupational and political upheaval? Abbink observes ethnic solidarity in Ethiopian drinking patterns which amounts to a statement of difference in the face of the ethnic "other." In Luning's case study, Christian converts in Burkino Faso deftly manage to retain a sense of rural sociability while evincing different interpretations of alcohol's symbolic relationship to the ancestors. Van Dijk demonstrates how Pentecostalism seeks "dividual" identity for new converts through disassociation from alcohol and the ancestors among Ghanaian migrants in Europe.

In several case studies presented in this volume, alcohol provides the rallying point for new notions of community. More egalitarian drink-laden village festivities in Guinea-Bissau are conducted within the discourse of democracy (van der Drift), while groups of Tanzanian women traders carefully legitimize their drinking in the discourse of maternal sacrifice (Pietilä). Kumasi's hard-drinking youth share a sense of community with older men who have also experienced economic marginalization (Akyeampong).

The local alcohol producers of East and southern Africa described by McCall, Tanzarn and Willis are trying to beat the process of economic marginalization by putting precedence on their market earnings from alcohol. Their communities are left struggling with the socially undesirable side-effects of this income-maximizing strategy.

The Romans depicted Bacchus with two faces, whereas in Africa he has at least three: one of joy, one of misery and one of pragmatism. The last twenty years have made alcohol a vital income-earning lifeline for people determined to survive labor redundancy and economic hardship. Alcohol has become an increasingly important component of economic livelihood and social leisure in much of Sub-Saharan Africa through these crisis-ridden decades. In many places, "integrative" and "constructive" alcohol usage has become tinged by "destructive" overuse, as the lifeline offered by income-generating alcohol production becomes a noose strangling consumers who fall under its addictive influence. At the outset of the twenty-first century, alcohol in Africa is providing a valuable economic fuel and social lubricant during hard times, but it is an inflammable substance, harboring the threat of individual tragedy and societal disarray.

NOTES

1. Haworth et al. 1981 redefined this to 8 cl for women and 12 cl for men in Zambia.

2. Much of the Western literature on alcohol centers on the nature of alcoholism, defined as a state of individual lack of control over when one starts or stops drinking. Controversy regarding the relevance of the concept of alcoholism to non-industrial societies has led many anthropologists to write defensively about alcohol, playing down its adverse effects. My definition of heavy drinking cultures is primarily concerned with the patterns and consequences of drinking on social groups rather than on individuals per se. This middle position circumvents the tendency of the alcoholism literature to portray alcohol excess as an outcome of weak-willed individuals and anthropologists' deflation of the problem (Room 1984).

3. Heath (1987: 43) infers that heavy drinking is more likely in periods of rapid social upheaval: "In any group or society in which the drinking customs, values, and sanctions—together with the attitudes of all segments of the group or society—are well established, known to and agreed upon by all, and are consistent with the rest of the culture, the rate of alcoholism will be low."

4. Nondrinkers in a drinking party are viewed uncomfortably because they not only demonstrate a lack of group solidarity but also retain a mental alertness that could prove advantageous at the expense of their drinking companions. They jeopardize social trust.

5. The association of religious conversion, work ethics and economic success is not unique to Pentecostalism. In rural settings, traditional social drinking could take up a great deal of time and place heavy demands on wealthier members of the community to supply alcohol to other members. Parkin (1972) documents how Islamic bans on alcohol gave a boost to coastal Kenyan Muslims' economic accumulation.

6. Personal communication, Mirjam de Bruijn, Afrika-Studiecentrum, Leiden, June 2000.

7. Percentages of the sampled teenagers and young adults who said they drank were: Ghanaian Catholic youth, 62 percent (Yangyuoru 1987); Nigerian secondary school students, 43 percent (Adejunmobi 1992); Botswanan secondary school students, 24 percent (felt to be underreported), whereas 37 percent said their friends drank (Molamu and Manyeneng 1988); Kenyan rural and urban youth, 55 percent had taken alcohol and 26 percent used it regularly (Acuda 1983); and South African black community youth (10–21 years old), 40 percent of boys and 32 percent of girls interviewed (Rocha-Silva et al. 1996); in Namibia, 50 percent of youths aged 13–16 experimented with alcohol and 33 percent abused it (UNDP 1999).

8. In Rocha-Silva et al.'s (1996: 41–62) South African study, youth used alcohol as a stepping stone to multiple substance usage. Their township survey provides a profile of youthful drinkers. Young people tended to begin drinking from fourteen onwards. On average male youth drank less than adults, but by international standards their intake was nonetheless high (7 cl pure alcohol per day). Attitudinally, youth expressed the view that drinking was not good for them, and 74 percent said they intended not to drink when they were older. Girls feared rape by intoxicated boys. Girls who drank were considered sexually promiscuous. Youth reported drinking for fun and enjoyment prompted by peer group pressure.

9. One particularly lethal batch of *kumi kumi* illicit spirit spiked with methanol killed over 100 Kenyan drinkers and permanently blinded others in a Nairobi slum in November 2000 ("Deadly Concoction," *Guardian* [London], 18 November 2000; "Worrying Facts about Methanol," *East African Standard* [Nairobi], 8 February 2001).

10. As Haworth et al. (1981: 75–78) described for Zambia: "[Drinking] sprees are part of an urban male folklore in Zambia, and they often coincide with the arrival of a worker's monthly pay. Although a man's wife is never part of a drinking spree, other women may be. We found no evidence that the presence of women in a group of male drinkers has a moderating influence on the amount of alcohol consumed. . . . Most of the few people who drink at all in Zambia drink so much that it becomes a problem both for themselves and for the rest of the community in which they live."

11. Obot's (1993) survey of drinking in the Middle Belt of Nigeria showed that men were more likely to drink than women, but among women drinkers, there was a high proportion of heavy drinkers.

12. In Molamu and Manyeneng's (1988) survey, 43 percent of industrial workers, 52 percent of middle management and 70 percent of professionals drank.

13. Multinational corporations have tried to capitalize on the strong association between masculine strength and alcohol. Diduk (1993) describes a prominent Guinness billboard in Cameroon depicting an African male athlete clothed in Guinness colors about to throw a javelin labeled with the word "FORCE."

14. Personal communication from Abdul Raufu Mustafa, Queen Elizabeth House, Oxford University, 29 March 2000.

15. UNDP (1999: 48) registered concern that the risks of HIV transmission are heightened by "the "disinhibiting" and other psychoactive effects of alcohol use . . . [which] . . . influence sexual activities and practices." Kilonzo (1990) suggested that alcohol may be a cofactor in HIV infection in Tanzania. In a case study of Winterveld, South Africa, wives worried about their risk of HIV infection through their husbands' liaisons with prostitutes at the local taverns (Naidoo 2000). A Zimbabwean secondary school teacher working in a peri-urban area of Harare observed: "AIDS came from outside this settlement. . . . It is not spread by traders *per se*. Rather it seems to be concentrated around pubs. For example, one pub I know witnessed the death of one lady of the night and one by one customers started dying" (interview with author, 2 February 2001).

16. As Heath (1987: 100) notes: "Surrounded with paradoxes, being often recognized as both a stimulant and a depressant, a food and a poison, its use symbolizes an enormous range of both positively and negatively valued things and feelings. Its rapid and sometimes dramatic effects on mood and behavior can easily be discerned by anyone."

REFERENCES

Acuda, S.W. 1983. "Alcoholism: Pattern of Use, Prevalence and Prevention." In Bernard Coche (ed.), *Mental Health*. Moshi, Tanzania: Kilimanjaro Christian Medical Centre.

———. 1985. "International Review Series: Alcohol and Alcohol Problems Research 1. East Africa." *British Journal of Addiction* 80: 121–26.

Adejunmobi, A. 1992. *Drug Use and the Nigerian Youth*. Ibadan: Nigerian Institute of Social and Economic Research.

Adomako, C.C. 1976. "Alcoholism: The African Scene." *Annals of the New York Academy of Sciences* 273: 39–46.

Akyeampong, E. 1996. *Drink, Power, and Cultural Change: A Social History of Alcohol in Ghana, c. 1800 to Recent Times*. Oxford: James Currey.

Ambler, C. 1990. "Alcohol, Racial Segregation and Popular Politics in Northern Rhodesia." *Journal of African History* 31: 295–313.

Baroin, C. 1996. "Religious Conflict in 1990–1993 among the Twa." *African Affairs* 95: 529–54.

Beckerleg, S. 1995. "'Brown Sugar' or Friday Prayers: Youth Choices and Community Building in Coastal Kenya." *African Affairs* 94 (374): 23–38.

Beckman, V. 1988. *Alcohol: Another Trap for Africa*. Örebro: Bokförlaget Libris.

Brody, H. 1974. *Inishkillane: Change and Decline in the West of Ireland*. New York: Schocken Books.

Bryceson, D.F. 1999. *Sub-Saharan Africa Betwixt and Between: Rural Livelihood Practices and Policies*. Leiden: Afrika-Studiecentrum, Working Paper 43.

Carlson, R.G. 1992. "Symbolic Mediation and Commoditization: A Critical Examination of Alcohol Use among the Haya of Bukoba, Tanzania." *Medical Anthropology* 15: 41–62.

Cobley, A.G. 1994. "Liquor and Leadership: Temperance, Drunkenness and the African Petty Bourgeoisie in South Africa." *South African Historical Journal* 31: 128–48.

Diduk, S. 1993. "European Alcohol, History, and the State in Cameroon." *African Studies Review* 36 (10): 1–42.

Douglas, M. 1987. "A Distinctive Anthropological Perspective." In M. Douglas (ed.), *Constructive Drinking: Perspectives on Drink from Anthropology*. Cambridge: Cambridge University Press, 3–15.

Ettore, E. 1997. *Women and Alcohol: A Private Pleasure or a Public Problem?* London: The Women's Press.

Glazer, I.M. 1997. "Alcohol and Politics in Urban Zambia: The Intersection of Gender and Class." In G. Mikell (ed.), *African Feminism: The Politics of Survival in Sub-Saharan Africa*. Philadelphia: University of Pennsylvania Press, 142–58.

Hall, D. 1999. "Impact Assessment of the Thaba Bosiu Alcohol and Drug Rehabilitation Centre." Mimeograph. Maseru, Lesotho: Sechaba Consultants.

Hausse, P. la. 1988. *Brewers, Beerhalls and Boycotts: A History of Liquor in South Africa*. Johannesburg: Ravan Press.

Haworth, A., M. Mwanalushi, and D. Todd. 1981, *Community Response to Alcohol-Related Problems in Zambia*. Lusaka: University of Zambia, Institute for African Studies, Community Health Research Unit.

Heald, S. 1986. "Mafias in Africa: The Rise of Drinking Companies and Vigilante Groups in Bugisu District, Uganda." *Africa* 56 (4): 446–66.

Heap, S. 1998. "'We Think Prohibition Is a Farce': Drinking in the Alcohol-Prohibited Zone of Colonial Northern Nigeria." *International Journal of African Historical Studies* 31 (1): 23–51.

Heath, D.B. 1987. "A Decade of Development in the Anthropological Study of Alcohol Use: 1970–1980." In M. Douglas (ed.), *Constructive Drinking: Perspectives on Drink from Anthropology*. Cambridge: Cambridge University Press, 16–69.

Huby, G. 1994. "Drinking and the Management of Problem Drinking among the Bari, Southern Sudan." In M. MacDonald (ed.), *Gender, Drink and Drugs*. Oxford: Berg.

Iliffe, J. 1987. *The African Poor: A History*. Cambridge: Cambridge University Press.

Karp, I. 1980. "Beer Drinking and Social Experience in an African Society." In I. Karp and C.S. Bird (eds.), *Explorations in African Systems of Thought*. Bloomington: Indiana University Press.

Kilonzo, G. Paul 1990. "Production and Consumption of Alcohol in Tanzania and Alcohol-Related Accidents." In J. Maula et al., *Alcohol in Developing Countries*. Helsinki: Nordic Council for Alcohol and Drug Research, 185–92.

Levy, J.E., and S.J. Kunitz. 1974. *Indian Drinking: Navaho Practices and Anglo-American Theories*. New York: John Wiley & Sons.

Mager, A. 1999. "The First Decade of "European Beer" in Apartheid South Africa: The State, the Brewers and the Drinking Public, 1962–72." *Journal of African History* 40: 367–88.

Malahleha, G.M. 1985. "Liquor Brewing: A Cottage Industry in Lesotho Shebeens." *Journal of Eastern African Research and Development* 15: 45–55.

Mamdani, M. 1984. "Analyzing the Agrarian Question: The Case of a Buganda Village." *Mawazo* (Kampala) 5 (3): 49–58.

McAllister, P. 1986. "'Releasing the Widow'—Xhosa Beer Drink Oratory and Status Change." *African Studies* 45 (2): 171–97.

Molamu, L., and W.G. Manyeneng. 1988. *Alcohol Use and Abuse in Botswana*. Gaborone: Government Printer.

Moser, C., and J. Holland. 1997, *Household Responses to Poverty and Vulnerability: Confronting Crisis in Chawama, Lusaka, Zambia*. Washington, DC: World Bank, Urban Management Programme.

Naidoo, K. 2000. "Households, Gender Relations and Changing Livelihoods in Winterveld." Paper presented at the Multiple Livelihoods and Social Change Workshop, University of Manchester, Institute for Development Policy and Management, June.

Ngokwey, N. 1987. "Varieties of Palm Wine among the Lele of the Kasai." In M. Douglas (ed.), *Constructive Drinking: Perspectives on Drink from Anthropology*. Cambridge: Cambridge University Press, 113–21.

Niger-Thomas, M. 2000. "Buying Futures: The Upsurge of Female Entrepreneurship Crossing the Formal-Informal Sector Divide in Southwest Cameroon." Ph.D. dissertation, Leiden University.

Njelekela, L.C.K. 1978. "Drinking Patterns in Selected Communities in Ludewa District, Iringa Region." Diploma dissertation in public health, University of Dar es Salaam.

Nti, K. 1998. "The Role of Alcohol in the 1905 Conflict Between the Anaafo and Ntsin Asafo Companies of Cape Coast." *Transactions of the Historical Society of Ghana*, New Series 2: 49–55.

Obot, I.S. 1990. "Substance Abuse, Health and Social Welfare in Africa: An Analysis of the Nigerian Experience." *Social Science and Medicine* 31 (6), 699–704.

———. 1993. *Drinking Behaviour and Attitudes in Nigeria.* Jos, Nigeria: University of Jos, Centre for Development Studies Monograph Series 1/93.

Odejide, A.O. 1986. "Alkohol i Nigeria: Produktion, Bruksmönster och Halsoeffekter." *Alkoholpolitik* 3 (1): 4–18.

Otieno, B., J.A. Owola, and O. Oduor. 1979. "A Study of Alcoholism in a Rural Setting in Kenya." *East African Medical Journal* 56: 665–70.

Parkin, D.J. 1972. *Palms, Wine, and Witnesses: Public Spirit and Private Gain in an African Farming Community.* San Francisco: Chandler.

Partanen, J. 1990. "Abstinence in Africa." In J. Maula et al., *Alcohol in Developing Countries.* Helsinki: Nordic Council for Alcohol and Drug Research, 70–85.

Reader, D.H., and J. May. 1971, *Drinking Patterns in Rhodesia: Highfield African Township Salisbury.* Salisbury: University of Rhodesia.

Rocha-Silva, L., S. de Miranda, and R. Erasmus. 1996. *Alcohol, Tobacco and Other Drug Use among Black Youth.* Pretoria: Human Science Research Council.

Room, R. 1968. "Cultural Contingencies of Alcoholism: Variations Between and Within Nineteenth-Century Urban Ethnic Groups in Alcohol-Related Death Rates." *Journal of Health and Social Behavior* 9: 106–11.

———. 1984. "Alcohol and Ethnography: A Case of Problem Deflation?" *Current Anthropology* 25 (2): 169–91.

Rootman, I., and J. Moser. 1984. *Community Response to Alcohol-Related Problems.* Washington, DC: U.S. Department of Health and Human Services/World Health Organization Project.

Said, H.I., and M. Last. 1991. *Youth and Health in Kano Today.* Kano: Bayero University.

Siiskonen, H. 1994. "Namibia and the Heritage of Colonial Alcohol Policy." *Nordic Journal of African Studies* 3 (1): 77–87.

Silberschmidt, M. 1990. "The Interaction Between Changing Male and Female Roles and Alcohol Problems in Rural Kenya: Observations from a Field Study in Kisii District." In J. Maula et al. (eds.), *Alcohol in Developing Countries.* Helsinki: Nordic Council for Alcohol and Drug Research, 134–50.

Stivers, R. 1976. *A Hair of the Dog: Irish Drinking and American Stereotype.* London: Pennsylvania State University Press.

Swantz, M-L. 1985. *Women in Development: A Creative Role Denied?* London: C. Hurst & Co.

Tayob, A.I. 1996. "Jihad Against Drugs in Cape Town: A Discourse-Centred Analysis." *Social Dynamics* 22 (2): 23–29.

Toit, B.M. du. 1991. *Cannabis, Alcohol, and the South African Student: Adolescent Drug Use, 1974–1985.* Athens: Ohio University Center for International Studies.

United Nations Development Program (UNDP). 1999. *Namibia: Human Development Report 1999.* Windhoek: UNDP.

White, S. 1996. *Russia Goes Dry: Alcohol, State and Society.* Cambridge: Cambridge University Press.

Whitehead, P.C., and C. Harvey. 1974. "Explaining Alcoholism: An Empirical Test and Reformulation." *Journal of Health and Social Behavior* 15: 57–65.

Wolcott, H.F. 1974. *The African Beer Gardens of Bulawayo*. New Brunswick, NJ: Rutgers Center of Alcohol Studies.

Yangyuoru, Y. 1987. "The Social Correlates of Psychotropic Substance Use by Contemporary Youth of Ghana." *Universitas* 9: 154–71.

Yguel, J., with S. Luciani, B. Duflo, C. M'Bamezoui, A. Froment, D. Bard and M. Gentilini. 1990. "Consumption of Alcoholic Drinks in Three Different Parts of Cameroon." In J. Maula et al. (eds.), *Alcohol in Developing Countries*. Helsinki: Nordic Council for Alcohol and Drug Research, 113–26.

Index

Accidents, 270
Accra, 16, 221
Addiction, 11
Advertising, 43, 280, 287
Africanization, 13, 32
African Party for the Independence of [Portuguese] Guinea and Cape Verde, 180, 185, 191
Agadagidi, 141
Age: general, 6, 10, 15, 31, 33, 56, 223, 279; generational conflict, 10, 13, 16, 60, 62, 186, 189–92, 226, 259–61, 276; intergenerational relationships, 57, 71, 180–82, 216
AIDS. *See* Disease
Akan, 215, 228
Akpeteshie, 27, 35, 218, 220–25, 227–28, 278
Alcohol: abstinence, 33, 107, 272–73, 279, 286; abuse, 12; adulteration, 46, 83, 195, 275, 286; attitudes towards, 4, 9, 195, 200, 231–45; brewed (*See* Breweries; Brewing); commodification, 14, 16, 29–32, 57–60, 80, 109, 167–71, 236, 244, 275, 281; connoisseur tastes, 274–75; content strength, 7, 24, 26–29, 42, 80–82, 89, 120–21, 130, 132, 147, 153, 165–67, 173, 175, 220, 271, 275, 279; control, 8, 12–13, 16, 26–27, 35, 39, 47, 107, 117–35, 190–91, 255, 267–69, 271–73, 275–76, 281; demand, 14, 36–37, 47, 66, 108, 117, 153, 277, 279, 282; distilled, 7–8, 24, 26, 28–30, 35, 38–39, 44, 47, 81–89, 139, 153, 162, 167–74, 180–81, 185–86, 193, 249, 253, 268, 271, 279, 281, 286; fermented, 7, 24, 26, 28, 30, 38–40, 81, 98–99, 140, 185, 271, 281; illegal, 38, 83, 90, 121–35, 153, 220, 278; imports, 5, 8, 15, 26–28, 37, 43, 139–57; intake, 7, 111, 270, 285–86; manufactured drinks (*See* Production: industrial); policy, 11–13, 267–69, 271, 277–80, 283–284; pricing, 26, 28–29, 34, 38, 40, 46, 61, 67–68, 82–83, 153, 171, 219, 228, 234, 268, 280–81; prohibition, 35, 127, 250–51, 258–62, 282; psycho-physical effect, 3–5, 7, 16, 287; supply, 14, 33, 36–37, 39, 44–45, 84, 269, 271, 282; symbolism, 5–6, 10, 16–17, 171–72, 236–39, 246, 251–53, 259, 262, 271, 283; temperance, 273, 282. *See also* Drinking; Beer; *and other named forms of alcohol*
Alcoholism, 9, 15, 18, 85–86, 107, 173, 193, 276–78, 280, 285
ALTERSIAL, 105
Amhara, 162–64, 175
Amin, Idi, 81
Ancestors, 3, 5–6, 16, 24, 139, 181, 187–88, 216, 231, 235, 239–44, 253, 257–59, 261, 273, 284
Angola, 47
Ankole, 76
Anthropology, 9–11, 13, 18, 239, 283

Apartheid, 32, 135
Aquavit, 270
Araqé, 166–67
Asante, 217–18
Australia, 23
Autonomy, 191, 201–2, 268–69

Babaton, 28
Baganda, 78
Balanta, 180–193
Baltic states, 47
Bamboo, 28, 40
Bananas, 15, 58, 77–79, 81, 85, 87, 104, 198
Barley, 27, 40, 166, 175
Bars, 38, 204–8, 216, 219–20, 224, 255, 257, 261, 287
Barter, 8
Beer: banana, 69, 81–82, 97; bottled, 7, 14, 27–28, 38, 40, 42, 46, 99, 109, 269, 275; club, 63, 65–66, 69, 72; general, 5–6, 8, 14, 24, 26, 28, 30, 33–34, 38, 45, 55–71, 80, 141, 162, 165–69, 204–208, 210, 253, 279, 281–82, 284; halls, 8, 33, 45, 61, 121, 131, 134–35, 274, 277; *kaffir*, 34, 120; lager, 27, 34–35, 42, 44, 46–47, 154–55, 221; opaque, 26, 28; perishability, 81, 108; sorghum, 7, 35, 46–47, 97, 111, 165. *See also* Breweries; Brewing; Distribution: beer
Beer bananas, 78–80, 84, 86
Bissau, 192
Blantyre, 17, 250, 255
Boké, 165
Bordé, 26, 166, 168–69, 175
Botswana, 34, 42–43, 46–47, 95, 100, 118, 272, 275, 280, 286
Bowker, Captain Octavus George, 124–35
Brandy, 8, 29
Braniger Brewery, Niger, 47
Brazil, 179
Breweries: general, 27, 47; multinational, 9, 42–43, 269, 280, 283, 287; South African Breweries, 35, 42, 45; state-owned, 27, 37, 42, 47
Brewing: bad brews, 38, 68 ; failures, 25; general, 8, 14–15, 27–28, 31–32, 37, 40, 80, 87, 93–111, 168, 231–45, 253, 255, 267; illegal, 13; official brews, 26; process, 25, 59, 61, 80, 96–103, 111, 121, 166, 236–37, 275; techniques, 25. *See also* Women: brewers
British West Africa, 143
Brussels Conference of 1890, 148
Buganda, 76–77, 81
Bunyoro, 75–90
Burkina Faso, 14, 17, 95, 231–48, 101, 105
Burukutu, 140
Business: capital, 62–63, 67–69; credit, 64; profit, 12, 43, 48, 61, 68–70, 82, 94, 127, 129; prospects, 25
Buzaa, 43, 47

Cameroon, 29, 46, 276, 278, 280, 287
Cana, 29 , 181, 186–88, 281
Cana de bordâo, 181
Cannabis, 25
Carlsberg, 101, 106, 255
Cashcropping, 30–31, 56, 60, 62–63, 78–79, 84, 88, 184–86, 219–20, 267
Cashew nuts, 16, 39, 179–80, 184–86, 189, 194–95
Cassava, 86, 90
Castle, 46, 106
Cattle, 63, 162, 164, 170, 189, 206
Celebrations. *See* Community
Central Africa, 75
Ceremonies. *See* Community
Chagga, 197–209, 269, 278
Chang'aa, 29, 35, 43
Chibuku, 27–28, 33–34, 40, 42–43, 46, 48, 109, 257
Chibuku Breweries, Zimbabwe, 109
Chiefs. *See* Government

Children, 7, 15–16, 64, 69, 71, 85, 88, 118, 200–201, 205–7, 217, 280
Christianity, 5, 17. *See also* Religion
Class: differentiation, 7, 42, 45; egalitarianism, 189; elite, 129, 167, 172, 217, 223, 280, 282; formation, 29, 36; general, 6, 10, 13, 15, 30; middle-class, 27, 30, 32, 34, 42–43, 46; working class, 30, 32–33, 35, 46, 220
Cocoa, 69, 151, 219, 221
Coconut, 28
Coffee, 60, 62, 63, 78, 84, 86, 163, 198, 206
Cognac, 35, 167
Colonial Development and Welfare Act 1940, 154
Colonialism: finance, 15; general, 9, 23, 29, 75–76, 117–35, 139–57, 172, 218, 232, 242, 251–53, 280; officials, 26; paternalism, 26; state, 15; taxation, 31, 139–54
Commodity production, 30
Community: ceremonial exchange, 24, 30; ceremonies, 25, 27, 29, 31, 97, 165, 187–188, 190, 216, 234, 253, 255, 259, 276; drinking norms, 27, 30–32, 165, 169–73, 186–93, 195, 218, 268, 270–71, 275–76, 280–81, 286; inheritance, 57; institutions, 17; welfare, 283–84. *See also* Ritual
Compagnie Française de l'Afrique Occidentale (CFAO), 154
Congo, Democratic Republic of, 46, 76, 110, 147, 274, 280
Consumption of alcohol: patterns, 23, 30; rates, 11, 193; seasonal, 24, 29; significance of, 188, 192, 272–73, 278. *See also* Drinking
Convention of St.-Germain-en-Laye 1919, 152
Conviviality, 6–7, 10, 16–17, 32, 35, 169–71, 192, 215, 224–25, 242–44, 269, 281, 284
Corporate investment, 13
Côte d'Ivoire, 105
Cotton, 78
Council for Scientific and Industrial Research (CSIR), 109
CPC Tongaat Foods, 111
Crevejas de Moçambique Limitada, 47
Currency, 8, 139
Custom duties, 142–57

Darbrew, Tanzania, 109
Dar es Salaam, 37–38, 46
Democracy, 16
Democratization, 191–93, 268, 284
Depression, 38, 124, 128–30, 153
Deviance, 11
Disease: AIDS, 269–70, 283, 287; cancer, 270; cholera, 47; diabetes, 270; general, 12, 85–86, 89; hypertension, 270; liver disease, 171
Distilling: controls, 26; general, 14, 27, 35, 37, 153, 162, 167–74, 180–81, 185–93, 268; hazards, 26, 81–82, 89–90; techniques, 26, 81–82, 89–90
Distribution: beer, 8, 34, 46, 61, 65–66, 69; general, 31, 83, 168; male-domination, 38, 48, 64–66, 69
Dizi, 162–63, 165, 169, 171
Dolo, 101, 110–11
Donors, 93, 110
Drinking: age, 6, 17, 85, 188, 195, 217, 278; binges, 24, 123, 219, 276, 281; competitive drinking, 219, 224, 281; constructive drinking, 9, 11, 166, 285; culture, 13, 267, 269–83, 285; female, 7, 33, 40–41, 48, 123, 132, 170, 200–209, 217, 234, 243, 269, 275–76, 279–80, 286–287; general, 55; heavy drinking, 6, 16–17, 33–34, 44, 215, 223, 227, 255, 269–71, 276–79, 285–87; informalized, 32; intake, 27–29, 46, 270, 285–86; 'integrative drinking,' 10, 285; modalities, 14, 23–45; patterns, 16, 23, 29–36, 45, 282–84;

Drinking (cont.), practices, 11, 16–17, 181, 218, 231–45, 271; seasonality (*See* Consumption: seasonal); single-sex drinking, 31; styles, 10, 16, 272–73; subculture, 12; taboos, 16–17, 188, 192; typology, 28–30
Drug use, 274, 282, 286
Drunkenness. *See* Inebriation
Dutch East India Company, 17, 277

East Africa, 5, 26–28, 31, 42, 55, 109, 285
Economies: crisis, 36–41, 59, 79, 128, 276, 279; exchange, 8; export earnings, 15; foreign investment, 48; income diversification, 39; international, 31, 271; local, 14–15, 40, 85, 94, 168–69, 199–200, 205, 217, 226, 234; purchasing power, 36; regional, 171; subsistence-based, 31, 86, 167–69, 275
Education, 63, 67, 69, 85, 90, 111, 216, 221, 223, 227, 250, 256, 268–69
Elders. *See* Men
Elite, 30, 135
Employment. *See* Labor
Environmental concerns, 15, 44, 93–111, 268
Ethanol, 25
Ethiopia, 10, 14, 16, 28, 47, 161–75, 284
Ethiopian People's Revolutionary Democratic Front, 174
Ethnicity, 10, 13, 15–16, 161–75, 279, 284
Euro, 29
Europe, 17, 47
European Union (EU), 104

Firewood, 44, 88, 93, 96–106, 167, 246, 268
Fiscal revenue, 3, 8–9, 13, 15, 27, 31, 64–66, 69–70, 72, 83–84, 121, 139–57, 167–68, 173, 201, 233
Food and Agricultural Organization, 38
Food security, 86–87, 233
Francophone Africa, 26
Fuel. *See* Firewood
Funi, 111

Gabon, 46
G.B. Ollivant, 154
Gender: division of labor, 39, 57, 87, 89, 165, 169–70, 175, 180, 187, 198, 207; double standards, 224, 275; drug use, 274; general, 6, 10, 13, 33; relations, 43, 58, 94, 182, 197–209, 224; resource use, 103; struggles, 15–16, 32, 55–56, 62–63, 71, 88, 205–8, 279; studies, 103–104, 107. *See also* Men; Women
Germany, 118
Gèso, 163, 166, 168–73, 175
Ghana, 14, 16, 27, 29, 32, 35, 41, 48, 215–230, 251, 276, 278, 280, 282, 284, 286
Ghia, 141
Gin, 8, 26–27, 29, 35, 43, 79, 81, 139, 141–143, 152, 167, 278
Globalization, 35, 41
Gold, 163, 217
Gold Coast, 143, 218
Gongo, 29, 37
Government: chiefs/headmen, 125–26, 182, 217, 232–233, 238, 242–43; general, 8, 12, 15, 17, 26; local, 70, 162–64, 174, 267–68, 283; municipal, 120–21, 124, 128–33, 217–18, 226, 267; national, 139–57, 173, 220–21, 267–68, 271, 283; village, 69, 107, 183
Grain: general, 24–25, 31, 40, 45, 62, 68, 94, 121, 129, 175, 198; shortages, 38; surplus, 30
GRET/GERES, 105
GTZ, 105
Guinea-Bissau, 14, 16, 29, 179–95, 268, 276, 281, 284
Guinea corn, 140

Guinness, 9, 42, 47, 111, 155, 270, 287
Gurage, 163

Hangovers, 28
Health and safety, 26
Heineken, 9, 42, 101, 106, 154
Herero, 118–35
Honey, 185

Ikamba, 81
Importation. *See* Alcohol: imports
Income generation. *See* Labor: informal sector; Production: cottage industry
Independence Brewery, Nigeria, 155
India, 179
Industry, 3. *See also* Production: industrial
Inebriation, 4–6, 10, 15, 23, 26, 32–33, 85, 117, 121, 123, 126–27, 132, 135, 141, 162, 171–72, 174, 249, 261, 270, 276, 280–81, 284
Inflation, 46
Informal sector. *See* Labor: informal sector; Production: cottage industry
Intermediate Technology Development Group (ITDG), 104–5
International Development Research Center (IRDC), 104
International Distillers of Uganda, 82
International donors, 15, 104–8, 267–68, 272, 283. *See also* World Bank
International Labor Office (ILO), 104
International Monetary Fund, 36, 41
Intoxication. *See* Inebriation
Ireland, 270
Islam, 5
Ivory Coast, 26, 46–47

Jego, 140
Johannesburg, 47
John Holt, Nigeria, 154

Kachasu, 29, 40, 253
Kampala, 82–83, 278
Kangala, 101
Kangara, 61, 66, 71, 101
Karagwe, 76
Katikala, 29, 162, 166–67, 169–74
Kenya, 12, 18, 27, 32, 35, 46–47, 81, 104, 111, 272, 274, 278, 280, 286
Khali, 28
Khari, 120–28, 135, 282
Kimpumu, 66
Kingsley, Mary, 143
Konyagi, 47
Korean war, 31
Kumasi, 6, 215–27, 268
Kumi kumi, 286
Kyela, 65–66, 69

Labor: employment, 38, 41, 43, 82, 119, 163, 206, 268; formal sector, 36, 41, 269, 279; general, 12; income generation, 7, 15, 23, 186, 199, 267, 281, 285 (*See also* Women: income earning); informal sector, 27, 36,–37, 46, 255, 269, 278; migrant labor, 31, 34, 60–61, 67, 120, 184, 233, 235, 274, 277, 284; payment in alcohol, 8, 12, 31, 59–60, 80, 168, 171, 194; proletarianization, 34; unemployment, 12, 17, 35–36, 193, 206, 221, 225, 268, 271, 278–79, 282–84; wage labor force, 31, 59, 120, 219. *See also* Work party
Laborers, 26
Lager, 34–35, 42, 139
Lagos, 143, 145, 155–56
Leisure, 6, 16, 24, 27, 29, 34, 40, 118, 132–133, 174, 225–26, 255, 268, 270–71, 277, 284–85
Lesotho, 47–48, 278
Libation. *See* Ritual
Liberalization, 14, 38, 41–44, 83, 185, 199, 268, 284

Licensing, 8, 27, 43, 62–64, 82–84, 108, 129, 149, 278
Livelihood. *See* Labor; Women: income earning
Liver disease. *See* Disease
Livestock, 58, 170
Local economy. *See* Economies: local
Local government, 66
Lonrho, 34
Lugard, Governor-General Frederick, 143, 151, 156, 282
Lusaka, 28, 33, 38

Maize, 25, 28, 40, 59, 61–62, 78, 81, 121, 127, 165–66
Maji, 163–69
Malawi, 14, 17, 40, 47, 249–64, 273
Malawi Congress Party, 260
Mali, 48, 110
Malnutrition. *See* Nutrition
Malt, 43, 46, 94, 236–37, 242
Mane, Brigdeiro Ansumane, 192
Manufacturing. *See* Production: industrial: *Marabi* culture, 35
Marijuana, 43, 225
Marital strife, 220, 222, 268, 270, 279, 283
Markets: expansion, 38, 168; general, 17; international, 39, 82, 180, 192; local, 82 (*See also* Economies: local); monopoly, 26, 45, 72, 108, 121; national, 82–83; regional, 14–15; urban (*See* Urban)
Masese, 40
Material culture, 3, 10
Mbamba, 28
Mbege, 28, 69, 97, 101, 203
Medical: health, 276, 283; literature, 9, 11, 14, 270; practice, 252. *See also* Disease
Me'en, 162–65, 171, 175
Men: brewing, 37, 47; drinking intake, 46, 286–87; elders, 14, 16, 24, 29, 186–87, 216, 223, 277–81, 284; general, 6, 32; male drinking groups, 31, 35, 171, 216–217, 268, 275, 278–79, 286; male elders, 14, 16, 24, 29; male identity, 6; masculinity, 6, 171, 223, 281–82, 287
Mengistu, Haile Mariam, 164, 167
Migration. *See* Labor; Urban: migration
Millet, 7, 25, 58–59, 61, 71, 78, 104, 111, 121, 166, 198, 233
Missionaries: general, 9, 242–43, 251–52, 255, 261, 275; Rhenish Mission, 122; schools, 63. *See also* Religion
Modernity, 10, 38, 42, 250, 272, 281
Monopolies, 8
Mooré, 235
Moose, 232, 242
Morality, 6, 9, 15, 25, 45, 106, 123, 131, 142, 146, 152, 171–72, 180, 201, 231, 249–62, 274
Mortality, 12, 219, 241–44, 269, 286
Moshi, 199, 209
Mowa, 253
Mozambique, 47, 101, 109
Mukonde, 28
Multinational corporations, 14, 34
Munkoyo, 28
Musa, 79–80, 89
Music: Congo jazz, 34; general, 110, 191, 219, 228; highlife, 34, 220–21, 224–25, 228

Nairobi, 27, 43
Namibia, 14–15, 42, 46–47, 117–35, 282
National Sorghum Breweries, South Africa, 109
Nationalism, 26, 31
Navaho, 270
Neoliberalism, 14, 36, 267
Niger, 47
Niger Coast Protectorate, 144–45, 156

Nigeria, 8, 14–15, 18, 28–29, 46–47, 139–57, 251, 272–73, 275, 280, 282, 286–87
Nigeria Brewery Limited (NBL), 154–55
Nigerian Breweries, 4, 7, 111
Njangi, 40
Nkrumah, Kwame, 27, 35
North America, 23
Nubia, 81
Nutrition, 7, 12, 26, 86, 121, 169, 204, 222
Nyakyusa, 55–73

Obote, President Milton, 77
Odoka, 224
Ogogoro, 153
Oil: boom, 27; crisis, 36, 46; general, 150, 155; palms, 28
Oromo, 162–63
Oti agbado, 141
Oti baba, 140
Oti ogede, 141
Oti-oka, 141
Otruppe. See Soldiers: *Otruppe*
Ougadougou, 7, 97–98, 101, 231–48
Ouzo, 167
OXFAM, 104

Palm kernels, 151
Palm oil, 151
Partido Africano para a Independência da Guinée do Cabo Verde (PAIGC). *See* African Party for the Independence of [Portuguese] Guinea and Cape Verde
Patterson Zochonis (PZ), 154
Peasant farmers, 39–41, 46, 58–70, 77–80, 89, 167–72, 179–93, 233–35
People's National Party, Ghana, 221
Pito, 140
Police, 43, 125, 127–28, 133–34, 143, 163, 282
Pombe, 28–37, 101, 110–111
Pombe za maji, 61
Porto Novo, 143
Portugal, 179, 185, 193
Post-modernism, 10
Poverty, 7, 17, 48, 76, 84, 122, 167, 179–80, 193, 220–27, 267, 269–70, 278–79, 281–82, 284–85
Power, 6, 13, 16, 31, 70, 88, 161, 167, 182, 218, 261
Precolonial period, 23–25, 215–18, 275
Price, 29
Privitization, 14, 41–44, 269
Problem drinking, 9, 11–12
Production: competition, 40, 275; co-operation, 40; cottage industry, 6, 8, 25–26, 28–30, 33, 36–41, 43–44, 47, 59–70, 80–85, 106–110, 149, 152, 267–68, 275, 283; distilling (*See* Distilling); general, 5, 14, 25–27, 36–44, 188; import substitution, 154–55; industrial, 5–6, 8, 26–27, 30, 34, 37–38, 43, 45–46, 82, 106, 109, 154–56, 255; seasonality, 84; technical innovation, 14, 25, 27, 59–60, 66, 81–82, 109, 153, 185, 271; turnkey factories, 27. *See also* Brewing; Breweries
Profit. *See* Business: profit
Prohibition, 38, 142, 148
Prostitution, 33, 38–39, 45, 279, 287
Pubs. *See* Bars
Puya, 101

Racism, 45, 135, 252
Rawlings, Flight Lieutenant J.J., 221
Religion: Catholicism, 17, 233–34, 242–46, 273, 286; Christianity, 17, 71, 118, 122–24, 143, 162, 164–65, 231–34, 241, 250, 272–73; conversion, 241–44, 272, 286; general, 3, 10, 17, 111, 231, 276, 282; Islam, 46, 81, 107, 148–49, 193, 233–34, 241, 245, 250, 273, 286; Pentecostalism, 249–62, 273, 282,

Religion (cont.) 284–85; Protestantism, 17, 107, 174, 233, 241–42, 245–46, 273. *See also* Missionaries
Rice, 81, 180–81, 183–84, 186–88, 194
Ritual: ceremonial libation, 24–25, 31, 186, 237; general, 118, 170, 183, 187–88, 195, 198, 231–45, 252–53, 258; libation, 5–6, 10, 32, 216, 228, 232, 237, 240, 246, 253, 259
Royal Niger Company, 140, 148
Rum, 8, 139, 141–43
Rural: areas, 3, 10–11, 16, 25–26, 29, 39–40, 43–44, 55–71, 75–90, 271; communities, 24, 30–31; drinking patterns, 31–34, 46, 85–86, 149, 181–93, 231–45, 272, 286; rural urban contrasts, 166, 173–74, 206, 219, 255; rural urban relations, 36; ties, 14
Russian, 270
Rwanda, 97

Sahel, 5, 17, 273–74
Sankoh, Foday, 282
Schnapps, 140
Selassie, Haile, 168
Sexual encounters: extramarital, 33–34, 287; illicit, 122, 204–5, 208; rape, 286; unwanted pregnancy, 270. *See also* Prostitution
Seychelles, 47
Shaky Shaky Enterprises, Zambia, 109
Shebeens, 26, 35, 109, 278
Shekete, 141
Shimeya, 28
Sierra Leone, 143–44, 282
Skokiaan, 28
Slave trade, 139, 149
Smuggling, 142–43, 194, 199
Sociability, 6, 10, 58. *See also* Conviviality
Social status, 6, 10, 139, 161–74, 217–18, 269–70, 280, 286
Social welfare, 8–9, 11, 13–14, 269, 276, 283–84
Société Commerciale de l'Ouest Africain (SCOA), 154
Sodabi, 29
Soldiers: alcohol consumption, 154, 219; general, 26, 167, 192, 281–82; *Otruppe,* 117–35
Solopi, 28
Sorghum, 7, 25, 28, 111, 121, 166, 233, 236, 238–39, 246, 279
South Africa, 8, 17, 26–28, 30, 32, 34, 42, 61, 109, 118–19, 125, 128, 274, 278, 280, 282, 287
South African Breweries, 35, 42, 45, 47, 109, 111
Southern Africa, 5, 8, 11–12, 18, 26, 31–32, 34, 42, 61, 109, 118, 231, 255, 277–78, 280, 283, 285
State, 26, 37. *See also* Government: monopolies
Structural adjustment, 16, 36–37, 41, 221, 267–69, 278–79, 284
Sudan, 81, 279
Sugar, 25, 28, 60–61, 66, 82, 124, 127, 141, 153, 166
Sugarcane, 47, 81
Suri, 162, 164–65, 168, 171, 173–75
Swahili, 63
Swaziland, 47

T'ädj, 28, 165, 168–69
T'älla, 165
Tanzania, 10, 14, 16, 32, 37–38, 41, 46–48, 55–73, 76, 95, 100, 101, 104, 107, 109, 197–212, 272, 276, 278, 284, 287
Tanzania Breweries, 42, 47
Tanzania Gender Network Programme (TGNP), 104
Taverns. *See* Bars
Tax. *See* Fiscal revenue
Technical innovations, 14

Tembo, 28
Temperance: advocates, 15, 124; general, 9
Tigrawi, 163
Tigray People's Liberation Front, 174
Tigrinya, 162
Tjwala, 129–30
Tobacco, 78, 108, 187, 257, 260, 269
Tombo, 28
Tonto, 79–80
Toro, 76
Tradition, 10
Traffic accidents, 11
Transport, 15, 24–25, 36, 39, 41, 43, 48, 79–80, 85, 88, 103, 109, 121, 168, 198
Tukuyu, 63, 65, 69

Uganda, 8, 14–15, 39, 41, 47–48, 75–90, 268, 282
Ulanzi, 28, 40
Unemployment. *See* Labor
UNIFEM, 104
Union Trading Company (UTC), 154
United Africa Company (UAC), 154
UN-NGO Group, 104
Upper Volta, *See* Burkina Faso
Urban: areas, 3, 7, 11, 16, 25–26, 43; drinking patterns, 32–36, 106, 117–35, 171, 173, 255, 272, 274, 278, 286; informal sector (*See* Economies: informal sector); markets, 15, 27, 36–37, 61–64, 82, 109, 171, 197–209, 215–16, 218; migration, 32, 180, 256, 281; poor, 48; popular culture, 219, 228, 250, 260; population, 30; supply, 39, 44, 55, 271; ties, 14, 222; urbanization, 13, 29, 44, 222, 255
Utshwala, 129

Vieira, President Joâo Bernard "Nino," 191–192
Violence, 162, 172, 174, 192
Vodka, 270

Wanzuki, 28
War: general, 184, 195, 218; World War I; 151; World War II, 81, 156, 255
Waragi, 8, 15, 29, 75, 79, 81–83, 88, 268, 278
West Africa, 5, 8, 26, 28–29, 34–35, 42, 104–105, 107, 179, 234, 236, 244, 282
West African Breweries, Nigeria, 155
Whisky, 26, 29, 35, 37, 139, 143, 167, 270
World Health Organization (WHO), 33
Windhoek, 15, 26, 117–35
Wine: banana, 5; general, 30, 38, 180; honey, 165; palm, 5–7, 24, 45, 140–41, 153, 216–18, 274–75, 281; sap, 28, 30; tots, 8
Women: barmaids, 38–39; brewers, 15, 25–27, 36–37, 47–48, 55, 63–71, 93–111, 117, 120–135, 140, 165, 168, 234–37, 245, 283; churchgoers, 123, 254; drinking intake (*See* Drinking: female); female heads of households, 48, 55, 134, 280; female identity, 6; general, 7, 13, 36; income earning, 14–15, 39, 47, 62–63, 67–70, 94–95, 123, 170, 202, 254, 276, 278; informal sector, 38; maternal identity, 16, 197–209, 284; menopausal, 17; ritual role, 190–91; traders, 40, 82, 199–210, 269, 280, 284; war survivors, 118; workload, 87
Work parties, 8, 59, 169–70, 194
World Bank, 36, 41, 48, 105, 221

Xhosa, 284

Yangan, 141
Yeast, 28, 237
Youth, 16–17, 32, 42, 110, 119, 122–23, 135, 170, 180–81, 187, 190–93, 198–99, 215–28, 250, 255–56, 260, 268, 273–75, 281–82, 285–86

Zaire, 26
Zambia, 8, 10, 28, 31–32, 34, 40, 46–47, 95, 109, 255, 272, 279
Zambia Breweries, 42
Zimbabwe, 34, 42, 47–48, 97, 99–101, 104, 109, 251, 272, 275, 287
Zulus, 7, 129, 240

About the Contributors

JON ABBINK is an anthropologist and senior researcher at the African Studies Centre, Leiden, and professor of African Ethnic Studies at the Vrije Universiteit, Amsterdam. He did fieldwork on ethnicity and social change in Israel and on agro-pastoralist and ethnic relations in Ethiopia. His interests are the history and ethnology of Ethiopia/Northeast Africa as well as culture and violence and sociopolitical change in Africa. He has published on the topics of the Beta Israel (Falasha), Ethiopian ethnology and African studies more generally. He recently coedited a book entitled *Meanings of Violence*. His current research is on local art/artefact traditions and on history and sociopolitical change in Ethiopia.

EMMANUEL AKYEAMPONG graduated with a B.A. in history and religions from the University of Ghana (1984), then attained his master's in European history from Wake Forest University (North Carolina, 1989) and a Ph.D. in African history from the University of Virginia (1993). He was appointed an assistant professor of African history at Harvard University in July 1993, and is currently the Hugh K. Foster Associate Professor of African Studies. He recently published *Between the Sea and the Lagoon: An Eco-Social History of the Anlo of Southeastern Ghana, 1850 to Recent Times* and is currently cowriting a history of African leisure with Charles Ambler.

DEBORAH FAHY BRYCESON is a senior researcher at the African Studies Centre, Leiden University, The Netherlands. She has a multidisciplinary background in geography, economic history and sociology. She studied for her first and second degrees at the University of Dar es Salaam before doing her Ph.D. at Oxford. Her work has spanned a number of areas, notably urbanization, food marketing, rural employment, rural transport and gender. Her recent books include *Women Wielding the Hoe, Farewell to Farms: De-agrarianisation and Employment in Africa* (edited with Vali Jamal) and *Disappearing Peasantries* (edited with Cris Kay and Jos Mooij).

JAN-BART GEWALD grew up in southern Africa. He completed his B.A. in African history and politics at Rhodes University, South Africa, and continued his studies at the University of Leiden, where, following stints as an exchange student at the Universities of Cologne, Germany, and Ghana, Legon, he completed his doctorate in 1996. He is currently employed at the University of Cologne, where his research deals with the sociocultural history of central Namibia in the first half of the twentieth century. Having lived and worked in West Africa, he maintains an interest in the history of Ghana and Niger.

SIMON HEAP is a senior researcher at INTRAC, the International NGO Training and Research Centre, Oxford. He was previously the Kirk-Greene Junior Research Fellow in Tropical African Studies at St. Antony's College, Oxford. He gained his doctorate on "The Liquor Trade and the Nigerian Economy" with a Leverhulme Trust Study Abroad Studentship from the University of Ibadan.

SABINE LUNING is a lecturer in the anthropology department and at the Research School for Asian, African and Amerindian Studies of the University of Leiden. She has done extensive fieldwork in Burkina Faso, and her Ph.D. dissertation deals with the annual ritual cycle of the Moose chiefdom Maane. The dynamics of ritual practices are her primary research interest.

MICHAEL K. McCALL is an associate professor in the social science division in ITC, Enschede, and is responsible for institutional and planning issues in natural resource management. He trained as a geographer in England and the United States and spent eight years teaching and researching at the University of Dar es Salaam, where he developed a practical knowledge of local brews. Currently his research interests are in local-level environmental management conflicts and options, focusing on rural eastern and southern Africa. This extends to developing training in operational environmental impact assessment, and to research in indigenous environmental knowledge, and the participatory use of geo-information systems at the local community level.

TUULIKKI PIETILÄ is a researcher in social anthropology in the Department of Sociology at the University of Helsinki. Her Ph.D. dissertation, "Gossip, Markets and Gender: The Dialogical Construction of Morality in Kilimanjaro," is a study of markets and market women in Kilimanjaro, Tanzania.

NITE BAZA TANZARN holds a B.Sc. in agricultural sciences and a master's in gender studies. She is currently working on her Ph.D., which is on the subject of gender analysis of labor-based methods in Ugandan roadworks. As a member of the Department of Gender Studies at Makerere University in Kampala, her time is mainly occupied with teaching and consultancy work for a variety of agencies including UNDP, UNICEF, FAO, Irish Aid and the United Kingdom's Department of International Development (DFID).

ROY VAN DER DRIFT is an anthropologist who has been working in West Africa since 1983. His Ph.D. research was on the crisis in mangrove rice farming, a study that broadened to an analysis of the interface among local peasant societies, the nation-state, the world market and development projects in Guinea-Bissau. Since 1996 he has been employed as a senior researcher and consultant at the National Institute for Studies and Research (INEP) in Guinea-Bissau, working on issues that include governance, decentralization, local power structures and gender. His work was disrupted by several episodes of recent conflict, and he and his colleagues witnessed heavy physical damage to INEP, which was used as a dormitory by Senegalese troops! Nevertheless, the staff have not lost their motivation and are currently working on the rehabilitation of the institute's infrastructure and restoring its vital role in Guinea-Bissau society.

RIJK VAN DIJK is an anthropologist working at the African Studies Centre, Leiden. He has done fieldwork in Malawi on the rise of charismatic Pentecostal movements in urban areas (*Young Malawian Puritans*). He has published articles on Pentecostalism, globalization and the anthropology of religion. His current research interest focuses on Pentecostal churches in Accra and Kumasi and their relations with Ghanaian diaspora communities in The Hague and in Botswana.

JUSTIN WILLIS is a senior research associate in the history department at the University of Durham. He has worked and published on a range of historical issues, specifically the social history of alcohol in East Africa, with the support of the Economic and Social Research Council and the British Institute in Eastern Africa.